World Philosophers on Death

D.J. Ciraulo
West Valley College

 KENDALL/HUNT PUBLISHING COMPANY
4050 Westmark Drive   Dubuque, Iowa 52002

↭ Contents ↢

✳ Appendix: Culture Criticism

Dedication

To my daughters,
Dina and Darlene.

❧ Preface ❧

*"Midway upon the journey of our life I found myself
in a dark wood, where the right way was lost!"*

DANTE

As the post war generation reach the dark wood of mid-life, one would naturally suppose a great deal of curiosity on their part concerning death. But what is most surprising is that so many young people, usually immune to a sense of vulnerability and mortality, are also eager to learn what the great thinkers and sages have said on this topic. The problem, however, has been one of access: usually one would go to a library, or peruse the Internet to find the exact book, article, or relevant pages where death is being discussed by a particular philosopher; and once this information is located, it would still be difficult to place the philosophical view in any coherent context. The present anthology seeks to remedy this situation.

First, since one's attitude toward death will necessarily take place within a larger world-view, the philosophers have been presented in four historical periods: the Classical, Medieval, Modern and Contemporary. Both Plato and Confucius, for instance, can best be understood and compared when seen from the Classical perspective. What they share in common is a cosmocentric point of view which puts an emphasis on one's participation in, and harmony with the laws of nature. This is quite different from Augustine's Medieval theocentric view of the world: at this historical juncture one no longer seeks harmony with nature, which is created and therefore contingent, but salvation from this world through God's moral law. With the advent of the 17th century—the Modern period—we begin to see a growing skepticism and a certain paradox concerning reason: along with the optimism which the great achievements of science and rationality bring, we also see the inherent limitations of reason to give any final metaphysical answers. So a thinker like Pascal finds himself alone and caught in a conflict between reason and faith. And finally, Contemporary philosophy reflects the 20th century preoccupation with logic, language and existence. On the one hand analytic philosophers, like Russell, believe that clear thinking and good arguments can alleviate most of life's conundrums. Those of the existential or continental persuasion, who like Heidegger practice a form of phenomenological description, see the human condition as essentially problematic. So by presenting the articles in this fashion, the reader will not only gain an historical and philosophical overview, but will also be able to make some important cross cultural comparisons. An appendix has also been added in order to supply a more critical analysis of the way we live, work and die in a capitalist society.

As one could well imagine, it took a great deal of time and effort to track down the exemplary books and articles on death and edit them in a way which would be understandable to lay readers in philosophy. In this regard, I would like to thank Christy Aguirre and Barbara Upton for their work, suggestions and help with this whole project. Also, thanks are due to the staff at Kendall/Hunt Publishing Company for guiding me through the process. And finally, nothing of this would be possible without Dr. Sandra LaFave, the chair of the Philosophy Department at West Valley College, who designed and created a course which has proved both successful and extremely popular—World Philosophers on Death.

✒ Introduction ✒

"All men are mortal," the simple but sublime major premise of Aristotle's famous syllogism, sets the tone and the parameter for this anthology, that is, that the human condition is finite. In fact, one could state the case even stronger and say that death is the defining condition of our humanity. How so? Does not everything come to an end—is not everything finite? Why, since plants and animals also die, would death constitute what is essentially human? Perhaps finitude is not at all essential to the human condition. What is special about death? Maybe there are beings from another galaxy who are immortal, and that we earthlings ourselves are on the brink of conquering death. If this is possible, then death would not at all be necessary to the human condition.

Whether the statement "all men are mortal" is analytic, that is, true by definition like "all bachelors are unmarried," or synthetic and therefore falsifiable as with the possibility of galactic immortals and future cyborgs, this way of framing the question is irrelevant to the issue of mortality and one's humanity. Whether we come to an end or not, or whether death is one empirical fact among others, is not the problem. The meaning of the term mortality when applied to humans does not merely mean that we cease to exist, but rather that we face our end as something held out in front of us as a possibility (Heidegger). In other words, finitude is an existential category—a way of being peculiar to being human. Animals die, but their mortality does not constitute a problem for them. "All dogs are mortal" has a strange ring to it. One can only be mortal when one recognizes the possibility of being otherwise—of being immortal. We should, therefore, distinguish between "death," a phenomenon most living things we know of undergo, and "mortality" which is peculiar to a possible being—a being whose being is in question and is, therefore, problematic.

Our furry friends solve problems, but their being is nonproblematic, that is, what and who they are is not in question. Fido can not be more or less a dog, but we can be more or less humane. This is probably why animals leave no history—no hieroglyphic scratchings—no residue of their existential anguish. The fact that they are not a problem to themselves and do not live in terms of their end is also why they do not squander their lives nor kill each other in great numbers for ideological reasons. But we humans are not so fortunate in that respect. We have a problem! Or, should one say we "are" a problem? Again, our being is problematic because we are not a fait accompli but a project yet to be—a strange exotic animal who, while scratching its head and wondering about who, what and where it is, erects monuments, creates laws, builds cathedrals to the heavens and splits the atom in desperate quest of an answer. What does one mean by the human spirit and the spectacle of its history but this peculiar and sometimes dangerous desire to break from the bonds of animality in an act of negation and often futile attempt at self-transcendence?

Now, the words "project," "possibility" and "transcendence" all imply a direction towards something. Towards what? Towards different ideas, objects and human ends. But all our human intentions and creations take place within, and are ultimately measured by, a larger bound-

ix

ary condition—our final end. It is not difficult to imagine a primal scene, a first sign and moment when Homo Problematicus recognizes a line which is drawn at death which says:

"Beyond here you can not know nor can not go."

This impenetrable wall and warning is the first indication of a taboo which marks the distinction between the sacred and the profane, the immortal and the mortal; it is the recognition of the possibility or impossibility of life beyond the line which engenders the question of our humanity—of how we will live out our allotted time here.

But what if we no longer need face nor fear our end? What if a way was found to live forever in this world, on this side of the line? There are at least three ways to view the possibility of an intraworldly immortality: Relative, Reductive and what could be called Absolute immortality. With Relative immortality we would, of course, not live forever but at least long enough to where our finitude would not really matter. The current advances in electro and biotechnology make it quite feasible to predict a life span of 150 to 300 years or more. One could imagine organ farms for replacement of body parts, manipulation of DNA and cures for most fatal and degenerative diseases; nanotechnology will also make possible the fusion of the organic with the inorganic thereby prolonging our existence beyond the current range. With this form of Relative immortality we would just get tired of living and refuse all further chip replacement—our end will simply not matter much! Or, is there something about our species—the ungrateful biped—which always wants more?

Some of us would certainly want more, for the latter kind of longevity can not eliminate the sense of contingency which remains. Along with the possibility of a long life there will still be earthquakes, falling pianos and killer asteroids to threaten our existence. What Homo Problematicus really wants is to rid itself once and for all of the anxiety which is intrinsic to being a possible and contingent being. In short, we want to be necessary beings—gods! Is this possible in the here and now? Maybe not in the now, but we can surely imagine a future condition, already represented by certain science fiction characters, where the emotional, overly reflective and anxious self is replaced by a kind of cool and spontaneous digital rationality. But instead of waiting for an intergalactic invasion, or the metamorphosis of our species, we would simply continue the biotechnic process of replacement and enhancement to the point where the current natural biological base of our existence is slowly transformed into a neonatural cybernetic base. If we want to totally eliminate the sense of contingency which haunts our existence, then the possible self will have to be absorbed and reduced to a factical condition—a condition in which the problematic nature of our existence would cease to be problematic and become merely a problem to be solved. We can call this Reductive immortality.

I am sure that for many of us the losses incurred by the above post-human cyborgian scenario would far outweigh the gains. We would be ridding ourselves of the anxiety concerning our end at the cost of what we experience as our freedom. In fact, if the possible is reduced to factical causal relations, the very notion of freedom would not be an issue for cyborg man (and by the way, if we create a cyborg, or android, whose circuitry is capable of producing the phenomenological effects of consciousness and existential angst, then we would have simply duplicated our problem). But is this what we really want? What we would like is to have our cake and eat it too—to be free possible beings while at the same time enjoying the nonanxious state of a gadget. Sartre calls this useless passion "bad faith." So, while having other interesting implications, neither the Relative nor Reductive forms of immortality seem to sever the existential connection between our finitude and the human condition. But perhaps there is a third way out.

We can call the third and most radical form of intraworldly immortality Absolute immortality. Keep in mind, however, that we are not talking about what may or may not happen after death but whether it is possible to eliminate finitude in this world. If we want to finally be free of the sense of contingency and existential angst without losing the freedom we experience as possible beings, we would have to eliminate the primary cause of our contingency—the elephant in the room has all along been the body. How then can we conquer the gravity of our somatic existence? It seems the only other way out would best be described as a form of atheistic process philosophy which would entail the separation of consciousness, and the correlative problematic phenomena we have been discussing, from its material base. The process view relies heavily on, and pushes to its furthest extreme, the implications of emergent evolution. It goes something like this: in the first millionth, or billionth of a second of the Big Bang (we will not concern ourselves here with the time discrepancy, it's just really fast), there was only a sea of neutrinos; but with every act of conjunction and complexification new phenomena like hydrogen began to emerge; now it took a long time for galactic gasses to solidify into stars and planets, but they did; and with the advent of planets came a new element called oxygen; when oxygen combined with hydrogen the miraculous new quality of water appeared. Remember, there was no moisture at the beginning. If we fast forward this process a bit, eventually some neuronal fibers came together in such a way to produce consciousness, and then self consciousness with its preoccupation with itself and its end. The upshot is that the stuff of the universe has combined in certain ways to produce nonstuff like ideas which tend to take on a life of their own through memory, culture and history. One could say that matter has managed to etherealize itself by producing a reflective ideational sphere which is not material in nature. Why would this process stop at this level of evolution? Just as the prospect of consciousness appears impossible when viewed from the primal subatomic level, so too does the notion of a superconsciousness separated from the contingency of the body seem strange.

Although there does seem to be something peculiar going on with matter which we do not fully understand, the emergent phenomena observed so far in nature are always tied to some arrangement of matter. How would nonstuff, or consciousness, sustain itself on its own? And if at some point it could, this last scenario offers no consolation to the present generation except, perhaps, the feeling of self sacrifice for the future. It would appear that there is no exit from death and its intrinsic connection to human existence. I suppose one could take up an attitude of nonchalance, be nonplussed and even annoyed by what seems to be a morbid concern about death. But this "I don't care" is already a way of taking up a position in regard to one's end—the refusal to let it count or give it meaning. But this refusal is in itself very telling and meaningful. What, for instance, would such a person say about the death of others?— about the conclusion to Aristotle's syllogism that Socrates suffered mortality. Would this kind of obliviousness be humane?

I

Classical West

Chapter 1

On the Trial and Death of Socrates

Plato

Whitehead said that all philosophy was but a footnote to Plato. Keep in mind when reading Plato that his style of thinking and questioning is not only relevant to the beginning of science and politics, but is foundational to the next two thousand years of theology. Plato was born in Athens around 428 B.C.E. into an aristocratic family; he was an Olympic wrestler, playwright and after seeing his mentor Socrates put to death, he dedicated the rest of his life to philosophy. He founded the Academy and died at the age of eighty-one in 347 B.C.E.

⚶ Apology ⚶

How you, O Athenians, have been affected by my accusers, I cannot tell; but I know that they almost made me forget who I was—so persuasively did they speak; and yet they have hardly uttered a word of truth. But of the many falsehoods told by them, there was one which quite amazed me;—I mean when they said that you should be upon your guard and not allow yourselves to be deceived by the force of my eloquence. To say this, when they were certain to be detected as soon as I opened my lips and proved myself to be anything but a great speaker, did indeed appear to me most shameless—unless by the force of eloquence they mean the force of truth; for if such is their meaning, I admit that I am eloquent. But in how different a way from theirs! Well, as I was saying, they have scarcely spoken the truth at all; but from me you shall hear the whole truth: not, however, delivered after their manner in a set oration duly ornamented with words and phrases. No, by heaven! but I shall use the words and arguments which occur to me at the moment; for I am confident in the justice of my cause:[1] at my time of life I ought not to be appearing before you, O men of Athens, in the character of a juvenile orator—let no one expect it of me. And I must beg of you to grant me a favour:—If I defend myself in my accustomed manner, and you hear me using the words which I have been in the habit of using in the agora, at the tables of the money-changers, or anywhere else, I would ask you not to be surprised, and not to interrupt me on this account. For I am more than seventy

---

The Dialogues of Plato.

years of age, and appearing now for the first time in a court of law, I am quite a stranger to the language of the place; and therefore I would have you regard me as if I were really a stranger, whom you would excuse if he spoke in his native tongue, and after the fashion of his country:—Am I making an unfair request of you? Never mind the manner, which may or may not be good; but, think only of the truth of my words, and give heed to that: let the speaker speak truly and the judge decide justly.

And first, I have to reply to the older charges and to my first accusers, and then I will go on to the later ones. For of old I have had many accusers, who have accused me falsely to you during many years; and I am more afraid of them than of Anytus and his associates, who are dangerous, too, in their own way. But far more dangerous are the others, who began when you were children, and took possession of your minds with their falsehoods, telling of one Socrates, a wise man, who speculated about the heaven above, and searched into the earth beneath, and made the worse appear the better cause. The disseminators of this tale are the accusers whom I dread; for their hearers are apt to fancy that such enquirers do not believe in the existence of the gods. And they are many, and their charges against me are of ancient date, and they were made by them in the days when you were more impressible than you are now—in childhood, or it may have been in youth—and the cause when heard went by default, for there was none to answer. And hardest of all, I do not know and cannot tell the names of my accusers; unless in the chance case of a Comic poet. All who from envy and malice have persuaded you—some of them having first convinced themselves—all this class of men are most difficult to deal with; for I cannot have them up here, and cross-examine them, and therefore I must simply fight with shadows in my own defence, and argue when there is no one who answers. I will ask you then to assume with me, as I was saying, that my opponents are of two kinds; one recent, the other ancient: and I hope that you will see the propriety of my answering the latter first, for these accusations you heard long before the others, and much oftener.

Well, then, I must make my defence, and endeavor to clear away in a short time, a slander which has lasted a long time. May I succeed, if to succeed be for my good and yours, or likely to avail me in my cause! The task is not an easy one; I quite understand the nature of it. And so leaving the event with God, in obedience to the law I will now make my defence.

I will begin at the beginning, and ask what is the accusation which has given rise to the slander of me, and in fact has encouraged Meletus to prefer this charge against me. Well, what do the slanderers say? They shall be my prosecutors, and I will sum up their words in an affidavit: 'Socrates is an evil-doer, and a curious person, who searches into things under the earth and in heaven, and he makes the worse appear the better cause; and he teaches the aforesaid doctrines to others.' Such is the nature of the accusation: it is just what you have yourselves seen in the comedy of Aristophanes,[2] who has introduced a man whom be calls Socrates, going about and saying that he walks in air, and talking a deal of nonsense concerning matters of which I do not pretend to know either much or little—not that I mean to speak disparagingly of any one who is a student of natural philosophy. I should be very sorry if Meletus could bring so grave a charge against me. But the simple truth is, O Athenians, that I have nothing to do with physical speculations. Very many of those here present are witnesses to the truth of this, and to them I appeal. Speak then, you who have heard me and tell your neighbours whether any of you have ever known me hold forth in few words or in many upon such matters.... You bear their answer. And from what they say of this part of the charge you will be able to judge of the truth of the rest.

As little foundation is there for the report that I am a teacher, and take money; this accusation has no more truth in it than the other. Although, if a man were really able to instruct mankind, to receive money for giving instruction would, in my opinion, be an honour to him. There is Gorgias of Leontium, and Prodicus of Ceos, and Hippias of Elis, who go the round of the cities, and are able to persuade the young men to leave their own citizens by whom they might be taught for nothing, and come to them whom they not only pay, but are thankful if they may be allowed to pay them. There is at this time, a Parian philosopher residing in Athens, of whom I have heard; and I came to hear of him in this way:—I came across a man who has spent a world of money on the Sophists, Callias, the son of Hipponicus, and knowing that he had sons, I asked him: 'Callias,' I said, 'if your two sons were foals or calves, there would be no difficulty in finding some one to put over them; we should hire a trainer of horses, or a farmer probably, who would improve and perfect them in their own proper virtue and excellence; but as they are human beings, whom are you thinking of placing over them? Is there any one who understands human and political virtue? You must have thought about the matter, for you have sons; is there any one?' 'There is,' he said. 'Who is he?' said I; 'and of what country? and what does he charge?' 'Evenus the Parian,' he replied; 'he is the man, and his charge is five minae.' Happy is Evenus, I said to myself, if he really has this wisdom, and teaches at such a moderate charge. Had I the same, I should have been very proud and conceited; but the truth is that I have no knowledge of the kind.

I dare say, Athenians, that some one among you will reply, 'Yes, Socrates, but what is the origin of these accusations which are brought against you; there must have been something strange which you have been doing? All these rumours and this talk about you would never have arisen if you had been like other men: tell us, then, what is the cause of them, for we should be sorry to judge hastily of you.' Now I regard this as a fair challenge, and I will endeavour to explain to you the reason why I am called wise and have such an evil fame. Please to attend then. And although some of you may think that I am joking, I declare that I will tell you the entire truth. Men of Athens, this reputation of mine has come of a certain sort of wisdom which I possess. If you ask me what kind of wisdom, I reply, wisdom such as may perhaps be attained by man, for to that extent I am inclined to believe that I am wise; whereas the persons of whom I was speaking have a superhuman wisdom, which I may fail to describe, because I have it not myself; and he who says that I have, speaks falsely, and is taking away my character. And here, O men of Athens, I must beg you not to interrupt me, even if I seem to say something extravagant. For the word which I will speak is not mine. I will refer you to a witness who is worthy of credit; that witness shall be the God of Delphi—he will tell you about my wisdom, if I have any, and of what sort it is. You must have known Chaerephon; he was early a friend of mine, and also a friend of yours, for he shared in the recent exile of the people, and returned with you. Well, Chaerephon, as you know, was very impetuous in all his doings, and he went to Delphi and boldly asked the oracle to tell him whether—as I was saying, I must beg you not to interrupt—he asked the oracle to tell him whether any one was wiser than I was, and the Pythian prophetess answered, that there was no man wiser. Chaerephon is dead himself; but his brother, who is in court, will confirm the truth of what I am saying.

Why do I mention this? Because I am going to explain to you why I have such an evil name. When I heard the answer, I said to myself, What can the god mean? and what is the interpretation of his riddle? for I know that I have no wisdom, small or great. What then can he mean when he says that I am the wisest of men? And yet he is a god, and cannot lie; that would be against his nature. After long consideration, I thought of a method of trying the question. I reflected that if I could only find a man wiser than myself then I might go to the god with a refutation in my hand. I should say to him, 'Here is a man who is wiser than I am; but you said that I was the wisest.' Accordingly I went to one who had the reputation of wisdom, and observed him—his name I need not mention; he was a politician whom I selected for examination—and the result was as follows: When I began to talk with him, I could not help thinking that he was not really wise, although he was thought wise by many, and still wiser by himself and thereupon I tried to explain to him that he thought himself wise, but was not really wise; and the consequence was that he hated me, and his enmity was shared by several who were present and heard me. So I left him, saying to myself, as I went away: Well, although I do not suppose that either of us knows anything really beautiful and good, I am better off than he is,—for he knows nothing, and thinks that he knows; I neither know nor think that I know. In this latter particular, then, I seem to have slightly the advantage of him. Then I went to another who had still higher pretensions to wisdom, and my conclusion was exactly the same. Whereupon I made another enemy of him, and of many others besides him.

Then I went to one man after another, being not unconscious of the enmity which I provoked, and I lamented and feared this: But necessity was laid upon me,—the word of God, I thought, ought to be considered first. And I said to myself, Go I must to all who appear to know, and find out the meaning of the oracle. And I swear to you, Athenians, by the dog I swear!—for I must tell you the truth—the result of my mission was just this: I found that the men most in repute were all but the most foolish; and that others less esteemed were really wiser and better. I will tell you the tale of my wanderings and of the 'Herculean' labours, as I may call them, which I endured only to find at last the oracle irrefutable. After the politicians, I went to the poets; tragic, dithyrambic, and all sorts. And there, I said to myself, you will be instantly detected; now you will find out that you are more ignorant than they are. Accordingly, I took them some of the most elaborate passages in their own writings, and asked what was the meaning of them—thinking that they would teach me something. Will you believe me? I am almost ashamed to confess the truth, but I must say that there is hardly a person present who would not have talked better about their poetry than they did themselves. Then I knew that not by wisdom do poets write poetry, but by a sort of genius and inspiration; they are like diviners or soothsayers who also say many fine things, but do not understand the meaning of them. The poets appeared to me to be much in the same case; and I further observed that upon the strength of their poetry they believed themselves to be the wisest of men in other things in which they were not wise. So I departed, conceiving myself to be superior to them for the same reason that I was superior to the politicians.

At last I went to the artisans, for I was conscious that I knew nothing at all, as I may say, and I was sure that they knew many fine things; and here I was not mistaken, for they did know many things of which I was ignorant, and in this they certainly were wiser than I was. But I observed that even the good artisans fell into the same error as the poets;—because they were good workmen they thought that they also knew all sorts of high matters, and this defect in them overshadowed their wisdom; and therefore I asked myself on behalf of the oracle, whether I would like to be as I was, neither having their knowledge nor their ignorance, or like them in both; and I made answer to myself and to the oracle that I was better off as I was.

This inquisition has led to my having many enemies of the worst and most dangerous kind, and has given occasion also to many calumnies. And I am called wise, for my hearers always imagine that I myself possess the wisdom which I find wanting in others: but the truth is, O men of Athens, that God only is wise; and by his answer he intends to show that the wisdom of men is worth little or nothing; he is not speaking of Socrates, he is only using my name by way of illustration, as if he said, He, O men, is the wisest, who, like Socrates, knows that his wisdom is in truth worth nothing. And so I go about the world, obedient to the god, and search and make enquiry into the wisdom of any one, whether citizen or stranger, who appears to be wise; and if he is not wise, then in vindication of the oracle I show him that he is not wise; and my occupation quite absorbs me, and I have no time to give either to any public matter of interest or to any concern of my own, but I am in utter poverty by reason of my devotion to the god.

There is another thing:—young men of the richer classes, who have not much to do, come about me of their own accord; they like to hear the pretenders examined, and they often imitate me, and proceed to examine others; there are plenty of persons, as they quickly discover, who think that they know something, but really know little or nothing; and then those who are examined by them instead of being angry with themselves are angry with me: This confounded Socrates, they say; this villainous misleader of youth!—and then if somebody asks them, Why, what evil does he practise or teach? they do not know, and cannot tell; but in order that they may not appear to be at a loss, they repeat the ready-made charges which are used against all philosophers about teaching things up in the clouds and under the earth, and having no gods, and making the worse appear the better cause; for they do not like to confess that their pretence of knowledge has been detected—which is the truth; and as they are numerous and ambitious and energetic, and are drawn up in battle array and have persuasive tongues, they have filled your ears with their loud and inveterate calumnies. And this is the reason why my three accusers, Meletus and Anytus and Lycon, have set upon me; Meletus, who has a quarrel with me on behalf of the poets; Anytus, on behalf of the craftsmen and politicians; Lycon, on behalf of the rhetoricians: and as I said at the beginning, I cannot expect to get rid of such a mass of calumny all in a moment. And this, O men of Athens, is the truth and the whole truth; I have concealed nothing, I have dissembled nothing. And yet, I know that my plainness of speech makes them hate me, and what is their hatred but a proof that I am speaking the truth?— Hence has arisen the prejudice against me; and this is the reason of it, as you will find out either in this or in any future enquiry.

I have said enough in my defence against the first class of my accusers; I turn to the second class. They are headed by Meletus, that good man and true lover of his country, as he calls himself. Against these, too, I must try to make a defence:—Let their affidavit be read: it contains something of this kind: It says that Socrates is a doer of evil, who corrupts the youth; and who does not believe in the gods of the state, but has other new divinities of his own. Such is the charge; and now let us examine the particular counts. He says that I am a doer of evil, and corrupt the youth; but I say, O men of Athens, that Meletus is a doer of evil, in that he pretends to be in earnest when he is only in jest, and is so eager to bring men to trial from a pretended zeal and interest about matters in which he really never had the smallest interest. And the truth of this I will endeavour to prove to you.

Come hither, Meletus, and let me ask a question of you. You think a great deal about the improvement of youth?

Yes, I do.

Tell the judges, then, who is their improver; for you must know, as you have taken the pains to discover their corrupter, and are citing and accusing me before them. Speak, then, and tell the judges who their improver is.—Observe, Meletus, that you are silent, and have nothing to say. But is not this rather disgraceful, and a very considerable proof of what I was saying, that you have no interest in the matter? Speak up, friend, and tell us who their improver is.

The laws.

But that, my good sir, is not my meaning. I want to know who the person is, who, in the first place, knows the laws.

The judges, Socrates, who are present in court.

What, do you mean to say, Meletus, that they are able to instruct and improve youth?

Certainly they are.

What, all of them, or some only and not others?

All of them.

By the goddess Herè, that is good news! There are plenty of improvers, then. And what do you say of the audience,—do they improve them?

Yes they do.

And the senators?

Yes, the senators improve them.

But perhaps the members of the assembly corrupt them?—or do they too improve them?

They improve them.

Then every Athenian improves and elevates them; all with the exception of myself; and I alone am their corrupter? Is that what you affirm?

That is what I stoutly affirm.

I am very unfortunate if you are right. But suppose I ask you a question: How about horses? Does one man do them harm and all the world good? Is not the exact opposite the truth? One man is able to do them good, or at least not many;—the trainer of horses, that is to say, does them good, and others who have to do with them rather injure them? Is not that true, Meletus, of horses, or of any other animals? Most assuredly it is; whether you and Anytus say yes or no. Happy indeed would be the condition of youth if they had one corrupter only, and all the rest of the world were their improvers. But you, Meletus, have sufficiently shown that you never had a thought about the young: your carelessness is seen in your not caring about the very things which you bring against me.

And now, Meletus, I will ask you another question—by Zeus I will: Which is better, to live among bad citizens, or among good ones? Answer, friend, I say; the question is one which may be easily answered. Do not the good do their neighbors good, and the bad do them evil?

Certainly.

And is there any one who would rather be injured than benefited by those who live with him? Answer, my good friend, the law requires you to answer—does any one like to be injured?

Certainly not.

And when you accuse me of corrupting and deteriorating the youth, do you allege that I corrupt them intentionally or unintentionally?

Intentionally, I say.

But you have just admitted that the good do their neighbours good, and evil do them evil. Now, is that a truth which your superior wisdom has recognized thus early in life, and am I, at my age, in such darkness and ignorance as not to know that if a man with whom I have to live is corrupted by me, I am very likely to be harmed by him; and yet I corrupt him, and intentionally, too—so you say, although neither I nor any other human being is ever likely to be convinced by you. But either I do not corrupt them, or I corrupt them unintentionally; and on either view of the case you lie. If my offence is unintentional, the law has no cognizance of unintentional offences: you ought to have taken me privately, and warned and admonished me; for if I had been better advised, I should have left off doing what I only did unintentionally— no doubt I should; but you would have nothing to say to me and refused to teach me. And now you bring me up in this court, which is a place not of instruction, but of punishment.

It will be very clear to you, Athenians, as I was saying, that Meletus has no care at all, great or small, about the matter. But still I should like to know, Meletus, in what I am affirmed to corrupt the young. I suppose you mean, as I infer from your indictment, that I teach them not to acknowledge the gods which the state acknowledges, but some other new divinities or, spiritual agencies in their stead. These are the lessons by which I corrupt the youth, as you say.

Yes, that I say emphatically.

Then, by the gods, Meletus, of whom we are speaking, tell me and the court, in somewhat plainer terms, what you mean! for I do not as yet understand whether you affirm that I teach other men to acknowledge some gods, and therefore that I do believe in gods, and am not an entire atheist—this you do not lay to my charge,—but only you say that they are not the same gods which the city recognizes—the charge is that they are different gods. Or, do you mean that I am an atheist simply, and a teacher of atheism?

I mean the latter—that you are a complete atheist.

What an extraordinary statement! Why do you think so, Meletus? Do you mean that I do not believe in the godhead of the sun or moon, like other men?

I assure you, judges, that he does not: for he says that the sun is stone, and the moon earth.

Friend Meletus, you think that you are accusing Anaxagoras: and you have but a bad opinion of the judges, if you fancy them illiterate to such a degree as not to know that these doctrines are found in the books of Anaxagoras the Clazomenian, which are full of them. And so, forsooth, the youth are said to be taught them by Socrates, when there are not unfrequently exhibitions of them at the theatre[3] (price of admission one drachma at the most); and they might pay their money, and laugh at Socrates if he pretends to father these extraordinary views. And so, Meletus, you really think that I do not believe in any god?

I swear by Zeus that you believe absolutely in none at all.

Nobody will believe you, Meletus, and I am pretty sure that you do not believe yourself. I cannot help thinking, men of Athens, that Meletus is reckless and impudent, and that he has written this indictment in a spirit of mere wantonness and youthful bravado. Has he not compounded a riddle, thinking to try me? He said to himself:—I shall see whether the wise Socrates will discover my facetious contradiction, or whether I shall be able to deceive him and the rest of them. For he certainly does appear to me to contradict himself in the indictment as much as if he said that Socrates is guilty of not believing in the gods, and yet of believing in them—but this is not like a person who is in earnest.

I should like you, O men of Athens, to join me in examining what I conceive to be his inconsistency; and do you, Meletus, answer. And I must remind the audience of my request that they would not make a disturbance if I speak in my accustomed manner:

Did ever man, Meletus, believe in the existence of human things, and not of human beings?...I wish, men of Athens, that he would answer, and not be always trying to get up an interruption. Did ever any man believe in horsemanship, and not in horses? or in flute-playing, and not in flute-players? No, my friend; I will answer to you and to the court, as you refuse to answer for yourself. There is no man who ever did. But now please to answer the next question: Can a man believe in spiritual and divine agencies, and not in spirits or demigods?

He cannot.

How lucky I am to have extracted that answer, by the assistance of the court! But then you swear in the indictment that I teach and believe in divine or spiritual agencies (new or old, no matter for that); at any rate, I believe in spiritual agencies,—so you say and swear in the affidavit; and yet if I believe in divine beings, how can I help believing in spirits or demigods;—must I not? To be sure I must; and therefore I may assume that your silence gives consent. Now what are spirits or demigods? are they not either gods or the sons of gods?

Certainly they are.

But this is what I call the facetious riddle invented by you: the demigods or spirits are gods, and you say first that I do not believe in gods, and then again that I do believe in gods; that is, if I believe in demigods. For if the demigods are the illegitimate sons of gods, whether by the nymphs or by any other mothers, of whom they are said to be the sons—what human being will ever believe that there are no gods if they are the sons of gods? You might as well affirm the existence of mules, and deny that of horses and asses. Such nonsense, Meletus, could only have been intended by you to make trial of me. You have put this into the indictment because you had nothing real of which to accuse me. But no one who has a particle of understanding will ever be convinced by you that the same men can believe in divine and superhuman things, and yet not believe that there are gods and demigods and heroes.

I have said enough in answer to the charge of Meletus: any elaborate defence is unnecessary; but I know only too well how many are the enmities which I have incurred, and this is what will be my destruction if I am destroyed;—not Meletus, nor yet Anytus, but the envy and detraction of the world, which has been the death of many good men, and will probably be the death of many more; there is no danger of my being the last of them.

Some one will say: And are you not ashamed, Socrates, of a course of life which is likely to bring you to an untimely end? To him I may fairly answer: There you are mistaken: a man who is good for anything ought not to calculate the chance of living or dying; he ought only to consider whether in doing anything he is doing right or wrong—acting the part of a good man or of a bad. Whereas, upon your view, the heroes who fell at Troy were not good for much, and the son of Thetis above all, who altogether despised danger in comparison with disgrace; and when he was so eager to slay Hector, his goddess mother said to him, that if he avenged his companion Patroclus, and slew Hector, he would die himself—'Fate,' she said, in these or the like words, 'waits for you next after Hector;' he, receiving this warning, utterly despised danger and death, and instead of fearing them, feared rather to live in dishonour, and not to avenge his friend. 'Let me die forthwith,' he replies, 'and be avenged of my enemy, rather than abide here by the beaked ships, a laughing-stock and a burden of the earth.' Had Achilles any thought of death and danger? For wherever a man's place is, whether the place which he has chosen or that in which he has been placed by a commander, there he ought to remain in the hour of danger; he should not think of death or of anything but of disgrace. And this, O men of Athens, is a true saying.

Strange, indeed, would be my conduct, O men of Athens, if I who, when I was ordered by the generals whom you chose to command me at Potidaea and Amphipolis and Delium, remained where they placed me, like any other man, facing death—if now, when, as I conceive and imagine, God orders me to fulfil the philosopher's mission of searching into myself and other men, I were to desert my post through fear of death, or any other fear; that would indeed be strange, and I might justly be arraigned in court for denying the existence of the gods, if I disobeyed the oracle because I was afraid of death, fancying that I was wise when I was not wise. For the fear of death is indeed the pretence of wisdom, and not real wisdom, being a pretence of knowing the unknown; and no one knows whether death, which men in their fear apprehend to be the greatest evil, may not be the greatest good. Is not this ignorance of a disgraceful sort, the ignorance which is the conceit that man knows what he does not know? And in this respect only I believe myself to differ from men in general, and may perhaps claim to be wiser than they are:—that whereas I know but little of the world below, I do not suppose that I know: but I do know that injustice and disobedience to a better, whether God or man, is evil and dishonourable, and I will never fear or avoid a possible good rather than a certain evil. And therefore if you let me go now, and are not convinced by Anytus, who said that since I had been prosecuted I must be put to death (or if not that I ought never to have been prosecuted at all) ; and that if I escape now, your sons will all be utterly ruined by listening to my words—if you say to me, Socrates, this time we will not mind Anytus, and you shall be let off, but upon one condition, that you are not to enquire and speculate in this way any more, and that if you are caught doing so again you shall die;—if this was the condition on which you let me go, I should reply: Men of Athens, I honour and love you; but I shall obey God rather than you, and while I have life and strength I shall never cease from the practice and teaching of philosophy, exhorting any one whom I meet and saying to him after my manner: You, my friend,—a citizen of the great and mighty and wise city of Athens,—are you not ashamed of heaping up the greatest amount of money and honour and reputation, and caring so little about wisdom and truth and the greatest improvement of the soul, which you never regard or heed at all? And if the person with whom I am arguing, says: Yes, but I do care; then I do not leave him or let him go at once; but I proceed to interrogate and examine and cross-examine him, and if I think that he has no virtue in him, but only says that he has, I reproach him with undervaluing the greater, and overvaluing the less. And I shall repeat the same words to every one whom I meet, young and old, citizen and alien, but especially to the citizens, inasmuch as they are my brethren. For know that this is the command of God; and I believe that no greater good has ever happened in the state than my service to the God. For I do nothing but go about persuading you all, old and young alike, not to take thought for your persons or your properties, but first and chiefly to care about the greatest improvement of the soul. I tell you that virtue is not given by money, but that from virtue comes money and every other good of man, public as well as private. This is my teaching, and if this is the doctrine which corrupts the youth, I am a mischievous person. But if any one says that this is not my teaching, he is speaking an untruth. Wherefore, O men of Athens, I say to you, do as Anytus bids or not as Anytus bids, and either acquit me or not; but whichever you do, understand that I shall never alter my ways, not even if I have to die many times.

Men of Athens, do not interrupt, but hear me; there was an understanding between us that you should hear me to the end: I have something more to say, at which you may be inclined to cry out; but I believe that to hear me will be good for you, and therefore I beg that you will not cry out. I would have you know, that if you kill such an one as I am, you will injure yourselves more than you will injure me. Nothing will injure me, not Meletus nor yet Anytus—they cannot, for a bad man is not permitted to injure a better than himself. I do not deny that Anytus may, perhaps, kill him, or drive him into exile, or deprive him of civil rights; and he may imagine, and others may imagine, that he is inflicting a great injury upon him: but there I do not agree. For the evil of doing as he is doing—the evil of unjustly taking away the life of another—is greater far.

And now, Athenians, I am not going to argue for my own sake, as you may think, but for yours, that you may not sin against the God by condemning me, who am his gift to you. For if you kill me you will not easily find a successor to me, who, if I may use such a ludicrous figure of speech, am a sort of gadfly, given to the state by God; and the state is a great and noble steed who is tardy in his motions owing to his very size, and requires to be stirred into life. I am that gadfly which God has attached to the state, and all day long and in all places am always fastening upon you, arousing and persuading and reproaching you. You will not easily find another like me, and therefore I would advise you to spare me. I dare say that you may feel out of temper (like a person who is suddenly awakened from sleep), and you think that you might easily strike me dead as Anytus advises, and then you would sleep on for the remainder of your lives, unless God in his care of you sent you another gadfly. When I say that I am given to you by God, the proof of my mission is this:—if I had been like other men, I should not have neglected all my own concerns or patiently seen the neglect of them during all these years, and have been doing yours, coming to you individually like a father or elder brother, exhorting you to regard virtue; such conduct, I say, would be unlike human nature. If I had gained anything, or if my exhortations had been paid, there would have been some sense in my doing so; but now, as you will perceive, not even the impudence of my accusers dares to say that I have ever exacted or sought pay of any one; of that they have no witness. And I have a sufficient witness to the truth of what I say—my poverty.

Some one may wonder why I go about in private giving advice and busying myself with the concerns of others, but do not venture to come forward in public and advise the state. I will tell you why. You have heard me speak at sundry times and in divers places of an oracle or sign which comes to me, and is the divinity which Meletus ridicules in the indictment. This sign, which is a kind of voice, first began to come to me when I was a child; it always forbids but never commands me to do anything which I am going to do. This is what deters me from being a politician. And rightly, as I think. For I am certain, O men of Athens, that if I had engaged in politics, I should have perished long ago, and done no good either to you or to myself. And do not be offended at my telling you the truth: for the truth is, that no man who goes to war with you or any other multitude, honestly striving against the many lawless and unrighteous deeds which are done in a state, will save his life; he who will fight for the right, if he would live even for a brief space, must have a private station and not a public one.

I can give you convincing evidence of what I say, not words only, but what you value far more—actions. Let me relate to you a passage of my own life which will prove to you that I should never have yielded to injustice from any fear of death, and that 'as I should have refused to yield' I must have died at once. I will tell you a tale of the courts, not very interesting perhaps, but nevertheless true. The only office of state which I ever held, O men of Athens, was that of senator: the tribe Antiochis, which is my tribe, had the presidency at the trial of the generals who had not taken up the bodies of the slain after the battle of Arginusae; and you proposed to try them in a body, contrary to law, as you all thought afterwards; but at the time I was the only one of the Prytanes who was opposed to the illegality, and I gave my vote against you; and when the orators threatened to impeach and arrest me, and you called and shouted, I made up my mind that I would run the risk, having law and justice with me, rather than take part in your injustice because I feared imprisonment and death. This happened in the days of the democracy. But when the oligarchy of the Thirty was in power, they sent for me and four others into the rotunda, and bade us bring Leon the Salaminian from Salamis, as they wanted to put him to death. This was a specimen of the sort of commands which they were always giving with the view of implicating as many as possible in their crimes; and then I showed, not in word only but in deed, that, if I may be allowed to use such an expression, I cared not a straw for death, and that my great and only care was lest I should do an unright-eous or unholy thing. For the strong arm of that oppressive power did not frighten me into doing wrong; and when we came out of the rotunda the other four went to Salamis and fetched Leon, but I went quietly home. For which I might have lost my life, had not the power of the Thirty shortly afterwards come to an end. And many will witness to my words.

Now do you really imagine that I could have survived all these years, if I had led a public life, supposing that like a good man I had always maintained the right and had made justice, as I ought, the first thing? No indeed, men of Athens, neither I nor any other man. But I have been always the same in all my actions, public as well as private, and never have I yielded any base compliance to those who are slanderously termed my disciples, or to any other. Not that I have any regular disciples. But if any one likes to come and hear me while I am pursuing my mission, whether he be young or old, he is not excluded. Nor do I converse only with those who pay; but any one, whether he be rich or poor, may ask and answer me and listen to my words; and whether he turns out to be a bad man or a good one, neither result can be justly imputed to me; for I never taught or professed to teach him anything. And if any one says that he has ever learned or heard anything from me in private which all the world has not heard, let me tell you that he is lying.

But I shall be asked, Why do people delight in continually conversing with you? I have told you already, Athenians, the whole truth about this matter: they like to hear the cross-examination of the pretenders to wisdom; there is amusement in it. Now this duty of cross-examining other men has been imposed upon me by God; and has been signified to me by oracles, visions, and in every way in which the will of divine power was ever intimated to any one. This is true, O Athenians; or, if not true, would be soon refuted. If I am or have been corrupting the youth, those of them who are now grown up and become sensible that I gave them bad advice in the days of their youth should come forward as accusers, and take their revenge; or if they do not like to come themselves, some of their relatives, fathers, brothers, or other kinsmen, should say what evil their families have suffered at my hands. Now is their time. Many of them I see in the court. There is Crito, who is of the same age and of the same deme with myself, and there is Critobulus his son, whom I also see. Then again there is Lysanias of Sphettus, who is the father of Aeschines—he is present; and also there is Antiphon of Cephisus, who is the father of Epigenes; and there are the brothers of several who have associated with me. There is Nicostratus the son of Theosdotides, and the brother of Theodotus (now Theodotus himself is dead, and therefore he, at any rate, will not seek to stop him); and there is Paralus the son of Demodocus, who had a brother Theages; and Adeimantus the son of Ariston, whose brother Plato is present; and Aeantodorus, who is the brother of Apollodorus, whom I also see. I might mention a great many others, some of whom Meletus should have produced as witnesses in the course of his speech; and let him still produce them, if he has forgotten—I will make way for him. And let him say, if he has any testimony of the sort which he can produce. Nay, Athenians, the very opposite is the truth. For all these are ready to witness on behalf of the corrupter, of the injurer of their kindred, as Meletus and Anytus call me; not the corrupted youth only—there might have been a motive for that—but their uncorrupted elder relatives. Why should they too support me with their testimony? Why, indeed, except for the sake of truth and justice, and because they know that I am speaking the truth, and that Meletus is a liar.

Well, Athenians, this and the like of this is all the defence which I have to offer. Yet a word more. Perhaps there may be some one who is offended at me, when he calls to mind how he himself on a similar, or even a less serious occasion, prayed and entreated the judges with many tears, and how he produced his children in court, which was a moving spectacle, together with a host of relations and friends; whereas I, who am probably in danger of my life, will do none of these things. The contrast may occur to his mind, and he may be set against me, and vote in anger because he is displeased at me on this account. Now if there be such a person among you,—mind, I do not say that there is,—to him I may fairly reply: My friend, I am a man, and like other men, a creature of flesh and blood, and not 'of wood or stone,' as Homer says; and I have a family, yes, and sons, O Athenians, three in number, one almost a man, and two others who are still young; and yet I will not bring any of them hither in order to petition you for an acquittal. And why not? Not from any self-assertion or want of respect for you. Whether I am or am not afraid of death is another question, of which I will not now speak. But, having regard to public opinion, I feel that such conduct would be discreditable to myself, and to you, and to the whole state. One who has reached my years, and who has a name for wisdom, ought not to demean himself. Whether this opinion of me be deserved or not, at any rate the world has decided that Socrates is in some way superior to other men. And if those among you who are said to be superior in wisdom and courage, and any other virtue, demean themselves in this way, how shameful is their conduct! I have seen men of reputation, when they have been condemned, behaving in the strangest manner: they seemed to fancy that they were going to suffer something dreadful if they died, and that they could be immortal if you only allowed them to live; and I think that such are a dishonour to the state, and that any stranger coming in would have said of them that the most eminent men of Athens, to whom the Athenians themselves give honour and command, are no better than women. And I say that these things ought not to be done by those of us who have a reputation; and if they are done, you ought not to permit them; you ought rather to show that you are far more disposed to condemn the man who gets up a doleful scene and makes the city ridiculous, than him who holds his peace.

But, setting aside the question of public opinion, there seems to be something wrong in asking a favour of a judge, and thus procuring an acquittal, instead of informing and convincing him. For his duty is, not to make a present of justice, but to give judgment; and he has sworn that he will judge according to the laws, and not according to his own good pleasure; and we ought not to encourage you, nor should you allow yourself to be encouraged, in this habit of perjury—there can be no piety in that. Do not then require me to do what I consider dishonourable and impious and wrong, especially now, when I am being tried for impiety on the indictment of Meletus. For if, O men of Athens, by force of persuasion and entreaty I could overpower your oaths, then I should be teaching you to believe that there are no gods, and in defending should simply convict myself of the charge of not believing in them. But that is not so—far otherwise. For I do believe that there are gods, and in a sense higher than that in which any of my accusers believe in them. And to you and to God I commit my cause, to be determined by you as is best for you and me.

There are many reasons why I am not grieved, O men of Athens, at the vote of condemnation. I expected it, and am only surprised that the votes are so nearly equal; for I had thought that the majority against me would have been far larger; but now, had thirty votes gone over to the other side, I should have been acquitted. And I may say, I think, that I have escaped Meletus. I may say more; for without the assistance of Anytus and Lycon, any one may see that he would not have had a fifth part of the votes, as the law requires, in which case he would have incurred a fine of a thousand drachmae.

And so he proposes death as the penalty. And what shall I propose on my part, O men of Athens? Clearly that which is my due. And what is my due? What return shall be made to the man who has never had the wit to be idle during his whole life; but has been careless of what the many care for—wealth, and family interests, and military offices, and speaking in the assembly, and magistracies, and plots, and parties. Reflecting that I was really too honest a man to be a politician and live, I did not go where I could do no good to you or to myself; but where I could do the greatest good privately to every one of you, thither I went, and sought to persuade every man among you that he must look to himself, and seek virtue and wisdom before he looks to his private interests, and look to the state before he looks to the interests of the state; and that this should be the order which he observes in all his actions. What shall be done to such an one? Doubtless some good thing, O men of Athens, if he has his reward; and the good should be of a kind suitable to him. What would be a reward suitable to a poor man who is your benefactor, and who desires leisure that he may instruct you? There can be no reward so fitting as maintenance in the Prytaneum, O men of Athens, a reward which he deserves far more than the citizen who has won the prize at Olympia in the horse or chariot race, whether the chariots were drawn by two horses or by many. For I am in want, and he has enough; and he only gives you the appearance of happiness, and I give you the reality. And if I am to estimate the penalty fairly, I should say that maintenance in the Prytaneum is the just return.

Perhaps you think that I am braving you in what I am saying now, as in what I said before about the tears and prayers. But this is not so. I speak rather because I am convinced that I never intentionally wronged any one, although I cannot convince you—the time has been too short; if there were a law at Athens, as there is in other cities, that a capital cause should not be decided in one day, then I believe that I should have convinced you. But I cannot in a moment refute great slanders; and, as I am convinced that I never wronged another, I will assuredly not wrong myself. I will not say of myself that I deserve any evil, or propose any penalty. Why should I? Because I am afraid of the penalty of death which Meletus proposes? When I do not know whether death is a good or an evil, why should I propose a penalty which would certainly be an evil? Shall I say imprisonment? And why should I live in prison, and be the slave of the magistrates of the year—of the Eleven? Or shall the penalty be a fine, and imprisonment until the fine is paid? There is the same objection. I should have to lie in prison, for money I have none, and cannot pay. And if I say exile (and this may possibly be the penalty which you will affix), I must indeed be blinded by the love of life, if I am so irrational as to expect that when you, who are my own citizens, cannot endure my discourses and words, and have found them so grievous and odious that you will have no more of them, others are likely to endure me. No indeed, men of Athens, that is not very likely. And what a life should I lead, at my age, wandering from city to city, ever changing my place of exile, and always being driven out! For I am quite sure that wherever I go, there, as here, the young men will flock to me; and if I drive them away, their elders will drive me out at their request; and if I let them come, their fathers and friends will drive me out for their sakes.

Some one will say: Yes, Socrates, but cannot you hold your tongue, and then you may go into a foreign city, and no one will interfere with you? Now I have great difficulty in making you understand my answer to this. For if I tell you that to do as you say would be a disobedience to the God, and therefore that I cannot hold my tongue, you will not believe that I am serious; and if I say again that daily to discourse about virtue, and of those other things about which you hear me examining myself and others, is the greatest good of man, and that the unexamined life is not worth living, you are still less likely to believe me. Yet I say what is true, although a thing of which it is hard for me to persuade you. Also, I have never been accustomed to think that I deserve to suffer any harm. Had I money I might have estimated the offence at what I was able to pay, and not have been much the worse. But I have none, and therefore I must ask you to proportion the fine to my means. Well, perhaps I could afford a mina, and therefore I propose that penalty: Plato, Crito, Critobulus, and Apollodorus, my friends here, bid me say thirty minae, and they will be the sureties. Let thirty minae be the penalty; for which sum they will be ample security to you.

Not much time will be gained, O Athenians, in return for the evil name which you will get from the detractors of the city, who will say that you killed Socrates, a wise man; for they will call me wise, even although I am not wise, when they want to reproach you. If you had waited a little while, your desire would have been fulfilled in the course of nature. For I am far advanced in years, as you may perceive, and not far from death. I am speaking now not to all of you, but only to those who have condemned me to death. And I have another thing to say to them: You think that I was convicted because I had no words of the sort which would have procured my acquittal—I mean, if I had thought fit to leave nothing undone or unsaid. Not so; the deficiency which led to my conviction was not of words—certainly not. But I had not the boldness or impudence or inclination to address you as you would have liked me to do, weeping and wailing and lamenting, and saying and doing many things which you have been accustomed to hear from others, and which, as I maintain, are unworthy of me. I thought at the time that I ought not to do anything common or mean when in danger: nor do I now repent of the style of my defence; I would rather die having spoken after my manner, than speak, in your manner and live. For neither in war nor yet at law ought I or any man to use every way of escaping death. Often in battle there can be no doubt that if a man will throw away his arms, and fall on his knees before his pursuers, he may escape death; and in other dangers there are other ways of escaping death, if a man is willing to say and do anything. The difficulty, my friends, is not to avoid death, but to avoid unrighteousness; for that runs faster than death. I am old and move slowly, and the slower runner has overtaken me, and my accusers are keen and quick, and the faster runner, who is unrighteousness, has overtaken them. And now I depart hence condemned by you to suffer the penalty of death,—they too go their ways condemned by the truth to suffer the penalty of villainy and wrong; and I must abide by my award—let them abide by theirs. I suppose that these things may be regarded as fated,—and I think that they are well.

And now, O men who have condemned me, I would fain prophesy to you; for I am about to die, and in the hour of death men are gifted with prophetic power. And I prophesy to you who are my murderers, that immediately after my departure punishment far heavier than you have inflicted on me will surely await you. Me you have killed because you wanted to escape the accuser, and not to give an account of your lives. But that will not be as you suppose: far otherwise. For I say that there will be more accusers of you than there are now; accusers whom hitherto I have restrained: and as they are younger they will be more inconsiderate with you, and you will be more offended at them. If you think that by killing men you can prevent some one from censuring your evil lives, you are mistaken; that is not a way of escape which is either possible or honourable; the easiest and the noblest way is not to be disabling others, but to be improving yourselves. This is the prophecy which I utter before my departure to the judges who have condemned me.

Friends, who would have acquitted me, I would like also to talk with you about the thing which has come to pass, while the magistrates are busy, and before I go to the place at which I must die. Stay then a little, for we may as well talk with one another while there is time. You are my friends, and I should like to show you the meaning of this event which has happened to me. O my judges—for you I may truly call judges—I should like to tell you of a wonderful circumstance. Hitherto the divine faculty of which the internal oracle is the source has constantly been in the habit of opposing me even about trifles, if I was going to make a slip or error in any matter; and now as you see there has come upon me that which may be thought, and is generally believed to be, the last and worst evil. But the oracle made no sign of opposition, either when I was leaving my house in the morning, or when I was on my way to the court, or while I was speaking, at anything which I was going to say; and yet I have often been stopped in the middle of a speech, but now in nothing I either said or did touching the matter in hand has the oracle opposed me. What do I take to be the explanation of this silence? I will tell you. It is an intimation that what has happened to me is a good, and that those of us who think that death is an evil are in error. For the customary sign would surely have opposed me had I been going to evil and not to good.

Let us reflect in another way, and we shall see that there is great reason to hope that death is a good; for one of two things—either death is a state of nothingness and utter unconsciousness, or, as men say, there is a change and migration of the soul from this world to another. Now if you suppose that there is no consciousness, but a sleep like the sleep of him who is undisturbed even by dreams, death will be an unspeakable gain. For if a person were to select the night in which his sleep was undisturbed even by dreams, and were to compare with this the other days and nights of his life, and then were to tell us how many days and nights he had passed in the course of his life better and more pleasantly than this one, I think that any man, I will not say a private man, but even the great king will not find many such days or nights, when compared with the others. Now if death be of such a nature, I say that to die is gain; for eternity is then only a single night. But if death is the journey to another place, and there, as men say, all the dead abide, what good, O my friends and judges, can be greater than this? If indeed when the pilgrim arrives in the world below, he is delivered from the professors of justice in this world, and finds the true judges who are said to give judgment there, Minos and Rhadamanthus and Aeacus and Triptolemus, and other sons of God who were righteous in their own life, that pilgrimage will be worth making. What would not a man give if he might converse with Orpheus and Musaeus and Hesiod and Homer? Nay, if this be true, let me die again and again. I myself, too, shall have a wonderful interest in there meeting and conversing with Palamedes, and Ajax the son of Telamon, and any other ancient hero who has suffered death through an unjust judgment; and there will be no small pleasure, as I think, in comparing my own sufferings with theirs. Above all, I shall then be able to continue my search into true and false knowledge; as in this world, so also in the next; and I shall find out who is wise, and who pretends to be wise, and is not. What would not a man give, O judges, to be able to examine the leader of the great Trojan expedition; or Odysseus or Sisyphus, or numberless others, men and women too! What infinite delight would there be in conversing with them and asking them questions! In another world they do not put a man to death for asking questions: assuredly not. For besides being happier than we are, they will be immortal, if what is said is true.

Wherefore, O judges, be of good cheer about death, and know of a certainty, that no evil can happen to a good man, either in life or after death. He and his are not neglected by the gods; nor has my own approaching end happened by mere chance. But I see clearly that the time had arrived when it was better for me to die and be released from trouble; wherefore the oracle gave no sign. For which reason, also, I am not angry with my condemners, or with my accusers; they have done me no harm, although they did not mean to do me any good; and for this I may gently blame them.

Still I have a favour to ask of them. When my sons are grown up, I would ask you, O my friends, to punish them; and I would have you trouble them, as I have troubled you, if they seem to care about riches, or anything, more than about virtue; or if they pretend to be something when they are really nothing,—then reprove them, as I have reproved you, for not caring about that for which they ought to care, and thinking that they are something when they are really nothing. And if you do this, both I and my sons will have received justice at your hands.

The hour of departure has arrived, and we go our ways—I to die, and you to live. Which is better God only knows.

◢ Crito ◣

SOCRATES. Why have you come at this hour, Crito? it must be quite early?
CRITO. Yes, certainly.
SOC. What is the exact time?
CR. The dawn is breaking.
SOC. I wonder that the keeper of the prison would let you in.
CR. He knows me, because I often come, Socrates; moreover, I have done him a kindness.
SOC. And are you only just arrived?
CR. No, I came some time ago.
SOC. Then why did you sit and say nothing, instead of at once awakening me?

CR.   I should not have liked myself, Socrates, to be in such great trouble and unrest as you are—indeed I should not: I have been watching with amazement your peaceful slumbers; and for that reason I did not awake you, because I wished to minimize the pain. I have always thought you to be of a happy disposition; but never did I see anything like the easy, tranquil manner in which you bear this calamity.

SOC.   Why, Crito, when a man has reached my age he ought not to be repining at the approach of death.

CR.   And yet other old men find themselves in similar misfortunes, and age does not prevent them from repining.

SOC.   That is true. But you have not told me why you come at this early hour.

CR.   I come to bring you a message which is sad and painful; not, as I believe, to yourself, but to all of us who are your friends, and saddest of all to me.

SOC.   What? Has the ship come from Delos, on the arrival of which I am to die?

CR.   No, the ship has not actually arrived, but she will probably be here to-day, as persons who have come from Sunium tell me that they left her there; and therefore to-morrow, Socrates, will be the last day of your life.

SOC.   Very well, Crito; if such is the will of God, I am willing; but my belief is that there will be a delay of a day.

CR.   Why do you think so?

SOC.   I will tell you. I am to die on the day after the arrival of the ship.

CR.   Yes; that is what the authorities say.

SOC.   But I do not think that the ship will be here until to-morrow; this I infer from a vision which I had last night, or rather only just now, when you fortunately allowed me to sleep.

CR.   And what was the nature of the vision?

SOC.   There appeared to me the likeness of a woman, fair and comely, clothed in bright raiment, who called to me and said: O Socrates,

'The third day hence to fertile Phthia shalt thou go.'[4]

CR.   What a singular dream, Socrates!

SOC.   There can be no doubt about the meaning, Crito, I think.

CR.   Yes; the meaning is only too clear. But, oh! my beloved Socrates, let me entreat you once more to take my advice and escape. For if you die I shall not only lose a friend who can never be replaced, but there is another evil: people who do not know you and me will believe that I might have saved you if I had been willing to give money, but that I did not care. Now, can there be a worse disgrace than this—that I should be thought to value money more than the life of a friend? For the many will not be persuaded that I wanted you to escape, and that you refused.

SOC.   But why, my dear Crito, should we care about the opinion of the many? Good men, and they are the only persons who are worth considering, will think of these things truly as they occurred.

CR.   But you see, Socrates, that the opinion of the many must be regarded, for what is now happening shows that they can do the greatest evil to any one who has lost their good opinion.

Soc.   I only wish it were so, Crito; and that the many could do the greatest evil; for then they would also be able to do the greatest good—and what a fine thing this would be! But in reality they can do neither; for they cannot make a man either wise or foolish; and whatever they do is the result of chance.

Cr.   Well, I will not dispute with you; but please to tell me, Socrates, whether you are not acting out of regard to me and your other friends: are you not afraid that if you escape from prison we may get into trouble with the informers for having stolen you away, and lose either the whole or a great part of our property; or that even a worse evil may happen to us? Now, if you fear on our account, be at ease; for in order to save you, we ought surely to run this, or even a greater risk; be persuaded, then, and do as I say.

Soc.   Yes, Crito, that is one fear which you mention, but by no means the only one.

Cr.   Fear not—there are persons who are willing to get you out of prison at no great cost; and as for the informers, they are far from being exorbitant in their demands—a little money will satisfy them. My means, which are certainly ample, are at your service, and if you have a scruple about spending all mine, here are strangers who will give you the use of theirs; and one of them, Simmias the Theban, has brought a large sum of money for this very purpose; and Cebes and many others are prepared to spend their money in helping you to escape. I say, therefore, do not hesitate on our account, and do not say, as you did in the court,[5] that you will have a difficulty in knowing what to do with yourself anywhere else. For men will love you in other places to which you may go, and not in Athens only; there are friends of mine in Thessaly, if you like to go to them, who will value and protect you, and no Thessalian will give you any trouble. Nor can I think that you are at all justified, Socrates, in betraying your own life when you might be saved; in acting thus you are playing into the hands of your enemies, who are hurrying on your destruction. And further I should say that you are deserting your own children; for you might bring them up and educate them; instead of which you go away and leave them, and they will have to take their chance; and if they do not meet with the usual fate of orphans, there will be small thanks to you. No man should bring children into the world who is unwilling to persevere to the end in their nurture and education. But you appear to be choosing the easier part, not the better and manlier, which would have been more becoming in one who professes to care for virtue in all his actions, like yourself. And indeed, I am ashamed not only of you, but of us who are your friends, when I reflect that the whole business will be attributed entirely to our want of courage. The trial need never have come on, or might have been managed differently; and this last act, or crowning folly, will seem to have occurred through our negligence and cowardice, who might have saved you, if we had been good for anything; and you might have saved yourself, for there was no difficulty at all. See now, Socrates, how sad and discreditable are the consequences, both to us and you. Make up your mind then, or rather have your mind already made up, for the time of deliberation is over, and there is only one thing to be done, which must be done this very night, and if we delay at all will be no longer practicable or possible; I beseech you therefore, Socrates, be persuaded by me, and do as I say.

Soc.   Dear Crito, your zeal is invaluable, if a right one; but if wrong, the greater the zeal the greater the danger; and therefore we ought to consider whether I shall or shall not do as you say. For I am and always have been one of those natures who must be guided by reason, whatever the reason may be which upon reflection appears to me to be the best; and now that this chance has befallen me, I cannot repudiate my own words: the principles which I have hitherto honoured and revered I still honour, and unless we can at once find other and better principles, I am certain not to agree with you; no, not even if the power of the multitude could inflict many more imprisonments, confiscations, deaths, frightening us like children with hobgoblin terrors.[6] What will be the fairest way of considering the question? Shall I return to your old argument about the opinions of men?—we were saying that some of them are to be regarded, and others not. Now were we right in maintaining this before I was condemned? And has the argument which was once good now proved to be talk for the sake of talking—mere childish nonsense? That is what I want to consider with your help, Crito:—whether, under my present circumstances, the argument appears to be in any way different or not; and is to be allowed by me or disallowed. That argument, which, as I believe, is maintained by many persons of authority, was to the effect, as I was saying, that the opinions of some men are to be regarded, and of other men not to be regarded. Now you, Crito, are not going to die to-morrow—at least, there is no human probability of this and therefore you are disinterested and not liable to be deceived by the circumstances in which you are placed. Tell me then, whether I am right in saying that some opinions, and the opinions of some men only, are to be valued, and that other opinions, and the opinions of other men, are not to be valued. I ask you whether I was right in maintaining this?

CR. Certainly.

SOC. The good are to be regarded, and not the bad?

CR. Yes.

SOC. And the opinions of the wise are good, and the opinions of the unwise are evil?

CR. Certainly.

SOC. And what was said about another matter? Is the pupil who devotes himself to the practice of gymnastics supposed to attend to the praise and blame and opinion of every man, or of one only—his physician or trainer, whoever he may be?

CR. Of one man only.

SOC. And he ought to fear the censure and welcome the praise of that one only, and not of the many?

CR. Clearly so.

SOC. And he ought to act and train, and eat and drink in the way which seems good to his single master who has understanding, rather than according to the opinion of all other men put together?

CR. True.

SOC. And if he disobeys and disregards the opinion and approval of the one, and regards the opinion of the many who have no understanding, will he not suffer evil?

CR. Certainly he will.

SOC. And what will the evil be, whither tending and what affecting, in the disobedient person?

CR. Clearly, affecting the body; that is what is destroyed by the evil.

SOC. Very good; and is not this true, Crito, of other things which we need not separately enumerate? In questions of just and unjust, fair and foul, good and evil, which are the subjects of our present consultation, ought we to follow the opinion of the many and to fear them; or the opinion of the one man who has understanding? ought we not to fear and reverence him more than all the rest of the world: and if we desert him shall we not destroy and injure that principle in us which may be assumed to be improved by justice and deteriorated by injustice;—there is such a principle?

CR. Certainly there is, Socrates.

SOC. Take a parallel instance:—if, acting under the advice of those who have no understanding, we destroy that which is improved by health and is deteriorated by disease, would life be worth having? And that which has been destroyed is—the body?

CR. Yes.

SOC. Could we live, having an evil and corrupted body?

CR. Certainly not.

SOC. And will life be worth having, if that higher part of man be destroyed, which is improved by justice and depraved by injustice? Do we suppose that principle, whatever it may be in man, which has to do with justice and injustice, to be inferior to the body?

CR. Certainly not.

SOC. More honourable than the body?

CR. Far more.

SOC. Then, my friend, we must not regard what the many say of us: but what he, the one man who has understanding of just and unjust, will say, and what the truth will say. And therefore you begin in error when you advise that we should regard the opinion of the many about just and unjust, good and evil, honourable and dishonourable.—'Well,' some one will say, 'but the many can kill us.'

CR. Yes, Socrates; that will clearly be the answer.

SOC. And it is true: but still I find with surprise that the old argument is unshaken as ever. And I should like to know whether I may say the same of another proposition—that not life, but a good life, is to be chiefly valued?

CR. Yes, that also remains unshaken.

SOC. And a good life is equivalent to a just and honourable one—that holds also?

CR. Yes, it does.

SOC. From these premises I proceed to argue the question whether I ought or ought not to try and escape without the consent of the Athenians: and if I am clearly right in escaping, then I will make the attempt; but if not, I will abstain. The other considerations which you mention, of money and loss of character and the duty of educating one's children, are, I fear, only the doctrines of the multitude, who would be as ready to restore people to life, if they were able, as they are to put them to death—and with as little reason. But now, since the argument has thus far prevailed, the only question which remains to be considered is, whether we shall do rightly either in escaping or in suffering others to aid in our escape and paying them in money and thanks, or whether in reality we shall not do rightly; and if the latter, then death or any other calamity which may ensue on my remaining here must not be allowed to enter into the calculation.

CR. I think that you are right, Socrates; how then shall we proceed?

SOC. Let us consider the matter together, and do you either refute me if you can, and I will be convinced; or else cease, my dear friend, from repeating to me that I ought to escape against the wishes of the Athenians: for I highly value your attempts to persuade me to do so, but I may not be persuaded against my own better judgment. And now please to consider my first position, and try how you can best answer me.

CR. I will.

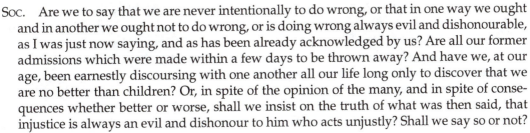

Soc.   Are we to say that we are never intentionally to do wrong, or that in one way we ought and in another we ought not to do wrong, or is doing wrong always evil and dishonourable, as I was just now saying, and as has been already acknowledged by us? Are all our former admissions which were made within a few days to be thrown away? And have we, at our age, been earnestly discoursing with one another all our life long only to discover that we are no better than children? Or, in spite of the opinion of the many, and in spite of consequences whether better or worse, shall we insist on the truth of what was then said, that injustice is always an evil and dishonour to him who acts unjustly? Shall we say so or not?

Cr.   Yes.

Soc.   Then we must do no wrong?

Cr.   Certainly not.

Soc.   Nor when injured injure in return, as the many imagine; for we must injure no one at all?[7]

Cr.   Clearly not.

Soc.   Again, Crito, may we do evil?

Cr.   Surely not, Socrates.

Soc.   And what of doing evil in return for evil, which is the morality of the many—is that just or not?

Cr.   Not just.

Soc.   For doing evil to another is the same as injuring him?

Cr.   Very true.

Soc.   Then we ought not to retaliate or render evil for evil to any one, whatever evil we may have suffered from him. But I would have you consider, Crito, whether you really mean what you are saying. For this opinion has never been held, and never will be held, by any considerable number of persons; and those who are agreed and those who are not agreed upon this point have no common ground, and can only despise one another when they see how widely they differ. Tell me, then, whether you agree with and assent to my first principle, that neither injury nor retaliation nor warding off evil by evil is ever right. And shall that be the premise of our argument? Or do you decline and dissent from this? For so I have ever thought, and continue to think; but, if you are of another opinion, let me hear what you have to say. If, however, you remain of the same mind as formerly, I will proceed to the next step.

Cr.   You may proceed, for I have not changed my mind.

Soc.   Then I will go on to the next point, which may be put in the form of a question:—Ought a man to do what he admits to be right, or ought he to betray the right?

Cr.   He ought to do what he thinks right.

Soc.   But if this is true, what is the application? In leaving the prison against the will of the Athenians, do I wrong any? or rather do I not wrong those whom I ought least to wrong? Do I not desert the principles which were acknowledged by us to be just—what do you say?

Cr.   I cannot tell, Socrates; for I do not know.

Soc.   Then consider the matter in this way:—Imagine that I am about to play truant (you may call the proceeding by any name which you like), and the laws and the government come and interrogate me: 'Tell us, Socrates,' they say; 'what are you about? are you not going by an act of yours to overturn us—the laws, and the whole state, as far as in you lies? Do you imagine that a state can subsist and not be overthrown, in which the decisions of law have no power, but are set aside and trampled upon by individuals?' What will be our answer, Crito, to these and the like words? Any one, and especially a rhetorician, will have a good deal to say on behalf of the law which requires a sentence to be carried out. He will argue that this law should not be set aside; and shall we reply, 'Yes; but the state has injured us and given an unjust sentence.' Suppose I say that?

CR.   Very good, Socrates.

SOC.   'And was that our agreement with you?' the law would answer; 'or were you to abide by the sentence of the state?' And if I were to express my astonishment at their words, the law would probably add: 'Answer, Socrates, instead of opening your eyes—you are in the habit of asking and answering questions. Tell us,—What complaint have you to make against us which justifies you in attempting to destroy us and the state? In the first place did we not bring you into existence? Your father married your mother by our aid and begat you. Say whether you have any objection to urge against those of us who regulate marriage?' None, I should reply. 'Or against those of us who after birth regulate the nurture and education of children, in which you also were trained? Were not the laws, which have the charge of education, right in commanding your father to train you in music and gymnastic?' Right, I should reply. 'Well then, since you were brought into the world and nurtured and educated by us, can you deny in the first place that you are our child and slave as your fathers were before you? And if this is true you are not on equal terms with us; nor can you think that you have a right to do to us what we are doing to you. Would you have any right to strike or revile or do any other evil to your father or your master, if you had one, because you have been struck or reviled by him, or received some other evil at his hands?—you would not say this? And because we think right to destroy you, do you think that you have any right to destroy us in return, and your country as far as in you lies? Will you, O professor of true virtue, pretend that you are justified in this? Has a philosopher like you failed to discover that our country is more to be valued and higher and holier far than mother or father or any ancestor, and more to be regarded in the eyes of the gods and of men of understanding? also to be soothed, and gently and reverently entreated when angry, even more than a father, and either to be persuaded, or if not persuaded, to be obeyed? And when we are punished by her, whether with imprisonment or stripes, the punishment is to be endured in silence; and if she leads us to wounds or death in battle, thither we follow as is right; neither may any one yield or retreat or leave his rank, but whether in battle or in a court of law, or in any other place, he must do what his city and his country order him; or he must change their view of what is just: and if he may do no violence to his father or mother, much less may he do violence to his country.' What answer shall we make to this, Crito? Do the laws speak truly, or do they not?

CR.   I think that they do.

SOC.   Then the laws will say, 'Consider, Socrates, if we are speaking truly that in your present attempt you are going to do us an injury. For, having brought you into the world, and nurtured and educated you, and given you and every other citizen a share in every good which we had to give, we further proclaim to any Athenian by the liberty which we allow him, that if he does not like us when he has become of age and has seen the ways of the city, and made our acquaintance, he may go where he pleases and take his goods with him. None of us laws will forbid him or interfere with him. Any one who does not like us and the city, and who wants to emigrate to a colony or to any other city, may go where he likes retaining his property. But he who has experience of the manner in which we order justice and administer the state, and still remains, has entered into an implied contract that he will do as we command him. And he who disobeys us is, as we maintain, thrice wrong; first, because in disobeying us he is disobeying his parents; secondly, because we are the authors of his education; thirdly, because he has made an agreement with us that he will duly obey our commands; and he neither obeys them nor convinces us that our commands are unjust; and we do not rudely impose them, but give him the alternative of obeying or convincing us;— that is what we offer, and he does neither.

'These are the sort of accusations to which, as we were saying, you, Socrates, will be exposed if you accomplish your intentions; you, above all other Athenians.' Suppose now I ask, why I rather than anybody else? they will justly retort upon me that I above all other men have acknowledged the agreement. 'There is clear proof,' they will say, 'Socrates, that we and the city were not displeasing to you. Of all Athenians you have been the most constant resident in the city, which, as you never leave, you may be supposed to love.[8] For you never went out of the city either to see the games, except once when you went to the Isthmus, or to any other place unless when you were on military service; nor did you travel as other men do. Nor had you any curiosity to know other states or their laws: your affections did not go beyond us and our state; we were your special favourites, and you acquiesced in our government of you; and here in this city you begat your children, which is a proof of your satisfaction. Moreover, you might in the course of the trial, if you had liked, have fixed the penalty at banishment; the state which refuses to let you go now would have let you go then. But you pretended that you preferred death to exile,[9] and that you were not unwilling to die. And now you have forgotten these fine sentiments, and pay no respect to us the laws, of whom you are the destroyer; and are doing what only a miserable slave would do, running away and turning your back upon the compacts and agreements which you made as a citizen. And first of all answer this very question: Are we right in saying that you agreed to be governed according to us in deed, and not in word only? Is that true or not?' How shall we answer, Crito? Must we not assent?

CR.   We cannot help it, Socrates.

SOC.   Then will they not say: 'You, Socrates, are breaking the covenants and agreements which you made with us at your leisure, not in any haste or under any compulsion or deception, but after you have had seventy years to think of them, during which time you were at liberty to leave the city, if we were not to your mind, or if our covenants appeared to you to be unfair. You had your choice, and might have gone either to Lacedaemon or Crete, both which states are often praised by you for their good government, or to some other Hellenic or foreign state. Whereas you, above all other Athenians, seemed to be so fond of the state, or, in other words, of us her laws (and who would care about a state which has no laws?), that you never stirred out of her; the halt, the blind, the maimed were not more stationary in her than you were. And now you run away and forsake your agreements. Not so, Socrates, if you will take our advice; do not make yourself ridiculous by escaping out of the city.

'For just consider, if you transgress and err in this sort of way, what good will you do either to yourself or to your friends? That your friends will be driven into exile and deprived of citizenship, or will lose their property, is tolerably certain; and you yourself, if you fly to one of the neighbouring cities, as, for example, Thebes or Megara, both of which are well governed, will come to them as an enemy, Socrates, and their government will be against you, and all patriotic citizens will cast an evil eye upon you, as a subverter of the laws, and you will confirm in the minds of the judges the justice of their own condemnation of you. For he who is a corrupter of the laws is more than likely to be a corrupter of the young and foolish portion of mankind. Will you then flee from well-ordered cities and virtuous men? and is existence worth having on these terms? Or will you go to them without shame, and talk to them, Socrates? And what will you say to them? What you say here about virtue and justice and institutions and laws being the best things among men? Would that be decent of you? Surely not. But if you go away from well-governed states to Crito's friends in Thessaly, where there is great disorder and licence, they will be charmed to hear the tale of your escape from prison, set off with ludicrous particulars of the manner in which you were wrapped in a goatskin or some other disguise, and metamorphosed as the manner is of runaways; but will there be no one to remind you that in your old age you were not ashamed to violate the most sacred laws from a miserable desire of a little more life? Perhaps not, if you keep them in a good temper; but if they are out of temper you will hear many degrading things; you will live, but how?—as the flatterer of all men, and the servant of all men; and doing what?—eating and drinking in Thessaly, having gone abroad in order that you may get a dinner. And where will be your fine sentiments about justice and virtue? Say that you wish to live for the sake of your children—you want to bring them up and educate them—will you take them into Thessaly and deprive them of Athenian citizenship? Is this the benefit which you will confer upon them? Or are you under the impression that they will be better cared for and educated here if you are still alive, although absent from them; for your friends will take care of them? Do you fancy that if you are an inhabitant of Thessaly they will take care of them, and if you are an inhabitant of the other world that they will not take care of them? Nay; but if they who call themselves friends are good for anything, they will—to be sure they will.

'Listen, then, Socrates, to us who have brought you up. Think not of life and children first, and of justice afterwards, but of justice first, that you may be justified before the princes of the world below. For neither will you nor any that belong to you be happier or holier or juster in this life, or happier in another, if you do as Crito bids. Now you depart in innocence, a sufferer and not a doer of evil; a victim, not of the laws but of men. But if you go forth, returning evil for evil, and injury for injury, breaking the covenants and agreements which you have made with us, and wronging those whom you ought least of all to wrong, that is to say, yourself, your friends, your country, and us, we shall be angry with you while you live, and our brethren, the laws in the world below, will receive you as an enemy; for they will know that you have done your best to destroy us. Listen, then, to us and not to Crito.'

This, dear Crito, is the voice which I seem to hear murmuring in my ears, like the sound of the flute in the ears of the mystic; that voice, I say, is humming in my ears, and prevents me from hearing any other. And I know that anything more which you may say will be vain. Yet speak, if you have anything to say.

CR.   I have nothing to say, Socrates.

SOC.   Leave me then, Crito, to fulfil the will of God, and to follow whither he leads.

Then tell me, Socrates, why is suicide held to be unlawful? as I have certainly heard Philolaus, about whom you were just now asking, affirm when he was staying with us at Thebes; and there are others who say the same, although I have never understood what was meant by any of them.

Do not lose heart, replied Socrates, and the day may come when you will understand. I suppose that you wonder why, when other things which are evil may be good at certain times and to certain persons, death is to be the only exception, and why, when a man is better dead, he is not permitted to be his own benefactor, but must wait for the hand of another.

Very true, said Cebes, laughing gently and speaking in his native Boeotian.

I admit the appearance of inconsistency in what I am saying; but there may not be any real inconsistency after all. There is a doctrine whispered in secret that man is a prisoner who has no right to open the door and run away; this is a great mystery which I do not quite understand. Yet I too believe that the gods are our guardians, and that we men are a possession of theirs. Do you not agree?

Yes, I quite agree, said Cebes.

And if one of your own possessions, an ox or an ass, for example, took the liberty of putting himself out of the way when you had given no intimation of your wish that he should die, would you not be angry with him, and would you not punish him if you could?

Certainly, replied Cebes.

Then, if we look at the matter thus, there may be reason in saying that a man should wait, and not take his own life until God summons him, as he is now summoning me.

Yes, Socrates, said Cebes, there seems to be truth in what you say. And yet how can you reconcile this seemingly true belief that God is our guardian and we his possessions, with the willingness to die which you were just now attributing to the philosopher? That the wisest of men should be willing to leave a service in which they are ruled by the gods who are the best of rulers, is not reasonable; for surely no wise man thinks that when set at liberty he can take better care of himself than the gods take of him. A fool may perhaps think so—he may argue that he had better run away from his master, not considering that his duty is to remain to the end, and not to run away from the good, and that there would be no sense in his running away. The wise man will want to be ever with him who is better than himself. Now this, Socrates, is the reverse of what was just now said; for upon this view the wise man should sorrow and the fool rejoice at passing out of life.

The earnestness of Cebes seemed to please Socrates. Here, said he, turning to us, is a man who is always enquiring, and is not so easily convinced by the first thing which he hears.

And certainly, added Simmias, the objection which he is now making does appear to me to have some force. For what can be the meaning of a truly wise man wanting to fly away and lightly leave a master who is better than himself? And I rather imagine that Cebes is referring to you; he thinks that you are too ready to leave us, and too ready to leave the gods whom you acknowledge to be our good masters.

Yes, replied Socrates; there is reason in what you say. And so you think that I ought to answer your indictment as if I were in a court?

We should like you to do so, said Simmias.

Then I must try to make a more successful defence before you than I did before the judges. For I am quite ready to admit, Simmias and Cebes, that I ought to be grieved at death, if I were not persuaded in the first place that I am going to other gods who are wise and good (of which I am as certain as I can be of any such matters), and secondly (though I am not so sure of this last) to men departed, better than those whom I leave behind; and therefore I do not grieve as I might have done, for I have good hope that there is yet something remaining for the dead, and as has been said of old, some far better thing for the good than for the evil.

But do you mean to take away your thoughts with you, Socrates? said Simmias. Will you not impart them to us?—for they are a benefit in which we too are entitled to share. Moreover, if you succeed in convincing us, that will be an answer to the charge against yourself.

I will do my best, replied Socrates. But you must first let me hear what Crito wants; he has long been wishing to say something to me.

Only this, Socrates, replied Crito:—the attendant who is to give you the poison has been telling me, and he wants me to tell you, that you are not to talk much; talking, he says, increases heat, and this is apt to interfere with the action of the poison; persons who excite themselves are sometimes obliged to take a second or even a third dose.

Then, said Socrates, let him mind his business and be prepared to give the poison twice or even thrice if necessary; that is all.

I knew quite well what you would say, replied Crito; but I was obliged to satisfy him.

Never mind him, he said.

And now, O my judges, I desire to prove to you that the real philosopher has reason to be of good cheer when he is about to die, and that after death he may hope to obtain the greatest good in the other world. And how this may be, Simmias and Cebes, I will endeavour to explain. For I deem that the true votary of philosophy is likely to be misunderstood by other men; they do not perceive that he is always pursuing death and dying; and if this be so, and he has had the desire of death all his life long, why when his time comes should he repine at that which he has been always pursuing and desiring?

Simmias said laughingly: Though not in a laughing humour, you have made me laugh, Socrates; for I cannot help thinking that the many when they hear your words will say how truly you have described philosophers, and our people at home will likewise say that the life which philosophers desire is in reality death, and that they have found them out to be deserving of the death which they desire.

And they are right, Simmias, in thinking so, with the exception of the words 'they have found them out;' for they have not found out either what is the nature of that death which the true philosopher deserves, or how he deserves or desires death. But enough of them:—let us discuss the matter among ourselves. Do we believe that there is such a thing as death?

To be sure, replied Simmias.

Is it not the separation of soul and body? And to be dead is the completion of this; when the soul exists in herself, and is released from the body and the body is released from the soul, what is this but death?

Just so, he replied.

There is another question, which will probably throw light on our present enquiry if you and I can agree about it:—Ought the philosopher to care about the pleasures—if they are to be called pleasures—of eating and drinking?

Certainly not, answered Simmias.

And what about the pleasures of love—should he care for them?

By no means.

And will he think much of the other ways of indulging the body, for example, the acquisition of costly raiment, or sandals, or other adornments of the body? Instead of caring about them, does he not rather despise anything more than nature needs? What do you say?

I should say that the true philosopher would despise them.

Would you not say that he is entirely concerned with the soul and not with the body? He would like, as far as he can, to get away from the body and to turn to the soul.

Quite true.

In matters of this sort philosophers, above all other men, may be observed in every sort of way to dissever the soul from the communion of the body.

Very true.

Whereas, Simmias, the rest of the world are of opinion that to him who has no sense of pleasure and no part in bodily pleasure, life is not worth having; and that he who is indifferent about them is as good as dead.

That is also true.

What again shall we say of the actual acquirement of knowledge?—is the body, if invited to share in the enquiry, a hinderer or a helper? I mean to say, have sight and hearing any truth in them? Are they not, as the poets are always telling us, inaccurate witnesses? and yet, if even they are inaccurate and indistinct, what is to be said of the other senses?—for you will allow that they are the best of them?

Certainly, he replied.

Then when does the soul attain truth?—for in attempting to consider anything in company with the body she is obviously deceived.

True.

Then must not true existence be revealed to her in thought, if at all?

Yes.

And thought is best when the mind is gathered into herself and none of these things trouble her—neither sounds nor sights nor pain nor any pleasure,—when she takes leave of the body, and has as little as possible to do with it, when she has no bodily sense or desire, but is aspiring after true being?

Certainly.

And in this the philosopher dishonours the body; his soul runs away from his body and desires to be alone and by herself?

That is true.

Well, but there is another thing, Simmias: Is there or is there not an absolute justice?

Assuredly there is.

And an absolute beauty and absolute good?

Of course.

But did you ever behold any of them with your eyes?

Certainly not.

Or did you ever reach them with any other bodily sense?—and I speak not of these alone, but of absolute greatness, and health, and strength, and of the essence or true nature of everything. Has the reality of them ever been perceived by you through the bodily organs? or rather, is not the nearest approach to the knowledge of their several natures made by him who so orders his intellectual vision as to have the most exact conception of the essence of each thing which he considers?

Certainly.

And he attains to the purest knowledge of them who goes to each with the mind alone, not introducing or intruding in the act of thought sight or any other sense together with reason, but with the very light of the mind in her own clearness searches into the very truth of each; he who has got rid, as far as he can, of eyes and ears and, so to speak, of the whole body, these being in his opinion distracting elements which when they infect the soul hinder her from acquiring truth and knowledge—who, if not he, is likely to attain to the knowledge of true being?

What you say has a wonderful truth in it, Socrates, replied Simmias.

And when real philosophers consider all these things, will they not be led to make a reflection which they will express in words something like the following? 'Have we not found,' they will say, 'a path of thought which seems to bring us and our argument to the conclusion, that while we are in the body, and while the soul is infected with the evils of the body, our desire will not be satisfied? and our desire is of the truth. For the body is a source of endless trouble to us by reason of the mere requirement of food; and is liable also to diseases which overtake and impede us in the search after true being: it fills us full of loves, and lusts, and fears, and fancies of all kinds, and endless foolery, and in fact, as men say, takes away from us the power of thinking at all. Whence come wars, and fightings, and factions? whence but from the body and the lusts of the body? Wars are occasioned by the love of money, and money has to be acquired for the sake and in the service of the body; and by reason of all these impediments we have no time to give to philosophy; and, last and worst of all, even if we are at leisure and betake ourselves to some speculation, the body is always breaking in upon us, causing turmoil and confusion in our enquiries, and so amazing us that we are prevented from seeing the truth. It has been proved to us by experience that if we would have pure knowledge of anything we must be quit of the body—the soul in herself must behold things in themselves: and then we shall attain the wisdom which we desire, and of which we say that we are lovers; not while we live, but after death; for if while in company with the body, the soul cannot have pure knowledge, one of two things follows—either knowledge is not to be attained at all, or, if at all, after death. For then, and not till then, the soul will be parted from the body and exist in herself alone. In this present life, I reckon that we make the nearest approach to knowledge when we have the least possible intercourse or communion with the body, and are not surfeited with the bodily nature, but keep ourselves pure until the hour when God himself is pleased to release us. And thus having got rid of the foolishness of the body we shall be pure and hold converse with the pure, and know of ourselves the clear light everywhere, which is no other than the light of truth.' For the impure are not permitted to approach the pure. These are the sort of words, Simmias, which the true lovers of knowledge cannot help saying to one another, and thinking. You would agree; would you not?

Undoubtedly, Socrates.

But, O my friend, if this be true, there is great reason to hope that, going whither I go, when I have come to the end of my journey, I shall attain that which has been the pursuit of my life. And therefore I go on my way rejoicing, and not I only, but every other man who believes that his mind has been made ready and that he is in a manner purified.

Certainly, replied Simmias.

And what is purification but the separation of the soul from the body, as I was saying before; the habit of the soul gathering and collecting herself into herself from all sides out of the body; the dwelling in her own place alone, as in another life, so also in this, as far as she can;—the release of the soul from the chains of the body?

Very true, he said.

And this separation and release of the soul from the body is termed death?

To be sure, he said.

And the true philosophers, and they only, are ever seeking to release the soul. Is not the separation and release of the soul from the body their especial study?

That is true.

And, as I was saying at first, there would be a ridiculous contradiction in men studying to live as nearly as they can in a state of death, and yet repining when it comes upon them.

Clearly.

And the true philosophers, Simmias, are always occupied in the practice of dying, wherefore also to them least of all men is death terrible. Look at the matter thus:—if they have been in every way the enemies of the body, and are wanting to be alone with the soul, when this desire of theirs is granted, how inconsistent would they be if they trembled and repined, instead of rejoicing at their departure to that place where, when they arrive, they hope to gain that which in life they desired—and this was wisdom—and at the same time to be rid of the company of their enemy. Many a man has been willing to go to the world below animated by the hope of seeing there an earthly love, or wife, or son, and conversing with them. And will he who is a true lover of wisdom, and is strongly persuaded in like manner that only in the world below he can worthily enjoy her, still repine at death? Will he not depart with joy? Surely he will, O my friend, if he be a true philosopher. For he will have a firm conviction that there, and there only, he can find wisdom in her purity. And if this be true, he would be very absurd, as I was saying, if he were afraid of death.

He would indeed, replied Simmias.

And when you see a man who is repining at the approach of death, is not his reluctance a sufficient proof that he is not a lover of wisdom, but a lover of the body, and probably at the same time a lover of either money or power, or both?

Quite so, he replied.

And is not courage, Simmias, a quality which is specially characteristic of the philosopher?

Certainly.

There is temperance again, which even by the vulgar is supposed to consist in the control and regulation of the passions, and in the sense of superiority to them—is not temperance a virtue belonging to those only who despise the body, and who pass their lives in philosophy?

Most assuredly.

For the courage and temperance of other men, if you will consider them, are really a contradiction.

How so?

Well, he said, you are aware that death is regarded by men in general as a great evil.

Very true, he said.

And do not courageous men face death because they are afraid of yet greater evils?

That is quite true.

Then all but the philosophers are courageous only from fear, and because they are afraid; and yet that a man should be courageous from fear, and because he is a coward, is surely a strange thing.

Very true.

And are not the temperate exactly in the same case? They are temperate because they are intemperate—which might seem to be a contradiction, but is nevertheless the sort of thing which happens with this foolish temperance. For there are pleasures which they are afraid of losing; and in their desire to keep them, they abstain from some pleasures, because they are overcome by others; and although to be conquered by pleasure is called by men intemperance, to them the conquest of pleasure consists in being conquered by pleasure. And that is what I mean by saying that, in a sense, they are made temperate through intemperance.

Such appears to be the case.

Yet the exchange of one fear or pleasure or pain for another fear or pleasure or pain, and of the greater for the less, as if they were coins, is not the exchange of virtue. O my blessed Simmias, is there not one true coin for which all things ought to be exchanged?—and that is wisdom; and only in exchange for this, and in company with this, is anything truly bought or sold, whether courage or temperance or justice. And is not all true virtue the companion of wisdom, no matter what fears or pleasures or other similar goods or evils may or may not attend her? But the virtue which is made up of these goods, when they are severed from wisdom and exchanged with one another, is a shadow of virtue only, nor is there any freedom or health or truth in her; but in the true exchange there is a purging away of all these things, and temperance, and justice, and courage, and wisdom herself are the purgation of them. The founders of the mysteries would appear to have had a real meaning, and were not talking nonsense when they intimated in a figure long ago that he who passes unsanctified and uninitiated into the world below will lie in a slough, but that he who arrives there after initiation and purification will dwell with the gods. For 'many,' as they say in the mysteries, 'are the thyrsus-bearers, but few are the mystics,'—meaning, as I interpret the words, 'the true philosophers.' In the number of whom, during my whole life, I have been seeking, according to my ability, to find a place;—whether I have sought in a right way or not, and whether I have succeeded or not, I shall truly know in a little while, if God will, when I myself arrive in the other world—such is my belief. And therefore I maintain that I am right, Simmias and Cebes, in not grieving or repining at parting from you and my masters in this world, for I believe that I shall equally find good masters and friends in another world. But most men do not believe this saying; if then I succeed in convincing you by my defence better than I did the Athenian judges, it will be well.

Cebes answered: I agree, Socrates, in the greater part of what you say. But in what concerns the soul, men are apt to be incredulous; they fear that when she has left the body her place may be nowhere, and that on the very day of death she may perish and come to an end—immediately on her release from the body, issuing forth dispersed like smoke or air and in her flight vanishing away into nothingness. If she could only be collected into herself after she has obtained release from the evils of which you were speaking, there would be good reason to hope, Socrates, that what you say is true. But surely it requires a great deal of argument and many proofs to show that when the man is dead his soul yet exists, and has any force or intelligence.

True, Cebes, said Socrates; and shall I suggest that we converse a little of the probabilities of these things?

I am sure, said Cebes, that I should greatly like to know your opinion about them.

I reckon, said Socrates, that no one who heard me now, not even if he were one of my old enemies, the Comic poets, could accuse me of idle talking about matters in which I have no concern:—If you please, then, we will proceed with the enquiry.

Suppose we consider the question whether the souls of men after death are or are not in the world below. There comes into my mind an ancient doctrine which affirms that they go from hence into the other world, and returning hither, are born again from the dead. Now if it be true that the living come from the dead, then our souls must exist in the other world, for if not, how could they have been born again? And this would be conclusive, if there were any real evidence that the living are only born from the dead; but if this is not so, then other arguments will have to be adduced.

Very true, replied Cebes.

Then let us consider the whole question, not in relation to man only, but in relation to animals generally, and to plants, and to everything of which there is generation, and the proof will be easier. Are not all things which have opposites generated out of their opposites? I mean such things as good and evil, just and unjust—and there are innumerable other opposites which are generated out of opposites. And I want to show that in all opposites there is of necessity a similar alternation; I mean to say, for example, that anything which becomes greater must become greater after being less.

True.

And that which becomes less must have been once greater and then have become less.

Yes.

And the weaker is generated from the stronger, and the swifter from the slower.

Very true.

And the worse is from the better, and the more just is from the more unjust.

Of course.

And is this true of all opposites? and are we convinced that all of them are generated out of opposites?

Yes.

And in this universal opposition of all things, are there not also two intermediate processes which are ever going on, from one to the other opposite, and back again; where there is a greater and a less there is also an intermediate process of increase and diminution, and that which grows is said to wax, and that which decays to wane?

Yes, he said.

And there are many other processes, such as division and composition, cooling and heating, which equally involve a passage into and out of one another. And this necessarily holds of all opposites, even though not always expressed in words—they are really generated out of one another, and there is a passing or process from one to the other of them?

Very true, he replied.

Well, and is there not an opposite of life, as sleep is the opposite of waking?

True, he said.

And what is it?

Death, he answered.

And these, if they are opposites, are generated the one from the other, and have their two intermediate processes also?

Of course.

Now, said Socrates, I will analyze one of the two pairs of opposites which I have mentioned to you, and also its intermediate processes, and you shall analyze the other to me. One of them I term sleep, the other waking. The state of sleep is opposed to the state of waking, and out of sleeping waking is generated, and out of waking, sleeping; and the process of generation is in the one case falling asleep, and in the other waking up. Do you agree?

I entirely agree.

Then, suppose that you analyze life and death to me in the same manner. Is not death opposed to life?

Yes.

And they are generated one from the other?

Yes.

What is generated from the living?

The dead.

And what from the dead?

I can only say in answer—the living.

Then the living, whether things or persons, Cebes, are generated from the dead?

That is clear, he replied.

Then the inference is that our souls exist in the world below?

That is true.

And one of the two processes or generations is visible—for surely the act of dying is visible?

Surely, he said.

What then is to be the result? Shall we exclude the opposite process? and shall we suppose nature to walk on one leg only? Must we not rather assign to death some corresponding process of generation?

Certainly, he replied.

And what is that process?

Return to life.

And return to life, if there be such a thing, is the birth of the dead into the world of the living?

Quite true.

Then here is a new way by which we arrive at the conclusion that the living come from the dead, just as the dead come from the living; and this, if true, affords a most certain proof that the souls of the dead exist in some place out of which they come again.

Yes, Socrates, he said; the conclusion seems to flow necessarily out of our previous admissions.

And that these admissions were not unfair, Cebes, he said, may be shown, I think, as follows: If generation were in a straight line only, and there were no compensation or circle in nature, no turn or return of elements into their opposites, then you know that all things would at last have the same form and pass into the same state, and there would be no more generation of them.

What do you mean? he said.

A simple thing enough, which I will illustrate by the case of sleep, he replied. You know that if there were no alternation of sleeping and waking, the tale of the sleeping Endymion would in the end have no meaning, because all other things would be asleep too, and he would not be distinguishable from the rest. Or if there were composition only, and no division of substances, then the chaos of Anaxagoras would come again. And in like manner, my dear Cebes, if all things which partook of life were to die, and after they were dead remained in the form of death, and did not come to life again, all would at last die, and nothing would be alive—what other result could there be? For if the living spring from any other things, and they too die, must not all things at last be swallowed up in death?[10]

There is no escape, Socrates, said Cebes; and to me your argument seems to be absolutely true.

Yes, he said, Cebes, it is and must be so, in my opinion; and we have not been deluded in making these admissions; but I am confident that there truly is such a thing as living again, and that the living spring from the dead, and that the souls of the dead are in existence, and that the good souls have a better portion than the evil.

Cebes added: Your favourite doctrine, Socrates, that knowledge is simply recollection, if true, also necessarily implies a previous time in which we have learned that which we now recollect. But this would be impossible unless our soul had been in some place before existing in the form of man; here then is another proof of the soul's immortality.

But tell me, Cebes, said Simmias, interposing, what arguments are urged in favour of this doctrine of recollection. I am not very sure at the moment that I remember them.

One excellent proof, said Cebes, is afforded by questions. If you put a question to a person in a right way, he will give a true answer of himself, but how could he do this unless there were knowledge and right reason already in him? And this is most clearly shown when he is taken to a diagram or to anything of that sort.[11]

But if, said Socrates, you are still incredulous, Simmias, I would ask you whether you may not agree with me when you look at the matter in another way;—I mean, if you are still incredulous as to whether knowledge is recollection?

Incredulous I am not, said Simmias; but I want to have this doctrine of recollection brought to my own recollection, and, from what Cebes has said, I am beginning to recollect and be convinced: but I should still like to hear what you were going to say.

This is what I would say, he replied:—We should agree, if I am not mistaken, that what a man recollects he must have known at some previous time.

Very true.

And what is the nature of this knowledge or recollection? I mean to ask, Whether a person who, having seen or heard or in any way perceived anything, knows not only that, but has a conception of something else which is the subject, not of the same but of some other kind of knowledge, may not be fairly said to recollect that of which he has the conception?

What do you mean?

I mean what I may illustrate by the following instance:—The knowledge of a lyre is not the same as the knowledge of a man?

True.

And yet what is the feeling of lovers when they recognize a lyre, or a garment, or anything else which the beloved has been in the habit of using? Do not they, from knowing the lyre, form in the mind's eye an image of the youth to whom the lyre belongs? And this is recollection. In like manner any one who sees Simmias may remember Cebes; and there are endless examples of the same thing.

Endless, indeed, replied Simmias.

And recollection is most commonly a process of recovering that which has been already forgotten through time and inattention.

Very true, he said.

Well; and may you not also from seeing the picture of a house or a lyre remember a man? and from the picture of Simmias, you may be led to remember Cebes;

True.

Or you may also be led to the recollection of Simmias himself?

Quite so.

And in all these cases, the recollection may be derived from things either like or unlike?

It may be.

And when the recollection is derived from like things, then another consideration is sure to arise, which is—whether the likeness in any degree falls short or not of that which is recollected?

Very true, he said.

And shall we proceed a step further, and affirm that there is such a thing as equality, not of one piece of wood or stone with another, but that, over and above this, there is absolute equality? Shall we say so?

Say so, yes, replied Simmias, and swear to it, with all the confidence in life.

And do we know the nature of this absolute essence?

To be sure, he said.

And whence did we obtain our knowledge? Did we not see equalities of material things, such as pieces of wood and stones, and gather from them the idea of an equality which is different from them? For you will acknowledge that there is a difference. Or look at the matter in another way:—Do not the same pieces of wood or stone appear at one time equal, and at another time unequal?

That is certain.

But are real equals ever equal? or is the idea of equality the same as of inequality?

Impossible, Socrates.

Then these (so-called) equals are not the same with the idea of equality?

I should say, clearly not, Socrates.

And yet from these equals, although differing from the idea of equality, you conceived and attained that idea?

Very true, he said.

Which might be like, or might be unlike them?

Yes.

But that makes no difference: whenever from seeing one thing you conceived another, whether like or unlike, there must surely have been an act of recollection?

Very true.

But what would you say of equal portions of wood and stone, or other material equals? and what is the impression produced by them? Are they equals in the same sense in which absolute equality is equal? or do they fall short of this perfect equality in a measure?

Yes, he said, in a very great measure too.

And must we not allow, that when I or any one, looking at any object, observes that the thing which he sees aims at being some other thing, but falls short of, and cannot be, that other thing, but is inferior, he who makes this observation must have had a previous knowledge of that to which the other, although, similar, was inferior.

Certainly.

And has not this been our own case in the matter of equals and of absolute equality?

Precisely.

Then we must have known equality previously to the time when we first saw the material equals, and reflected that all these apparent equals strive to attain absolute equality, but fall short of it?

Very true.

And we recognize also that this absolute equality has only been known, and can only be known, through the medium of sight or touch, or of some other of the senses, which are all alike in this respect?

Yes, Socrates, as far as the argument is concerned, one of them is the same as the other.

From the senses then is derived the knowledge that all sensible things aim at an absolute equality of which they fall short?

Yes.

Then before we began to see or hear or perceive in any way, we must have had a knowledge of absolute equality, or we could not have referred to that standard the equals which are derived from the senses?—for to that they all aspire, and of that they fall short.

No other inference can be drawn from the previous statements.

And did we not see and hear and have the use of our other senses as soon as we were born?

Certainly.

Then we must have acquired the knowledge of equality at some previous time?

Yes.

That is to say, before we were born, I suppose?

True.

And if we acquired this knowledge before we were born and were born having the use of it, then we also knew before we were born and at the instant of birth not only the equal or the greater or the less, but all other ideas; for we are not speaking only of equality, but of beauty, goodness, justice, holiness, and of all which we stamp with the name of essence in the dialectical process, both when we ask and when we answer questions. Of all this we may certainly affirm that we acquired the knowledge before birth?

We may.

But if, after having acquired, we have not forgotten what in each case we acquired, then we must always have come into life having knowledge, and shall always continue to know as long as life lasts—for knowing is the acquiring and retaining knowledge and not forgetting. Is not forgetting, Simmias, just the losing of knowledge?

Quite true, Socrates.

But if the knowledge which we acquired before birth was lost by us at birth, and if afterwards by the use of the senses we recovered what we previously knew, will not the process which we call learning be a recovering of the knowledge which is natural to us, and may not this be rightly termed recollection?

Very true.

So much is clear—that when we perceive something, either by the help of sight, or hearing, or some other sense, from that perception we are able to obtain a notion of some other thing like or unlike which is associated with it but has been forgotten. Whence, as I was saying, one of two alternatives follows:—either we had this knowledge at birth, and continued to know through life; or, after birth, those who are said to learn only remember, and learning is simply recollection.

Yes, that is quite true, Socrates.

And which alternative, Simmias, do you prefer? Had we the knowledge at our birth, or did we recollect the things which we knew previously to our birth?

I cannot decide at the moment.

At any rate you can decide whether he who has knowledge will or will not be able to render an account of his knowledge? What do you say?

Certainly, he will.

But do you think that every man is able to give an account of these very matters about which we are speaking?

Would that they could, Socrates, but I rather fear that to-morrow, at this time, there will no longer be any one alive who is able to give an account of them such as ought to be given.

Then you are not of opinion, Simmias, that all men know these things?

Certainly not.

They are in process of recollecting that which they learned before?

Certainly.

But when did our souls acquire this knowledge?—not since we were born as men?

Certainly not.

And therefore, previously?

Yes.

Then, Simmias, our souls must also have existed without bodies before they were in the form of man, and must have had intelligence.

Unless indeed you suppose, Socrates, that these notions are given us at the very moment of birth; for this is the only time which remains.

Yes, my friend, but if so, when do we lose them? for they are not in us when we are born—that is admitted. Do we lose them at the moment of receiving them, or if not at what other time?

No, Socrates, I perceive that I was unconsciously talking nonsense.

Then may we not say, Simmias, that if, as we are always repeating, there is an absolute beauty, and goodness, and an absolute essence of all things; and if to this, which is now discovered to have existed in our former state, we refer all our sensations, and with this compare them, finding these ideas to be pre-existent and our inborn possession—then our souls must have had a prior existence, but if not, there would be no force in the argument? There is the same proof that these ideas must have existed before we were born, as that our souls existed before we were born; and if not the ideas, then not the souls.

Yes, Socrates; I am convinced that there is precisely the same necessity for the one as for the other; and the argument retreats successfully to the position that the existence of the soul before birth cannot be separated from the existence of the essence of which you speak. For there is nothing which to my mind is so patent as that beauty, goodness, and the other notions of which you were just now speaking, have a most real and absolute existence; and I am satisfied with the proof.

Well, but is Cebes equally satisfied? for I must convince him too.

I think, said Simmias, that Cebes is satisfied: although he is the most incredulous of mortals, yet I believe that he is sufficiently convinced of the existence of the soul before birth. But that after death the soul will continue to exist is not yet proven even to my own satisfaction. I cannot get rid of the feeling of the many to which Cebes was referring—the feeling that when the man dies the soul will be dispersed, and that this may be the extinction of her. For admitting that she may have been born elsewhere, and framed out of other elements, and was in existence before entering the human body, why after having entered in and gone out again may she not herself be destroyed and come to an end?

Very true, Simmias, said Cebes; about half of what was required has been proven; to wit, that our souls existed before we were born:—that the soul will exist after death as well as before birth is the other half of which the proof is still wanting, and has to be supplied; when that is given the demonstration will be complete.

But that proof, Simmias and Cebes, has been already given, said Socrates, if you put the two arguments together—I mean this and the former one, in which we admitted that everything living is born of the dead. For if the soul exists before birth, and in coming to life and being born can be born only from death and dying, must she not after death continue to exist, since she has to be born again?—Surely the proof which you desire has been already furnished. Still I suspect that you and Simmias would be glad to probe the argument further. Like children, you are haunted with a fear that when the soul leaves the body, the wind may really blow her away and scatter her; especially if a man should happen to die in a great storm and not when the sky is calm.

Cebes answered with a smile: Then, Socrates, you must argue us out of our fears—and yet, strictly speaking, they are not our fears, but there is a child within us to whom death is a sort of hobgoblin: him too we must persuade not to be afraid when he is alone in the dark.

Socrates said: Let the voice of the charmer be applied daily until you have charmed away the fear.

And where shall we find a good charmer of our fears, Socrates, when you are gone?

Hellas, he replied, is a large place, Cebes, and has many good men, and there are barbarous races not a few: seek for him among them all, far and wide, sparing neither pains nor money; for there is no better way of spending your money. And you must seek among yourselves too; for you will not find others better able to make the search.

The search, replied Cebes, shall certainly be made. And now, if you please, let us return to the point of the argument at which we digressed.

By all means, replied Socrates; what else should I please?

Very good.

Must we not, said Socrates, ask ourselves what that is which, as we imagine, is liable to be scattered, and about which we fear? and what again is that about which we have no fear? And then we may proceed further to enquire whether that which suffers dispersion is or is not of the nature of soul—our hopes and fears as to our own souls will turn upon the answers to these questions.

Very true, he said.

Now the compound or composite may be supposed to be naturally capable, as of being compounded, so also of being dissolved; but that which is uncompounded, and that only, must be, if anything is, indissoluble.

Yes; I should imagine so, said Cebes.

And the uncompounded may be assumed to be the same and unchanging, whereas the compound is always changing and never the same.

I agree, he said.

Then now let us return to the previous discussion. Is that idea or essence, which in the dialectical process we define as essence or true existence—whether essence of equality, beauty, or anything else—are these essences, I say, liable at times to some degree of change? or are they each of them always what they are, having the same simple self-existent and unchanging forms, not admitting of variation at all, or in any way, or at any time?

They must be always the same, Socrates, replied Cebes.

And what would you say of the many beautiful—whether men or horses or garments or any other things which are named by the same names and may be called equal or beautiful,—are they all unchanging and the same always, or quite the reverse? May they not rather be described as almost always changing and hardly ever the same, either with themselves or with one another?

The latter, replied Cebes; they are always in a state of change.

And these you can touch and see and perceive with the senses, but the unchanging things you can only perceive with the mind—they are invisible and are not seen?

That is very true, he said.

Well then, added Socrates, let us suppose that there are two sorts of existences—one seen, the other unseen.

Let us suppose them.

The seen is the changing, and the unseen is the unchanging?

That may be also supposed.

And, further, is not one part of us body, another part soul?

To be sure.

And to which class is the body more alike and akin?

Clearly to the seen—no one can doubt that.

And is the soul seen or not seen?

Not by man, Socrates.

And what we mean by 'seen' and 'not seen' is that which is or is not visible to the eye of man?

Yes, to the eye of man.

And is the soul seen or not seen?

Not seen.

Unseen then?

Yes.

Then the soul is more like to the unseen, and the body to the seen?

That follows necessarily, Socrates.

And were we not saying long ago that the soul when using the body as an instrument of perception, that is to say, when using the sense of sight or hearing or some other sense (for the meaning of perceiving through the body is perceiving through the senses)—were we not saying that the soul too is then dragged by the body into the region of the changeable, and wanders and is confused; the world spins round her, and she is like a drunkard, when she touches change?

Very true.

But when returning into herself she reflects, then she passes into the other world, the region of purity, and eternity, and immortality, and unchangeableness, which are her kindred, and with them she ever lives, when she is by herself and is not let or hindered; then she ceases from her erring ways, and being in communion with the unchanging is unchanging. And this state of the soul is called wisdom?

That is well and truly said, Socrates, he replied.

And to which class is the soul more nearly alike and akin, as far as may be inferred from this argument, as well as from the preceding one?

I think, Socrates, that, in the opinion of every one who follows the argument, the soul will be infinitely more like the unchangeable—even the most stupid person will not deny that.

And the body is more like the changing?

Yes.

Yet once more consider the matter in another light: When the soul and the body are united, then nature orders the soul to rule and govern, and the body to obey and serve. Now which of these two functions is akin to the divine? and which to the mortal? Does not the divine appear to you to be that which naturally orders and rules, and the mortal to be that which is subject and servant?

True.

And which does the soul resemble?

The soul resembles the divine, and the body the mortal—there can be no doubt of that, Socrates.

Then reflect, Cebes: of all which has been said is not this the conclusion?—that the soul is in the very likeness of the divine, and immortal, and intellectual, and uniform, and indissoluble, and unchangeable; and that the body is in the very likeness of the human, and mortal, and unintellectual, and multiform, and dissoluble, and changeable. Can this, my dear Cebes, be denied?

It cannot.

But if it be true, then is not the body liable to speedy dissolution? and is not the soul almost or altogether indissoluble?

Certainly.

And do you further observe, that after a man is dead, the body, or visible part of him, which is lying in the visible world, and is called a corpse, and would naturally be dissolved and decomposed and dissipated, is not dissolved or decomposed at once, but may remain for some time, nay even for a long time, if the constitution be sound at the time of death, and the season of the year favourable? For the body when shrunk and embalmed, as the manner is in Egypt, may remain almost entire through infinite ages; and even in decay, there are still some portions, such as the bones and ligaments, which are practically indestructible:—Do you agree?

Yes.

And is it likely that the soul, which is invisible, in passing to the place of the true Hades, which like her is invisible, and pure, and, noble, and on her way to the good and wise God, whither, if God will, my soul is also soon to go,—that the soul, I repeat, if this be her nature and origin, will be blown away and destroyed immediately on quitting the body, as the many say? That can never be, my dear Simmias and Cebes. The truth rather is, that the soul which is pure at departing and draws after her no bodily taint, having never voluntarily during life had connection with the body, which she is ever avoiding, herself gathered into herself;—and making such abstraction her perpetual study—which means that she has been a true disciple of philosophy; and therefore has in fact been always engaged in the practice of dying? For is not philosophy the study of death?—

Certainly—

That soul, I say, herself invisible, departs to the invisible world—to the divine and immortal and rational; thither arriving, she is secure of bliss and is released from the error and folly of men, their fears and wild passions and all other human ills, and for ever dwells, as they say of the initiated, in company with the gods.[12] Is not this true, Cebes?

Yes, said Cebes, beyond a doubt.

But the soul which has been polluted, and is impure at the time of her departure, and is the companion and servant of the body always, and is in love with and fascinated by the body and by the desires and pleasures of the body, until she is led to believe that the truth only exists in a bodily form, which a man may touch and see and taste, and use for the purposes of his lusts,—the soul, I mean, accustomed to hate and fear and avoid the intellectual principle, which to the bodily eye is dark and invisible, and can be attained only by philosophy;—do you suppose that such a soul will depart pure and unalloyed?

Impossible, he replied.

She is held fast by the corporeal, which the continual association and constant care of the body have wrought into her nature.

Very true.

And this corporeal element, my friend, is heavy and weighty and earthy, and is that element of sight by which a soul is depressed and dragged down again into the visible world, because she is afraid of the invisible and of the world below—prowling about tombs and sepulchres, near which, as they tell us, are seen certain ghostly apparitions of souls which have not departed pure, but are cloyed with sight and therefore visible.[13]

That is very likely, Socrates.

Yes, that is very likely, Cebes; and these must be the souls, not of the good, but of the evil, which are compelled to wander about such places in payment of the penalty of their former evil way of life; and they continue to wander until through the craving after the corporeal which never leaves them, they are imprisoned finally in another body. And they may be supposed to find their prisons in the same natures which they have had in their former lives.

What natures do you mean, Socrates?

What I mean is that men who have followed after gluttony, and wantonness, and drunkenness, and have had no thought of avoiding them, would pass into asses and animals of that sort. What do you think?

I think such an opinion to be exceedingly probable.

And those who have chosen the portion of injustice, and tyranny, and violence, will pass into wolves, or into hawks and kites;—whither else can we suppose them to go?

Yes, said Cebes; with such natures, beyond question.

And there is no difficulty, he said, in assigning to all of them places answering to their several natures and propensities?

There is not, he said.

Some are happier than others; and the happiest both in themselves and in the place to which they go are those who have practised the civil and social virtues which are called temperance and justice, and are acquired by habit and attention without philosophy and mind.[14]

Why are they the happiest?

Because they may be expected to pass into some gentle and social kind which is like their own, such as bees or wasps or ants, or back again into the form of man, and just and moderate men may be supposed to spring from them.

Very likely.

No one who has not studied philosophy and who is not entirely pure at the time of his departure is allowed to enter the company of the Gods, but the lover of knowledge only. And this is the reason, Simmias and Cebes, why the true votaries of philosophy abstain from all fleshly lusts, and hold out against them and refuse to give themselves up to them,—not because they fear poverty or the ruin of their families, like the lovers of money, and the world in general; nor like the lovers of power and honour, because they dread the dishonour or disgrace of evil deeds.

No, Socrates, that would not become them, said Cebes.

No indeed, he replied; and therefore they who have any care of their own souls, and do not merely live moulding and fashioning the body, say farewell to all this; they will not walk in the ways of the blind: and when philosophy offers them purification and release from evil, they feel that they ought not to resist her influence, and whither she leads they turn and follow.

What do you mean, Socrates?

I will tell you, he said. The lovers of knowledge are conscious that the soul was simply fastened and glued to the body—until philosophy received her, she could only view real existence through the bars of a prison, not in and through herself; she was wallowing in the mire of every sort of ignorance, and by reason of lust had become the principal accomplice in her own captivity. This was her original state; and then, as I was saying, and as the lovers of knowledge are well aware, philosophy, seeing how terrible was her confinement, of which she was to herself the cause, received and gently comforted her and sought to release her, pointing out that the eye and the ear and the other senses are full of deception, and persuading her to retire from them, and abstain from all but the necessary use of them, and be gathered up and collected into herself, bidding her trust in herself and her own pure apprehension of pure existence, and to mistrust whatever comes to her through other channels and is subject to variation; for such things are visible and tangible, but what she sees in her own nature is intelligible and invisible. And the soul of the true philosopher thinks that she ought not to resist this deliverance, and therefore abstains from pleasures and desires and pains and fears, as far as she is able; reflecting that when a man has great joys or sorrows or fears or desires, he suffers from them, not merely the sort of evil which might be anticipated—as for example, the loss of his health or property which he has sacrificed to his lusts—but an evil greater far, which is the greatest and worst of all evils, and one of which he never thinks.

What is it, Socrates? said Cebes.

The evil is that when the feeling of pleasure or pain is most intense, every soul of man imagines the objects of this intense feeling to be then plainest and truest: but this is not so, they are really the things of sight.

Very true.

And is not this the state in which the soul is most enthralled by the body?

How so?

Why, because each pleasure and pain is a sort of nail which nails and rivets the soul to the body, until she becomes like the body, and believes that to be true which the body affirms to be true; and from agreeing with the body and having the same delights she is obliged to have the same habits and haunts, and is not likely ever to be pure at her departure to the world below, but is always infected by the body; and so she sinks into another body and there germinates and grows, and has therefore no part in the communion of the divine and pure and simple.

Most true, Socrates, answered Cebes.

And this, Cebes, is the reason why the true lovers of knowledge are temperate and brave; and not for the reason which the world gives.

Certainly not.

Certainly not! The soul of a philosopher will reason in quite another way; she will not ask philosophy to release her in order that when released she may deliver herself up again to the thraldom of pleasures and pains, doing a work only to be undone again, weaving instead of unweaving her Penelope's web. But she will calm passion, and follow reason, and dwell in the contemplation of her, beholding the true and divine (which is not matter of opinion), and thence deriving nourishment. Thus she seeks to live while she lives, and after death she hopes to go to her own kindred and to that which is like her, and to be freed from human ills. Never fear, Simmias and Cebes, that a soul which has been thus nurtured and has had these pursuits, will at her departure from the body be scattered and blown away by the winds and be no-where and nothing.

When Socrates had done speaking, for a considerable time there was silence; he himself appeared to be meditating, as most of us were, on what had been said; only Cebes and Simmias spoke a few words to one another. And Socrates observing them asked what they thought of the argument, and whether there was anything wanting? For, said he, there are many points still open to suspicion and attack, if any one were disposed to sift the matter thoroughly. Should you be considering some other matter I say no more, but if you are still in doubt do not hesitate to say exactly what you think, and let us have anything better which you can suggest; and if you think that I can be of any use, allow me to help you.

Simmias said: I must confess, Socrates, that doubts did arise in our minds, and each of us was urging and inciting the other to put the question which we wanted to have answered but which neither of us liked to ask, fearing that our importunity might be troublesome at such a time.

Socrates replied with a smile: O Simmias, what are you saying? I am not very likely to persuade other men that I do not regard my present situation as a misfortune, if I cannot even persuade you that I am no worse off now than at any other time in my life. Will you not allow that I have as much of the spirit of prophecy in me as the swans? For they, when they perceive that they must die, having sung all their life long, do then sing more lustily than ever, rejoicing in the thought that they are about to go away to the god whose ministers they are. But men, because they are themselves afraid of death, slanderously affirm of the swans that they sing a lament at the last, not considering that no bird sings when cold, or hungry, or in pain, not even the nightingale, nor the swallow, nor yet the hoopoe; which are said indeed to tune a lay of sorrow, although I do not believe this to be true of them any more than of the swans. But because they are sacred to Apollo, they have the gift of prophecy, and anticipate the good things of another world; wherefore they sing and rejoice in that day more than ever they did before. And I too, believing myself to be the consecrated servant of the same God, and the fellow-servant of the swans, and thinking that I have received from my master gifts of prophecy which are not inferior to theirs, would not go out of life less merrily than the swans.

Now these rivers are many, and mighty, and diverse, and there are four principal ones, of which the greatest and outermost is that called Oceanus, which flows round the earth in a circle; and in the opposite direction flows Acheron, which passes under the earth through desert places into the Acherusian lake: this is the lake to the shores of which the souls of the many go when they are dead, and after waiting an appointed time, which is to some a longer and to some a shorter time, they are sent back to be born again as animals. The third river passes out between the two, and near the place of outlet pours into a vast region of fire, and forms a lake larger than the Mediterranean Sea, boiling with water and mud; and proceeding muddy and turbid, and winding about the earth, comes, among other places, to the extremities of the Acherusian lake, but mingles not with the waters of the lake, and after making many coils about the earth plunges into Tartarus at a deeper level. This is that Pyriphlegethon, as the stream is called, which throws up jets of fire in different parts of the earth. The fourth river goes out on the opposite side, and falls first of all into a wild and savage region, which is all of a dark blue colour, like lapis lazuli; and this is that river which is called the Stygian river, and falls into and forms the Lake Styx, and after falling into the lake and receiving strange powers in the waters, passes under the earth, winding round in the opposite direction, and comes near the Acherusian lake from the opposite side to Pyriphlegethon. And the water of this river too mingles with no other, but flows round in a circle and falls into Tartarus over against Pyriphlegethon; and the name of the river, as the poets say, is Cocytus.
Such is the nature of the other world; and when the dead arrive at the place to which the genius of each severally guides them, first of all, they have sentence passed upon them, as they have lived well and piously or not. And those who appear to have lived neither well nor ill, go to the river Acheron, and embarking in any vessels which they may find, are carried in them to the lake, and there they dwell and are purified of their evil deeds, and having suffered the penalty of the wrongs which they have done to others, they are absolved, and receive the rewards of their good deeds, each of them according to his deserts. But those who appear to be incurable by reason of the greatness of their crimes—who have committed many and terrible deeds of sacrilege, murders foul and violent, or the like—such are hurled into Tartarus which

is their suitable destiny, and they never come out. Those again who have committed crimes, which, although great, are not irremediable—who in a moment of anger, for example, have done some violence to a father or a mother, and have repented for the remainder of their lives, or, who have taken the life of another under the like extenuating circumstances—these are plunged into Tartarus, the pains of which they are compelled to undergo for a year, but at the end of the year the wave casts them forth—mere homicides by way of Cocytus, parricides and matricides by Pyriphlegethon—and they are borne to the Acherusian lake, and there they lift up their voices and call upon the victims whom they have slain or wronged, to have pity on them, and to be kind to them, and let them come out into the lake. And if they prevail, then they come forth and cease from their troubles; but if not, they are carried back again into Tartarus and from thence into the rivers unceasingly, until they obtain mercy from those whom they have wronged: for that is the sentence inflicted upon them by their judges. Those too who have been pre-eminent for holiness of life are released from this earthly prison, and go to their pure home which is above, and dwell in the purer earth; and of these, such as have duly purified themselves with philosophy live henceforth altogether without the body, in mansions fairer still, which may not be described, and of which the time would fail me to tell.

Wherefore, Simmias, seeing all these things, what ought not we to do that we may obtain virtue and wisdom in this life? Fair is the prize, and the hope great!

A man of sense ought not to say, nor will I be very confident, that the description which I have given of the soul and her mansions is exactly true. But I do say that, inasmuch as the soul is shown to be immortal, he may venture to think, not improperly or unworthily, that something of the kind is true. The venture is a glorious one, and he ought to comfort himself with words like these, which is the reason why I lengthen out the tale. Wherefore, I say, let a man be of good cheer about his soul, who having cast away the pleasures and ornaments of the body as alien to him and working harm rather than good, has sought after the pleasures of knowledge; and has arrayed the soul, not in some foreign attire, but in her own proper jewels, temperance, and justice, and courage, and nobility, and truth—in these adorned she is ready to go on her journey to the world below, when her hour comes. You, Simmias and Cebes, and all other men, will depart at some time or other. Me already, as a tragic poet would say, the voice of fate calls. Soon I must drink the poison; and I think that I had better repair to the bath first, in order that the women may not have the trouble of washing my body after I am dead.

When he had done speaking, Crito said: And have you any commands for us, Socrates—anything to say about your children, or any other matter in which we can serve you?

Nothing particular, Crito, he replied: only, as I have always told you, take care of yourselves; that is a service which you may be ever rendering to me and mine and to all of us, whether you promise to do so or not. But if you have no thought for yourselves, and care not to walk according to the rule which I have prescribed for you, not now for the first time, however much you may profess or promise at the moment, it will be of no avail.

We will do our best, said Crito: And in what way shall we bury you?

In any way that you like; but you must get hold of me, and take care that I do not run away from you. Then he turned to us, and added with a smile:—I cannot make Crito believe that I am the same Socrates who have been talking and conducting the argument; he fancies that I am the other Socrates whom he will soon see, a dead body—and he asks, How shall he bury me? And though I have spoken many words in the endeavour to show that when I have drunk the poison I shall leave you and go to the joys of the blessed,—these words of mine, with which I was comforting you and myself, have had, as I perceive, no effect upon Crito. And therefore I want you to be surety for me to him now, as at the trial he was surety to the judges for me: but let the promise be of another sort; for he was surety for me to the judges that I would remain, and you must be my surety to him that I shall not remain, but go away and depart; and then he will suffer less at my death, and not be grieved when he sees my body being burned or buried. I would not have him sorrow at my hard lot, or say at the burial, Thus we lay out Socrates, or, Thus we follow him to the grave or bury him; for false words are not only evil in themselves, but they infect the soul with evil. Be of good cheer then, my dear Crito, and say that you are burying my body only, and do with that whatever is usual, and what you think best.

When he had spoken these words, he arose and went into a chamber to bathe; Crito followed him and told us to wait. So we remained behind, talking and thinking of the subject of discourse, and also of the greatness of our sorrow; he was like a father of whom we were being bereaved, and we were about to pass the rest of our lives as orphans. When he had taken the bath his children were brought to him—(he had two young sons and an elder one); and the women of his family also came, and he talked to them and gave them a few directions in the presence of Crito; then he dismissed them and returned to us.

Now the hour of sunset was near, for a good deal of time had passed while he was within. When he came out, he sat down with us again after his bath, but not much was said. Soon the jailer, who was the servant of the Eleven, entered and stood by him, saying:—To you, Socrates, whom I know to be the noblest and gentlest and best of all who ever came to this place, I will not impute the angry feelings of other men, who rage and swear at me, when, in obedience to the authorities, I bid them drink the poison—indeed, I am sure that you will not be angry with me; for others, as you are aware, and not I, are to blame. And so fare you well, and try to bear lightly what must needs be—you know my errand. Then bursting into tears he turned away and went out.

Socrates looked at him and said: I return your good wishes, and will do as you bid. Then turning to us, he said, How charming the man is: since I have been in prison he has always been coming to see me, and at times he would talk to me, and was as good to me as could be, and now see how generously he sorrows on my account. We must do as he says, Crito; and therefore let the cup be brought, if the poison is prepared: if not, let the attendant prepare some.

Yet, said Crito, the sun is still upon the hill-tops, and I know that many a one has taken the draught late, and after the announcement has been made to him, he has eaten and drunk, and enjoyed the society of his beloved; do not hurry—there is time enough.

Socrates said: Yes, Crito, and they of whom you speak are right in so acting, for they think that they will be gainers by the delay; but I am right in not following their example, for I do not think that I should gain anything by drinking the poison a little later; I should only be ridiculous in my own eyes for sparing and saving a life which is already forfeit. Please then to do as I say, and not to refuse me.

Crito made a sign to the servant, who was standing by; and he went out, and having been absent for some time, returned with the jailer carrying the cup of poison. Socrates said: You, my good friend, who are experienced in these matters, shall give me directions how I am to proceed. The man answered: You have only to walk about until your legs are heavy, and then to lie down, and the poison will act. At the same time he handed the cup to Socrates, who in the easiest and gentlest manner, without the least fear or change of colour or feature, looking at the man with all his eyes. Echecrates, as his manner was, took the cup and said: What do you say about making a libation out of this cup to any god? May I, or not? The man answered: We only prepare, Socrates, just so much as we deem enough. I understand, he said: but I may and must ask the gods to prosper my journey from this to the other world—even so—and so be it according to my prayer. Then raising the cup to his lips, quite readily and cheerfully he drank off the poison. And hitherto most of us had been able to control our sorrow; but now when we saw him drinking, and saw too that he had finished the draught, we could no longer forbear, and in spite of myself my own tears were flowing fast; so that I covered my face and wept, not for him, but at the thought of my own calamity in having to part from such a friend. Nor was I the first; for Crito, when he found himself unable to restrain his tears, had got up, and I followed; and at that moment, Apollodorus, who had been weeping all the time, broke out in a loud and passionate cry which made cowards of us all. Socrates alone retained his calmness: What is this strange outcry? he said. I sent away the women mainly in order that they might not misbehave in this way, for I have been told that a man should die in peace. Be quiet then, and have patience. When we heard his words we were ashamed, and refrained our tears; and he walked about until, as he said, his legs began to fail, and then he lay on his back, according to the directions, and the man who gave him the poison now and then looked at his feet and legs; and after a while he pressed his foot hard, and asked him if he could feel; and he said, No; and then his leg, and so upwards and upwards, and showed us that he was cold and stiff. And he felt them himself, and said: When the poison reaches the heart, that will be the end. He was beginning to grow cold about the groin, when he uncovered his face, for he had covered himself up, and said—they were his last words—he said: Crito, I owe a cock to Asclepius; will you remember to pay the debt? The debt shall be paid, said Crito; is there anything else? There was no answer to this question; but in a minute or two a movement was heard, and the attendants uncovered him; his eyes were set, and Crito closed his eyes and mouth.

Such was the end, Echecrates, of our friend; concerning whom I may truly say, that of all the men of his time whom I have known, he was the wisest and justest and best.

Notes

1. Or, I am certain that I am right in taking this course.
2. Aristoph., Clouds, 225 ff.
3. Probably in allusion to Aristophanes who caricatured, and to Euripides who borrowed the notions of Anaxagoras, as well as to other dramatic poets.
4. Homer, Il. ix. 363.
5. Cp. Apol. 37 C, D.
6. Cp. Apol. 30 C.
7. e.g. cp. Rep. i. 335 E.
8. Cp. Phaedr. 230 C.
9. Cp. Apol. 37 D.
10. But cp. Rep. x. 611 A.
11. Cp. Meno 83 ff.

12. Cp. Apol. 40 E.
13. Compare Milton, Comus, 463 foll.:—

> 'But when lust,
> By unchaste looks, loose gestures, and foul talk,
> But most by lewd and lavish act of sin,
> Lets in defilement to the inward parts,
> The soul grows clotted by contagion,
> Imbodies, and imbrutes, till she quite lose,
> The divine property of her first being.
> Such are those thick and gloomy shadows damp
> Oft seen in charnel vaults and sepulchres,
> Lingering, and sitting by a new made grave,
> As loath to leave the body that it lov'd,
> And linked itself by carnal sensuality
> To a degenerate and degraged state.'

14. Cp. Rep. x. 619 C.

Suggested Readings

The Collected Dialogues of Plato. Ed. Edith Hamilton and Huntington Cairns. Princeton: Princeton University Press, 1961.

Gribe, G. M. A. *Plato's Thoughts*. Indianapolis: Hackett, 1980.

Findlay, J. N. *Plato: The Written and Unwritten Doctrine*. New York: Humanities Press, 1974.

Chapter 2

Materialism and the Denial of Immortality

Epicurus

Epicurus was born on the island of Samos in 341 B.C.E. He went to Athens and studied
with both the students of Plato and Aristotle. He rejected their views in favor of the
materialistic philosophy of Democritus. He adopted the quite modern empiricist view that
if all things are essentially reducible to atoms, then there would be no need to fear death
nor an afterlife. His disciples gathered in the Garden of Epicurus to pursue philosophy
and the higher pleasures of the mind (hedonism).

◀ Letter to Herodotus ▶

First of all, Herodotus, we must grasp the ideas attached to words, in order that we may be
able to refer to them and so to judge the inferences of opinion or problems of investigation or
reflection, so that we may not either leave everything uncertain and go on explaining to infinity or use words devoid of meaning. For this purpose it is essential that the first mental image
associated with each word should be regarded, and that there should be no need of explanation, if we are really to have a standard to which to refer a problem of investigation or reflection or a mental inference. And besides we must keep all our investigations in accord with our
sensations, and in particular with the immediate apprehensions whether of the mind or of any
one of the instruments of judgement, and likewise in accord with the feelings existing in us, in
order that we may have indications whereby we may judge both the problem of sense-perception
and the unseen.

Having made these points clear, we must now consider things imperceptible to the senses.
First of all, that nothing is created out of that which does not exist: for if it were, everything
would be created out of everything with no need of seeds. And again, if that which disappears

From Epicurus: *The Extant Remains* translated by Cyril Bailey (1926) pp. 19-55. Reprinted by permission of Oxford
University Press.

were destroyed into that which did not exist, all things would have perished, since that into which they were dissolved would not exist. Furthermore, the universe always was such as it is now, and always will be the same. For there is nothing into which it changes: for outside the universe there is nothing which could come into it and bring about the change.

Moreover, the universe is (bodies and space): for that bodies exist, sense itself witnesses in the experience of all men, and in accordance with the evidence of sense we must of necessity judge of the imperceptible by reasoning, as I have already said. And if there were not that which we term void and place and intangible existence, bodies would have nowhere to exist and nothing through which to move, as they are seen to move. And besides these two nothing can even be thought of either by conception or on the analogy of things conceivable such as could be grasped as whole existences and not spoken of as the accidents or properties of such existences. Furthermore, among bodies some are compounds, and others those of which compounds are formed. And these latter are indivisible and unalterable (if, that is, all things are not to be destroyed into the non-existent, but something permanent is to remain behind at the dissolution of compounds): they are completely solid in nature, and can by no means be dissolved in any part. So it must needs be that the first-beginnings are indivisible corporeal existences.

Moreover, the universe is boundless. For that which is bounded has an extreme point: and the extreme point is seen against something else. So that as it has no extreme point, it has no limit; and as it has no limit, it must be boundless and not bounded. Furthermore, the infinite is boundless both in the number of the bodies and in the extent of the void. For if on the one hand the void were boundless, and the bodies limited in number, the bodies could not stay anywhere, but would be carried about and scattered through the infinite void, not having other bodies to support them and keep them in place by means of collisions. But if, on the other hand, the void were limited, the infinite bodies would not have room wherein to take their place.

Besides this the indivisible and solid bodies, out of which too the compounds are created and into which they are dissolved, have an incomprehensible number of varieties in shape: for it is not possible that such great varieties of things should arise from the same (atomic) shapes, if they are limited in number. And so in each shape the atoms are quite infinite in number, but their differences of shape are not quite infinite, but only incomprehensible in number.

And the atoms move continuously for all time, some of them (falling straight down, others swerving, and other recoiling from their collisions. And of the latter, some are borne on) separating to a long distance from one another, while others again recoil and recoil, whenever they chance to be checked by the interlacing with others, or else shut in by atoms interfaced around them. For on the one hand the nature of the void which separates each atom by itself brings this about, as it is not able to afford resistance, and on the other hand the hardness which belongs to the atoms makes them recoil after collision to as great a distance as the interlacing permits separation after the collision. And these motions have no beginning, since the atoms and the void are the cause.

These brief sayings, if all these points are borne in mind, afford a sufficient outline for our understanding of the nature of existing things.

Furthermore, there are infinite worlds both like and unlike this world of ours. For the atoms being infinite in number, as was proved already, are borne on far out into space. For those atoms, which are of such nature that a world could be created out of them or made by them, have not been used up either on one world or on a limited number of worlds, nor again on all the worlds which are alike, or on those which are different from these. So that there nowhere exists an obstacle to the infinite number of the worlds.

Moreover, there are images like in shape to the solid bodies, far surpassing perceptible things in their subtlety of texture. For it is not impossible that such emanations should be formed in that which surrounds the objects, nor that there should be opportunities for the formation of such hollow and thin frames, nor that there should be effluences which preserve the respective position and order which they had before in the solid bodies: these images we call idols.

Next, nothing among perceptible things contradicts the belief that the images have unsurpassable fineness of texture. And for this reason they have also unsurpassable speed of motion, since the movement of all their atoms is uniform, and besides nothing or very few things hinder their emission by collisions, whereas a body composed of many or infinite atoms is at once hindered by collisions. Besides this (nothing contradicts the belief) that the creation of the idols takes place as quick as thought. For the flow of atoms from the surface of bodies is continuous, yet it cannot be detected by any lessening in the size of the object because of the constant filling up of what is lost. The flow of images preserves for a long time the position and order of the atoms in the solid body, though it is occasionally confused. Moreover compound idols are quickly formed in the air around, because it is not necessary for their substance to be filled in deep inside: and besides there are certain other methods in which existences of this sort are produced. For not one of these beliefs is contradicted by our sensations, if one looks to see in what way sensation will bring us the clear visions from external objects, and in what way again the corresponding sequence of qualities and movements.

Now we must suppose too that it is when something enters us from external objects that we not only see but think of their shapes. For external objects could not make on us an impression of the nature of their own colour and shape by means of the air which lies between us and them, nor again by means of the rays or effluences of any sort which pass from us to them— nearly so well as if models, similar in colour and shape, leave the objects and enter according to their respective size either into our sight or into our mind; moving along swiftly, and so by this means reproducing the image of a single continuous thing and preserving the corresponding sequence of qualities and movements from the original object as the result of their uniform contact with us, kept up by the vibration of the atoms deep in the interior of the concrete body.

And every image which we obtain by an act of apprehension on the part of the mind or of the sense-organs, whether of shape or of properties, this image is the shape (or the properties) of the concrete object, and is produced by the constant repetition of the image or the impression it has left. Now falsehood and error always lie in the addition of opinion with regard to (what is waiting) to be confirmed or not contradicted, and then is not confirmed (or is contradicted). For the similarity between the things which exist, which we call real, and the images received as a likeness of things and produced either in sleep or through some other acts of apprehension on the part of the mind or the other instruments of judgement, could never be, unless there were some effluences of this nature actually, brought into contact with our senses. And error would not exist unless another kind of movement too were produced inside ourselves, closely linked to the apprehension of images, but differing from it; and it is owing to this, supposing it is not confirmed, or is contradicted, that falsehood arises; but if it is confirmed or not contradicted, it is true. Therefore we must do our best to keep this doctrine in mind, in order that on the one hand the standards of judgement dependent on the clear visions may not be undermined, and on the other error may not be as firmly established as truth and so throw all into confusion.

Moreover, hearing too results when a current is carried off from the object speaking or sounding or making a noise, or causing in any other way a sensation of hearing. Now this current is split up into particles, each like the whole, which at the same time preserve a correspondence of qualities with one another and a unity of character which stretches right back to the object which emitted the sound: this unity it is which in most cases produces comprehension in the recipient, or, if not, merely makes manifest the presence of the external object. For without the transference from the object of some correspondence of qualities, comprehension of this nature could not result. We must not then suppose that the actual air is moulded into shape by the voice which is emitted or by other similar sounds—for it will be very far from being so acted upon by it—but that the blow which takes place inside us, when we emit our voice, causes at once a squeezing out of certain particles, which produce a stream of breath, of such a character as to afford us the sensation of hearing.

Furthermore, we must suppose that smell too, just like hearing, could never bring about any sensation unless there were certain particles carried off from the object of suitable size to stir this sense-organ, some of them in a manner disorderly and alien to it, others in a regular manner and akin in nature.

Next, referring always to the sensations and the feelings (for in this way you will obtain the most trustworthy ground of belief), you must consider that the soul is a body of fine particles distributed throughout the whole structure, and most resembling wind with a certain admixture of heat, and in some respects like to one of these and in some to the other. There is also the part which is many degrees more advanced even than these in fineness of composition, and for this reason is more capable of feeling in harmony with the rest of the structure as well. Now all this is made manifest by the activities of the soul and the feelings and the readiness of its movements and its processes of thought and by what we lose at the moment of death. Further, you must grasp that the soul possesses the chief cause of sensation: yet it could not have acquired sensation, unless it were in some way enclosed by the rest of the structure. And this in its turn having afforded the soul this cause of sensation acquires itself too a share in this contingent capacity from the soul. Yet it does not acquire all the capacities which the soul possesses: and therefore when the soul is released from the body, the body no longer has sensation. For it never possessed this power in itself, but used to afford opportunity for it to another existence, brought into being at the same time with itself: and this existence, owing to the power now consummated within itself as a result of motion, used spontaneously to produce for itself the capacity of sensation and then to communicate it to the body as well, in virtue of its contact and correspondence of movement, as I have already said. Therefore, so long as the soul remains in the body, even though some other part of the body be lost, it will never lose sensation; nay more, whatever portions of the soul may perish too, when that which enclosed it is removed either in whole or in part, if the soul continues to exist at all, it will retain sensation. On the other hand the rest of the structure, though it continues to exist either as a whole or in part, does not retain sensation, if it has once lost that sum of atoms, however small it be, which together goes to produce the nature of the soul. Moreover, if the whole structure is dissolved, the soul is dispersed and no longer has the same powers nor performs its movements, so that it does not possess sensation either. For it is impossible to imagine it with sensation, if it is not in this organism and cannot effect these movements, when what encloses and surrounds it is no longer the same as the surroundings in which it now exists and performs these movements. Furthermore, we must clearly comprehend as well, that the incorporeal in the general acceptation of the term is applied to that which could be thought of as such as an independent existence. Now it is impossible to conceive the incorporeal as a separate in existence, except the void: and the void can neither act nor be acted upon, but only provides opportunity of motion through itself to bodies. So that those who say that the soul is incorporeal are talking idly. For it would not be able to act or be acted on in any respect, if it were of this nature. But as it is, both these occurrences are clearly distinguished in respect of the soul. Now if one refers all these reasonings about the soul to the standards of feeling and sensation and remembers what was said at the outset, he will see that they are sufficiently embraced in these general formulae to enable him to work out with certainty on this basis the details of the system as well.

Furthermore, the motions of the heavenly bodies and their turnings and eclipses and risings and settings, and kindred phenomena to these, must not be thought to be due to any being who controls and ordains or has ordained them and at the same time enjoys perfect bliss together with immortality (for trouble and care and anger and kindness are not consistent with a life of blessedness, but these things come to pass where there is weakness and fear and dependence on neighbours). Nor again must we believe that they, which are but fire agglomerated in a mass, possess blessedness, and voluntarily take upon themselves these movements. But we must preserve their full majestic significance in all expressions which we apply to such conceptions, in order that there may not arise out of them opinions contrary to this notion of majesty. Otherwise this very contradiction will cause the greatest disturbance in men's souls. Therefore we must believe that it is due to the original inclusion of matter in such agglomerations during the birth-process of the world that this law of regular succession is also brought about.

Furthermore, we must believe that to discover accurately the cause of the most essential facts is the function of the science of nature, and that blessedness for us in the knowledge of celestial phenomena lies in this and in the understanding of the nature of the existences seen in these celestial phenomena, and of all else that is akin to the exact knowledge requisite for our happiness: in knowing too that what occurs in several ways or is capable of being otherwise has no place here, but that nothing which suggests doubt or alarm can be included at all in that which is naturally immortal and blessed. Now this we can ascertain by our mind is absolutely the case. But what falls within the investigation of risings and settings and turnings and eclipses, and all that is akin to this, is no longer of any value for the happiness which knowledge brings, but persons who have perceived all this, but yet do not know what are the natures of these things and what are the essential causes, are still in fear, just as if they did not know these things at all: indeed, their fear may be even greater, since the wonder which arises out of the observation of these things cannot discover any solution or realize the regulation of the essentials. And for this very reason, even if we discover several causes for turnings and settings and risings and eclipses and the like, as has been the case already in our investigation of detail, we must not suppose that our inquiry into these things has not reached sufficient accuracy to contribute to our peace of mind and happiness. So we must carefully consider in how many ways a similar phenomenon is produced on earth, when we reason about the causes of celestial phenomena and all that is imperceptible to the senses; and we must despise those persons who do not recognize either what exists or comes into being in one way only, or that which may occur in several ways in the case of things which can only be seen by us from a distance, and further are not aware under what conditions it is impossible to have peace of mind. If, therefore, we think that a phenomenon probably occurs in some such particular way, and that in circumstances under which it is equally possible for us to be at peace, when we realize that it may occur in several ways, we shall be just as little disturbed as if we know that it occurs in some such particular way.

And besides all these matters in general we must grasp this point, that the principal disturbance in the minds of men arises because they think that these celestial bodies are blessed and immortal, and yet have wills and actions and motives inconsistent with these attributes; and because they are always expecting or imagining some everlasting misery, such as is depicted in legends, or even fear the loss of feeling in death as though it would concern them themselves; and, again, because they are brought to this pass not by reasoned opinion, but rather by some irrational presentiment, and therefore, as they do not know the limits of pain, they suffer a disturbance equally great or even more extensive than if they had reached this belief by opinion. But peace of mind is being delivered from all this, and having a constant memory of the general and most essential principles.

Wherefore we must pay attention to internal feelings and to external sensations in general and in particular, according as the subject is general or particular, and to every immediate intuition in accordance with each of the standards of judgement. For if we pay attention to these, we shall rightly trace the causes whence arose our mental disturbance and fear, and, by learning the true causes of celestial phenomena and all other occurrences that come to pass from time to time, we shall free ourselves from all which produces the utmost fear in other men.

Here, Herodotus, is my treatise on the chief points concerning the nature of the general principles, abridged so that my account would be easy to grasp with accuracy. I think that, even if one were unable to proceed to all the detailed particulars of the system, he would from this obtain an unrivalled strength compared with other men. For indeed he will clear up for himself many of the detailed points by reference to our general system, and these very principles, if he stores them in his mind, will constantly aid him. For such is their character that even those who are at present engaged in working out the details to a considerable degree, or even completely, will be able to carry out the greater part of their investigations into the nature of the whole by conducting their analysis in reference to such a survey as this. And as for all who are not fully among those on the way to being perfected, some of them can from this summary obtain a hasty view of the most important matters without oral instruction so as to secure peace of mind.

⚓ Epicurus to Menoeceus ⚓

Let no one when young delay to study philosophy, nor when he is old grow weary of his study. For no one can come too early or too late to secure the health of his soul. And the man who says that the age for philosophy has either not yet come or has gone by is like the man who says that the age for happiness is not yet come to him, or has passed away. Wherefore both when young and old a man must study philosophy, that as he grows old he may be young in blessings through the grateful recollection of what has been, and that in youth he may be old as well, since he will know no fear of what is to come. We must then meditate on the things that make our happiness, seeing that when that is with us we have all, but when it is absent we do all to win it.

The things which I used unceasingly to commend to you, these do and practice, considering them to be the first principles of the good life. First of all believe that god is a being immortal and blessed, even as the common idea of a god is engraved on men's minds, and do not assign to him anything alien to his immortality or ill-suited to his blessedness: but believe about him everything that can uphold his blessedness and immortality. For gods there are, since the knowledge of them is by clear vision. But they are not such as the many believe them to be: for indeed they do not consistently represent them as they believe them to be. And the impious man is not he who denies the gods of the many, but he who attaches to the gods the beliefs of the many. For the statements of the many about the gods are not conceptions derived from sensation, but false suppositions, according to which the greatest misfortunes befall the wicked and the greatest blessings (the good) by the gift of the gods. For men being accustomed always to their own virtues welcome those like themselves, but regard all that is not of their nature as alien.

Become accustomed to the belief that death is nothing to us. For all good and evil consists in sensation, but death is deprivation of sensation. And therefore a right understanding that death is nothing to us makes the mortality of life enjoyable, not because it adds to it an infinite span of time, but because it takes away the craving for immortality. For there is nothing terrible in life for the man who has truly comprehended that there is nothing terrible in not living. So that the man speaks but idly who says that he fears death not because it will be painful when it comes, but because it is painful in anticipation. For that which gives no trouble when it comes, is but an empty pain in anticipation. So death, the most terrifying of ills, is nothing to us, since so long as we exist, death is not with us; but when death comes, then we do not exist. It does not then concern either the living or the dead since for the former it is not, and the latter are no more.

But the many at one moment shun death as the greatest of evils, at another (yearn for it) as a respite from the (evils) in life. (But the wise man neither seeks to escape life) nor fears the cessation of life, for neither does life offend him nor does the absence of life seem to be any evil. And just as with food he does not seek simply the larger share and nothing else, but rather the most pleasant, so he seeks to enjoy not the longest period of time, but the most pleasant.

And he who counsels the young man to live well, but the old man to make a good end, is foolish, not merely because of the desirability of life, but also because it is the same training which teaches to live well and to die well. Yet much worse still is the man who says it is good not to be born, but

'once born make haste to pass the gates of Death.'

For if he says this from conviction why does he not pass away out of life? For it is open to him to do so, if he had firmly made up his mind to this. But if he speaks in jest, his words are idle among men who cannot receive them.

We must then bear in mind that the future is neither ours, nor yet wholly not ours, so that we may not altogether expect it as sure to come, nor abandon hope of it, as if it will certainly not come.

We must consider that of desires some are natural, others vain, and of the natural some are necessary and others merely natural; and of the necessary some are necessary for happiness, others for the repose of the body, and others for very life. The right understanding of these facts enables us to refer all choice and avoidance to the health of the body and (the soul's) freedom from disturbance, since this is the aim of the life of blessedness. For it is to obtain this end that we always act, namely, to avoid pain and fear. And when this is once secured for us, all the tempest of the soul is dispersed, since the living creature has not to wander as though in search of something that is missing, and to look for some other thing by which he can fulfil the good of the soul and the good of the body. For it is then that we have need of pleasure, when we feel pain owing to the absence of pleasure; (but when we do not feel pain), we no longer need pleasure. And for this cause we call pleasure the beginning and end of the blessed life. For we recognize pleasure as the first good innate in us, and from pleasure we begin every act of choice and avoidance, and to pleasure we return again, using the feeling as the standard by which we judge every good.

And since pleasure is the first good and natural to us, for this very reason we do not choose every pleasure, but sometimes we pass over many pleasures, when greater discomfort accrues to us as the result of them: and similarly we think many pains better than pleasures, since a greater pleasure comes to us when we have endured pains for a long time. Every pleasure then because of its natural kinship to us is good, yet not every pleasure is to be chosen: even as every pain also is an evil, yet not all are always of a nature to be avoided. Yet by a scale of comparison and by the consideration of advantages and disadvantages we must form our judgement on all these matters. For the good on certain occasions we treat as bad, and conversely the bad as good.

And again independence of desire we think a great good—not that we may at all times enjoy but a few things, but that, if we do not possess many, we may enjoy the few in the genuine persuasion that those have the sweetest pleasure in luxury who least need it, and that all that is natural is easy to be obtained, but that which is superfluous is hard. And so plain savours bring us a pleasure equal to a luxurious diet, when all the pain due to want is removed; and bread and water produce the highest pleasure, when one who needs them puts them to his lips. To grow accustomed therefore to simple and not luxurious diet gives us health to the full, and makes a man alert for the needful employments of life, and when after long intervals we approach luxuries disposes us better towards them, and fits us to be fearless of fortune.

When, therefore, we maintain that pleasure is the end, we do not mean the pleasures of profligates and those that consist in sensuality, as is supposed by some who are either ignorant or disagree with us or do not understand, but freedom from pain in the body and from trouble in the mind. For it is not continuous drinkings and revellings, nor the satisfaction of lusts, nor the enjoyment of fish and other luxuries of the wealthy table, which produce a pleasant life, but sober reasoning, searching out the motives for all choice and avoidance, and banishing mere opinions, to which are due the greatest disturbance of the spirit.

Of all this the beginning and the greatest good is prudence. Wherefore prudence is a more precious thing even than philosophy: for from prudence are sprung all the other virtues, and it teaches us that it is not possible to live pleasantly without living prudently and honourably and justly, (nor, again, to live a life of prudence, honour, and justice) without living pleasantly. For the virtues are by nature bound up with the pleasant life, and the pleasant life is inseparable from them. For indeed who, think you, is a better man than he who holds reverent opinions concerning the gods, and is at all times free from fear of death, and has reasoned out the end ordained by nature? He understands that the limit of good things is easy to fulfil and easy to attain, whereas the course of ills is either short in time or slight in pain: he laughs at (destiny), whom some have introduced as the mistress of all things. (He thinks that with us lies the chief power in determining events, some of which happen by necessity) and some by chance, and some are within our control; for while necessity cannot be called to account, he sees that chance is inconstant, but that which is in our control is subject to no master, and to it are naturally attached praise and blame. For, indeed, it were better to follow the myths about the gods than to become a slave to the destiny of the philosophers: for the former suggests a hope of placating the gods by worship, whereas the latter involves a necessity which knows no placation. As to chance, he does not regard it as a god as most men do (for in a god's acts there is no disorder), nor as an uncertain cause (of all things): for he does not believe that good and evil are given by chance to man for the framing of a blessed life, but that opportunities for great good and great evil are afforded by it. He therefore thinks it better to be unfortunate in reasonable action than to prosper in unreason. For it is better in a man's actions that what is well chosen (should fail, rather than that what is ill chosen) should be successful owing to chance.

Meditate therefore on these things and things akin to them night and day by yourself, and with a companion like to yourself, and never shall you be disturbed waking or asleep, but you shall live like a god among men. For a man who lives among immortal blessings is not like to a mortal being.

Suggested Readings

Rist, J. M. *Epicurus: An Introduction*. Cambridge: Cambridge University Press, 1972.
Mitsis, P. *Epicurus' Ethical Theory*. Ithaca: Cornell University Press, 1988.
Zeller, Eduard. *The Stoics, Epicureans and Sceptics*. New York: Russell and Russell, Inc., 1962.

Chapter 3

The Stoic View of Life and Death

Marcus Aurelius

The Roman emperor Marcus Aurelius, born in 121 C.E., comes very close to Plato's ideal of the philosopher king. Romans, like Cicero, Seneca and Aurelius adopted the Greek Stoic motto of Zeno's to "live according to nature." This saying does not mean to follow one's impulses, but rather, to follow nature's rational laws and be apathetic, or detached from our passions. It is the Stoic cosmopolitan philosophy of fraternal equality under natural law which grounds our constitutional system.

Begin the morning by saying to thyself, I shall meet with the busybody, the ungrateful, arrogant, deceitful, envious, unsocial. All these things happen to them by reason of their ignorance of what is good and evil. But I who have seen the nature of the good that it is beautiful, and of the bad that it is ugly, and the nature of him who does wrong, that it is akin to me, not [only] of the same blood or seed, but that it participates in [the same] intelligence and [the same] portion of the divinity, I can neither be injured by any of them, for no one can fix on me what is ugly, nor can I be angry with my kinsman, nor hate him. For we are made for co-operation, like feet, like hands, like eyelids, like the rows of the upper and lower teeth.[1] To act against one another then is contrary to nature; and it is acting against one another to be vexed and to turn away.

2. Whatever this is that I am, it is a little flesh and breath, and the ruling part. Throw away thy books; no longer distract thyself: it is not allowed; but as if thou wast now dying, despise the flesh; it is blood and bones and a network, a contexture of nerves, veins and arteries. See the breath also, what kind of a thing it is; air, and not always the same, but every moment sent out and again sucked in. The third then is the ruling part: consider thus: Thou art an old man; no longer let this be a slave, no longer be pulled by the strings like a puppet to unsocial movements, no longer, be either dissatisfied with thy present lot, or shrink from the future.

3. All that is from the gods is full of providence. That which is from fortune is not separated from nature or without an interweaving and involution with the things which are ordered by Providence. From thence all things flow; and there is besides necessity, and that

---

The Meditations by Marcus Aurelius.

which is for the advantage of the whole universe, of which thou art a part. But that is good for every part of nature which the nature of the whole brings, and what serves to maintain this nature. Now the universe is preserved, as by the changes of the elements so by the changes of things compounded of the elements. Let these principles be enough for thee; let them always be fixed opinions. But cast away the thirst after books, that thou mayest not die murmuring, but, cheerfully, truly, and from thy heart thankful to the gods.

4. Remember how long thou hast been putting off these things, and how often thou hast received an opportunity from the gods, and yet dost not use it. Thou must now at last perceive of what universe thou art a part, and of what administrator of the universe thy existence is an efflux, and that a limit of time is fixed for thee, which if thou dost not use for clearing away the clouds from thy mind, it will go and thou wilt go, and it will never return.

5. Every moment think steadily as a Roman and a man to do what thou hast in band with perfect and simple dignity, and feeling of affection, and freedom, and justice; and to give thyself relief from all other thoughts. And thou wilt give thyself relief, if thou doest every act of thy life as if it were the last, laying aside all carelessness and passionate aversion from the commands of reason, and all hypocrisy, and self-love, and discontent with the portion which has been given to thee. Thou seest how few the things are, the which if a man lays hold of, he is able to live a life which flows in quiet, and is like the existence of the gods; for the gods on their part will require nothing more from him who observes these things.

6. Do wrong[2] to thyself, do wrong to thyself, my soul; but thou wilt no longer have the opportunity of honoring thyself. Every man's life is sufficient.† But thine is nearly finished, though thy soul reverences not itself, but places thy felicity in the souls of others.

7. Do the things external which fall upon thee distract thee? Give thyself time to learn something new and good, and cease to be whirled around. But then thou must also avoid being carried about the other way. For those too are triflers who have wearied themselves in life by their activity, and yet have no object to which to direct every movement, and, in a word, all their thoughts.

8. Through not observing what is in the mind of another a man has seldom been seen to be unhappy; but those who do not observe the movements of their own minds must of necessity be unhappy.

9. This thou must always bear in mind, what is the nature of the whole, and what is my nature, and how this is related to that, and what kind of a part it is of what kind of a whole; and that there is no one who hinders thee from always doing and saying the things which are according to the nature of which thou art a part.

10. Theophrastus, in his comparison of bad acts—such a comparison as one would make in accordance with the common notions of mankind—says, like a true philosopher, that the offenses which are committed through desire are more blameable than those which are committed through anger. For he who is excited by anger seems to turn away from reason with a certain pain and unconscious contraction; but he who offends through desire, being overpowered by pleasure, seems to be in a manner more intemperate and more womanish in his offenses. Rightly then, and in a way worthy of philosophy, he said that the offense which is committed with pleasure is more blameable than that which is committed with pain; and on the whole the one is more like a person who has been first wronged and through pain is com-

pelled to be angry; but the other is moved by his own impulse to do wrong, being carried toward doing something by desire.

11. Since it is possible[3] that thou mayest depart from life this very moment, regulate every act and thought accordingly.[4] But to go away from among men, if there are gods, is not a thing to be afraid of, for the gods will not involve thee in evil; but if indeed they do not exist, or if they have no concern about human affairs, what is it to me to live in a universe devoid of gods or devoid of providence? But in truth they do exist, and they do care for human things and they have put all the means in man's power to enable him not to fall into real evils. And as to the rest, if there was anything evil, they would have provided for this also, that it should be altogether in a man's power not to fall into it. Now, that which does not make a man worse, how can it make a man's life worse? But neither through ignorance, nor having the knowledge, but not the power to guard against or correct these things, is it possible that the nature of the universe has overlooked them; nor is it possible that it has made so great a mistake, either through want of power or want of skill, that good and evil should happen indiscriminately to the good and the bad. But death certainly, and life, honor and dishonor, pain and pleasure, all these things equally happen to good men and bad, being things which make us neither better nor worse. Therefore they are neither good nor evil.

12. How quickly all these things disappear, in the universe the bodies themselves, but in time the remembrance of them; what is the nature of all sensible things, and particularly those which attract with the bait of pleasure or terrify by pain, or are noised abroad by vapory fame; how worthless, and contemptible, and sordid and perishable, and dead they are—all this it is the part of the intellectual faculty to observe. To observe too who these are whose opinions and voices give reputation; what death is, and the fact that, if a man looks at it in itself, and by the abstractive power of reflection receives into their parts all the things which present themselves to the imagination in it, he will then consider it to be nothing else than all operation of nature; and if any one is afraid of an operation of nature he is a child. This, however, is not only an operation of nature, but it is also a thing which conduces to the purposes of nature. To observe, too, how man comes near to the deity, and by what part of him, and when this part of man is so disposed† (vi. 28).

13. Nothing is more wretched than a man who traverses everything in a round, and pries into the things beneath the earth, as the poet[5] says, and seeks by conjecture what is in the minds of his neighbors, without perceiving that it is sufficient to attend to the demon within him, and to reverence it sincerely. And reverence of the demon consists in keeping it pure from passion and thoughtlessness, and dissatisfaction with what comes from gods and men. For the things from the gods merit veneration for their excellence; and the things from men should be dear to us by reason of kinship; and sometimes even, in a manner, they move our pity by reason of men's ignorance of good and bad; this defect being not less than that which deprives us of the power of distinguishing things that are white and black.

14. Though thou shouldest be going to live three thousand years, and as many times ten thousand years, still remember that no man loses any other life than this which he now lives, nor lives any other than this which he now loses. The longest and shortest are thus brought to the same. For the present is the same to all, though that which perishes is not the same;† and so that which is lost appears to be a mere moment. For a man cannot lose either the past or the future: for what a man has not, how can any one take this from him? These two things then

thou must bear in mind: the one, that all things from eternity are of like forms and come round in a circle, and it makes no difference whether a man shall see the same things during a hundred years or two hundred, or an infinite time; and the second, that the longest liver and he who will die soonest lose just the same. For the present is the only thing of which a man can be deprived, if it is true that this is the only thing which he has, and that a man cannot lose a thing if he has it not.

15. Remember that all is opinion. For what was said by the Cynic Monimus is manifest: and manifest too is the use of what was said, if a man receives what may be got out of it as far as it is true.

16. The soul of man does violence to itself, first of all, when it becomes an abscess and, as it were, a tumor on the universe, so far as it can. For to be vexed at anything which happens is a separation of ourselves from nature, in some part of which the natures of all other things are contained. In the next place, the soul does violence to itself when it turns away from any man, or even moves toward him with the intention of injuring, such as are the souls of those who are angry. In the third place, the soul does violence to itself when it is overpowered by pleasure or by pain. Fourthly, when it plays a part, and does or says anything insincerely and untruly. Fifthly when it allows any act of its own and any movement to be without an aim, and does anything thoughtlessly and without considering what it is, it being right that even the smallest things be done with reference to an end; "and the end of rational animals is to follow the reason and the law of the most ancient city and polity."

17. Of human life the time is a point, and the substance is in a flux, and the perception dull, and the composition of the whole body subject to putrefaction, and the soul a whirl, and fortune hard to divine, and fame a thing devoid of judgment. And, to say all in a word, everything which belongs to the body is a stream, and what belongs to the soul is a dream and vapor, and life is a warfare and a stranger's sojourn, and afterfame is oblivion. What, then, is that which is able to conduct a man? One thing and only one—philosophy. But this consists in keeping, the demon within a man free from violence and unharmed, superior to pains and pleasures, doing nothing without a purpose, nor yet falsely and with hypocrisy, not feeling the need of another man's doing or not doing anything; and besides, accepting all that happens, and all that is allotted, as coming from thence, wherever it is, from whence he himself came; and, finally, waiting for death with a cheerful mind, as being nothing else than a dissolution of the elements of which every living being is compounded. But if there is no harm to the elements themselves in each continually changing into another, why should a man have any apprehension about the change and dissolution of all the elements? For it is according to nature, and nothing is evil which is according to nature.

This in Carnuntum.[6]

48. Think continually how many physicians are dead after often contracting their eyebrows over the sick; and how many astrologers after predicting with great pretensions the deaths of others; and how many philosophers after endless discourses on death or immortality; how many heroes after killing thousands; and how many tyrants who have used their power over men's lives with terrible insolence as if they were immortal; and how many cities are entirely dead, so to speak, Helice[7] and Pompeii and Herculaneum, and others innumerable. Add to the reckoning all whom thou hast known, one after another. One man after burying

another has been laid out dead, and another buries him; and all this in a short time. To conclude, always observe how ephemeral and worthless human things are, and what was yesterday a little mucus, tomorrow will be a mummy or ashes. Pass then through this little space of time conformably to nature, and end thy journey in content, just as an olive falls off when it is ripe, blessing nature who produced it, and thanking the tree on which it grew.

49. Be like the promotory against which the waves continually break, but it stands firm and tames the fury of the water around it.

Unhappy am I, because this has happened to me—Not so, but Happy am I, though this has happened to me, because I continue free from pain, neither crushed by the present nor fearing the future. For such a thing as this might have happened to every man; but every man would not have continued free from pain on such an occasion. Why, then, is that rather a misfortune than this a good fortune? And dost thou in all cases call that a man's misfortune, which is not a deviation from man's nature? And does a thing seem to thee to be a deviation from man's nature, when it is not contrary to the will of man's nature? Well, thou knowest the will of nature. Will then this which has happened prevent thee from being just, magnanimous, temperate, prudent, secure against inconsiderate opinions and falsehood; will it prevent thee from having modesty, freedom, and everything else, by the presence of which man's nature obtains all that is its own? Remember, too, on every occasion which leads thee to vexation to apply this principle: not that this is a misfortune, but that to bear it nobly is good fortune.

50. It is a vulgar, but still a useful help toward contempt of death, to pass in review those who have tenaciously stuck to life. What more then have they gained than those who have died early? Certainly they lie in their tombs somewhere at last, Cadicianus, Fabius, Julianus, Lepidus, or any one else like them, who have carried out many to be buried, and then were carried out themselves. Altogether the interval is small [between birth and death]; and consider with how much trouble, and in company with what sort of people, and in what a feeble body this interval is laboriously passed. Do not then consider life a thing of any value.† For look to the immensity of time behind thee, and to the time which is before thee, another boundless space. In this infinity then what is the difference between him who lives three days and him who lives three generations?[8]

51. Always run to the short way; and the short way is the natural: accordingly say and do everything in conformity with the soundest reason. For such a purpose frees a man from trouble,† and warfare, and all artifice and ostentatious display.

Notes

1. Xenophon, Mem. ii. 3. 18.
2. Perhaps it should be "thou art doing violence to thyself."
3. Or it may mean "since it is in thy power to depart;" which gives a meaning somewhat different.
4. See Cicero, Tuscul. i. 49.
5. Pindar in the Theætetus of Plato. See xi. 1.
6. Carnuntum was a town of Pannonia, on the south side of the Danube, about thirty miles east of Vindobona (Vienna). Orosius (vii. 15) and Eutropius (viii. 13) say that Antoninus remained three years at Carnuntum during his war with the Marcomanni.

7. Ovid, Met. xv. 293:
   Si quaeras Hellicen et Burin Achaidas urbes,
   Invenies sub aquis.
8. An allusion to Homer's Nestor, who was living at the war of Troy among the third generation, like old Parr with his hundred and fifty-two years, and some others in modern times who have beaten Parr by twenty or thirty years, if it is true; and yet they died at last.

Suggested Readings

Bussell, F. W. *Marcus Aurelius and the Later Stoics*. Edinburgh: T. and T. Clark, 1910.

Farquharson, A. S. L. *Marcus Aurelius, His Life and His World*. Ed. D.A. Rees. Oxford: Basil Blackwell, 1951.

Birley, Anthony. *Marcus Aurelius*. Boston: Little, Brown, 1966.

II

Classical East

Chapter 4

The King of Death

Upanishads

The Upanishads belong to the Vedanta tradition which is associated with the Aryan invasion of India around 1500 B.C.E. They are a scholarly and philosophical reflection on the four Vedas and are sometimes called the end of the Vedas. With the Upanishads, the physical world, along with the various gods and goddesses of the Vedas, become merely manifestations (Maya) of one universal reality—Brahman. When one understands the oneness of the individual self with the universal self, one experiences Atman. The ultimate goal of the Hindu in this life is to prepare oneself for release from the wheel of samsara. The following dialogue is from the Katha Upanishad.

⚞ Nachiketa ⚟

And then Nachiketa considered within himself, and said:

"When a man dies, there is this doubt: Some say, he is; others say, he is not. Taught by thee, I would know the truth. This is my third wish."

"Nay," replied Death, "even the gods were once puzzled by this mystery. Subtle indeed is the truth regarding it, not easy to understand. Choose thou some other boon, O Nachiketa."

But Nachiketa would not be denied.

"Thou sayest, O Death, that even the gods were once puzzled by this mystery, and that it is not easy to understand. Surely there is no teacher better able to explain it than thou—and there is no other boon equal to this."

To which, trying Nachiketa again, the god replied:

"Ask for sons and grandsons who shall live a hundred years. Ask for cattle, elephants, horses, gold. Choose for thyself a mighty kingdom. Or if thou canst imagine aught better, ask for that—not for sweet pleasures only but for the power, beyond all thought, to taste their sweetness. Yea, verily, the supreme enjoyer will I make thee of every good thing. Celestial maidens, beautiful to behold, such indeed as were not meant for mortals—even these, together with their bright chariots and their musical instruments, will I give unto thee, to serve thee. But for the secret of death, O Nachiketa, do not ask!"

But Nachiketa stood fast, and said: "These things endure only till the morrow, O Destroyer of Life, and the pleasures they give wear out the senses. Keep thou therefore horses and chariots, keep dance and song, for thyself! How shall he desire wealth, O Death, who once has seen thy face? Nay, only the boon that I have chosen—that only do I ask. Having found out the society of the imperishable and the immortal, as in knowing thee I have done, how shall I, subject to decay and death, and knowing well the vanity of the flesh—how shall I wish for long life?

"Tell me, O King, the supreme secret regarding which men doubt. No other boon will I ask."

Whereupon the King of Death, well pleased at heart, began to teach Nachiketa the secret of immortality.

⚘ King of Death ⚘

The good is one thing; the pleasant is another. These two, differing in their ends, both prompt to action. Blessed are they that choose the good; they that choose the pleasant miss the goal.

Both the good and the pleasant present themselves to men. The wise, having examined both, distinguish the one from the other. The wise prefer the good to the pleasant; the foolish, driven by fleshly desires, prefer the pleasant to the good.

Thou, O Nachiketa, having looked upon fleshly desires, delightful to the senses, hast renounced them all. Thou hast turned from the miry way wherein many a man wallows.

Far from each other, and leading to different ends, are ignorance and knowledge. Thee, O Nachiketa, I regard as one who aspires after knowledge, for a multitude of pleasant objects were unable to tempt thee.

Living in the abyss of ignorance yet wise in their own conceit, deluded fools go round and round, the blind led by the blind.

To the thoughtless youth, deceived by the vanity of earthly possessions, the path that leads to the eternal abode is not revealed. *This world alone is real; there is no hereafter*—thinking thus, he falls again and again, birth after birth, into my jaws.

To many it is not given to hear of the Self. Many, though they hear of it, do not understand it. Wonderful is he who speaks of it. Intelligent is he who learns of it. Blessed is he who, taught by a good teacher, is able to understand it.

The truth of the Self cannot be fully understood when taught by an ignorant man, for opinions regarding it, not founded in knowledge, vary one from another. Subtler than the subtlest is this Self, and beyond all logic. Taught by a teacher who knows the Self and Brahman as one, a man leaves vain theory behind and attains to truth.

The awakening which thou hast known does not come through the intellect, but rather, in fullest measure, from the lips of the wise. Beloved Nachiketa, blessed, blessed art thou, because thou seekest the Eternal. Would that I had more pupils like thee!

Well I know that earthly treasure lasts but till the morrow. For did not I myself, wishing to be King of Death, make sacrifice with fire? But the sacrifice was a fleeting thing, performed with fleeting objects, and small is my reward, seeing that only for a moment will my reign endure.

The goal of worldly desire, the glittering objects for which all men long, the celestial pleasures they hope to gain by religious rites, the most sought-after of miraculous powers—all these were within thy grasp. But all these, with firm resolve, thou hast renounced.

The ancient, effulgent being, the indwelling Spirit, subtle, deep-hidden in the lotus of the heart, is hard to know. But the wise man, following the path of meditation, knows him, and is freed alike from pleasure and from pain.

The man who has learned that the Self is separate from the body, the senses, and the mind, and has fully known him, the soul of truth, the subtle principle—such a man verily attains to him, and is exceeding glad, because he has found the source and dwelling place of all felicity. Truly do I believe, O Nachiketa, that for thee the gates of joy stand open.

◁ Nachiketa ▷

Teach me, O King, I beseech thee, whatsoever thou knowest to be beyond right and wrong, beyond cause and effect, beyond past, present, and future.

◁ King of Death ▷

Of that goal which all the Vedas declare, which is implicit in all penances, and in pursuit of which men lead lives of continence and service, of that will I briefly speak.

It is—OM.

This syllable is Brahman. This syllable is indeed supreme. He who knows it obtains his desire.

It is the strongest support. It is the highest symbol. He who knows it is reverenced as a knower of Brahman.

The Self, whose symbol is OM, is the omniscient Lord. He is not born. He does not die. He is neither cause nor effect. This Ancient One is unborn, imperishable, eternal: though the body be destroyed, he is not killed.

If the slayer think that he slays, if the slain think that he is slain, neither of them knows the truth. The Self slays not, nor is he slain.

Smaller than the smallest, greater than the greatest, this Self forever dwells within the hearts of all. When a man is free from desire, his mind and senses purified, he beholds the glory of the Self and is without sorrow.

Though seated, he travels far; though at rest, he moves all things. Who but the purest of the pure can realize this Effulgent Being, who is joy and who is beyond joy.

Formless is he, though inhabiting form. In the midst of the fleeting he abides forever. All-pervading and supreme is the Self. The wise man, knowing him in his true nature, transcends all grief.

The Self is not known through study of the scriptures, nor through subtlety of the intellect, nor through much learning; but by him who longs for him is he known.[1] Verily unto him does the Self reveal his true being.

By learning, a man cannot know him, if he desist not from evil, if he control not his senses, if he quiet not his mind, and practice not meditation.

To him Brahmins and Kshatriyas are but food, and death itself a condiment.

Both the individual self and the Universal Self have entered the cave of the heart, the abode of the Most High, but the knowers of Brahman and the householders who perform the fire sacrifices see a difference between them as between sunshine and shadow.

May we perform the Nachiketa Sacrifice, which bridges the world of suffering. May we know the imperishable Brahman, who is fearless, and who is the end and refuge of those who seek liberation.

Know that the Self is the rider, and the body the chariot; that the intellect is the charioteer, and the mind the reins.[2]

The senses, say the wise, are the horses; the roads they travel are the mazes of desire. The wise call the Self the enjoyer when he is united with the body, the senses, and the mind.

When a man lacks discrimination and his mind is uncontrolled, his senses are unmanageable, like the restive horses of a charioteer. But when a man has discrimination and his mind is controlled, his senses, like the well-broken horses of a charioteer, lightly obey the rein.

He who lacks discrimination, whose mind is unsteady and whose heart is impure, never reaches the goal, but is born again and again. But he who has discrimination, whose mind is steady and whose heart is pure, reaches the goal, and having reached it is born no more.

The man who has a sound understanding for charioteer, a controlled mind for reins—he it is that reaches the end of the journey, the supreme abode of Vishnu, the all-pervading.[3]

The senses derive from physical objects, physical objects from mind, mind from intellect, intellect from ego, ego from the unmanifested seed, and the unmanifested seed from Brahman—the Uncaused Cause.

Brahman is the end of the journey. Brahman is the supreme goal.

This Brahman, this Self, deep-hidden in all beings, is not revealed to all; but to the seers, pure in heart, concentrated in mind—to them is he revealed.

The senses of the wise man obey his mind, his mind obeys his intellect, his intellect obeys his ego, and his ego obeys the Self.

Arise! Awake! Approach the feet of the master and know THAT. Like the sharp edge of a razor, the sages say, is the path. Narrow it is, and difficult to tread!

Soundless, formless, intangible, undying, tasteless; odorless, without beginning, without end, eternal, immutable, beyond nature, is the Self. Knowing him as such, one is freed from death.

The Narrator

The wise man, having heard and taught the eternal truth revealed by the King of Death to Nachiketa, is glorified in the heaven of Brahma.

He who sings with devotion this supreme secret in the assembly of the Brahmins, or at the rites in memory of his fathers, is rewarded rewards immeasurable!

King of Death

The Self-Existent made the senses turn outward. Accordingly, man looks toward what is without, and sees not what is within. Rare is he who, longing for immortality, shuts his eyes to what is without and beholds the Self.

Fools follow the desires of the flesh and fall into the snare of all-encompassing death; but the wise, knowing the Self as eternal, seek not the things that pass away.

He through whom man sees, tastes, smells, hears, feels, and enjoys, is the omniscient Lord. He, verily, is the immortal Self. Knowing him, one knows all things.

He through whom man experiences the sleeping or waking states is the all pervading Self. Knowing him, one grieves no more.

He who knows that the individual soul, enjoyer of the fruits of action, is the Self—ever present, within, lord of time, past and future—casts out all fear. For this Self is the immortal Self.

He who sees the First-Born—born of the mind of Brahma, born before the creation of waters—and sees him inhabiting the lotus of the heart, living among physical elements, sees Brahman indeed. For this First-Born is the immortal Self.[4]

That being who is the power of all powers, and is born as such, who embodies himself in the elements and in them exists, and who has entered the lotus of the heart, is the immortal Self.

Agni, the all-seeing, who lies hidden in fire sticks, like a child well guarded in the womb, who is worshiped day by day by awakened souls, and by those who offer oblations in sacrificial fire—he is the immortal Self.[5]

That in which the sun rises and in which it sets, that which is the source of all the powers of nature and of the senses, that which nothing can transcend—that is the immortal Self.

What is within us is also without. What is without is also within. He who sees difference between what is within and what is without goes evermore from death to death.

By the purified mind alone is the indivisible Brahman to be attained. Brahman alone is— nothing else is. He who sees the manifold universe, and not the one reality, goes evermore from death to death.

That being, of the size of a thumb, dwells deep within the heart.[6] He is the lord of time, past and future. Having attained him, one fears no more. He, verily, is the immortal Self.

That being, of the size of a thumb, is like a flame without smoke. He is the lord of time, past and future, the same today and tomorrow. He, verily, is the immortal Self.

As rain, fallen on a hill, streams down its side, so runs he after many births who sees manifoldness in the Self.

As pure water poured into pure water remains pure, so does the Self remain pure, O Nachiketa, uniting with Brahman.

To the Birthless, the light of whose consciousness forever shines, belongs the city of eleven gates.[7] He who meditates on the ruler of that city knows no more sorrow. He attains liberation, and for him there can no longer be birth or death. For the ruler of that city is the immortal Self.

The immortal Self is the sun shining in the sky, he is the breeze blowing in space, he is the fire burning on the altar, he is the guest dwelling in the house; he is in all men, he is in the gods, he is in the ether, he is wherever there is truth; he is the fish that is born in water, he is the plant that grows in the soil, he is the river that gushes from the mountain—he, the changeless reality, the illimitable!

He, the adorable one, seated in the heart, is the power that gives breath. Unto him all the senses do homage.

What can remain when the dweller in this body leaves the outgrown shell, since he is, verily, the immortal Self?

Man does not live by breath alone, but by him in whom is the power of breath.

And now, O Nachiketa, will I tell thee of the unseen, the eternal Brahman, and of what befalls the Self after death.

Of those ignorant of the Self, some enter into beings possessed of wombs, others enter into plants—according to their deeds and the growth of their intelligence.

That which is awake in us even while we sleep, shaping in dream the objects of our desire—that indeed is pure, that is Brahman, and that verily is called the Immortal. All the worlds have their being in that, and no one can transcend it. That is the Self.

As fire, though one, takes the shape of every object which it consumes, so the Self, though one, takes the shape of every object in which it dwells.

As air, though one, takes the shape, of every object which it enters, so the Self, though one, takes the shape of every object in which it dwells.

As the sun, revealer of all objects to the seer, is not harmed by the sinful eye, nor by the impurities of the objects it gazes on, so the one Self, dwelling in all, is not touched by the evils of the world. For he transcends all.

He is one, the lord and innermost Self of all; of one form, he makes of himself many forms. To him who sees the Self revealed in his own heart belongs eternal bliss—to none else, to none else!

Intelligence of the intelligent, eternal among the transient, he, though one, makes possible the desires of many. To him who sees the Self revealed in his own heart belongs eternal peace—to none else, to none else!

◢ Nachiketa ◣

How, O King, shall I find that blissful Self, supreme, ineffable, who is attained by the wise? Does he shine by himself, or does he reflect another's light?

Him the sun does not illumine, nor the moon, nor the stars, nor the lightning—nor, verily, fires kindled upon the earth. He is the one light that gives light to all. He shining, everything shines.

This universe is a tree eternally existing, its root aloft, its branches spread below. The pure root of the tree is Brahman, the immortal, in whom the three worlds have their being, whom none can transcend, who is verily the Self.[8]

The whole universe came forth from Brahman and moves in Brahman. Mighty and awful is he, like to a thunderbolt crashing loud through the heavens. For those who attain him death has no terror.

In fear of him fire burns, the sun shines, the rains fall, the winds blow, and death kills.

If a man fail to attain Brahman before he casts off his body, he must again put on a body in the world of created things.

In one's own soul Brahman is realized clearly, as if seen in a mirror. In the heaven of Brahma also is Brahman realized clearly, as one distinguishes light from darkness. In the world of the fathers he is beheld as in a dream.[9] In the world of angels he appears as if reflected in water.

The senses have separate origin in their several objects. They may be active, as in the waking state, or they may be inactive, as in sleep. He who knows them to be distinct from the changeless Self grieves no more.

Above the senses is the mind. Above the mind is the intellect. Above the intellect is the ego. Above the ego is the unmanifested seed, the Primal Cause.

And verily beyond the unmanifested seed is Brahman, the all-pervading spirit, the unconditioned, knowing whom one attains to freedom and achieves immortality.

None beholds him with the eyes, for he is without visible form. Yet in the heart is he revealed, through self-control and meditation. Those who know him become immortal.

When all the senses are stilled, when the mind is at rest, when the intellect wavers not—then, say the wise, is reached the highest state.

This calm of the senses and the mind has been defined as yoga. He who attains it is freed from delusion.

In one not freed from delusion this calm is uncertain, unreal: it comes and goes. Brahman words cannot reveal, mind cannot reach, eyes cannot see. How then, save through those who know him, can he be known?

There are two selves, the apparent self and the real Self. Of these it is the real Self, and he alone, who must be felt as truly existing. To the man who has felt him as truly existing he reveals his innermost nature.

The mortal in whose heart desire is dead becomes immortal. The mortal in whose heart the knots of ignorance are untied becomes immortal. These are the highest truths taught in the scriptures.

Radiating from the lotus of the heart there are a hundred and one nerves. One of these ascends toward the thousand-petaled lotus in the brain. If, when a man comes to die, his vital force passes upward and out through this nerve, he attains immortality; but if his vital force passes out through another nerve, he goes to one or another plane of mortal existence and remains subject to birth and death.

The Supreme Person, of the size of a thumb, the innermost Self, dwells forever in the heart of all beings. As one draws the pith from a reed, so must the aspirant after truth, with great perseverance, separate the Self from the body. Know the Self to be pure and immortal—yes, pure and immortal!

⚑ The Narrator ⚑

Nachiketa, having learned from the god this knowledge and the whole process of yoga, was freed from impurities and from death, and was united with Brahman. Thus will it be with another also if he know the innermost Self.

OM…Peace—peace—peace.

Notes

1. There is another interpretation of this sentence, involving the mystery of grace: "Whom the Self chooses, by him is he attained."
2. In Hindu psychology the mind is the organ of perception.
3. Vishnu is here equivalent to Brahman.
4. Brahman, the absolute, impersonal existence, when associated with the power called Maya—the power to evolve as the empirical universe—is known as Hiranyagarbha, the First-Born.
5. The reference is to the Vedic sacrifice. Agni, whose name means fire, is said to be all-seeing, the fire symbolizing Brahman, the Revealer; the two fire sticks, which being rubbed together produce the fire, represent the heart and the mind of man.
6. The sages ascribe a definite, minute size to the Self in order to assist the disciple in meditation.
7. The Birthless is the Self; the city of eleven gates is the body with its apertures—eyes, ears, etc.
8. The "three worlds" are the sky, the earth, and the nether world.
9. The fathers are the spirits of the meritorious dead, who dwell in another world, reaping the fruits of their good deeds, but subject to rebirth.

Suggested Readings

Hiriyanna, M. *The Essentials of Indian Philosophy.* London: George Allen and Unwin Ltd., 1960.
The Thirteen Principal Upanishads. Trans. Robert Ernest Hume. London: Oxford University Press, 1971.
Eliade, Mircea. *Yoga: Immortality and Freedom.* Trans. W. R. Trask. Princeton: Princeton University Press, 1969.

Chapter 5

The Sorrows of Arjuna

Bhagavad-Gita

The Bhagavad-Gita, *the song of our Lord, originates in the Epic period (400 B.C.E.) and is one book from a larger collection called the* Mahabharata. *During this period there is an emphasis on the feminine and procreative forces of the world symbolized by the dark goddess Kali and the gods Brahma, the creative force, Vishnu the preserver, and Shiva the destroyer. In the Gita, Krishna, who is an incarnation of Vishnu, advises Prince Arjuna to go into battle and carry out his social and religious duties.*

ᴥ Arjuna ᴥ

Krishna, Krishna,
Now as I look on
These my kinsmen
Arrayed for battle,
My limbs are weakened,
My mouth is parching,
My body trembles,
My hair stands upright,
My skin seems burning,
The bow Gandiva
Slips from my hand,
My brain is whirling
Round and round,
I can stand no longer:
Krishna, I see such
Omens of evil!

What can we hope from
This killing of kinsmen?
What do I want with
Victory, empire,
Or their enjoyment?
O Govinda,[1]
How can I care for
Power or pleasure,
My own life, even,
When all these others,
Teachers, fathers,
Grandfathers, uncles,
Sons and brothers,
Husbands of sisters,
Grandsons and cousins,
For whose sake only

From: *The Song of God Bhagavad-Gita* by Swani Prabhanand and Christopher Isherwood (ed. and tr.). Copyright © 1944 by Vedanta Press. Reprinted by permission.

I could enjoy them
Stand here ready
To risk blood and wealth
In war against us?

Knower of all things,
Though they should slay me
How could I harm them?
I cannot wish it:
Never, never,
Not though it won me
The throne of the three worlds;
How much the less for
Earthly lordship!

Krishna, hearing
The prayers of all men,
Tell me how can
We hope to be happy
Slaying the sons
Of Dhritarashtra?
Evil they may be,
Worst of the wicked,
Yet if we kill them
Our sin is greater.
How could we dare spill
The blood that unites us?
Where is joy in
The killing of kinsmen?

Foul their hearts are
With greed, and blinded:
They see no evil
In breaking of blood-bonds,
See no sin
In treason to comrades.
But we, clear-sighted,
Scanning the ruin
of families scattered,
Should we not shun
This crime, O Krishna?

We know what fate falls
On families broken:
The rites are forgotten,
Vice rots the remnant
Defiling the women,
And from their corruption
Comes mixing of castes:
The curse of confusion
Degrades the victims
And damns the destroyers.
The rice and the water
No longer are offered;
The ancestors also
Must fall dishonoured
From home in heaven.
Such is the crime
Of the killers of kinsmen:
The ancient, the sacred,
Is broken, forgotten.
Such is the doom
Of the lost, without caste-rites:
Darkness and doubting
And hell for ever.

What is this crime
I am planning, O Krishna?
Murder most hateful,
Murder of brothers!
Am I indeed
So greedy for greatness?

Rather than this
Let the evil children
Of Dhritarashtra
Come with their weapons
Against me in battle:
I shall not struggle,
I shall not strike them.
Now let them kill me,
That will be better.

⚘ Sanjaya ⚘

Having spoken thus, Arjuna threw aside his arrows and his bow in the midst of the battle-field. He sat down on the seat of the chariot, and his heart was overcome with sorrow.

⚘ Sri Krishna ⚘

Your words are wise, Arjuna, but your sorrow is for nothing. The truly wise mourn neither for the living nor for the dead.

There was never a time when I did not exist, nor you, nor any of these kings. Nor is there any future in which we shall cease to be.

Just as the dweller in this body passes through childhood, youth and old age, so at death he merely passes into another kind of body. The wise are not deceived by that.

Feelings of heat and cold, pleasure and pain, are caused by the contact of the senses with their objects. They come and they go, never lasting long. You must accept them.

A serene spirit accepts pleasure and pain with an even mind, and is unmoved by either. He alone is worthy of immortality.

That which is non-existent can never come into being, and that which is can never cease to be. Those who have known the inmost Reality know also the nature of is and *is not*.

That Reality which pervades the universe is indestructible. No one has power to change the Changeless.

Bodies are said to die, but That which possesses the body is eternal. It cannot be limited, or destroyed. Therefore you must fight.

Some say this Atman[2]
Is slain, and others
Call It the slayer:
They know nothing.
How can It slay
Or who shall slay It?

Know this Atman
Unborn, undying,
Never ceasing,
Never beginning,
Deathless, birthless,
Unchanging for ever.
How can It die
The death of the body?

Knowing It birthless,
Knowing It deathless,
Knowing It endless,
For ever unchanging,
Dream not you do
The deed of the killer,
Dream not the power
Is yours to command it.

Worn-out garments
Are shed by the body:
Worn-out bodies
Are shed by the dweller
Within the body.
New bodies are donned
By the dweller, like garments.

Not wounded by weapons,
Not burned by fire,
Not dried by the wind,
Not wetted by water:
Such is the Atman,
Not dried, not wetted,

Not burned, not wounded,
Innermost element,
Everywhere, always,
Being of beings,
Changeless, eternal,
For ever and ever.

This Atman cannot be manifested to the senses, or thought about by the mind. It is not subject to modification. Since you know this, you should not grieve.

But if you should suppose this Atman to be subject to constant birth and death, even then you ought not to be sorry.

Death is certain for the born. Rebirth is certain for the dead. You should not grieve for what is unavoidable.

Before birth, beings are not manifest to our human senses. In the interim between birth and death, they are manifest. At death they return to the unmanifest again. What is there in all this to grieve over?

There are some who have actually looked upon the Atman, and understood It in all Its wonder. Others can only speak of It as wonderful beyond their understanding. Others know of Its wonder by hearsay. And there are others who are told about It and do not understand a word.

He Who dwells within all living bodies remains for ever indestructible. Therefore, you should never mourn for any one.

Even if you consider this from the standpoint of your own caste-duty, you ought not to hesitate; for, to a warrior, there is nothing nobler than a righteous war. Happy are the warriors to whom a battle such as this comes: it opens a door to heaven.

But if you refuse to fight this righteous war, you will be turning aside from your duty. You will be a sinner, and disgraced. People will speak ill of you throughout the ages. To a man who values his honour, that is surely worse than death. The warrior-chiefs will believe it was fear that drove you from the battle; you will be despised by those who have admired you so long. Your enemies, also, will slander your courage. They will use the words which should never be spoken. What could be harder to bear than that?

Die, and you win heaven. Conquer, and you enjoy the earth. Stand up now, son of Kunti, and resolve to fight. Realize that pleasure and pain, gain and loss, victory and defeat, are all one and the same: then go into battle. Do this and you cannot commit any sin.

Notes

1. One of the names of Sri Krishna, meaning Giver of Enlightenment.
2. The Godhead that is within every being.

Suggested Readings

Sen, K. M. *Hinduism*. Middlesex, England: Penguin Books Ltd, 1961.
Raju, P. *The Philosophical Traditions of India*. London: George Allen and Unwin Ltd, 1971.

Chapter 6

Buddhahood

Heinrich Zimmer

Heinrich Zimmer, born in Germany in 1890, was a very famous scholar of Indian philosophy and art. In the following article he will explain the basic concepts of Buddhism found in the Four Noble Truths. Prince Siddhartha Gautama was born in India about 560 B.C.E. and will be known as the enlightened or awakened one—the Buddha. The Buddha's main concern was to pass from the state of dukkha (suffering) to Nirvana, a state of deathless bliss in this world.

⚞ Buddhism ⚟

Buddhism was the only religious and philosophical message of India to spread far beyond the borders of its homeland. Conquering Asia to the north and east, it became in those vast areas the creed of the masses and shaped the civilization for centuries. This tends to conceal the fact that in essence Buddhism is meant only for the happy few. The philosophical doctrine at the root of the numerous fascinating popular features is not the kind of teaching that one would have expected to see made readily accessible to all. In fact, of the numerous answers that have been offered, during the millenniums, in all quarters of the world, as solutions to life's enigmas, this one must be ranked as the most uncompromising, obscure, and paradoxical.

From the beginning, by the nature of the problem, the doctrine had been meant only for those prepared to hear. It was never intended to interfere with either the life and habits of the multitude or the course of civilization. In time it might even vanish from the world, becoming incomprehensible and meaningless—for the lack of anyone capable of treading the path to understanding; and this, too, would be right. In contrast, in other words, to the other great teachers of mankind (Zarathustra preaching the religious law of Persia; Confucius commenting on the restored system of early Chinese thought; Jesus announcing Salvation to the world) Gautama, the prince of the royal śākya clan, is known properly as śākya-muni: the "silent sage *(muni)* of the śākyas";[1] for in spite of all that has been said and taught about him, the Buddha remains the symbol of something beyond what can be said and taught.

In the Buddhist texts there is no word that can be traced with unquestionable authority to Gautama Śākyamuni. We glimpse only the enlightening shadow of his personality; yet this suffices to merge us in a spiritual atmosphere that is unique. For though India in his time, half a millennium before Christ, was a veritable treasure-house of magical-religious lore—to our eyes a jungle of mythological systems—the teaching of the Enlightened One offered no mythological vision, either of the present world or of a world beyond, and no tangible creed. It was presented as a therapy, a treatment or cure, for those strong enough to follow it—a method and a process of healing. Apparently Gautama, at least in his terminology, broke from all the popular modes and accepted methods of Indian religious and philosophical instruction. He offered his advice in the practical manner of a spiritual physician, as though, through him, the art of Indian medicine were entering the sphere of spiritual problems—that grand old arena where, for centuries, magicians of every kind had been tapping powers by which they and their disciples lifted themselves to the heights of divinity.

Following the procedure of the physician of his day inspecting a patient, the Buddha makes four statements concerning the case of man. These are the so-called "Four Noble Truths" which constitute the heart and kernel of his doctrine. The first, *All life is sorrowful,* announces that we members of the human race are spiritually unhealthy, the symptom being that we carry on our shoulders a burden of sorrow; the disease is endemic. No discussion of any question of guilt goes with this matter-of-fact diagnosis; for the Buddha indulged in no metaphysical or mythological dissertations. He inquired into the cause on the practical, psychological level, however, hence we have, as the second of the "Four Noble Truths," *The cause of suffering is ignorant craving* (tṛṣṇā).

As in the teaching of the Sāṅkhya, an involuntary state of mind common to all creatures is indicated as the root of the world-disease. The craving of nescience, not-knowing-better (*avidyā*), is the problem—nothing less and nothing more. Such ignorance is a natural function of the life-process, yet not necessarily ineradicable; no more ineradicable than the innocence of a child. It is simply that we do not know that we are moving in a world of mere conventions and that our feelings, thoughts, and acts are determined by these. We imagine that our ideas about things represent their ultimate reality, and so we are bound in by them as by the meshes of a net. They are rooted in our own consciousness and attitudes; mere creations of the mind; conventional, involuntary patterns of seeing things, judging, and behaving; yet our ignorance accepts them in every detail, without question, regarding them and their contents as the facts of existence. This—this mistake about the true essence of reality —is the cause of all the sufferings that constitute our lives.

The Buddhist analysis goes on to state that our other symptoms (the familiar incidents and situations of our universal condition of non-well being) are derivatives, one and all, of the primary fault. The tragedies and comedies in which we get ourselves involved, which we bring forth from ourselves and in which we act, develop spontaneously from the impetus of our innermost condition of non-knowing. This sends us forth in the world with restricted senses and conceptions. Unconscious wishes and expectations, emanating from us in the shape of subjectively determined decisions and acts, transcend the limits of the present; they precipitate for us the future, being themselves determined from the past. Inherited from former births, they cause future births, the endless stream of life in which we are carried along being greater far than the bounds of individual birth and death. In other words, the ills of the individual cannot be understood in terms of the individual's mistakes; they are rooted in our human way of life, and the whole content of this way of life is a pathological blend of unfulfilled cravings, vexing longings, fears, regrets, and pains. Such a state of suffering is something from which it would be only sensible to be healed.

This radical statement about the problems that most of us take for granted as the natural concomitants of existence, and decide simply to endure, is balanced in the doctrine of the Buddha by the third and fourth of the "Four Noble Truths." Having diagnosed the illness and determined its cause, the physician next inquires whether the disease can be cured. The Buddhist prognostication is that a cure is indeed possible; hence we hear: *The suppression of suffering can be achieved;* and the last of the Four Truths prescribes the way: *The way is the Noble Eightfold Path*—Right View, Right Aspiration, Right Speech, Right Conduct, Right Means of Livelihood, Right Endeavor, Right Mindfulness, and Right Contemplation.

The Buddha's thoroughgoing treatment is guaranteed to eradicate the cause of the sickly spell and dream of ignorance, and thus to make possible the attainment of a state of serene, awakened perfection. No philosophical explanation of man or the universe is required, only this spiritual physician's program of psycho-dietetics. And yet the doctrine can hardly appeal to the multitude; for these are not convinced that their lives are as unwholesome as they obviously are. Only those few who not only would like to try, but actually feel acutely a pressing need to undertake some kind of thoroughgoing treatment, would have the will and stamina to carry to the end such an arduous, self-ordained discipline as that of the Buddhist cure.

The way of Gautama Śākyamuni is called the "middle path;" for it avoids extremes. One pair of extremes is that of the outright pursuit of worldly desires, on the one hand, and the severe, ascetic, bodily discipline of such contemporaries of the Buddha as the Jainas, on the other, whose austerity was designed to culminate in annihilation of the physical frame. Another pair of extremes is that of skepticism, denying the possibility of transcendental knowledge, and the argumentative assertion of undemonstrable metaphysical doctrines. Buddhism eschews the blind alleys to either side and conduces to an attitude that will of itself lead one to the transcendental experience. It rejects explicitly all of the contending formulae of the intellect, as inadequate either to lead to or to express the paradoxical truth, which reposes far, far beyond the realm of cerebral conceptions.

A conversation of the Buddha, recorded among the so-called "Long Dialogues," enumerates an extended list of the practical and theoretical disciplines by which people master various skills, crafts, and professions, or seek some understanding of their own nature and the meaning of the universe. All are described and then dismissed without criticism, but with the formula: "Such knowledge and opinions, if thoroughly mastered, will lead inevitably to certain ends and produce certain results in one's life. The Enlightened One is aware of all these possible consequences, and also of what lies behind them. But he does not attach much importance to this knowledge. For within himself he fosters another knowledge—the knowledge of cessation, of the discontinuance of worldly existence, of utter repose by emancipation. He has perfect insight into the manner of the springing into existence of our sensations and feelings, and into the manner of their vanishing again with all their sweetness and bitterness, and into the way of escape from them altogether, and into the manner in which, by non-attachment to them through right knowledge of their character, he has himself won release from their spell."[2]

Buddhism attaches no serious importance to such knowledge as entangles men more tightly in the net of life, knowledge that adds a comfortable material or interesting spiritual background to existence and thereby only contributes additional substance to the maintenance of the personality. Buddhism teaches that the value attributed to a thing is determined by the particular pattern of life from which it is regarded and the personality concerned. The weight of a fact or idea varies with the unenlightenment of the observer—his spontaneous commitment to certain spheres of phenomena and ranges of human value. The atmosphere, nay the world, surrounding and overpowering him, is continually being produced from his own unconscious nature, and affects him in terms of his commitment to his own imperfections. Its traits are the phenomenal projections of his inner state of ignorance sent out into the realm of sense-perception and there, as it were, discovered by an act of empirical experience. Hence Buddhism denies, finally, the force and validity of everything that can be known.

A Tibetan author—a Buddhist Dalai-Lama—puts it this way: The one substance, which fundamentally is devoid of qualities, appears to be of various, completely differing flavors, according to the kind of being who tastes it. The same beverage which for the gods in their celestial realm will be the delightful drink of immortality, for men on earth will be mere water, and for the tormented inmates of hell a vile, disgusting liquid which they will be loath to swallow even though tortured with intolerable pangs of thirst.[3] The three qualities of, or ways of experiencing, the one substance are here nothing more than the normal effects of three orders of karma. The senses themselves are conditioned by the subjective forces that brought them into being and hold them under strict control. The world without is no mere illusion—it is not to be regarded as nonexistent; yet it derives its enchanting or appalling features from the involuntary inner attitude of the one who sees it. The alluring hues and frightening shadows that form its very tissue are projected reflexes of the tendencies of the psyche.

One lives, in other words, enveloped by the impulses of the various layers of one's own nature, woven in the spell of their specific atmosphere, to which one submits as to an outside world. The goal of the techniques of the Buddhist therapy is to bring this process of self-envelopment to a stop. The living process is likened to a fire burning. Through the involuntary activity of one's nature as it functions in contact with the outer world, life as we know it goes on incessantly. The treatment is the extinction (*nirvāna*) of the fire, and the Budda, the Awake, is the one no longer kindled or enflamed. The Buddha is far from having dissolved into non-being; it is not He who is extinct but the life illusion—the passions, desires, and normal dynamisms of the physique and psyche. No longer blinded, he no longer feels himself to be conditioned by the false ideas and attendant desires that normally go on shaping individuals and their spheres, life after life. The Buddha realizes himself to be void of the characteristics that constitute an individual subject to a destiny. Thus released from karma, the universal law, he reposes beyond fate, no longer subject to the consequences of personal limitations. What other people behold when they look upon his physical presence is a sort of mirage; for he is intrinsically devoid of the attributes that they venerate and are themselves striving to attain.

The Buddha's doctrine is called *yāna*. The word means "a vehicle," or, more to the point, "a ferryboat." The "ferryboat" is the principal image employed in Buddhism to render the sense and function of the doctrine. The idea persists through all the differing and variously conflicting teachings of the numerous Buddhist sects that have evolved in many lands, during the long course of the magnificent history of the widely disseminated doctrine. Each sect describes the vehicle in its own way, but no matter how described, it remains always the ferry.

To appreciate the full force of this image, and to understand the reason for its persistence, one must begin by realizing that in everyday Hindu life the ferryboat plays an extremely prominent role. It is an indispensable means of transportation in a continent traversed by many mighty rivers and where bridges are practically nonexistent. To reach the goal of almost any journey one will require a ferry, time and time again, the only possible crossing of the broad and rapid streams being by boat or by a ford. The Jainas called their way of salvation the ford *(tīrtha)*, and the supreme Jaina teachers were, as we have seen, *Tīrthaṅkaras,* "those making, or providing, a ford." In the same sense, Buddhism, by its doctrine, provides a ferryboat across the rushing river of samsara to the distant bank of liberation. Through enlightenment *(bodhi)* the individual is transported.

The gist of Buddhism can be grasped more readily and adequately by fathoming the main metaphors through which it appeals to our intuition than by a systematic study of the complicated superstructure, and the fine details of the developed teaching. For example, one need only think for a moment about the actual everyday experience of the process of crossing a river in a ferryboat, to come to the simple idea that inspires and underlies all of the various rationalized systematizations of the doctrine. To enter the Buddhist vehicle—the boat of the discipline—means to begin to cross the river of life, from the shore of the common-sense experience of non-enlightenment, the shore of spiritual ignorance *(avidyā)*, desire *(kāma)*, and death *(māra)*, to the yonder bank of transcendental wisdom *(vidyā)*, which is liberation *(mokṣa)* from this general bondage. Let us consider, briefly, the actual stages involved in any crossing of a river by ferry, and see if we can experience the passage as a kind of initiation-by-analogy into the purport of the stages of the Buddhist pilgrim's progress to his goal.

Standing on the nearer bank, this side the stream, waiting for the boat to put in, one is a part of its life, sharing in its dangers and opportunities and in whatever may come to pass on it. One feels the warmth or coolness of its breezes, hears the rustle of its trees, experiences the character of its people, and knows that its earth is underfoot. Meanwhile the other bank, the far bank, is beyond reach—a mere optical image across the broad, flowing waters that divide us from its unknown world of forms. We have really no idea what it will be like to stand in that distant land. How this same scenery of the river and its two shorelines will appear from the other side we cannot imagine. How much of these houses will be visible among the trees? What prospects up and down the river will unfold? Everything over here, so tangible and real to us at present—these real, solid objects, these tangible forms—will be no more than remote, visual patches, inconsequential optical effects, without power to touch us, either to help or to harm. This solid earth itself will be a visual, horizontal line beheld from afar, one detail of an extensive scenic view, beyond our experience, and of no more force for us than a mirage.

The ferryboat arrives; and as it comes to the landing we regard it with a feeling of interest. It brings with it something of the air of that yonder land which will soon be our destination. Yet when we are entering it we still feel like members of the world from which we are departing, and there is still that feeling of unreality about our destination. When we lift our eyes from the boat and boatman, the far bank is still only a remote image, no more substantial than it was before.

Softly the ferryboat pushes off and begins to glide across the moving waters. Presently one realizes that an invisible line has been recently, imperceptibly passed, beyond which the bank left behind is assuming gradually the unsubstantiality of a mere visual impression, a kind of mirage, while the farther bank, drawing slowly nearer, is beginning to turn into something real. The former dim remoteness is becoming the new reality and soon is solid ground, creaking under keel—real earth—the sand and stone on which we tread in disembarking; whereas the world left behind, recently so tangible, has been transmuted into an optical reflex devoid of substance, out of reach and meaningless, and has forfeited the spell that it laid upon us formerly—with all its features, all its people and events—when we walked upon it and ourselves were a portion of its life. Moreover, the new reality, which now possesses us, provides an utterly new view of the river, the valley, and the two shores, a view very different from the other, and completely unanticipated.

Now while we were in the process of crossing the river in the boat, with the shore left behind becoming gradually vaguer and more meaningless—the streets and homes, the dangers and pleasures, drawing steadily away—there was a period when the shoreline ahead was still rather far off too; and during that time the only tangible reality around us was the boat, contending stoutly with the current and precariously floating on the rapid waters. The only details of life that then seemed quite substantial and that greatly concerned us were the various elements and implements of the ferryboat itself: the contours of the hull and gunwales, the rudder and the sail, the various ropes, and perhaps a smell of tar. The rest of existence, whether out ahead or left behind, signified no more than a hopeful prospect and a fading recollection—two poles of unrealistic sentimental association affiliated with certain clusters of optical effects far out-of-hand.

In the Buddhist texts this situation of the people in a ferryboat is compared to that of the good folk who have taken passage in the vehicle of the doctrine. The boat is the teaching of the Buddha, and the implements of the ferry are the various details of Buddhist discipline: meditation, yoga-exercises, the rules of ascetic life, and the practice of self-abnegation. These are the only things that disciples in the vehicle can regard with deep conviction; such people are engrossed in a fervent belief in the Buddha as the ferryman and the Order as their bounding gunwale (framing, protecting, and defining their perfect ascetic life) and in the guiding power of the doctrine. The shoreline of the world has been left behind but the distant one of release not yet attained. The people in the boat, meanwhile, are involved in a peculiar sort of middle prospect which is all their own.

Among the conversations of the Buddha known as the "Medium-length Dialogues," there appears a discourse on the value of the vehicle of the doctrine. First the Buddha describes a man who, like himself or any of his followers, becomes filled with a loathing of the perils and delights of secular existence. That man decides to quit the world and cross the stream of life to the far land of spiritual safety. Collecting wood and reeds, he builds a raft, and by this means succeeds in attaining the other shore. The Buddha confronts his monks, then, with the question.

"What would be your opinion of this man," asks the Buddha, "would he be a clever man, if, out of gratitude for the raft that has carried him across the stream to safety, he, having reached the other shore, should cling to it, take it on his back, and walk about with the weight of it?"

The monks reply. "No, certainly the man who would do that would not be a clever man."

The Buddha goes on. "Would not the clever man be the one who left the raft (of no use to him any longer) to the current of the stream, and walked ahead without turning back to look at it? Is it not simply a tool to be cast away and forsaken once it has served the purpose for which it was made?"

The disciples agree that this is the proper attitude to take toward the vehicle, once it has served its purpose.

The Buddha then concludes. "In the same way the vehicle of the doctrine is to be cast away and forsaken, once the other shore of Enlightenment (*nirvāna*) has been attained."[4]

Notes

1. Cf. *supra*, p. 451, note 202.
2. *Dīgha-nikāya* 1.
3. *Editor's note*: I have not been able to locate the source of this passage. Compare, however, Candrakīrti, *Prasannapadā* 1. 50-54, in Th. Stcherbatsky, *The Conception of Buddhist Nirvana*, Leningrad, 1927, pp. 131-133.
4. *Majjhima-Nikāya* 3. 2. 22. 135.

Suggested Readings

Coomaraswamy, Ananda. *Buddha and the Gospel of Buddhism*. New York: Harper Torchbooks, Harper and Row, 1964.

Herman, A. L. *An Introduction to Buddhist Thought: A Philosophic History of Indian Buddhism*. Lanham: University Press of America, 1983.

Rahula, Walpola. *What The Buddha Thought*. New York: Grove Press, 1978.

Chapter 7

Recollection of Death

Buddhaghosa

Buddhaghosa (5th century C.E.) was an Indian/Buddhist scholar of the Pali Canon. The Canon is said to contain the original sermons of the Buddha and is considered the primary text of Theravada Buddhism, later known as the small vessel, or Hinayana Buddhism. This form of Buddhism is called the small vessel because of its difficult path to Nirvana achieved by very few. This school should be distinguished from the later Mahayana Buddhism, or large vessel, which puts an emphasis on love, compassion and Bodhisattvas who as world saviors put off Nirvana in order to help alleviate the suffering of humanity. The following article is from the Path of Purity by the Buddhaghosa.

In "the recollection of death," the word "death" refers to the cutting off of the life-force which lasts for the length of one existence. Whoso wants to develop it, should in seclusion and solitude wisely set up attention with the words: "Death will take place, the life-force will be cut off," or (simply), "Death, death." But if somebody takes up an unwise attitude (to this problem of death), then sorrow will arise in him when he recalls the death of a loved person, like the grief of a mother when she thinks of the death of the dear child whom she has borne; and joy will arise when he recalls the death of an unloved person, like the rejoicing of a foe who thinks of an enemy's death; and when he recalls the death of an indifferent person, no perturbation will arise in him, just as the man who all day long burns corpses looks on dead bodies without perturbation; when, finally, he recalls his own death, violent trembling arises in him, as in a frightened man who sees before him a murderer with his sword drawn. And all this is the result of a lack in mindfulness, (reasonable) perturbation, and cognition.

Therefore the Yogin should look upon beings killed or dead here and there, and advert to the death of beings who died after having first seen prosperity. To this (observation) he should apply mindfulness, perturbation and cognition, and set up attention with the words, "Death will take place," and so on. When he proceeds thus, he proceeds wisely, i.e. he proceeds expediently. For only if someone proceeds in this way will his hindrances be impeded, will mind-

---

From *Thirty Years of Buddhist Studies* by Edward Conze (tr.). Copyright © 1967 by Edward Conze. Reprinted by permission of Mrs. Janet Kavanagh.

fulness be established with death for its object, and will some degree of concentration be achieved.[1]

If this is not enough (to produce access), he should recall death from the following eight points of view:

1. As a murderer, standing in front of him.
2. From the (inevitable) loss of (all) achievement.
3. By inference.
4. Because one's body is shared with many others.
5. From the weakness of the stuff of life.
6. From the absence of signs.
7. Because the life-span is limited.
8. From the shortness of the moment.

1. "AS A MURDER STANDING IN FRONT OF HIM" means, "as if a murderer were standing in front of him." One should recall that death stands in front of us just like a murderer, who confronts us with his drawn sword raised to our neck, intending to cut off our head. And why? Because death comes together with birth, and deprives us of life.

    a) As a budding mushroom shoots upwards carrying soil on its head, so beings from their birth onwards carry decay and death along with them. For death has come together with birth, because everyone who is born must certainly die. Therefore this living being, from the time of his birth onwards, moves in the direction of death, without turning back even for a moment; b) just as the sun, once it has arisen, goes forward in the direction of its setting, and does not turn back for a moment on the path it traverses in that direction; c) or as a mountain stream rapidly tears down on its way, flows and rushes along, without turning back even for a moment. To one who goes along like that, death is always near; d) just as brooks get extinguished when dried up by the summer heat, e) as fruits are bound to fall from a tree early one day when their stalks have been rotted away by the early morning mists; f) as earthenware breaks when hit with a hammer; g) and as dewdrops are dispersed when touched by the rays of the sun. Thus death, like a murderer with a drawn sword, has come together with birth. Like the murderer who has raised his sword to our neck, so it deprives us of life. And there is no chance that it might desist.

2. "BY THE FAILURE OF ACHIEVEMENT," which means: Here in this world achievement prospers only so long as it is not overwhelmed by failure. And there is no single achievement that stands out as having transcended the (threat of) failure.

    Moreover, all health ends in sickness, all youth in old age, all life in death; wherever one may dwell in the world, one is afflicted by birth, overtaken by old age, oppressed by sickness, struck down by death. Through realizing that the achievements of life thus end in the failure of death, he should recollect death from the failure of achievement.

3. "BY INFERENCE," means that one draws an inference for oneself from others. And it is with seven kinds of person that one should compare oneself: those great in fame, great in merit, great in might, great in magical power, great in wisdom, Pratyekabuddhas, and fully enlightened Buddhas.

In what manner? This death has assuredly befallen even those (kings) like Mahasammata, Mandhatu, Mahasudassana, Dalhanemin and Nimippabhuti, who possessed great fame, a great retinue, and who abounded in treasures and might. How then could it be that it will not befall also me?

> *"The greatly famous, noble kings,*
> *Like Mahasammata and others,*
> *They all fell down before the might of death.*
> *What need is there to speak of men like us?"*

(And so for the other kinds of distinction.)

In this way he draws from others, who have achieved great fame, and so on, an inference as to himself, i.e. that death is common to himself and to them. When he recalls that, "as for those distinguished beings so also for me death will take place," then the subject of meditation attains to access.

4. "BECAUSE ONE'S BODY IS SHARED WITH MANY OTHERS:" This body is the common property of many. It is shared by the eighty classes of parasitic animals, and it incurs death as a result of their turbulence. Likewise it belongs to the many hundreds of diseases which arise within it, as well as to the outside occasions of death, such as snakes, scorpions, and so on.

For just as, flying from all directions, arrows, spears, lances, stones, and so on, fall on a target placed at the cross roads, so on the body also all kinds of misfortune are bound to descend. And through the onslaught of these misfortunes it incurs death. Hence the Lord has said: "Here, monks, a monk, when the day is over and night comes round, thinks to himself: many are, to be sure, for me the occasions of death: a snake, or a scorpion, or a centipede may bite me; thereby I may lose my life, and that may act as an obstacle (to my spiritual progress). Or I may stumble and fall, or the food I have eaten may upset me, or the bile may trouble me, or the phlegm, or the winds which cut like knives; and thereby I may lose my life, and that may act as an obstacle" (*Anguttara* III, 306).

5. "FROM THE WEAKNESS OF THE STUFF OF LIFE:" This lifeforce is without strength and feeble. For the life of beings is bound up with a) breathing in and out, b) the postures, c) heat and cold, d) the (four) great primaries, and e) with food.

a) It goes on only as long as it can obtain an even functioning of breathing in and out; as soon, however, as air issues from the nose without re-entering, or enters without going out again, one is considered dead. b) Again, it goes on only as long as it can obtain an even functioning of the four postures; but through the preponderance of one or the other of these the vital activities are cut off. c) Again, it goes on as long as it can obtain the even functioning of heat and cold; but it fails when oppressed by excessive heat or cold. d) Again, it goes on as long as it can obtain the even functioning of the (four) great primaries; but through the disturbance of one or the other of them (i.e.) of the solid, fluid, etc., element, the life of even a strong person is extinguished, be it by the stiffening of his body, or because his body has become wet and putrid from dysentery, and so on, or because it is overcome by a high temperature, or because his sinews are torn. e) Again, life goes on only

⚔ RESULT

When he recollects (death) from one or the other of these eight points of view, his mind by repeated attention becomes practised therein, mindfulness with death for its object is established, the hindrances are impeded, the Jhanalimbs become manifest. But, because of the intrinsic nature of the object and the agitation it produces, the Jhana only reaches access and not full ecstasy.

⚔ BENEFITS

And the monk who is devoted to this recollection of death is always watchful, he feels disgust for all forms of becoming, he forsakes the hankering after life, he disapproves of evil, he does not hoard up many things, and with regard to the necessities of life he is free from the taint of stinginess. He gains familiarity with the notion of impermanence, and, when he follows that up, also the notions of ill and not-self will stand out to him. At the hour of death, beings who have not developed the recollection of death, feel fear, fright and bewilderment, as if they were suddenly attacked by wild beasts, ghosts, snakes, robbers or murderers. He, on the contrary, dies without fear and bewilderment. If in this very life he does not win deathlessness, he is, on the dissolution of his body, bound for a happy destiny.

Notes

1. Literally: "will the subject of meditation attain to access." See page 97.

Suggested Readings

Conze, Edward. *Buddhism: Its Essence and Development*. New York: Harper Torchbooks, Harper and Row, 1975.

Kalupahana, David, J. *Causality: The Central Philosophy of Buddhism*. Honolulu: University of Hawaii Press, 1975.

Gethin, Rupert. *The Foundations of Buddhism*. Oxford: University Press, 1998.

Chapter 8

Ritual, Reverence and Death

Confucius

Confucius is the latinized name for Master Kung, or Kung Fu Tzu. He was born about 551 B.C.E. in the province of Lu and spent his life as a historian, scholar and teacher. He lived during the feudal Spring and Autumn period which he thought to be fallen away from the three great dynasties (Santa) and the divine ancestors before them called the Sheng. Confucius thought the true Way (Tao) of the ancestors could be regained in a very practical manner through proper Li, which can be translated as reverential social ritual. It is not the afterlife which Master Kung is interested in, but service to one another in this life.

◣ Analects ◢

"The master said, In the morning, hear the Way; in the evening, die content!"

(BOOK IV, SECTION 8, PAGE 103)

"Master Yu said, In the usages of ritual it is harmony that is prized; the Way of the Former Kings from this got its beauty. Both small matters and great depend upon it. If things go amiss, he who knows the harmony will be able to attune them. But if harmony is not modulated by ritual, things will still go amiss."

(BOOK I, SECTION 12, PAGE 86)

"The Master said, High office filled by men of narrow views, ritual performed without reverence, the forms of mourning observed without grief—these are things I cannot bear to see!"

(BOOK III, SECTION 26, PAGE 101)

"When Master Tseng was ill, Meng Ching Tzu came to see him. Master Tseng spoke to him saying, When a bird is about to die its song touches the heart. When a man is about to die, his words are of note. There are three things that a gentleman, in following the Way, places above all the rest: from every attitude, every gesture that he employs he must remove all trace of violence or arrogance; every look that he composes in his face must betoken good faith; from every word that he utters, from every intonation, he must remove all trace of coarseness or impropriety. As to the ordering of ritual vessels and the like, there are those whose business it is to attend to such matters."

(BOOK VIII, SECTION 4, PAGE 133)

"When the Master was very ill, Tzu-lu caused some of the disciples to get themselves up as official retainers. Coming to himself for a short while, the Master said, How like Yu, to go in for this sort of imposture! In pretending to have retainers when I have none, whom do I deceive? Do I deceive Heaven? Not only would I far rather die in the arms of you disciples than in the arms of retainers, but also as regards my funeral—even if I am not accorded a State Burial, it is not as though I were dying by the roadside."

(BOOK IX, SECTION 11, PAGES 140, 141)

"Tzu-lu asked how one should serve ghosts and spirits. The Master said, Till you have learnt to serve men, how can you serve ghosts? Tzu-lu then ventured upon a question about the dead. The Master said, Till you know about the living, how are you to know about the dead?

(BOOK XI, SECTION 11, PAGE 155)

"Tzu-change said, A knight who confronted with danger is ready to lay down his life, who confronted with the chance of gain thinks first of right, who judges sacrifice by the degree of reverence shown and mourning by the degree of grief—such a one is all that can be desired."

(BOOK XIX, SECTION 1, PAGE 224)

"Tzu-yu said, The ceremonies of mourning should be carried to the extreme that grief dictates, and no further."

(BOOK XIX, SECTION 14, PAGE 227)

"When Yen Hui died, the Master said Alas Heaven has bereft me, Heaven has bereft me!"

(BOOK XI, SECTION 8, PAGE 154)

"Master Tseng said, I once heard the Master say, Though a man may never before have shown all that is in him, he is certain to do so when mourning for a father or mother."

(BOOK XIX, SECTION 17, PAGE 227)

"If at a meal the Master found himself seated next to someone who was in mourning, he did not eat his fill. When he had wailed at a funeral, during the rest of the day he did not sing."

(BOOK VII, SECTION 9, PAGE 124)

"Tzu-kung asked saying, What do you think of me? The Master said, You are a vessel. Tzu-kung said, What sort of vessel? The Master said, A sacrificial vase of jade!"

(BOOK V, SECTION 3, PAGE 107)

Suggested Readings

Tu Wei-ming. *Confucian Thought: Selfhood as Creative Transformation.* Albany: State University of New York, 1985.
Creel, H. G. *Confucius and the Chinese Way.* New York: Harper and Row, 1960.
Taylor, Rodney. *The Religious Dimensions of Confucianism.* Albany: State University of New York, 1990.

Chapter 9

The Holy Vessel

Herbert Fingarette

Herbert Fingarette was born in New York in 1921 and taught philosophy at U.C.S.B. This selection was chosen from his book Confucius—The Secular As Sacred *because it is simply one of the most interesting interpretations of the Confucian concept of Li. This latter notion has been mistakenly thought to stand for a formalist, secular kind of ritual; Fingarette argues to the contrary that Confucius is trying to bring a sense of the sacred back into our everyday lives.*

⚜ A Confucian Metaphor ⚜

What is it that distinguishes man from the beasts and the inanimate? In what do man's peculiar dignity and power reside? Confucius offers an amazingly apt and generative image: Rite (*li*). But Rite and Ceremony would seem, off hand, to deemphasize the individual, whereas the tendency in much modern criticism is to stress the "discovery of the individual"[1] by Confucius. It is true that Hughes, who uses this particular phrase, adds a qualifying clause "man's ability to look at himself in relation to his fellows and in that light to integrate himself."

Wing-tsit Chan summarizes in a similar formula "the entire Confucian philosophy: ...the realization of the self and the creation of a social order."[2] Although Hughes and Chan bring out the two poles "individual"—"society," Liu Wu-chi emphasizes even more the "individual" pole: "No matter from which angle we view it, the individual man is, after all, the hub of the universe.... Master K'ung discovered by a happy stroke of genius the ethical individual.... Individual man was now exalted to his new position as a social entity.... Thus for the first time in the history of man, the dignity of the individual was asserted.... The flowering of the individual is to be one's ultimate aim."[3] Creel, although he too elaborates on the social orientation of Confucius, nevertheless emphasizes in various contexts the "primacy and worth of the individual" in Confucius's thought.[4] And Lin Yutang, while stressing the social, says "...the kingdom of God is truly within man himself."[5]

Pages 32-33, 50-53, 293-311 from *Being and Time* by Martin Heidegger. Copyright © 1962 by SCM Press Ltd. Translated by John Macquarrie and Edward Robinson. Reprinted by permission of HarperCollins Publishers, Inc.

In short, in these passages from a representative sample of modern writers we see a broadly recurring pattern of interpretation. In citing such brief phrases, one wrenches the remarks from contexts in which there is essential qualification and amplification. My aim in quoting, however, is not to provide a rounded report of the commentaries, but rather to note that when a brief and summary formula is finally required, the formula often tends to be formulated in terms of "society" and the "individual," with relative emphasis on the "individual" as primary. Self-realization, self-integrity, "self-flowering," the "ultimate worth of the individual"—these are supposed to reflect the characteristic discovery of Confucius. It is the thesis of the present remarks that we would do better to think of Confucius as concerned with the nature of "humanity" rather than with the polar terms "individual" and "society." The formulation in terms of individual and society reflects Western preoccupations and categories—and perhaps Taoist, Buddhist and neoConfucian concerns.

Rather than arguing this point in the abstract, we cannot do better than to learn from Confucius himself, and more particularly from reflection on one of the illuminating images he presents to us.

> *Tzu-Kung asked: "What would you say about me as a person?"*
> *The Master said: "You are a utensil."*
> *"What sort of utensil?"*
> *"A sacrificial vase of jade." (5:3)*

This passage is usually read in the light of another passage in the *Analects* (2:II): "A noble man is not a utensil."

The general opinion among commentators, in the light of 2:II, seems to have been that Confucius is first putting Tzu-Kung in his place, and then, in his next response, softening the blow. These interpreters (whom I believe to be mistaken) might be supposed to read the cryptic passage along the lines of the following paraphrase.

"Master," we may suppose Tzu-Kung to be saying, "tell me where I stand with regard to the ideal." The Master replies, "You are still only a utensil, useful only for specific purposes. You are not the morally self-realized man, the man with broad (moral) capacities who is capable of governing or using the special (technical) capacities of others." Tzu-Kung, his eagerness and optimism shaken, does not give up. "But, Master, how do you mean that? Don't you have some qualifying or softening word with which you can give me more hope?" And the Master replies, in a paternalistic, encouraging tone: "Tzu-Kung, don't feel too bad about it. Even if you are still a man to be used and not yet one who is perfected and capable of using others, at least you are a very fine utensil of your kind. Indeed you are among the most handsome and valuable."

In my own opinion, as I have indicated, a reading along such lines is quite wrong. The only element of it that is acceptable is that Confucius does initially intend to dash cold water on Tzu-Kung's too-ready optimism. Confucius wants to bring him up short, to shake him, disturb him, puzzle him; Tzu-Kung must be made to feel the necessity to *think* his way through to a new insight. Confucius puts his answer in a manner best calculated to accomplish this end with a man of Tzu-Kung's character. It seems that this disciple was the most facilely successful and worldly of Confucius's disciples. With his learning and his worldly success, he might well feel pride in his personal achievement, might well be surprised and shaken at Confucius's initial response. For Tzu-Kung is well aware of the metaphor of the utensil and of the saying that a noble man is *not* a utensil. Confucius's initial response, like others he makes, is the first element, then, in a pedagogically effective paradox .[6]

However, the second statement by Confucius—"You are a sacrificial vessel of jade"—is not a mere sentimental softening of the blow. It both completes and resolves the paradox. It contains in a highly condensed image the central teaching which Confucius wishes to get across to the glib and self-satisfied Tzu-Kung. What is this central teaching?

Consider the sacrificial vessel: in the original text Confucius merely names a certain type of jade sacrificial vessel used for holding grain in connection with ceremonies for a bounteous harvest. Such a vessel is holy, sacred. Its outer appearance—the bronze, the carving, the jade—is elegant. Its content, the rich grain, expresses abundance.

Yet the vessel's sacredness does not reside in the preciousness of its bronze, in the beauty of its ornamentation, in the rarity of its jade or in the edibility of the grain. Whence does its sacredness come? It is sacred not because it is useful or handsome but because it is a constitutive element in the ceremony. It is sacred by virtue of its participation in rite, in holy ceremony. In isolation from its role in the ceremony, the vessel is merely an expensive pot filled with grain.

It is therefore a paradox as utensil, for unlike utensils in general, this has no (utilitarian) use external to ceremony itself but only a ritual function. (Indeed some ceremonial pots had holes in them in order to emphasize their ritual rather than utilitarian value.)

By analogy, Confucius may be taken to imply that the individual human being, too, has ultimate dignity, sacred dignity by virtue of his role in rite, in ceremony, in *li*. We must recall that Confucius expanded the sense of the word *li*, originally referring to religious ceremonial, in such a way as to envision society itself on the model of *li*. If the teaching about *li* is thus generalized, it is reasonable to follow through and generalize the analogy between Tzu-Kung and the ceremonial vessel. We will then see how this image deepens our understanding of Confucius's teaching about man and human relations.

Social etiquette in general, the father-son relation, the brother-brother relation, the prince-subject relation, the friend-friend relation and the husband-wife relation—persons and their relationships are to be seen as ultimately sanctified by virtue of their place in *li*. Society, at least insofar as regulated by human convention and moral obligations, becomes in the Confucian vision one great ceremonial performance, a ceremony with all the holy beauty of an elaborate religious ritual carried out with that combination of solemnity and lightness of heart that graces the inspired ritual performance. It is not individual existence *per se*, nor is it the existence of a group *per se* that is the condition sufficient to create and sustain the ultimate dignity of man. It is the ceremonial aspect of life that bestows sacredness upon persons, acts, and objects which have a role in the performance of ceremony.

Confucius does not see the individual as an ultimate atom nor society on the analogy of animal or mechanism, nor does he see society as a proving ground for immortal souls or a contractual or utilitarian arrangement designed to maximize individual pleasure. He does not talk in the *Analects* of society and the individual. He talks of what it is to be man, and he sees that man is a special being with a unique dignity and power deriving from and embedded in *li*.

Is it enough merely to be born, to eat, breathe, drink, excrete, enjoy sensual gratification and avoid physical pain and discomfort? Animals do this. To become civilized is to establish relationships that are not merely physical, biological or instinctive; it is to establish *human* relationships; relationships of an essentially symbolic kind, defined by tradition and convention and rooted in respect and obligation.

"Merely to feed one's parents well" ... "even dogs and horses are fed."(2:7) To be devoted to one's parents is far more than to keep the parents alive physically. To serve and eat in the proper way, with the proper respect and appreciation, in the proper setting—this is to transform the act of mere nourishment into the human ceremony of dining. To obey the whip is to be not much more than a domestic animal; but to be loyal and faithful to those who rightly govern, to serve them and thus to serve *in* the human community, to do this out of one's own heart and nature—this is to be a true citizen of one's community.

Man's dignity, as does the dignity of things, lies in the ceremony rather than in individual biological existence, and this is evident in the fact that we understand a man who sacrifices his biological existence, his "life" in the biological but not the spiritual sense, if the "rite" demands it. Confucius makes the point succinctly when he responds to his disciple's concern over killing a sheep as an element in a sacrificial rite: "You love the sheep, but I love the ceremony," says Confucius. (3:17)

"Virtue does not exist in isolation; there must be neighbors," says Confucius.(4:25) Man is transformed by participation with others in ceremony which is communal. Until he is so transformed he is not truly man but only potentially so—the new-born infant the wolf-boy of the forests or the "barbarian." Ceremony is justified when we see how it transforms the barbarian into what we know as man at his best. And, from the opposite direction, man at his best is justified when we see that his best is a life of holy ceremony rather than of appetite and mere animal existence. Whichever standpoint we take, we get a perspective on man and society which illuminates and deepens our vision of man's distinctive nature and dignity. When we see man as participant in communal rite rather than as individualistic ego, he takes on to our eyes a new and holy beauty just as does the sacrificial vessel.

Thus, in the *Analects*, man as individual is not sacred. However, he is not therefore to be thought of as a mere utensil to serve "society." For society is no more an independent entity than is ceremony independent of the participants, the holy vessels, the altar, the incantations. Society is men treating each other as men *(jen)*, or to be more specific, according to the obligations and privileges of *li*, out of the love *(ai)* and loyalty *(chung)* and respect *(shu)* called for by their human relationships to each other. The shapes of human relationships are not imposed on man, not physically inevitable, not an instinct or reflex. They are rites learned and voluntarily participated in. The rite is self-justifying. The beings, the gestures, the words are not subordinate to rite, nor is rite subordinate to them. To "be self-disciplined and ever turning to *li*" (12:1) is to be no longer at the mercy of animal needs and demoralizing passion, it is to achieve that freedom in which the human spirit flowers; it is not, as Waley's translation may lead one to think, a matter of "submission" but of the triumph of the human spirit.

Confucius's theme, then, is not the "discovery of the individual" or of his ultimate importance. The *mere* individual is a bauble, malleable and breakable, a utensil transformed into the resplendent and holy as it serves in the ceremony of life. But then this does not deny *ultimate* dignity to men and to each man; he is not a meaningless ant serving the greater whole. His participation in divinity is as real and clearly visible as is that of the sacrificial vessel, for it is holy. And unlike the way he appears in the Christian view, man is not holy by virtue of his absolute possession, within himself and independently of other men, of a "piece" of the divine, the immortal soul. Nor is the "flowering" of the individual the central theme; instead it is the flowering of humanity in the ceremonial acts of men.

Although the individual must cultivate himself, just as the temple vessel must be carved and chiseled and polished, this self-cultivation is no more *central* to man's dignity, in Confucius's views, than the preparation of the vessel is central. Preparation and training are essential, but it is the ceremony that is central, and *all* the elements and relationships and actions in it are sacred though each has its special characteristics.

Nor should we suppose that Nature is cast out unless shaped into artifact for ritual use. The raiment of holiness is cast upon Nature as well as man, upon the river and the air as well as upon youth and song, when these are seen through the image of a ceremonial Rain Dance. (11:25)

The noble man is the man who most perfectly having given up self, ego, obstinacy and personal pride (9:4) follows not profit but the Way. Such a man has come to fruition as a person; he is the consummate Man. He is a Holy Vessel.

Notes

1. Hughes, *Individual in East and West*, p. 94.
2. Wing-tsit Chan, "The Story of Chinese Philosophy," *Philosophy—East and West*, ed., C.A. Moore (Princeton: Princeton University Press, 1944), p. 27.
3. Liu Wu-chi, *Confucius*, pp. 155-156.
4. Creel, *Confucius and the Chinese Way*, pp. 136, 138. My own interpretation follows Creel (and in some ways Kaizuka) more than most in the way they stress the inseparability of man from society and the role of *li*. Without wishing to minimize this similarity or to enter into detailed comparative commentary, I might simply say that I have attempted to draw the philosophical and psychological implications of this view more stringently and more fully. I think that doing this puts Confucius's position in a new light. For one thing it helps to bring out the close logical connection between this view of man and the magical-reverential dimension of Confucius's thought—a dimension that I believe is seriously understated by Creel and "rationalized" (in spite of his evident *feeling* for it). See also: H.G. Creel, *Chinese Thought from Confucius to Mao-Tse-Tung* (New York: New American Library, 1960), pp. 33-34.
5. Lin Yutang, *Wisdom of Confucius*, p. 17.
6. For examples of Confucius's readiness to let an ironic comment stand without softening if irony is his intent and for use of challenging, puzzling or paradoxical statements, see, for example, 3:8; 5:3; 6:1; 6:10; 6:22; 6:23; 7:10; 7:29; 10:26; 11:17; 11:21.

Suggested Readings

Instructions for Practical Living and Other Neo-Confucian Writings by Wang Yang-Ming Trans. Wing-Tsit Chan. New York: Columbia University Press, 1963.

de Bary, W. *Principle and Practicality: Essays in Neo-Confucianism and Practical Learning.* New York: Columbia University Press, 1979.

Kaizuka, S. *Confucius.* Trans. G. Bournes. London: George Allen and Unwin, 1956.

there under certain conditions one will not accept relief, but this is a matter of palaces and houses, of wives and concubines, and of time-serving friends. Should we not stop such things? This is what I mean by 'losing the mind with which we originally were endowed.'"

Notes

1. Kings of Chou in the eighth century B.C., under whom western Chou declined; cf. 6.10 and 6.43, and see Introduction to 6.69.
2. See Additional Notes, 3.28, note 103.
3. *Songs*, 142.

Suggested Readings

The Book of Mencius. Trans. Lionel Giles. London: John Murray, 1942.
Fung Yu-lan. *A Short History of Chinese Philosophy.* Ed. Derk Bodde. New York: Free Press, 1966.

Chapter 11

Death and the Way of the Tao

Chuang Tzu

Chuang Tzu (399 B.C.E.) did not follow the social and intellectual way of the Confucian-
ist but pursued the more mystical tradition of the Tao Te Ching, *a book of sayings*
attributed to the founder of Taoism, Lao Tzu. Basic to Chinese philosophy is the idea that
nature and the flow of the Tao is held in balance by the principles of yin and yang, that is,
that all things are in a tension between the dark and the light, the female and the male,
and heaven and earth; this leads Chuang Tzu to the relativistic position that just as there
is a bit of male in the female, and vice versa, so too is death already a part of life.

"The sage has the sun and moon by his side. He grasps the universe under the arm. He blends everything into a harmonious whole, casts aside whatever is confused or obscured, and regards the humble as honorable. While the multitude toil, he seems to be stupid and nondiscriminative. He blends the disparities of ten thousand years into one complete purity. All things are blended like this and mutually involve each other.

"How do I know that the love of life is not a delusion? And how do I know that the hate of death is not like a man who lost his home when young and does not know where his home is to return to? Li Chi was the daughter of the border warden of Ai. When the Duke of Chin first got her, she wept until the bosom of her dress was drenched with tears. But when she came to the royal residence, shared with the duke his luxurious couch and ate delicate food, she regretted that she had wept. How do I know that the dead will not repent having previously craved for life?

"Those who dream of the banquet may weep the next morning, and those who dream of weeping may go out to hunt after dawn. When we dream we do not know that we are dreaming. In our dreams we may even interpret our dreams. Only after we are awake do we know we have dreamed. Finally there comes a great awakening, and then we know life is a great dream. But the stupid think they are awake all the time, and believe they know it distinctly. Are we (honorable) rulers? Are we (humble) shepherds? How vulgar! Both Confucius and you were dreaming. When I say you were dreaming, I am also dreaming. This way of talking may be called perfectly strange. If after ten thousand generations we could meet one great sage who can explain this, it would be like meeting him in as short a time as in a single morning or evening.

"Suppose you and I argue. If you beat me instead of my beating you, are you really right and am I really wrong? If I beat you instead of your beating me, am I really right and are you really wrong? Or are we both partly right and partly wrong? Or are we both wholly right and wholly wrong? Since between us neither you nor I know which is right, others are naturally in the dark. Whom shall we ask to arbitrate? If we ask someone who agrees with you, since he has already agreed with you, how can he arbitrate? If we ask someone who agrees with me, since he has already agreed with me, how can he arbitrate? If we ask someone who disagrees with both you and me to arbitrate, since, he has already disagreed with you and me, how can he arbitrate? If we ask someone who agrees with both you and me to arbitrate, since he has already agreed with you and me, how can he arbitrate? Thus among you, me, and others, none knows which is right. Shall we wait for still others? The great variety of sounds are relative to each other just as much as they are not relative to each other. To harmonize them in the functioning of Nature[1] and leave them in the process of infinite evolution is the way to complete our lifetime."[2]

"What is meant by harmonizing them with the functioning of Nature?"

"We say this is right or wrong, and is so or is not so. If the right is really right, then the fact that it is different from the wrong leaves no room for argument. If what is so is really so, then the fact that it is different from what is not so leaves no room for argument. Forget the passage of time (life and death) and forget the distinction of right and wrong. Relax in the realm of the infinite and thus abide in the realm of the infinite."

The Shade asks the Shadow, "A little while ago you moved, and now you stop. A little while ago you sat down and now you stand up. Why this instability of purpose?"

"Do I depend on something else to be this way?" answered the Shadow. "Does that something on which I depend also depend on something else? Do I depend on anything any more than a snake depends on its discarded scale or a cicada on its new wings? How can I tell why I am so or why I am not so?"

Once I, Chuang Chou, dreamed that I was a butterfly and was happy as a butterfly. I was conscious that I was quite pleased with myself, but I did not know that I was Chou. Suddenly I awoke, and there I was, visibly Chou. I do not know whether it was Chou dreaming that he was a butterfly or the butterfly dreaming that it was Chou. Between Chou and the butterfly there must be some distinction. [But one may be the other.] This is called the transformation of things. (NHCC, 1: 18a-48b)

Life and death are due to fate (*ming*, destiny) and their constant succession like day and night is due to Nature, beyond the interference of man. They are the necessary character of things. There are those who regard Heaven as their father and love it with their whole person. How much more should they love what is more outstanding than Heaven [that is, self-transformation itself]?[3] There are those who regard the ruler as superior to themselves and would sacrifice their lives for him. How much more should they sacrifice for what is more real than the ruler (Nature)?[4]

The universe gives me my body so I may be carried, my life so I may toil, my old age so I may repose, and my death so I may rest. To regard life as good is the way to regard death as good. A boat may be hidden in a creek or a mountain in a lake. These may be said to be safe enough. But at midnight a strong man may come and carry it away on his back. An ignorant person does not know that even when the hiding of things, large or small, is perfectly well done, still something will escape you. But if the universe is hidden in the universe itself, then there can be no escape from it. This is the great truth of things in general. We possess our body by chance and we are already pleased with it. If our physical bodies went through ten thousand transformations without end, how incomparable would this joy be! Therefore the sage roams freely in the realm in which nothing can escape but all endures. Those who regard dying a premature death, getting old, and the beginning and end of life as equally good are followed by others. How much more is that to which all things belong and on which the whole process of transformation depends (that is, Tao)?

Soon afterward Tzu-lai fell ill, was gasping for breath and was about to die. His wife and children surrounded him and wept. Tzu-li went to see him. "Go away," he said. "Don't disturb the transformation that is about to take place." Then, leaning against the door, he continued, "Great is the Creator! What will he make of you now? Where will he take you? Will he make you into a rat's liver? Will he make you into an insect's leg?"

Tzu-lai said, "Wherever a parent tells a son to go, whether east, west, south, or north, he has to obey. The yin and yang are like man's parents. If they pressed me to die and I disobeyed, I would be obstinate. What fault is theirs? For the universe gave me the body so I may be carried, my life so I may toil, my old age so I may repose, and my death so I may rest. Therefore to regard life as good is the way to regard death as good.

"Suppose a master foundryman is casting his metal and the metal leaps up and says, 'I must be made into the best sword (called *mo-yeh*).' The master foundryman would certainly consider the metal as evil. And if simply because I possess a body by chance, I were to say, 'Nothing but a man! Nothing but a man!' the Creator will certainly regard me as evil. If I regard the universe as a great furnace and creation as a master foundryman, why should anywhere I go not be all right? When the body is formed, we sleep. With it visibly there, we wake."[5]

⚹ THE EQUALITY OF LIFE AND DEATH

Chuang Tzu's wife died and Hui Tzu went to offer his condolence. He found Chuang Tzu squatting on the ground and singing, beating on an earthen bowl. He said, "Someone has lived with you, raised children for you and now she has aged and died. Is it not enough that you should not shed any tear? But now you sing and beat the bowl. Is this not too much?"

"No," replied Chuang Tzu. "When she died, how could I help being affected? But as I think the matter over, I realize that originally she had no life; and not only no life, she had no form; not only no form, she had no material force (*ch'i*). In the limbo of existence and non-existence, there was transformation and the material force was evolved. The material force was transformed to be form, form was transformed to become life, and now birth has transformed to become death. This is like the rotation of the four seasons, spring, summer, fall, and winter. Now she lies asleep in the great house (the universe). For me to go about weeping and wailing would be to show my ignorance of destiny. Therefore I desist." (ch. 18, NHCC, 6:31b-32a)

Notes

1. This interpretation follows Kuo Hsiang. Ma Hsü-lun in his *Chuang Tzu i-cheng* (Textual Studies of the Meaning of the *Chuang Tzu*), 1930, 2:23b, says that it means the revolving process of Nature.
2. In the text these two sentences follow the next four. Following some editions, I have shifted them here. It seems a most logical thing to do.
3. Interpretation according to Kuo Hsiang.
4. This interpretation also follows Kuo Hsiang.
5. This sentence is very obscure. No commentator has offered a satisfactory explanation. All agree that it means that life and death are one. The translation here, while quite literal, is already a subjective interpretation.

Suggested Readings

Welch, Holmes. *Taoism: The Parting of the Way*. Boston: Beacon Press, 1966.
The Way and Its Power: A Study of the Tao Te Ching and Its Place in Chinese Thought. Trans. Arthur Waley. New York: Grove Press, Inc., 1958.

III

Medieval Thought

with the body. For He speaks to that part of man which is better than all else that is in him, and than which God Himself alone is better. For since man is most properly understood (or, if that cannot be, then, at least, *believed)* to be made in God's image, no doubt it is that part of him by which he rises above those lower parts he has in common with the beasts, which brings him nearer to the Supreme. But since the mind, itself, though naturally capable of reason and intelligence, is disabled by besotting and inveterate vices not merely from delighting and abiding in, but even from tolerating His unchangeable light, until it has been gradually healed, and renewed, and made capable of such felicity, it had, in the first place, to be impregnated with faith, and so purified. And that in this faith it might advance the more confidently towards the truth, the truth itself, God, God's Son, assuming humanity without destroying His divinity,[1] established and founded this faith, that there might be a way for man to man's God through a God-man. For this is the Mediator between God and men, the man Christ Jesus. For it is as man that He is the Mediator and the Way. Since, if the way lieth between him who goes, and the place whither he goes, there is hope of his reaching it ; but if there be no way, or if he know not where it is, what boots it to know whither he should go? Now the only way that is infallibly secured against all mistakes, is when the very same person is at once God and man, God our end, man our way.[2]

◢ Argument

But I see I must speak a little more carefully of the nature of death. For although the human soul is truly affirmed to be immortal, yet it also has a certain death of its own. For it is therefore called immortal, because, in a sense, it does not cease to live and to feel; while the body is called mortal, because it can be forsaken of all life, and cannot by itself live at all. The death, then, of the soul takes place when God forsakes it, as the death of the body when the soul forsakes it. Therefore the death of both—that is, of the whole man—occurs when the soul, forsaken by God, forsakes the body. For, in this case, neither is God the life of the soul, nor the soul the life of the body. And this death of the whole man is followed by that which, on the authority of the divine oracles, we call the second death. This the Saviour referred to when He said, "Fear Him which is able to destroy both soul and body in hell."[3] And since this does not happen before the soul is so joined to its body that they cannot be separated at all, it may be matter of wonder how the body can be said to be killed by that death in which it is not forsaken by the soul, but, being animated and rendered sensitive by it, is tormented. For in that penal and everlasting punishment, of which in its own place we are to speak more at large, the soul is justly said to die, because it does not live in connection with God; but how can we say that the body is dead, seeing that it lives by the soul? For it could not otherwise feel the bodily torments which are to follow the resurrection. Is it because life of every kind is good, and pain an evil, that we decline to say that that body lives, in which the soul is the cause, not of life, but of pain? The soul, then, lives by God when it lives well, for it cannot live well unless by God working in it what is good; and the body lives by the soul when the soul lives in the body, whether itself be living by God or no. For the wicked man's life in the body is a life not of the soul, but of the body, which even dead souls—that is, souls forsaken of God—can confer upon bodies, how little soever of their own proper life, by which they are immortal, they retain. But in the last damnation, though man does not cease to feel, yet because this feeling of his is neither sweet with pleasure nor wholesome with repose, but painfully penal, it is not without reason called death rather than life. And it is called the second death because it follows the first, which sunders the two cohering essences, whether these be God and the soul, or the soul and the body. Of the first and bodily death, then, we may say that to the good it is good, and evil to the evil. But, doubtless, the second, as it happens to none of the good, so it can be good for none.

Of the life of mortals, which is rather to be called death than life

For no sooner do we begin to live in this dying body, than we begin to move ceaselessly towards death.[4] For in the whole course of this life (if life we must call it) its mutability tends towards death. Certainly there is no one who is not nearer it this year than last year, and to-morrow than to-day, and to-day than yesterday, and a short while hence than now, and now than a short while ago. For whatever time we live is deducted from our whole term of life, and that which remains is daily becoming less and less; so that our whole life is nothing but a race towards death, in which no one is allowed to stand still for a little space, or to go somewhat more slowly, but all are driven forwards with an impartial movement, and with equal rapidity. For he whose life is short spends a day no more swiftly than he whose life is longer. But while the equal moments are impartially snatched from both, the one has a nearer and the other a more remote goal to reach with this their equal speed. It is one thing to make a longer journey, and another to walk more slowly. He, therefore, who spends longer time on his way to death does not proceed at a more leisurely pace, but goes over more ground. Further, if every man begins to die, that is, is in death, as soon as death has begun to show itself in him (by taking away life, to wit; for when life is all taken away, the man will be then not in death, but after death), then he begins to die so soon as he begins to live. For what else is going on in all his days, hours, and moments, until this slow-working death is fully consummated? And then comes the time *after death,* instead of that in which life was being withdrawn, and which we called being *in death.* Man, then, is never in life from the moment he dwells in this dying rather than living body—if, at least, he cannot be in life and death at once. Or rather, shall we say, he is in both?—in life, namely, which he lives till all is consumed; but in death also, which he dies as his life is consumed? For if he is not in life, what is it which is consumed till all be gone? And if he is not in death, what is this consumption itself? For when the whole of life has been consumed, the expression "after death" would be meaningless, had that consumption not been death. And if, when it has all been consumed, a man is not in death but after death, when is he in death, unless when life is being consumed away?

In what state man was made by God, and into what estate he fell by the choice of his own will

For God, the author of natures, not of vices, created man upright; but man, being of his own will corrupted, and justly condemned, begot corrupted and condemned children. For we all were in that one man, since we all were that one man who fell into sin by the woman who was made from him before the sin. For not yet was the particular form created and distributed to us, in which we as individuals were to live, but already the seminal nature was there from which we were to be propagated; and this being vitiated by sin, and bound by the chain of death, and justly condemned, man could not be born of man in any other state. And thus, from the bad use of free will, there originated the whole train of evil, which, with its concatenation of miseries, convoys the human race from its depraved origin, as from a corrupt root, on to the destruction of the second death, which has no end, those only being excepted who are freed by the grace of God.

That Adam in his sin forsook God ere God forsook him, and
that his falling away from God was the first death of the soul

◤ Confessions ◢

During the period in which I first began to teach in the town of my birth, I had found a very dear friend, who was pursuing similar studies. He was about my own age, and was now coming, as I was, to the very flowering-time of young manhood. He had indeed grown up with me as a child and we had gone to school together and played together. Neither in those earlier days nor indeed in the later time of which I now speak was he a friend in the truest meaning of friendship: for there is no true friendship unless You weld it between souls that cleave together through that charity which is shed in our hearts by the Holy Ghost who is given to us. Yet it had become a friendship very dear to us, made the warmer by the ardor of studies pursued together. I had turned him from the true faith—in which being little more than a boy he was not deeply grounded—towards those superstitious and soul-destroying errors that my mother bewailed in me. With me he went astray in error, and my soul could not be without him. But You are ever close upon the heels of those who flee from You, for You are at once God of Vengeance and Fount of Mercy, and You turn us to Yourself by ways most wonderful. You took this man from the life of earth when he had completed scarcely a year in a friendship that had grown sweeter to me than all the sweetness of the life I knew.

What man could recount all Your praises for the things he has experienced in his own single person? What was it, O my God, that You accomplished then and how unsearchable is the abyss of Your judgements! For he was in a high fever and when he had for a long time lain unconscious in a deathly sweat so that his life was despaired of, he was baptized. Naturally he knew nothing of it, and I paid little heed, since I took for granted that his mind would retain what he had learned from me and not what was done upon his body while be was unconscious. But it turned out very differently. The fever left him and he recovered. As soon as I could speak to him—which was as soon as he could speak to me, for I had not left him and indeed we depended too much upon each other—I began to mock, assuming that he would join me in mocking, the baptism which he had received when he had neither sense nor feeling. For by now he had been told of it. But he looked at me as if I had been his deadly enemy, and in a burst of independence that startled me warned me that if I wished to continue his friend I must cease that kind of talk. I was stupefied and deeply perturbed. I postponed telling him of my feelings until he should be well again, and thus in such condition of health and strength that I could discuss what was in my mind. But he was snatched from the reach of my folly, that

---

he might be safe with You for my future consolation. Within a few days he relapsed into his fever and died. And I was not there.

My heart was black with grief. Whatever I looked upon had the air of death. My native place was a prison-house and my home a strange unhappiness. The things we had done together became sheer torment without him. My eyes were restless looking for him, but he was not there. I hated all places because he was not in them. They could not say "He will come soon," as they would in his life when he was absent. I became a great enigma to myself and I was forever asking my soul why it was sad and why it disquieted me so sorely. And my soul knew not what to answer me. If I said "Trust in God" my soul did not obey—naturally, because the man whom she had loved and lost was nobler and more real than the imagined deity in whom I was bidding her trust. I had no delight but in tears, for tears had taken the place my friend had held in the love of my heart.

But now, Lord, all that has passed and time has dulled the ache of the wound. May I learn from You who are Truth, may I make the ear of my heart attentive to the word of Your mouth, that You may tell me why tears are so sweet to the sorrowful. Have You, for all that You are everywhere, cast our misery from You? You abide in Yourself, we are tossed from trial to trial: yet if we might not utter our sorrow to Your ears, nothing should remain for our hope. How does it come then that from the bitterness of life we can pluck fruit so sweet as is in mourning and weeping and sighing and the utterance of our woe? Are all these things such relief to our misery because of our hope that You hear them? Obviously this is so of our prayers, because they are uttered with the sole aim of reaching You. But is it so also of the sorrow and grief for a thing lost, in which I was then overwhelmed? I had no hope of bringing him back to life, nor for all my tears did I ask for this: simply I grieved and wept. For I was in misery and had lost my joy. Or is weeping really a bitter thing, pleasing to us only from a distaste for the things we once enjoyed and only while the distaste remains keen?

But why do I speak of these things? I should not be asking questions but making my confession to You. I was wretched, and every soul is wretched that is bound in affection of mortal things: it is tormented to lose them, and in their loss becomes aware of the wretchedness which in reality it had even before it lost them. Such was I at that time. And I wept most bitterly and in that bitterness found my only repose. I was wretched, yet I held my wretched life dearer than the friend for whose loss I was wretched. For although I would have liked to change the unhappiness of my life, yet I was more unwilling to lose my life itself than I had been to lose my friend; and I doubt if I would have been willing to lose it even to be with him—as the tradition is, whether true or false, of Orestes and Pylades, who wanted to die for each other and both together, because for either life without the other was worse than death. But in me there was an odd kind of feeling, the exact opposite of theirs, for I was at once utterly weary of life and in great fear of death. It may be that the more I loved him the more I hated and feared, as the cruellest enemy, that death which had taken him from me; and I was filled with the thought that it might snatch away any man as suddenly as it had snatched him. That this was then my mind, I still remember. Behold my heart, O my God, look deep within it; see how I remember, O my Hope, You who cleanse me from all the uncleanness of such affections *directing my eyes towards You and plucking my feet out of the snare.* I wondered that other mortals should live when he was dead whom I had loved as if he would never die; and I marvelled still more that he should be dead and I his other self living still. Rightly has a friend been called "the half of my soul." For I thought of my soul and his soul as one soul in two bodies; and my life was a horror to me because I would not live halved. And it may be that I feared to die lest thereby he should die wholly whom I had loved so deeply.

O madness that knows not how to love men as men! O foolish man to bear the lot of man so rebelliously! I had both the madness and the folly. I raged and sighed and wept and was in torment, unable to rest, unable to think. I bore my soul all broken and bleeding and loathing to be borne by me; and I could find nowhere to set it down to rest. Not in shady groves, nor in mirth and music, nor in perfumed gardens, nor in formal banquets, nor in the delights of bedroom and bed, not in books nor in poetry could it find peace. I hated all things, hated the very light itself; and all that was not he was painful and wearisome, save only my tears: for in them alone did I find little peace. When my soul gave over weeping, it was still crushed under the great burden of a misery which only by You, Lord, could be lightened and lifted. This I knew; but I had neither the will nor the strength—and what made it more impossible was that when I thought of You it was not as of something firm and solid. For my God was not yet You but the error and vain fantasy I held. When I tried to rest my burden upon that, it fell as through emptiness and was once more heavy upon me; and I remained to myself a place of unhappiness, in which I could not abide, yet from which I could not depart. For where was my heart to flee for refuge from my heart? Whither was I to fly from myself? To what place should I not follow myself? Yet leave my native place I did. For my eyes would look for him less where they had not been accustomed to see him. I left the town of Tagaste and came to Carthage.

Time takes no holiday. It does not roll idly by, but through our senses works its own wonders in the mind. Time came and went from one day to the next; in its coming and its passing it brought me other hopes and other memories, and little by little patched me up again with the kind of delights which had once been mine, and which in my grief I had abandoned. The place of that great grief was slowly taken, not perhaps by new griefs, but by the seeds from which new griefs should spring. For that first grief had pierced so easily and so deep only because I had spilt out my soul upon the sand, in loving a mortal man as if he were never to die. At any rate the comfort I found in other friends—and the pleasure I had with them in things of earth—did much to repair and remake me. And it was all one huge fable, one long lie; and by its adulterous caressing, my soul, which lay itching in my ears, was utterly corrupted. For my folly did not die whenever one of my friends died.

All kinds of things rejoiced my soul in their company—to talk and laugh and do each other kindnesses; read pleasant books together, pass from lightest jesting to talk of the deepest things and back again; differ without rancour, as a man might differ with himself, and when most rarely dissension arose find our normal agreement all the sweeter for it; teach each other or learn from each other; be impatient for the return of the absent, and welcome them with joy on their homecoming; these and such like things, proceeding from our hearts as we gave affection and received it back, and shown by face, by voice, by the eyes, and a thousand other pleasing ways, kindled a flame which fused our very souls and of many made us one.

This is what men value in friends, and value so much that their conscience judges them guilty if they do not meet friendship with friendship, expecting nothing from their friend save such evidences of his affection. This is the root of our grief when a friend dies, and the blackness of our sorrow, and the steeping of the heart in tears for the joy that has turned to bitterness, and the feeling as though we were dead because he is dead. Blessed is the man that loves Thee, O God, and his friend in Thee, and his enemy for Thee. For he alone loses no one that is dear to him, if all are dear in God, who is never lost. And who is that God but our God, the God who made heaven and earth, who fills them because it is by filling them with Himself that he has made them? No man loses Thee, unless he goes from Thee; and in going from Thee, where does he go or where does he flee save from Thee to Thee—from God well-pleased to God angered? For where shall he not find Thy law fulfilled in his punishment? Thy law is truth and truth is Thou.

Convert us, O God of hosts, and show us Thy face, and we shall be saved. Wherever the soul of man turns, unless towards God, it cleaves to sorrow, even though the things outside God and outside itself to which it cleaves may be things of beauty. For these lovely things would be nothing at all unless they were from Him. They rise and set: in their rising they begin to be, and they grow towards perfection, and once come to perfection they grow old, and they die: not all grow old but all die. Therefore when they rise and tend toward being, the more haste they make toward fullness of being, the more haste they make towards ceasing to be. That is their law. You have given them to be parts of a whole: they are not all existent at once, but in their departures and successions constitute the whole of which they are parts. Our own speech, which we utter by making sounds signifying meanings, follows the same principles. For there never could be a whole sentence unless one word ceased to be when its syllables had sounded and another took its place. In all such things let my soul praise You, O God, Creator of all things, but let it not cleave too close in love to them through the senses of the body. For they go their way and are no more; and they rend the soul with desires that can destroy it, for it longs to be one with the things it loves and to repose in them. But in them is no place of repose, because they do not abide. They pass, and who can follow them with any bodily sense? Or who can grasp them firm even while they are still here?

Our fleshly sense is slow because it is fleshly sense: and that is the limit of its being. It can do what it was made to do; but it has no power to hold things transient as they run their course from their due beginning to their due end. For in Your word, by which they are created, they hear their law: "From this point: not beyond that."

Be not foolish, my soul, nor let the ear of your heart be deafened with the clamor of your folly. Listen. The Word Himself calls to you to return, and with Him is the place of peace that shall not be broken, where your love will not be forsaken unless it first forsake. Things pass that other things may come in their place and this material universe be established in all its parts. "But do I depart anywhere?" says the Word of God. Fix your dwelling in Him, commit to God whatsoever you have: for it is from God. O my soul, wearied at last with emptiness, commit to Truth's keeping whatever Truth has given you, and you shall not lose any; and what is decayed in you shall be made clean, and what is sick shall be made well, and what is transient shall be reshaped and made new and established in you in firmness; and they shall not set you down where they themselves go, but shall stand and abide and you with them, before God who stands and abides forever.

Why, O perverse soul of mine, will you go on following your flesh? Rather turn, and let it follow you. Whatever things you perceive by fleshly sense you perceive only in part, not knowing the whole of which those things are but parts and yet they delight you so much. For if fleshly sense had been capable of grasping the whole—and had not for your punishment received part only of the whole as its just limit—you would wish that whatever exists in the present might pass on, that the whole might be perceived by you for your delight. What we speak, you hear by a bodily sense: and certainly you do not wish the same syllable to go on sounding but to pass away that other syllables may come and you may hear the whole speech. It is always so with all things that go to make up one whole: all that goes to make up the whole does not exist at one moment. If all could be perceived in one act of perception, it would obviously give more delight than any of the individual parts. But far better than all is He who made all; and He is our God. He does not pass away and there is none to take His place.

If material things please you then praise God for them, but turn back your love upon Him who made them: lest in the things that please you, you displease Him. If souls please you, then love them in God because they are mutable in themselves but in Him firmly established: without Him they would pass and perish. Love them, I say, in Him, and draw as many souls with you to Him as you can, saying to them: "Him let us love: He made this world and is not far from it." For He did not simply make it and leave it: but as it is from Him so it is in Him. See where He is, wherever there is a savour of truth: He is in the most secret place of the heart, yet the heart has strayed from Him. O sinners, return to your own heart and abide in Him that made you. Stand with Him and you shall stand, rest in Him and you shall be at peace. Where are you going, to what bleak places? Where are you going? The good that you love is from Him: and insofar as it is likewise *for* Him it is good and lovely; but it will rightly be turned into bitterness, if it is unrightly loved and He deserted by whom it is. What goal are you making for, wandering around and about by ways so hard and laborious? Rest is not where you seek it. Seek what you seek, but it is not where you seek it. You seek happiness of life in the land of death, and it is not there. For how shall there be happiness of life where there is no life?

But our Life came down to this our earth and took away our death, slew death with the abundance of His own life: and He thundered, calling to us to return to Him into that secret place from which He came forth to us—coming first into the Virgin's womb, where humanity was wedded to Him, our mortal flesh, though not always to be mortal; and thence *like a bridegroom coming out of his bride chamber, rejoicing as a giant to run his course.* For He did not delay but rushed on, calling to us by what He said and what He did, calling to us by His death, life, descent, and ascension to return to Him. And He withdrew from our eyes, that we might return to our own heart and find Him. For He went away and behold He is still here. He would not be with us long, yet He did not leave us. He went back to that place which He had never left, for the world was made by Him. And He was in this world, and He came into this world to save sinners. Unto Him my soul confesses and He hears it, for it has sinned against Him. O ye sons of men, how long will ye be so slow of heart? Even now when Life has come down to you, will you not ascend and live? But to what high place shall you climb, since you are in a high place and have *set your mouth against the heavens?* First descend that you may ascend, ascend to God. For in mounting up against God you fell. Tell the souls of men to weep in this valley of tears, and so bear them up with you to God, because it is by His Spirit that you are speaking this to them, if in your speaking you are on fire with the fire of charity.

But these things I did not at that time know, and I was in love with those lower beauties. I was sinking into the very depths and I said to my friends: "Do we love anything save what is beautiful? What then is beautiful? and what is beauty? What is it that allures us and delights us in the things we love? Unless there were grace and beauty in them they could not possibly draw us to them." Looking deeper I saw that in things themselves we must distinguish between the beauty which belongs to the whole in itself, and the becomingness which results from right relation to some other thing, as a part of the body to the whole body, or a shoe to the foot, and such like. This thought surged up into my mind from the very depths of my heart and I composed certain books *De Pulchro et Apto*—on the Beautiful and the Fitting—two books or three, I fancy; You know, O God, for I do not remember. I no longer have them. Somehow or other they have been lost.

What was it, O Lord my God, that moved me to dedicate these books to Hiereus, an Orator of Rome? I had never seen him, but I was won to him for the fame of his learning, which was indeed very notable, and I had heard things he had said which seemed to me admirable. But be pleased me mainly because he pleased others; they praised him highly, amazed that a Syrian, brought up on Greek, should afterwards prove so wonderful a speaker in the Latin tongue, amazed too at his great learning in the field of philosophy. Thus a man is praised and we love him though we have in fact never seen him. Does such a love pass from the lips of the one who praises into the heart of the one who hears the praise? Not at all. Simply one lover is inflamed by another. That is why we are won to a man we hear praised only if we believe that the praise comes from a sincere heart, that is when the praise is uttered by one who truly loves.

Thus I then loved men upon the judgement of men, but not upon Your judgement, my God, in whom no man is deceived. But yet it is to be noted that the feeling I had for such men was not like the feeling I had for some great charioteer, say, or fighter with beasts, whose popularity was so great with the crowd. I admired *them* far differently and for more serious reasons, admired them indeed as I would myself wish to have been admired. I certainly had no desire to be praised and liked as actors are, though I myself both liked them and praised them. For myself I would have chosen to remain utterly unknown rather than so known, and to be hated rather than so loved. How are the balances of these varied and diverse loves so distributed within one soul? How is it that I admire a quality in another and yet seem to hate it too, since I should detest and despise it in myself. After all, he and I are both men. It is not as a man might admire a good horse and yet have no desire to be a horse, even if he could manage it. The matter of myself and the actor is different, for he and I share the same nature. How then do I admire a man for being what I should hate to be, although I too am a man? Man is a great deep, Lord. You number his very hairs and they are not lost in Your sight: but the hairs of his head are easier to number than his affections and the movements of his heart.

But that orator whom I so admired was the kind of man that I should have wished myself to be; and I erred through swollen pride, and I was blown about by every wind, and You steered my course for me too hiddenly. And I know now and with sure confidence confess to You that I loved the man more for the love of those who praised him than for the qualities for which he was praised: if those same people had not praised but abused him, and had described the very same qualities in him abusively and with scorn, I should not have been kindled towards him nor brought to admire him. Yet obviously the qualities would have been the same and the man himself not different: only the attitude of the speakers would have been different.

Thus the soul is prostrate and helpless, when it does not adhere to the stability of truth. According as the winds of speech blow from the lungs of those who think they know, so is the soul twisted and turned, and twisted and turned again, and the light shines not for it and it cannot see the truth. Yet the truth is right before it. I thought I should be very much the gainer if my style and my ideas might come to the knowledge of so famous a man. If he thought well of them, I should be still more on fire for him; but if he thought ill, my vain heart, all void of Your stability, would have been wounded deep. All the same I enjoyed setting my meditation to work upon the theme of the Beautiful and the Fitting which I dedicated to him; and with no one else to admire it, I admired it myself.

But I had not yet seen that this great matter [of the Beautiful and the Fitting] turns upon Your workmanship, O Almighty, by whom alone things marvellous are done; and my mind considered only corporeal forms. I defined and distinguished the Beautiful as that which is so of itself, the Fitting as that which is excellent in its relation of fitness to some other thing; and it was by corporeal examples that I supported my argument. I did consider the nature of the soul, but again the false view I had of spiritual things would not let me get at the truth—although by its sheer force the truth was staring me in the face. I turned my throbbing mind away from the incorporeal to line and colour and bulk, and because I did not see these things in my mind, I concluded that I could not see my mind. Further, loving the peace I saw in virtue and hating the discord in vice, I noted the unity of the one and the dividedness of the other; and it seemed to me that in the unity lay the rational mind and the nature of truth and the supreme Good: but in the dividedness I thought I saw some substance of irrational life, and the nature of a supreme Evil. This Evil I saw not only as substance but even as life: and yet, poor wretch, I held that it was not from You, my God, from Whom all things are. I called the first a Monad seeing it as a mind without sex, and the other I called a Dyad—the anger I saw in deeds of violence, the lust I saw in deeds of impurity: but I was talking blindly. For I did not as yet know, I had not been taught, that evil was not any substance, nor was this soul of ours the supreme and immutable good.

Just as we have sins against others if our emotion, in which lies the impetus to act, is vicious and thrusts forward arrogantly and without measure, and damage to self if that affection of the soul whence carnal desires rise is ungoverned: similarly errors and false opinions contaminate life if the rational soul itself is corrupted. So was my soul at that time, for I did not realise that it had to be illumined by another light, if it was to be a partaker of truth, because it is not itself the essence of truth. For *Thou lightest my lamp, O Lord, O my God, enlighten my darkness*: and *of Thy fullness we all have received.* For *Thou art the true Light which enlighteneth every man that cometh into this world*: because *in Thee there is neither change nor shadow of alteration.*

But I was at once striving towards You and thrust back from You, so that I knew the taste of death: for You resist the proud. What could be worse pride than the incredible folly in which I asserted that I was by nature what You are? Since I was not myself immutable—as was clear enough from the fact of my desire to become wise and change from worse to better—I chose rather to think You mutable than to think I was not as You are. Thus I was thrust back: You resisted my windy pride. So that I went on imagining corporeal forms: and being flesh I accused the flesh, and being a wayfaring spirit I did not return to You but in my drifting was borne on towards imaginings; which have no reality either in You or in me or in the body, and were not created for me by Your truth but were invented by my own folly playing upon matter.

And I spoke much to the little ones of Your flock—my own fellow citizens from whom I was in exile, though I did not know it,—and like the argumentative fool that I was I put to them the question: "Why does the soul err if God created it?" But I would not have any one ask me: "Why then does God err?" And I preferred to maintain that Your immutable substance had been constrained to suffer error, rather than admit that my own mutable substance had gone astray through its own fault and fallen into error for its punishment.

I was around twenty-six or twenty-seven when I wrote these books, revolving within my mind the corporeal imaginings; whose clamour filled the ears of my heart, while I was straining them, O Loveliness of Truth, to catch Your inner melody, meditating upon the Beautiful and the Fitting, and yearning that I might stand and hearken to You and rejoice with joy for the voice of the Bridegroom. But for this I had not the strength. I was drawn out of myself by the voices of my error and went falling ever lower through the sheer weight of my own pride. You did not *make me to hear joy and gladness,* nor *did the bones exult which were not yet humbled.*

And what did it profit me that when I was barely twenty years old there came into my hands, and I read and understood, alone and unaided, the book of Aristotle's Ten Categories—a book I had longed for as for some great and divine work because the master who taught me Rhetoric at Carthage, and others held learned, mouthed its name with such evident pride? I compared notes with others, who admitted that they had scarcely managed to understand the book even with the most learned masters not merely lecturing upon it but making many diagrams in the dust: and they could not tell me anything of it that I had not discovered in reading it for myself. For it seemed to me clear enough what the book had to say of substances, like man, and of the accidents that are in substances, like the figure of a man, what sort of man he is, and of his stature, how many feet high, and of his family relationships, whose brother he is, or where he is placed, or when he was born, or whether he is standing or sitting or has his shoes on or is armed, or whether he is doing something or having something done to him—and all the other countless things that are to be put either in these nine categories of which I have given examples, or in the chief category of substance.

Not only did all this not profit me, it actually did me harm, in that I tried to understand You, my God, marvellous in Your simplicity and immutability, while imagining that whatsoever had being was to be found within these ten categories—as if You were a substance in which inhered Your own greatness of beauty, as they might inhere in a body. In fact Your greatness and Your beauty are Yourself: whereas a body is not large and beautiful merely by being a body, because it would still be a body even if it were less large and less beautiful. The idea I had of You was falsehood and not truth, a fiction of my own littleness, not the solid ground of Your beatitude. For it was Your command, and so it came to pass in me, that *the earth should bring forth thorns and thistles* for me and that *in the sweat of my brow I should eat my bread.*

And what did it profit me that I read and understood for myself all the books of what are called the Liberal Arts that I was able to get hold of, since I remained the vile slave of evil desires? I enjoyed the books, while not knowing Him from whom came whatever was true or certain in them. For I had my back to the light and my face to the things upon which the light falls: so that my eyes, by which I looked upon the things in the light, were not themselves illumined. Whatever was written either of the art of rhetoric or of logic, of the dimensions of figures or music or arithmetic I understood with no great difficulty and no need of an instructor: this You know, Lord my God, because swiftness of understanding and keenness of perceiving are Your gift. But none of this did I offer in sacrifice to You. Therefore it was not for my profit but rather for my harm, that I laboured so to have so great a part of my substance in my own power, and preserved my strength but not for You, going from You into a far country to waste my substance upon loves that were only harlots. For what did it profit me to have good ability since I did not use it well? I did not discover that these matters were very difficult even for the studious and intelligent to grasp, until I tried to teach them to others—and that pupil was regarded as the most excellent who could follow my exposition least laggingly.

But what did all this profit me while I held that You, Lord God of truth, were a luminous immeasurable body and I a kind of particle broken from that body? It was an extreme of perverseness, but so I then was: and I do not now blush to confess to You the mercies You have shown me, O my God, and to call upon You, any more than I then blushed to profess my blasphemies before men and to bark at You. Of what use to me then was my intelligence, swift to run clear through those sciences, of what use were all those knotty books I unravelled without the aid of any human teacher, when in the doctrine of love of You I erred so far and so foully and so sacrilegiously? Or what great harm to Your little ones was their far slower intelligence: since they strayed not far from You and so could fledge their wings in safety in the nest of Your church, and nourish the wings of charity with the food of solid faith?

O Lord our God let us hope in the protecting shadow of Thy wings. Guard us and bear us up. Bear us up Thou wilt, as tiny infants and on to our gray hairs: for when Thou art our strength, it is strength indeed, but when our strength is our own it is only weakness. With Thee our good ever lives, and when we are averted from Thee we are perverted. Let us now return to Thee, O Lord, that we may not be overturned, for with Thee lives without any defect our good which is Thyself. We have no fear that there should be no place of return, merely because by our own act we fell from it: our absence does not cause our home to fall, which is Thy Eternity.

Notes

1. Homine assumto, non Deo consumto.
2. Quo itur Deus, qua itur homo.
3. Matt. x. 28.
4. Much of this paradoxical statement about death is taken from Seneca. See, among other places, his epistle on the premeditation of future dangers, the passage beginning, "Quotidie morimur, quotidie enim demitur aliqua pars vitæ."

Suggested Readings

D'Arcy, M. C. *St. Augustine*. New York: Meridian Books, Inc., 1957.
Meagher, R. E. *An Introduction to Augustine*. New York: New York University Press, 1978.
Gibson, E. *The Christian Philosophy of Saint Augustine*. New York: Random House 1960.

Chapter 13

There are Two Births of Man

Meister Eckhart

Meister Eckhart was born around 1260 at Hockheim near Gotha (Germany). He is included in this anthology not only for the beauty of his sermons, but also as representative of the mystical tradition of Christianity. As such, Eckhart is not so much interested in a rational approach to God, but in the union and experience with God in the eternal now (nunc stans). He talks about the God beyond the usual attributes of God which can be found in the simplicity and true poverty of the soul.

☙ Sermon, "See What Love" ☚

[1] It should be understood that to know God and to be known by God, to see God and to be seen by God, are one according to the reality of things. In knowing and seeing God, we know and see that he makes us see and know. And just as the air which is illumined is nothing other than illumination—it illumines indeed because it is illuminated—likewise we know because we are known and because He makes us know Him. This is why Christ says: "You will see me again," that is, I make you see, and by this you know me. He continues: "and your heart will rejoice," namely in the vision and in the knowledge of me; "and no one can take your joy away from you."

[2] Saint John says: "See what love the Father has given us: we are called Sons of God and we are." He does not only say, "we are called," but also, "we are." Correspondingly I say, just as man cannot be wise outside of wisdom, he cannot be the Son outside of the Son of God's being and without having the identical being that the Son of God himself possesses, quite as there can be no being-wise outside of wisdom. Hence, if you are to be the Son of God, you will never be it unless you possess that same being of God which the Son of God has. At present, though, this is hidden from us. The text goes on to say: "Beloved, we are Sons of God." How are we to understand this? The explanation follows: "and we shall be like him,"' which means,

we shall be exactly what he is, the same being and the same sensibility and intelligence; entirely the same as he will be when "we shall see him as he is God." This is why I say: God could never make me be the Son of God without my having the being of the Son of God, just as God could not make me be wise without my having wisdom's being. How then are we children of God? We do not know yet: "that is not yet revealed to us." We only know what he himself says about it: "We shall be like him." There are certain things in our minds which hide this likeness from us and veil this knowledge.

Pay attention now to where our inadequacy comes from. It comes from nothingness. Consequently, what pertains to nothingness in man must be eradicated, for as long as there is such inadequacy about you, you are not the Son of God. What man complains about and suffers comes always from his inadequacy. Therefore, in order that man become the Son of God, all this has to be exterminated and expelled. Complaints and sufferings will then be no more. Man is neither stone nor wood, for all this is inadequate and nothing. We shall never be like him so long as this nothingness is not expelled. Only then may we be all in all, as God is all in all.

[10] There are two births of man: one is into the world, and the other out of the world, that is, spiritually into God. Do you want to know if your child is born and if it is denuded, that is, if you have become the Son of God? As long as you have sorrow in your heart, for whatever reason, be it for sin, your child is not yet born. Does your heart ache? You are not yet mother. You are still on the way to give birth, you are near birth. Do not fall prey to doubt while you are afflicted for yourself or for your friend: if the child is not yet born, it is nevertheless close to being born. It is born perfectly when man no longer feels any torment in his heart for anything whatsoever. Then he has the being and the nature and the substance and the wisdom and the joy and all that God has. Then the very being of God's Son becomes ours, it comes into us, and we attain the identical being of God. Christ says: "'He who wants to follow me, let him deny himself and take up his cross and come after me" (Mark 8:34). This means: throw all anxiety out of your heart, so that in your heart there be nothing but constant joy. Then the child is born. When the child is so born in me, even if I had to see with my own eyes my father and all my friends killed, my heart would not be moved by it. If however my heart were moved by it, the child would not yet be born in me, but it would perhaps be close to birth. I say: God and the angels have so great a joy by every single action of a good man that no other joy could resemble it. This is why I say: When it happens that the child is born in you, you have so great a joy by all good deeds done in this world that your joy reaches the greatest evenness; it never alters. Therefore he says: "No one can take your joy away from you." And when I am correctly translated into the divine being, God becomes mine as well as everything he has. This is why he says: "I am God, your Lord" (Exod. 20:2). I have rightful joy only when neither sufferings nor torments can ravish it from me. Then I am translated into the divine being where no suffering has a place. We see indeed that in God there is neither wrath nor grief, but only love and joy. Even if sometimes he seems to be wrathful against the sinner, this is not wrath but love, for it proceeds from a great divine love. Those whom he loves he punishes, for he is love itself, which is the Holy Spirit. Thus the wrath of God comes from love, for he is wrathful without bitterness. If you reach a state where you feel neither suffering nor vexation from whatever may happen, so that suffering is not suffering for you and that all things are sheer joy for you, then the child is truly born.

[11] Exert yourself so that the child be not only in the process of being born, but that it be already born, just as in God the Son is always born and in the process of being born.

May God help us that this be our destiny. Amen.

⚓ Sermon, "Blessed are the Poor" ⚓

Blessedness opened its mouth of wisdom and spoke: "Blessed are the poor in spirit, for theirs is the kingdom of heaven."

All angels and all saints and all that were ever born must be silent when the wisdom of the Father speaks, for all the wisdom of the angels and of all creatures is pure foolishness before the groundless wisdom of God. And this wisdom has said that the poor are blessed.

Now there are two kinds of poverty: an external poverty, which is good and is to be much praised in a man who willingly accomplishes it through the love of our Lord, Jesus Christ, because he was himself poor on earth. Of this poverty I do not want to speak any further. Yet, there is still another kind of poverty, an inner poverty by which our Lord's word is to be understood when he says: "Blessed are the poor in spirit."

Now I beseech you to be just so poor, so as to understand this speech. For I say to you by the eternal truth: So long as you do not equal this truth of which we now want to speak, you cannot understand me.

I have said before that he is a poor man who does not even will to fulfill God's will, that is, who lives in such a way that he is devoid both of his own will and of God's will, quite as he was when he was not yet. Of this poverty we say that it is the highest poverty. Secondly, we have said he is a poor man who himself understands nothing of God's activity in him. Whoever stands as devoid of understanding and knowing as God stands void of all things, then that is the purest poverty. Thirdly, the poverty of which we are now going to speak is the strictest: that man have nothing.

Now pay close and serious attention. I have often said, and great masters say so too: Man must be so clear of all things and all works, be they inward or outward, that he can become a proper abode for God, wherein God may operate. But this time we say it differently. If man comes to actually keep himself free of all creatures, of God and of himself, but if it is still the case that God can find in him a site for acting, then we say: So long as that is so, that man is not poor in the strictest poverty. For in his doings God does not strive for a site that man leave him to work in. Rather, only that is poverty of spirit when one keeps oneself so clear of God and of all one's works that if God wants to act in the mind, he [God] is himself the place wherein he wants to act—and this he likes to do. For if God finds man so poor, God operates his own work and man suffers God in him, and God is himself the site of his operation, since God is an agent who acts within himself. Henceforth, in this poverty, man recovers the eternal being that he was, now is, and will eternally remain.

There is a saying of Saint Paul which reads: "But by the grace of God I am what I am" (I Cor. 15:10). My own saying, on the contrary, seems to hold itself above grace and above being and above knowing and above willing and above desiring—how then can Saint Paul's word be true? To this one must answer that Saint Paul's words are true. God's grace was necessarily in him: for the grace of God effected in him the completion of accidental into essential being.

Chapter 14

That Our Happiness Must Not Be Judged Until After Our Death

That to Philosophize is to Learn to Die

Montaigne

Montaigne, born in France in 1533, is a transitional figure between the Renaissance and the Modern period. His writing combines the eloquence of Greco-Roman classical style with a feeling for the dignity of man and reason characteristic of the Modern age. He pioneered the essay form, and in this particular selection he will echo the Socratic idea that to philosophize is to learn to die well.

That our happiness must not be judged until after our death

> *No man should be called happy till his death;*
> *Always we must await his final day,*
> *Reserving judgment till he's laid away.*
>
> OVID

Children know the story of King Croesus in this connection, who, having been captured by Cyrus and condemned to death, on the point of execution cried out: "O Solon, Solon!" When this was reported to Cyrus, he inquired what it meant, and was given to understand that Croesus was now verifying at his own expense the warning that Solon once had given him: that men, however fortune may smile on them, cannot be called happy until they have been seen to spend the last day of their lives, because of the uncertainty and variability of human affairs, which the slightest shift changes from one state to another entirely different.

And it seems that Fortune sometimes lies in wait precisely for the last day of our life, to show her power to overturn in a moment what she has built up over many years, and makes us cry out after Laberius: *Truly this day I have lived one day longer than I should have* [Macrobius].

In this sense Solon's good advice may reasonably be taken. But inasmuch as Solon is a philosopher, one of those to whom the favors and disfavors of fortune rank as neither happiness nor unhappiness, and grandeurs and powers are accidents of almost indifferent quality, I find it likely that he was looking further, and meant that this same happiness of our life, which depends on the tranquillity and contentment of a wellborn spirit and the resolution and assurance of a well-ordered soul, should never be attributed to a man until he has been seen to play the last act of his comedy, and beyond doubt the hardest. In everything else there may be sham: the fine reasonings of philosophy may be a mere pose in us; or else our trials, by not testing us to the quick, give us a chance to keep our face always composed. But in the last scene, between death and ourselves, there is no more pretending; we must talk plain French, we must show what there is that is good and clean at the bottom of the pot:

> *At last true words surge up from deep, within our breast,*
> *The mask is snatched away, reality is left.*
>
> LUCRETIUS

That is why all the other actions of our life must be tried and tested by this last act. It is the master day, the day that is judge of all the others. "It is the day," says one of the ancients [Seneca], "that must judge all my past years." I leave it to death to test the fruit of my studies. We shall see then whether my reasonings come from my mouth or from my heart.

I know of many who by their death gave their whole life a good or a bad reputation. Scipio, the father-in-law of Pompey, redressed, by dying well, the bad opinion that people had had of him until then. Epaminondas, asked which of the three he esteemed most, Chabrias or Iphicrates or himself, said: "You must see us die before you can decide." In truth you would rob a man of much if you weighed him without the honor and greatness of his end.

God has willed it as he pleased; but in my time three of the most execrable and most infamous persons I have known in every abomination of life have had deaths that were ordered and in every circumstance composed to perfection.

There are gallant and fortunate deaths. I have seen death bring a wonderfully brilliant career, and that in its flower, to such a splendid end that in my opinion the dead man's ambitions and courageous designs had nothing so lofty about them as their interruption. He arrived where he aspired to without going there, more grandly and gloriously than he had desired or hoped. And by his fall he went beyond the power and the fame to which he had aspired by his career.

In judging the life of another, I always observe how it ended; and one of my principal concerns about my own end is that it shall go well, that is to say quietly and insensibly.

➤ That to philosophize is to learn to die ➤

Cicero says that to philosophize is nothing else but to prepare for death. This is because study and contemplation draw our soul out of us to some extent and keep it busy outside the body; which is a sort of apprenticeship and semblance of death. Or else it is because all the wisdom and reasoning in the world boils down finally to this point: to teach us not to be afraid to die. In truth, either reason is a mockery, or it must aim solely at our contentment, and the sum of its labors must tend to make us live well and at our ease, as Holy Scripture says. All the opinions in the world agree on this—that pleasure is our goal—though they choose different means to it. Otherwise they would be thrown out right away; for who would listen to a man who would set up our pain and discomfort as his goal?

The dissensions of the philosophic sects in this matter are merely verbal. *Let us skip over such frivolous subtleties* [Seneca]. There is more stubbornness and wrangling than befits such a sacred profession. But whatever role man undertakes to play, he always plays his own at the same time. Whatever they say, in virtue itself the ultimate goal we aim at is voluptuousness. I like to beat their ears with that word, which so goes against their grain. And if it means a certain supreme pleasure and excessive contentment, this is due more to the assistance of virtue than to any other assistance. This voluptuousness, for being more lusty, sinewy, robust, and manly, is only the more seriously voluptuous. And we should have given virtue the name of pleasure, a name more favorable, sweet, and natural; not that of vigor, as we have named it. That other baser sort of voluptuousness, if it deserved that beautiful name, should have acquired it in competition, not as a privilege. I find it less free of inconveniences and obstacles than virtue. Besides the fact that its enjoyment is more momentary, watery, and weak, it has its vigils, its fasts, and its hardships, its sweat and blood; and, more particularly, its poignant sufferings of so many kinds, and an accompanying satiety so heavy that it is the equivalent of penance. We are very wrong to suppose that these disadvantages act as a spur and a spice to its sweetness, as in nature a thing is enlivened by its opposite, and to say, when we come to virtue, that similar consequences and difficulties oppress it, make it austere and inaccessible; whereas, much more than in the case of voluptuousness, they ennoble, whet, and heighten the divine and perfect pleasure that virtue affords us. That man is surely very unworthy of its acquaintance who balances its cost against its fruits; he knows neither its graces nor its use. Those who go on teaching us that the quest of it is rugged and laborious, though the enjoyment of it is agreeable, what are they doing but telling us that it is always disagreeable? For what human means ever attained the enjoyment of virtue? The most perfect have been quite content to aspire to it and to approach it, without possessing it. But those others are wrong; since in all the pleasures that we know, even the pursuit is pleasant. The attempt is made fragrant by the quality of the thing it aims at, for it is a good part of the effect, and consubstantial with it. The happiness and blessedness that shines in virtue fills all its appurtenances and approaches even to the first entrance and the utmost barrier.

Now among the principal benefits of virtue is disdain for death, a means that furnishes our life with a soft tranquillity and gives us a pure and pleasant enjoyment of it, without which all other pleasures are extinguished. That is why all rules meet and agree at this point. And though they all with one accord lead us also to scorn pain, poverty, and other accidents to which human life is subject, it is not with equal insistence; partly because these accidents are not so inevitable (most men spend their life without tasting poverty, and some also without feeling pain and illness, like Xenophilus the musician, who lived a hundred and six years in complete health), and also because at worst, whenever we please, death can put an end, and deny access, to all our other woes. But as for death itself, it is inevitable.

> *We are all forced down the same road. Our fate,*
> *Tossed in the urn, will spring out soon or late,*
> *And force us helpless into Charon's bark,*
> *Passengers destined for eternal dark.*

HORACE

And consequently, if it frightens us, it is a continual source of torment which cannot be alleviated at all. There is no place from which it may not come to us; we may turn our heads constantly this way and that as in a suspicious country: *death always hangs over us, like the stone over Tantalus* [Cicero]. Our law courts often send criminals to be executed at the place where the crime was committed. On the way, take them past beautiful houses, give them as good a time as you like—

> *Not even a Sicilian feast*
> *Can now produce for him a pleasant taste,*
> *Nor song of birds, nor music of the lyre*
> *Restore his sleep*

HORACE

—do you think that they can rejoice in these things, and that the final purpose of their trip, being steadily before their eyes, will not have changed and spoiled their taste for all these pleasures?

> *He hears it as it comes, counts days, measures the breath*
> *Of life upon their length, tortured by coming death.*

CLAUDIAN

The goal of our career is death. It is the necessary object of our aim. If it frightens us, how is it possible to go a step forward without feverishness? The remedy of the common herd is not to think about it. But from what brutish stupidity can come so gross a blindness! They have to bridle the ass by the tail,

> *Who sets his mind on moving only backward.*

LUCRETIUS

It is no wonder they are so often caught in the trap. These people take fright at the mere mention of death, and most of them cross themselves at that name, as at the name of the devil. And because death is mentioned in wills, don't expect them to set about writing a will until the doctor has given them their final sentence; and then, between the pain and the fright, Lord knows with what fine judgment they will concoct it.

Because this syllable struck their ears too harshly and seemed to them unlucky, the Romans learned to soften it or to spread it out into a periphrasis. Instead of saying "He is dead," they say to live, "He has lived." Provided it is life, even past life, they take comfort. We have borrowed from them our "late Mr. John."[1]

Perhaps it is true that, as the saying goes, the delay is worth the money. I was born between eleven o'clock and noon on the last day of February, 1533, as we reckon time now,[2] beginning the year in January. It was only just two weeks ago that I passed the age of thirty-nine years, and I need at least that many more; but to be bothered meanwhile by the thought of a thing so far off would be folly. After all, young and old leave life on the same terms. None goes out of it otherwise than as if he had just entered it. And besides, there is no man so decrepit that as long as he sees Methuselah ahead of him, he does not think he has another twenty years left in his body. Furthermore, poor fool that you are, who has assured you the term of your life? You are building on the tales of doctors. Look rather at facts and experience. By the ordinary run of things, you have been living a long time now by extraordinary favor. You have passed the accustomed limits of life. And to prove this, count how many more of your acquaintances have died before your age than have attained it. And even for those who have glorified their lives by renown, make a list, and I'll wager I'll find more of them who died before thirty-five than after. It is completely reasonable and pious to take our example from the humanity of Jesus Christ himself; now be finished his life at thirty-three. The greatest man that was simply a man, Alexander, also died at that age.

How many ways has death to surprise us!

> *Man never can plan fully to avoid*
> *What any hour may bring.*
> HORACE

With such frequent and ordinary examples passing before our eyes, how can we possibly rid ourselves of the thought of death and of the idea that at every moment it is gripping us by the throat?

What does it matter, you will tell me, how it happens, provided we do not worry about it? I am of that opinion; and in whatever way we can put ourselves in shelter from blows, even under a calf's skin, I am not the man to shrink from it. For it is enough for me to spend my life comfortably; and the best game I can give myself I'll take, though it be as little glorious and exemplary as you like:

> *If but my faults could trick and please*
> *My wits, I'd rather seem a fool at ease,*
> *Than to be wise and rage.*
> HORACE

But it is folly to expect to get there that way. They go, they come, they trot, they dance—of death no news. All that is fine. But when it comes, either to them or to their wives, children, or friends, surprising them unprepared and defenseless, what torments, what cries, what frenzy, what despair overwhelms them! Did you ever see anything so dejected, so changed, so upset? We must provide for this earlier; and this brutish nonchalance, even if it could lodge in the head of a man of understanding—which I consider entirely impossible—sells us its wares too dear. If it were an enemy we could avoid, I would advise us to borrow the arms of cowardice. But since that cannot be, since it catches you just the same, whether you flee like a coward or act like a man—

> As surely it pursues the man that flees,
> Nor does it spare the haunches slack
> Of warless youth, or its timid back
>
> HORACE

—and since no kind of armor protects you—

> Hide as he will, cautious, in steel and brass,
> Still death will drag his head outside at last
>
> PROPERTIUS

—let us learn to meet it steadfastly and to combat it. And to begin to strip it of its greatest advantage against us, let us take an entirely different way from the usual one. Let us rid it of its strangeness, come to know it, get used to it. Let us have nothing on our minds as often as death. At every moment let us picture it in our imagination in all its aspects. At the stumbling of a horse, the fall of a tile, the slightest pin prick, let us promptly chew on this: Well, what if it were death itself? And thereupon let us tense ourselves and make an effort. Amid feasting and gaiety let us ever keep in mind this refrain, the memory of our condition; and let us never allow ourselves to be so carried away by pleasure that we do not sometimes remember in how many ways this happiness of ours is a prey to death, and how death's clutches threaten it. Thus did the Egyptians, who, in the midst of their feasts and their greatest pleasures, had the skeleton of a dead man brought before them, to serve as a reminder to the guests.

> Look on each day as if it were your last,
> And each unlooked-for hour will seem a boon.
>
> HORACE

It is uncertain where death awaits us; let us await it everywhere. Premeditation of death is premeditation of freedom. He who has learned how to die has unlearned how to be a slave. Knowing how to die frees us from all subjection and constraint. There is nothing evil in life for the man who has thoroughly grasped the fact that to be deprived of life is not an evil. Aemilius Paulus replied to the messenger sent by that miserable king of Macedon, his prisoner, to beg him not to lead him in his triumph: "Let him make that request of himself."

In truth, in all things, unless nature lends a hand, it is hard for art and industry to get very far. I am by nature not melancholy, but dreamy. Since my earliest days, there is nothing with which I have occupied my mind more than with images of death. Even in the most licentious season of my life,

> *When blooming youth enjoyed a gladsome spring,*
>
> CATULLUS

amid ladies and games, someone would think me involved in digesting some jealousy by myself, or the uncertainty of some hope, while I was thinking about I don't remember whom, who had been overtaken a few days before by a hot fever and by death, on leaving a similar feast, his head full of idleness, love, and a good time, like myself; and thinking that the same chance was hanging from my ear:

> *And soon it will have been, past any man's recall.*
>
> LUCRETIUS

I did not wrinkle my forehead any more over that thought than any other. It is impossible that we should fail to feel the sting of such notions at first. But by handling them and going over them, in the long run we tame them beyond question. Otherwise for my part I should be in continual fright and frenzy; for never did a man so distrust his life, never did a man set less faith in his duration. Neither does health, which thus far I have enjoyed in great vigor and with little interruption, lengthen my hope of life, nor do illnesses shorten it. Every minute I seem to be slipping away from myself. And I constantly sing myself this refrain: Whatever can be done another day can be done today. Truly risks and dangers bring us little or no nearer our end; and if we think how many million accidents remain hanging over our heads, not to mention this one that seems to threaten us most, we shall conclude that lusty or feverish, on sea or in our houses, in battle or in rest, death is equally near us. *No man is frailer than another, no man more certain of the morrow* [Seneca]. To finish what I have to do before I die, even if it were one hour's work, any leisure seems short to me.

Someone, looking through my tablets the other day, found a memorandum about something I wanted done after my death. I told him what was true, that although only a league away from my house, and hale and hearty, I had hastened to write it there, since I could not be certain of reaching home. Since I am constantly brooding over my thoughts and settling them within me, I am at all times about as well prepared as I can be. And the coming of death will teach me nothing new.

We must be always booted and ready to go, so far as it is in our power, and take especial care to have only ourselves to deal with then:

> *Why aim so stoutly at so many things*
> *In our short life?*
>
> HORACE

Our religion has no surer human foundation than contempt for life. Not only do the arguments of reason invite us to it; for why should we fear to lose a thing which once lost can not be regretted? And since we are threatened by so many kinds of death, is there not more pain in fearing them all than in enduring one?[3]

What does it matter when it comes, since it is inevitable? To the man who told Socrates, "The tyrants have condemned you to death," he replied: "And nature, them."

What stupidity to torment ourselves about passing into exemption from all torment! As our birth brought us the birth of all things, so will our death bring us the death of all things. Wherefore it is as foolish to lament that we shall not be alive a hundred years from now as it is to lament that we were not alive a hundred years ago. Death is the origin of another life. Just so did we weep, just so did we struggle against entering this life, just so did we strip off our former veil when we entered it.

Nothing can be grievous that happens only once. Is it reasonable so long, to fear a thing so short? Long life and short life are made all one by death. For there is no long or short for things that are no more. Aristotle says that there are little animals by the river Hypanis that live only a day. The one that dies at eight o'clock in the morning dies in its youth; the one that dies, at five in the afternoon dies in its decrepitude. Which of us does not laugh to see this moment of duration considered in terms of happiness or unhappiness? The length or shortness of our duration, if we compare it with eternity, or yet with the duration of mountains, rivers, stars, trees, and even of some animals, is no less ridiculous.

But Nature forces us to it.[4] Go out of this world, she says, as you entered it. The same passage that you made from death to life, without feeling or fright, make it again from life to death. Your death is a part of the order of the universe; it is a part of the life of the world.

> *Our lives we borrow from each other...*
> *And men, like runners, pass along the torch of life.*
>
> LUCRETIUS

Wherever your life ends, it is all there. The advantage of living is not measured by length, but by use; some men have lived long, and lived little; attend to it while you are in it. It lies in your will, not in the number of years, for you to have lived enough. Did you think you would never arrive where you never ceased going? Yet there is no road but has its end. And if company can comfort you, does not the world keep pace with you?

> *All things, their life being done, will follow you.*
>
> LUCRETIUS

Does not everything move with your movement? Is there anything that does not grow old along with you? A thousand men, a thousand animals, and a thousand other creatures die at the very moment when you die:

> *No night has ever followed day, no day the night,*
> *That has not heard, amid the newborn infants' squalls,*
> *The wild laments that go with death and funerals.*
>
> LUCRETIUS

Why do you recoil, if you cannot draw back? You have seen enough men who were better off for dying, thereby avoiding great miseries. Have you found any man that was worse off? How simple-minded it is to condemn a thing that you have not experienced yourself or through anyone else. Why do you complain of me and of destiny? Do we wrong you? Is it for you to govern us, or us you? Though your age is not full-grown, your life is. A little man is a whole man, just like a big one. Neither men nor their lives are measured by the ell.

Chiron refused immortality when informed of its conditions by the very god of time and duration, his father Saturn. Imagine honestly how much less bearable and more painful to man would be an everlasting life than the life I have given him. If you did not have death, you would curse me incessantly for having deprived you of it. I have deliberately mixed with it a little bitterness to keep you, seeing the convenience of it, from embracing it too greedily and intemperately. To lodge you in that moderate state that I ask of you, of neither fleeing life nor fleeing back from death, I have tempered both of them between sweetness and bitterness.

I taught Thales, the first of your sages, that life and death were matters of indifference; wherefore, to the man who asked him why then he did not die, he replied very wisely: "Because it is indifferent."

Water, earth, air, fire, and the other parts of this structure of mine are no more instruments of your life than instruments of your death. Why do you fear your last day? It contributes no more to your death than each of the others. The last step does not cause the fatigue, but reveals it. All days travel toward death, the last one reaches it.

Such are the good counsels of our mother Nature. Now I have often pondered how it happens that in wars the face of death, whether we see it in ourselves or in others, seems to us incomparably less terrifying than in our houses—otherwise you would have an army of doctors and snivelers—and, since death is always the same, why nevertheless there is much more assurance against it among villagers and humble folk than among others. I truly think it is those dreadful faces and trappings with which we surround it, that frighten us more than death itself: an entirely new way of living; the cries of mothers, wives, and children; the visits of people dazed and benumbed by grief; the presence of a number of pale and weeping servants; a darkened room; lighted candles; our bedside besieged by doctors and preachers; in short, everything horror and fright around us. There we are already shrouded and buried. Children fear even their friends when they see them masked, and so do we ours. We must strip the mask from things as well as from persons; when it is off, we shall find beneath only that same death which a valet or a mere chambermaid passed through not long ago without fear. Happy the death that leaves no leisure for preparing such ceremonies!

Notes

1. The French for *late* in this sense is *feu*, from Latin *fatutus*. Montaigne seems to think it comes from Latin *fuit* (*was*), Old French *feut*.
2. In 1563 Charles IX set January 1 as the beginning of the year, and this decree took full effect in 1567. Until then the year had officially begun at Easter.
3. Montaigne's argument is that not only reason but also nature urges us to accept death gracefully. The following three paragraphs, which interrupt his movement, are additions to the original version.
4. Nature's speech, which extends to "the last one reaches it" almost at the end of this chapter (p. 67), is largely a paraphrase of Seneca and Lucretius, and especially Lucretius.

Suggested Readings

Burke, Peter. *Montaigne*. New York: Hill and Wang, 1982.

Quint, David. *Montaigne and the Quality of Mercy*. Princeton: Princeton University Press, 1998.

Regosin, Richard. *The Matter of My Book: Montaigne's Essays as the Book of the Self*. Berkeley: University of California Press, 1977.

Chapter **15**

Of the Necessity of the Wager

Blaise Pascal

Born in 1623, Pascal was a mathematician and philosopher contemporary with both Newton and Descartes. Along with these thinkers, and the new scientific understanding of the immensity and complexity of the universe, comes an overwhelming sense of metaphysical loneliness and alienation. Pascal simply cannot understand one's indifference to the finite and contingent nature of our existence. These aphorisms are from his Pensées.

Let us imagine a number of men in chains and all condemned to death, where some are killed each day in the sight of the others, and those who remain see their own fate in that of their fellows and wait their turn, looking at each other sorrowfully and without hope. It is an image of the condition of men.

When I consider the short duration of my life, swallowed up in the eternity before and after, the little space which I fill and even can see, engulfed in the infinite immensity of spaces of which I am ignorant and which know me not, I am frightened and am astonished at being here rather than there; for there is no reason why here rather than there, why now rather than then. Who has put me here? By whose order and direction have this place and time been allotted to me? *Memoria hospitis unius diei prætereuntis.*[1]

We are fools to depend upon the society of our fellow-men. Wretched as we are, powerless as we are, they will not aid us; we shall die alone. We should therefore act as if we were alone, and in that case should we build fine houses, etc. We should seek the truth without hesitation; and, if we refuse it, we show that we value the esteem of men more than the search for truth.

Man is but a reed, the most feeble thing in nature; but he is a thinking reed. The entire universe need not arm itself to crush him. A vapour, a drop of water suffices to kill him. But, if the universe were to crush him, man would still be more noble than that which killed him, because he knows that he dies and the advantage which the universe has over him; the universe knows nothing of this.

All our dignity consists, then, in thought. By it we must elevate ourselves, and not by space and time which we cannot fill. Let us endeavour, then, to think well; this is the principle of morality.

The immortality of the soul is a matter which is of so great consequence to us and which touches us so profoundly that we must have lost all feeling to be indifferent as to knowing what it is. All our actions and thoughts must take such different courses, according as there are or are not eternal joys to hope for, that it is impossible to take one step with sense and judgment unless we regulate our course by our view of this point which ought to be our ultimate end.

Thus our first interest and our first duty is to enlighten ourselves on this subject, whereon depends all our conduct. Therefore among those who do not believe, I make a vast difference between those who strive with all their power to inform themselves and those who live without troubling or thinking about it.

I can have only compassion for those who sincerely bewail their doubt, who regard it as the greatest of misfortunes, and who, sparing no effort to escape it, make of this inquiry their principal and most serious occupation.

But as for those who pass their life without thinking of this ultimate end of life, and who, for this sole reason that they do not find within themselves the lights which convince them of it, neglect to seek them elsewhere, and to examine thoroughly whether this opinion is one of those which people receive with credulous simplicity, or one of those which, although obscure in themselves, have nevertheless a solid and immovable foundation, I look upon them in a manner quite different.

This carelessness in a matter which concerns themselves, their eternity, their all, moves me more to anger than pity; it astonishes and shocks me; it is to me monstrous. I do not say this out of the pious zeal of a spiritual devotion. I expect, on the contrary, that we ought to have this feeling from principles of human interest and self-love; for this we need only see what the least enlightened persons see.

We do not require great education of the mind to understand that here is no real and lasting satisfaction; that our pleasures are only vanity; that our evils are infinite; and, lastly, that death, which threatens us every moment, must infallibly place us within a few years under the dreadful necessity of being for ever either annihilated or unhappy.

There is nothing more real than this, nothing more terrible. Be we as heroic as we like, that is the end which awaits the noblest life in the world. Let us reflect on this and then say whether it is not beyond doubt that there is no good in this life but in the hope of another; that we are happy only in proportion as we draw near it; and that, as there are no more woes for those who have complete assurance of eternity, so there is no more happiness for those who have no insight into it.

Surely then it is a great evil thus to be in doubt, but it is at least an indispensable duty to seek when we are in such doubt; and thus the doubter who does not seek is altogether completely unhappy and completely wrong. And if besides this he is easy and content, professes to be so, and indeed boasts of it; if it is this state itself which is the subject of his joy and vanity, I have no words to describe so silly a creature.

How can people hold these opinions? What joy can we find in the expectation of nothing but hopeless misery? What reason for boasting that we are in impenetrable darkness? And how can it happen that the following argument occurs to a reasonable man?

"I know not who put me into the world, nor what the world is, nor what I myself am. I am in terrible ignorance of everything. I know not what my body is, nor my senses, nor my soul, not even that part of me which thinks what I say, which reflects on all and on itself, and knows itself no more than the rest. I see those frightful spaces of the universe which surround me, and I find myself tied to one corner of this vast expanse, without knowing why I am put in this place rather than in another, nor why the short time which is given me to live is assigned to me at this point rather than at another of the whole eternity which was before me or which shall come after me. I see nothing but infinites on all sides, which surround me as an atom and as a shadow which endures only for an instant and returns no more. All I know is that I must soon die, but what I know least is this very death which I cannot escape.

"As I know not whence I come, so I know not whither I go. I know only that, in leaving this world, I fall for ever either into annihilation or into the hands of an angry God, without knowing to which of these two states I shall be for ever assigned. Such is my state, full of weakness and uncertainty. And from all this I conclude that I ought to spend all the days of my life without caring to inquire into what must happen to me. Perhaps I might find some solution to my doubts, but I will not take the trouble, nor take a step to seek it; and after treating with scorn those who are concerned with this care, I will go without foresight and without fear to try the great event, and let myself be led carelessly to death, uncertain of the eternity of my future state."

Who would desire to have for a friend a man who talks in this fashion? Who would choose him out from others to tell him of his affairs? Who would have recourse to him in affliction? And indeed to what use in life could one put him?

In truth, it is the glory of religion to have for enemies men so unreasonable; and their opposition to it is so little dangerous that it serves, on the contrary, to establish its truths. For the Christian faith goes mainly to establish these two facts: the corruption of nature, and redemption by Jesus Christ. Now I contend that, if these men do not serve to prove the truth of the redemption by the holiness of their behaviour, they at least serve admirably to show the corruption of nature by sentiments so unnatural.

Nothing is so important to man as his own state, nothing is so formidable to him as eternity; and thus it is not natural that there should be men indifferent to the loss of their existence, and to the perils of everlasting suffering. They are quite different with regard to all other things. They are afraid of mere trifles; they foresee them; they feel them. And this same man who spends so many days and nights in rage and despair for the loss of office, or for some imaginary insult to his honour, is the very one who knows without anxiety and without emotion that he will lose all by death. It is a monstrous thing to see, in the same heart and at the same time this sensibility to trifles and this strange insensibility to the greatest objects. It is an incomprehensible enchantment, and a supernatural slumber, which indicates as its cause an all-powerful force.

There must be a strange confusion in the nature of man, that he should boast of being in that state in which it seems incredible that a single individual should be. However, experience has shown me so great a number of such persons that the fact would be surprising, if we did not know that the greater part of those who trouble themselves about the matter are disingenuous and not, in fact, what they say. They are people who have heard it said that it is the fashion to be thus daring. It is what they call "shaking off the yoke," and they try to imitate this. But it would not be difficult to make them understand how greatly they deceive themselves in thus seeking esteem. This is not the way to gain it, even I say among those men of the world who take a healthy view of things and who know that the only way to succeed in this life is to make ourselves appear honourable, faithful, judicious, and capable of useful service to a friend; because naturally men love only what may be useful to them. Now, what do we gain by hearing it said of a man that he has now thrown off the yoke, that he does not believe there is a God who watches our actions, that he considers himself the sole master of his conduct, and that he thinks he is accountable for it only to himself? Does he think that he has thus brought us to have henceforth complete confidence in him and to look to him for consolation, advice, and help in every need of life? Do they profess to have delighted us by telling us that they hold our soul to be only a little wind and smoke, especially by telling us this in a haughty and self-satisfied tone of voice? Is this a thing to say gaily? Is it not, on the contrary, a thing to say sadly, as the saddest thing in the world?

If they thought of it seriously, they would see that this is so bad a mistake, so contrary to good sense, so opposed to decency, and so removed in every respect from that good breeding which they seek, that they would be more likely to correct than to pervert those who had an inclination to follow them. And, indeed, make them give an account of their opinions, and of the reasons which they have for doubting religion, and they will say to you things so feeble and so petty, that they will persuade you of the contrary. The following is what a person one day said to such a one very appositely: "If you continue to talk in this manner, you will really make me religious." And he was right, for who would not have a horror of holding opinions in which he would have such contemptible persons as companions!

Thus those who only feign these opinions would be very unhappy, if they restrained their natural feelings in order to make themselves the most conceited of men. If, at the bottom of their heart, they are troubled at not having more light, let them not disguise the fact; this avowal will not be shameful. The only shame is to have none. Nothing reveals more an extreme weakness of mind than not to know the misery of a godless man. Nothing is more indicative of a bad disposition of heart than not to desire the truth of eternal promises. Nothing is more dastardly than to act with bravado before God. Let them then leave these impieties to those who are sufficiently ill-bred to be really capable of them. Let them at least be honest men, if they cannot be Christians. Finally, let them recognise that there are two kinds of people one can call reasonable; those who serve God with all their heart because they know Him, and those who seek Him with all their heart because they do not know Him.

But as for those who live without knowing Him and without seeking Him, they judge themselves so little worthy of their own care, that they are not worthy of the care of others; and it needs all the charity of the religion which they despise, not to despise them even to the point of leaving them to their folly. But because this religion obliges us always to regard them, so long as they are in this life, as capable of the grace which can enlighten them, and to believe that they may, in a little time, be more replenished with faith than we are, and that, on the other hand, we may fall into the blindness wherein they are, we must do for them what we would they should do for us if we were in their place, and call upon them to have pity upon themselves, and to take at least some steps in the endeavour to find light. Let them give to reading this some of the hours which they otherwise employ so uselessly; whatever aversion they may bring to the task, they will perhaps gain something, and at least will not lose much. But as for those who bring to the task perfect sincerity and a real desire to meet with truth, those I hope will be satisfied and convinced of the proofs of a religion so divine, which I have here collected, and in which I have followed somewhat after this order...

Before entering into the proofs of the Christian religion, I find it necessary to point out the sinfulness of those men who live in indifference to the search for truth in a matter which is so important to them, and which touches them so nearly.

Of all their errors, this doubtless is the one which most convicts them of foolishness and blindness, and in which it is easiest to confound them by the first glimmerings of common sense and by natural feelings.

For it is not to be doubted that the duration of this life is but a moment; that the state of death is eternal, whatever may be its nature; and that thus all our actions and thoughts must take such different directions, according to the state of that eternity, that it is impossible to take one step with sense and judgement, unless we regulate our course by the truth of that point which ought to be our ultimate end.

There is nothing clearer than this; and thus, according to the principles of reason, the conduct of men is wholly unreasonable, if they do not take another course.

On this point, therefore, we condemn those who live without thought of the ultimate end of life, who let themselves be guided by their own inclinations and their own pleasures without reflection and without concern, and, as if they could annihilate eternity by turning away their thought from it, think only of making themselves happy for the moment.

Yet this eternity exists, and death, which must open into it and threatens them every hour, must in a little time infallibly put them under the dreadful necessity of being either annihilated or unhappy for ever, without knowing which of these eternities is for ever prepared for them.

This is a doubt of terrible consequence. They are in peril of eternal woe and thereupon, as if the matter were not worth the trouble, they neglect to inquire whether this is one of those opinions which people receive with too credulous a facility, or one of those which, obscure in themselves, have a very firm, though hidden, foundation. Thus they know not whether there be truth or falsity in the matter, nor whether there be strength or weakness in the proofs. They have them before their eyes; they refuse to look at them; and in that ignorance they choose all that is necessary to fall into this misfortune if it exists, to await death to make trial of it, yet to be very content in this state, to make profession of it, and indeed to boast of it. Can we think seriously of the importance of this subject without being horrified at conduct so extravagant?

This resting in ignorance is a monstrous thing, and they who pass their life in it must be made to feel its extravagance and stupidity, by having it shown to them, so that they may be confounded by the sight of their folly. For this is how men reason, when they choose to live in such ignorance of what they are and without seeking enlightenment. "I know not," they say...

Let us now speak according to natural lights.

If there is a God, He is infinitely incomprehensible, since, having neither parts nor limits, He has no affinity to us. We are then incapable of knowing either what He is or if He is. This being so, who will dare to undertake the decision of the question? Not we, who have no affinity to Him.

Who then will blame Christians for not being able to give a reason for their belief, since they profess a religion for which they cannot give a reason? They declare, in expounding it to the world, that it is a foolishness, *stultitiam;*[2] and then you complain that they do not prove it! If they proved it, they would not keep their word; it is in lacking proofs that they are not lacking in sense. "Yes, but although this excuses those who offer it as such and takes away from them the blame of putting it forward without reason, it does not excuse those who receive it." Let us then examine this point, and say, "God is, or He is not." But to which side shall we incline? Reason can decide nothing here. There is an infinite chaos which separates us. A game is being played at the extremity of this infinite distance where heads or tails will turn up. What will you wager? According to reason, you can do neither the one thing nor the other; according to reason, you can defend neither of the propositions.

Do not, then, reprove for error those who have made a choice; for you know nothing about it. "No, but I blame them for having made, not this choice, but a choice; for again both he who chooses heads and he who chooses tails are equally at fault, they are both in the wrong. The true course is not to wager at all."

Yes; but you must wager. It is not optional. You are embarked. Which will you choose then? Let us see. Since you must choose, let us see which interests you least. You have two things to lose, the true and the good; and two things to stake, your reason and your will, your knowledge and your happiness; and your nature has two things to shun, error and misery. Your reason is no more shocked in choosing one rather than the other, since you must of necessity choose. This is one point settled. But your happiness? Let us weigh the gain and the loss in wagering that God is. Let us estimate these two chances. If you gain, you gain all; if you lose, you lose nothing. Wager, then, without hesitation that He is. "That is very fine. Yes, I must wager; but I may perhaps wager too much." Let us see. Since there is an equal risk of gain and of loss, if you had only to gain two lives, instead of one, you might still wager. But if there were three lives to gain, you would have to play (since you are under the necessity of playing), and you would be imprudent, when you are forced to play, not to chance your life to gain three at a game where there is an equal risk of loss and gain. But there is an eternity of life and happiness. And this being so, if there were an infinity of chances, of which one only would be for you, you would still be right in wagering one to win two, and you would act stupidly, being obliged to play, by refusing to stake one life against three at a game in which out of an infinity of chances there is one for you, if there were an infinity of an infinitely happy life to gain. But there is here an infinity of an infinitely happy life to gain, a chance of gain against a finite number of chances of loss, and what you stake is finite. It is all divided; whereever the infinite is and there is not an infinity of chances of loss against that of gain, there is no time to hesitate, you must give all. And thus, when one is forced to play, he must renounce reason to preserve his life, rather than risk it for infinite gain, as likely to happen as the loss of nothingness.

For it is no use to say it is uncertain if we will gain, and it is certain that we risk, and that the infinite distance between the *certainty* of what is staked and the *uncertainty* of what will be gained, equals the finite good which is certainly staked against the uncertain infinite. It is not so, as every player stakes a certainty to gain an uncertainty, and yet he stakes a finite certainty to gain a finite uncertainty, without transgressing against reason. There is not an infinite distance between the certainty staked and the uncertainty of the gain; that is untrue. In truth, there is an infinity between the certainty of gain and the certainty of loss. But the uncertainty of the gain is proportioned to the certainty of the stake according to the proportion of the chances of gain and loss. Hence it comes that, if there are as many risks on one side as on the other, the course is to play even; and then the certainty of the stake is equal to the uncertainty of the gain, so far is it from fact that there is an infinite distance between them. And so our proposition is of infinite force, when there is the finite to stake in a game where there are equal risks of gain and of loss, and the infinite to gain. This is demonstrable; and if men are capable of any truths, this is one.

"I confess it, I admit it. But, still, is there no means of seeing the faces of the cards?" Yes, Scripture and the rest, etc. "Yes, but I have my hands tied and my mouth closed; I am forced to wager, and am not free. I am not released, and am so made that I cannot believe. What, then, would you have me do?"

True. But at least learn your inability to believe, since reason brings you to this, and yet you cannot believe. Endeavour, then, to convince yourself, not by increase of proofs of God, but by the abatement of your passions. You would like to attain faith and do not know the way; you would like to cure yourself of unbelief and ask the remedy for it. Learn of those who have been bound like you, and who now stake all their possessions. These are people who know the way which you would follow, and who are cured of an ill of which you would be cured. Follow the way by which they began; by acting as if they believed, taking the holy water, having masses said, etc. Even this will naturally make you believe, and deaden your acuteness. "But this is what I am afraid of." And why? What have you to lose?

But to show you that this leads you there, it is this which will lessen the passions, which are your stumbling-blocks.

The end of this discourse.—Now, what harm will befall you in taking this side? You will be faithful, honest, humble, grateful, generous, a sincere friend, truthful. Certainly you will not have those poisonous pleasures, glory and luxury; but will you not have others? I will tell you that you will thereby gain in this life, and that, at each step you take on this road, you will see so great certainty of gain, so much nothingness in what you risk, that you will at last recognise that you have wagered for something certain and infinite, for which you have given nothing.

"Ah! This discourse transports me, charms me," etc.

If this discourse pleases you and seems impressive, know that it is made by a man who has knelt, both before and after it, in prayer to that Being, infinite and without parts, before whom he lays all he has, for you also to lay before Him all you have for your own good and for His glory, that so strength may be given to lowliness.

Notes

1. Wisd. of Sol. 5.15. "The remembrance of a guest that tarrieth but a day."
2. I Cor. I.21.

Suggested Readings

Morris, Thomas. *Making Sense of It All: Pascal and the Meaning of Life*. Grand Rapids: W. B. Eerdmans, 1992.

Goldman, Lucien. *The Hidden God: A Study of Tragic Vision in the Pensee's of Pascal and the Tragedies of Racine*. Trans. Philip Thody. New York: Humanities Press, 1964.

Bishop, Morris. *Blaise Pascal*. New York: Dell Publishing Co., 1966.

V

Late Modern

Chapter 16

Death and the Historical Process of the Spirit

G. W. F. Hegel

Hegel, born in 1770, shared the German intellectual scene with such giants as Kant, Goethe, Schelling, Schiller and Hölderlin. He is probably the most influential and controversial thinker of the 19th century. His dialectical philosophy of history influenced both Marxism and Fascism with their monumental consequences for the 20th century. Although Hegel does not address personal mortality directly, his system implies a larger historical process of life, death and resurrection in which we are involved.

The inquiry into the *essential destiny* of Reason—as far as it is considered in reference to the World—is identical with the question, *what is the ultimate design of the World?* And the expression implies that that design is destined to be realized. Two points of consideration suggest themselves; first, the *import* of this design—its abstract definition; and secondly, its *realization*.

It must be observed at the outset, that the phenomenon we investigate—Universal History—belongs to the realm of *Spirit*. The term *"World,"* includes both physical and psychical Nature. Physical Nature also plays its part in the World's History, and attention will have to be paid to the fundamental natural relations thus involved. But Spirit, and the course of its development, is our substantial object. Our task does not require us to contemplate Nature as a Rational System in itself—though in its own proper domain it proves itself such—but simply in its relation to *Spirit*.

The nature of Spirit may be understood by a glance at its direct opposite—*Matter*. As the essence of Matter is Gravity, so, on the other hand, we may affirm that the substance, the essence of Spirit is Freedom. All will readily assent to the doctrine that Spirit, among other properties, is also endowed with Freedom; but philosophy teaches that all the qualities of Spirit exist only through Freedom; that all are but means for attaining Freedom; that all seek and produce this and this alone. It is a result of speculative Philosophy, that Freedom is the sole truth of Spirit. Matter possesses gravity in virtue of its tendency toward a central point. It is essentially composite; consisting of parts that *exclude* each other. It seeks its Unity; and therefore exhibits itself as self-destructive, as verging toward its opposite [an indivisible point]. If it could attain this, it would be Matter no longer, it would have perished. It strives after the realization of its Idea; for in Unity it exists *ideally*. Spirit, on the contrary, may be defined as that which has its centre in itself. It has not a unity outside itself, but has already found it; it exists *in* and *with itself*. Matter has its essence out of itself; Spirit is *self-contained existence* (Bei-sich-selbst-seyn). Now this is Freedom, exactly. For if I am dependent, my being is referred to something else which I am not; I cannot exist independently of something external. I am free, on the contrary, when my existence depends upon myself. This self-contained existence of Spirit is none other than self-consciousness—consciousness of one's own being. Two things must be distinguished in consciousness; first, the fact *that I know*; secondly, *what I know*. In *self* consciousness these are merged in one; for Spirit *knows itself*. It involves an appreciation of its own nature, as also an energy enabling it to realize itself; to make itself *actually* that which it is *potentially*. According to this abstract definition it may be said of Universal History, that it is the exhibition of Spirit in the process of working out the knowledge of that which it is potentially. And as the germ bears in itself the whole nature of the tree, and the taste and form of its fruits, so do the first traces of Spirit virtually contain the whole of that History. The Orientals have not attained the knowledge that Spirit—Man *as such*—is free; and because they do not know this, they are not free. They only know that *one is free*. But on this very account, the freedom of that one is only caprice; ferocity—brutal recklessness of passion, or a mildness and tameness of the desires, which is itself only an accident of Nature—mere caprice like the former.—That *one* is therefore only a Despot; not a *free man*. The consciousness of Freedom first arose among the Greeks, and therefore they were free; but they, and the Romans likewise, knew only that *some* are free—not man as such. Even Plato and Aristotle did not know this. The Greeks, therefore, had slaves; and their whole life and the maintenance of their splendid liberty, was implicated with the institution of slavery: a fact moreover, which made that liberty on the one hand only an accidental, transient and limited growth; on the other hand, constituted it a rigorous thraldom of our common nature—of the Human. The German nations, under the influence of Christianity, were the first to attain the consciousness, that man, as man, is free: that it is the *freedom* of Spirit which constitutes its essence. This consciousness arose first in religion, the inmost region of Spirit; but to introduce the principle into the various relations of the actual world, involves a more extensive problem than its simple implantation; a problem whose solution and application require a severe and lengthened process of culture. In proof of this, we may note that slavery did not cease immediately on the reception of Christianity. Still less did liberty predominate in States; or Governments and Constitutions adopt a rational organization, or recognize freedom as their basis. That application of the principle to political relations; the thorough moulding and interpenetration of the constitution of society by it, is a process identical with history itself. I have already directed attention to the distinction here involved, between a principle as such, and its *application; i.e.,* its introduction and carrying out in the actual phenomena of Spirit and Life. This is a point of fundamental importance in our science, and one which must be constantly respected as essential. And in the same way as this distinction has attracted attention in view of the *Christian* principle of self-consciousness—Freedom; it also shows itself as an essential one, in view of the principle of Freedom *generally*. The History of the world is none other than the progress of the consciousness of Freedom; a progress whose development according to the necessity of its nature, it is our business to investigate.

The course of the World's History.—The mutations which history presents have been long characterized in the general, as an advance to something better, more perfect. The changes that take place in Nature—how infinitely manifold soever they may be—exhibit only a perpetually self-repeating cycle; in Nature there happens "nothing new under the sun," and the multiform play of its phenomena so far induces a feeling of *ennui*; only in those changes which take place in the region of Spirit does anything new arise. This peculiarity in the world of mind has indicated in the case of man an altogether different destiny from that of merely natural objects—in which we find always one and the same stable character, to which all change reverts;—namely, a *real* capacity for change, and that for the better—an impulse of *perfectibility*.

History in general is therefore the development of Spirit in *Time,* as Nature is the development of the Idea in *Space.*

If then we cast a glance over the World's-History generally, we see a vast picture of changes and transactions; of infinitely manifold forms of peoples, states, individuals, in unresting succession. Everything that can enter into and interest the soul of man—all our sensibility to *goodness, beauty, and greatness*—is called into play. On every hand aims are adopted and pursued, which we recognize, whose accomplishment we desire—we hope and fear for them. In all these occurrences and changes we behold human action and suffering predominant; everywhere something akin to ourselves, and therefore everywhere something that excites our interest for or against. Sometimes it attracts us by beauty, freedom, and rich variety, sometimes by energy such as enables even vice to make itself interesting. Sometimes we see the more comprehensive mass of some general interest advancing with comparative slowness, and subsequently sacrificed to an infinite complication of trifling circumstances, and so dissipated into atoms. Then, again, with a vast expenditure of power a trivial result is produced; while from what appears unimportant a tremendous issue proceeds. On every hand there is the motliest throng of events drawing us within the circle of its interest, and when one combination vanishes another immediately appears in its place.

The general thought—the category which first presents itself in this restless mutation of individuals and peoples, existing for a time and then vanishing—is that of *change* at large. The sight of the ruins of some ancient sovereignty directly leads us to contemplate this thought of change in its negative aspect. What traveller among the ruins of Carthage, of Palmyra, Persepolis, or Rome, has not been stimulated to reflections on the transiency of kingdoms and men, and to sadness at the thought of a vigorous and rich life now departed—a sadness which does not expend itself on personal losses and the uncertainty of one's own undertakings, but is a disinterested sorrow at the decay of a splendid and highly cultured national life! But the next consideration which allies itself with that of change, is, that change while it imports dissolution, involves at the same time the rise of a *new life*—that while death is the issue of life, life is also the issue of death. This is a grand conception; one which the Oriental thinkers attained, and which is perhaps the highest in their metaphysics. In the idea of *Metempsychosis* we find it evolved in its relation to individual existence; but a myth more generally known, is that of the *Phoenix* as a type of the Life of *Nature;* eternally preparing for itself its funeral pile, and consuming itself upon it; but so that from its ashes is produced the new, renovated, fresh life. But this image is only Asiatic; oriental not occidental. Spirit—consuming the envelope of its existence—does not merely pass into another envelope, nor rise rejuvenescent from the ashes of its previous form; it comes forth exalted, glorified, a purer spirit. It certainly makes war upon itself—consumes its own existence; but in this very destruction it works up that existence into a new form, and each successive phase becomes in its turn a material, working on which it exalts itself to a new grade.

The very essence of Spirit is activity; it realizes its potentiality—makes itself its own deed, its own work—and thus it becomes an object to itself; contemplates itself as an objective existence. Thus is it with the Spirit of a people: it is a Spirit having strictly defined characteristics, which erects itself into an objective world, that exists and persists in a particular religious form of worship, customs, constitution, and political laws—in the whole complex of its institutions—in the events and transactions that make up its history. That is its work—that is what this particular Nation *is*. Nations are what their deeds are. Every Englishman will say: We are the men who navigate the ocean, and have the commerce of the world; to whom the East Indies belong and their riches; who have a parliament, juries, etc.—The relation of the individual to that Spirit is that he appropriates to himself this substantial existence; that it becomes his character and capability, enabling him to have a definite place in the world—to be *something*. For he finds the being of the people to which he belongs an already established, firm world—objectively present to him—with which he has to incorporate himself. In this its work, therefore—its world—the Spirit of the people enjoys its existence and finds its satisfaction.—A Nation is moral—virtuous—vigorous—while it is engaged in realizing its grand objects, and defends its work against external violence during the process of giving to its purposes an objective existence. The contradiction between its potential, subjective being—its inner aim and life—and its *actual* being is removed; it has attained full reality, has itself objectively present to it. But this having been attained, the activity displayed by the Spirit of the people in question is no longer needed; it has its desire. The Nation can still accomplish much in war and peace at home and abroad; but the living substantial soul itself may be said to have ceased its activity. The essential, supreme interest has consequently vanished from its life, for interest is present only where there is opposition. The nation lives the same kind of life as the individual when passing from maturity to old age—in the enjoyment of itself—in the satisfaction of being exactly what it desired and was able to attain. Although its imagination might have transcended that limit, it nevertheless abandoned any such aspirations as objects of *actual endeavor,* if the real world was less than favorable to their attainment—and restricted its aim by the conditions thus imposed. This mere *customary life* (the watch wound up and going on of itself) is that which brings on natural death. Custom is activity without opposition, for which there remains only a formal duration; in which the fullness and zest that originally characterized the aim of life are out of the question—a merely external sensuous existence which has ceased to throw itself enthusiastically into its object. Thus perish individuals, thus perish peoples by a natural death; and though the latter may continue in being, it is an existence without intellect or vitality; having no need of its institutions, because the need for them is satisfied—a political nullity and tedium. In order that a truly universal interest may arise, the Spirit of a People must advance to the adoption of some new purpose; but whence can this new purpose originate? It would be a higher, more comprehensive conception of itself—a transcending of its principle—but this very act would involve a principle of a new order, a new National Spirit.

Spirit is essentially the result of its own activity: its activity is the transcending of immediate, simple, unreflected existence—the negation of that existence, and the returning into itself. We may compare it with the seed; for with this the plant begins, yet it is also the result of the plant's entire life. But the weak side of life is exhibited in the fact that the commencement and the result are disjoined from each other. Thus also is it in the life of individuals and peoples. The life of a people ripens a certain fruit; its activity aims at the complete manifestation of the principle which it embodies. But this fruit does not fall back into the bosom of the people that produced and matured it; on the contrary, it becomes a poison-draught to it. That poison-draught it cannot let alone, for it has an insatiable thirst for it: the taste of the draught is its annihilation, though at the same time the rise of a new principle.

We have already discussed the final aim of this progression. The principles of the successive phases of Spirit that animate the Nations in a necessitated gradation, are themselves only steps in the development of the one universal Spirit, which through them elevates and completes itself to a self-comprehending *totality*.

While we are thus concerned exclusively with the Idea of Spirit, and in the History of the World regard everything as only its manifestation, we have, in traversing the past—however extensive its periods—only to do with what is *present*; for philosophy, as occupying itself with the True, has to do with the *eternally present*. Nothing in the past is lost for it, for the Idea is ever present; Spirit is immortal; with it there is no past, no future, but an essential *now*. This necessarily implies that the present form of Spirit comprehends within it all earlier steps. These have indeed unfolded themselves in succession independently; but what Spirit is it has always been essentially; distinctions are only the development of this essential nature. The life of the ever present Spirit is a circle of progressive embodiments, which looked at in one aspect still exist beside each other, and only as looked at from another point of view appear as past. The grades which Spirit seems to have left behind it, it still possesses in the depths of its present.

Suggested Readings

Stace, W. T. *The Philosophy of Hegel*. New York: Dover Publications, Inc., 1923.
Taylor, C. *Hegel*. New York: Cambridge University Press, 1975.
Findlay, J. N. *Hegel: A Re-examination*. New York: Collier Books, 1962.

Chapter 17

Life and the Passion of the Infinite

Soren Kierkegaard

Kierkegaard, often called the melancholy Dane, was born in Copenhagen in 1813. Dissatisfied with Hegel's all consuming Idealistic system in which the individual is lost in a world-historical process, Kierkegaard once again raised the issue of the concrete person. What does it mean to exist authentically? For Kierkegaard the truth about one's faith in God and the authenticity of one's existence is measured not by objective proof but through inward subjective passion.

The Subjective Truth: Inwardness
⚶ Truth is Subjectivity ⚶

When *the question of truth is raised in an objective manner, reflection is directed objectively to the truth, as an object to which the knower is related. Reflection is not focused upon the relationship, however, but upon the question of whether it is the truth to which the knower is related. If only the object to which he is related is the truth, the subject is accounted to be in the truth. When the question of the truth is raised subjectively, reflection is directed subjectively to the nature of the individual's relationship: if only the mode of this relationship is in the truth, the individual is in the truth, even if he should happen to be thus related to what is not true.*[1] Let us take as an example the knowledge of God. Objectively, reflection is directed to the problem of whether this object is the true God; subjectively, reflection is directed to the question whether the individual is related to a something *in such a manner* that his relationship is in truth a God-relationship. On which side is the truth now to be found? Ah, may we not here resort to a mediation, and say: It is on neither side, but in the mediation of both? Excellently well said, provided we might have it explained how an existing individual manages to be in a state of mediation. For to be in a state of mediation is to be finished, while to exist is to become. Nor can an existing individual be in two places at the same time—he cannot be an identity of subject and object. When he is nearest to being in two

---

places at the same time he is in passion; but passion is merely momentary, and passion is also the highest expression of subjectivity.

The existing individual who chooses to pursue the objective way enters upon the entire approximation-process by which it is proposed to bring God to light objectively. But this is in all eternity impossible, because God is a subject, and therefore exists only for subjectivity in inwardness. The existing individual who chooses the subjective way apprehends instantly the entire dialectical difficulty involved in having to use some time, perhaps a long time, in finding God objectively; and he feels this dialectical difficulty in all its painfulness, because he must use God at that very moment, since every moment is wasted in which he does not have God.[2] That very instant he has God, not by virtue of any objective deliberation but by virtue of the infinite passion of inwardness. The objective inquirer, on the other hand, is not embarrassed by such dialectical difficulties as are involved in devoting an entire period of investigation to finding God—since it is possible that the inquirer may die tomorrow; and if he lives he can scarcely regard God as something to be taken along if convenient, since God is precisely that which one takes *a tout prix*, which in the understanding of passion constitutes the true inward relationship to God.

It is at this point, so difficult dialectically, that the way swings off for everyone who knows what it means to think, and to think existentially; which is something very different from sitting at a desk like a fantastical being and writing about what one has never done, something very different from writing *de omnibus dubitandum,* and at the same time being as existentially credulous as the most sensuous of men. Here is where the way swings off, and the change is marked by the fact that, while objective knowledge rambles comfortably on by way of the long road of approximation without being impelled by the urge of passion, subjective knowledge counts every delay a deadly peril, and the decision so infinitely important and so instantly pressing that it is as if the opportunity had already passed unutilized.

Now when the problem is to reckon up on which side there is most truth, whether on the side of one who seeks the true God objectively, and pursues the approximate truth of the God-idea; or on the side of one who, driven by the infinite passion of his need of God, feels an infinite concern for his own relationship to God in truth (and to be at one and the same time on both sides equally is, as we have noted, not possible for an existing individual, but is merely the happy delusion of an imaginary I-am-I): the answer cannot be in doubt for anyone who has not been demoralized with the aid of science. If one who lives in the midst of Christianity goes up to the house of God, the house of the true God, with the true conception of God in his knowledge, and prays, but prays in a false spirit; and one who lives in an idolatrous community prays with the entire passion of the infinite, although his eyes rest upon the image of an idol: where is there most truth? The one prays in truth to God though he worships an idol; the other prays falsely to the true God, and hence worships in fact an idol.

When one man investigates objectively the problem of immortality, and another embraces an uncertainty with the passion of the infinite: where is there most truth, and who has the greater certainty? The one has entered upon a never-ending approximation, for the certainty of immortality lies precisely in the subjectivity of the individual; the other is immortal, and fights for his immortality by struggling with the uncertainty. Let us consider Socrates. Nowadays everyone dabbles in a few proofs; some have several such proofs, others fewer. But Socrates! He puts the question objectively in a problematic manner: *if* there is an immortality. Must he therefore be accounted a doubter in comparison with one of our modern thinkers with the three proofs? By no means. On this "if" he risks his entire life, he has the courage to meet death, and he has with the passion of the infinite so determined the pattern of his life that it must be found acceptable—*if* there is an immortality. Can any better proof be given for the immortality of the soul? But those who have the three proofs do not at all determine their lives in conformity therewith; if there is an immortality, it must feel disgust over their manner of life: can any better refutation be given of the three proofs? The "bit" of uncertainty that Socrates had helped him, because he himself contributed the passion of the infinite; the three proofs that the others have do not profit them at all, because they are and remain dead to spirit and enthusiasm, and their three proofs, in lieu of proving anything else, prove just this. A young girl may enjoy all the sweetness of love on the basis of what is merely a weak hope; but she is beloved, because she rests everything on this weak hope; but many a wedded matron more than once subjected to the strongest expressions of love has in so far indeed had proofs, but strangely enough has not enjoyed *quod erat demonstrandum.* The Socratic ignorance, which Socrates held fast with the entire passion of his inwardness, was thus an expression for the principle that the eternal truth is related to an existing individual, and that this truth must therefore be a paradox for him as long as he exists; and yet it is possible that there was more truth in the Socratic ignorance as it was in him, than in the entire objective truth of the System, which flirts with what the times demand and accommodates itself to *Privatdocents.*

The objective accent falls on WHAT is said, the subjective accent on HOW it is said. This distinction holds even in the aesthetic realm, and receives definite expression in the principle that what is in itself true may in the mouth of such and such a person become untrue. In these times this distinction is particularly worthy of notice for, if we wish to express in a single sentence the difference between ancient times and our own, we should doubtless have to say: "In ancient times only an individual here and there knew the truth; now all know it, but the inwardness of its appropriation stands in an inverse relationship to the extent of its dissemination. Aesthetically the contradiction that truth becomes untruth in this or that person's mouth is best construed comically. In the ethico-religious sphere, the accent is again on the "how." But this is not to be understood as referring to demeanor, expression, delivery, or the like; rather it refers to the relationship sustained by the existing individual, in his own existence, to the content of his utterance. Objectively the interest is focused merely on the thought-content, subjectively on the inwardness. At its maximum this inward "how" is the passion of the infinite, and the passion of the infinite is the truth. But the passion of the infinite is precisely subjectivity, and thus subjectivity becomes the truth. Objectively there is no infinite decision, and hence it is objectively in order to annul the difference between good and evil, together with the principle of contradiction, and therewith also the infinite difference between the true and the false. Only in subjectivity is there decision, to seek objectivity is to be in error. It is the passion of the infinite that is the decisive factor and not its content, for its content is precisely itself. In this manner subjectivity and the subjective "how" constitute the truth.

But the "how" which is thus subjectively accentuated, precisely because the subject is an existing individual, is also subject to a dialectic with respect to time. In the passionate moment of decision, where the road swings away from objective knowledge, it seems as if the infinite decision were thereby realized. But in the same moment the existing individual finds himself in the temporal order, and the subjective "how" is transformed into a striving, a striving which receives indeed its impulse and a repeated renewal from the decisive passion of the infinite, but is nevertheless a striving.

When subjectivity is the truth, the conceptual determination of the truth must include an expression for the antithesis to objectivity, a memento of the fork in the road where the way swings off; this expression will also indicate the tension of the subjective inwardness. Here is such a definition of truth: *An objective uncertainty held fast in an appropriation-process of the most passionate inwardness is the truth,* the highest truth attainable for an *existing individual.* At the point where the way swings off (and where this is cannot be specified objectively, since it is a matter of subjectivity), there objective knowledge is placed in abeyance. Thus the subject merely has, objectively, the uncertainty; but it is this which precisely increases the tension of that infinite passion which constitutes his inwardness. The truth is precisely the venture which chooses an objective uncertainty with the passion of the infinite. I contemplate nature in the hope of finding God, and I see omnipotence and wisdom; but I also see much else that disturbs my mind and excites anxiety. The sum of all this is an objective uncertainty. But it is for this very reason that the inwardness becomes as intense as it is, for it embraces this objective uncertainty with the entire passion of the infinite. In the case of a mathematical proposition the objectivity is given, but for this reason the truth of such a proposition is also an indifferent truth.

But the above definition of truth is an equivalent expression for faith. Without risk there is no faith. Faith is precisely the contradiction between the infinite passion of the individual's inwardness and the objective uncertainty. If I am capable of grasping God objectively, I do not believe, but precisely because I cannot do this I must believe. If I wish to preserve myself in faith I must constantly be intent upon holding fast the objective uncertainty, so that in the objective uncertainty I am out "upon the seventy thousand fathoms of water," and yet believe.

In the principle that subjectivity, inwardness, is the truth, there is comprehended the Socratic wisdom, whose everlasting merit it was to have become aware of the essential significance of existence, of the fact that the knower is an existing individual. For this reason Socrates was in the truth by virtue of his ignorance, in the highest sense in which this was possible within paganism. To attain to an understanding of this, to comprehend that the misfortune of speculative philosophy is again and again to have forgotten that the knower is an existing individual, is in our objective age difficult enough. "But to have made an advance upon Socrates, without ever having understood what he understood, is at any rate not Socratic."

Notes

1. The reader will observe that the question here is about essential truth, or about the truth which is essentially related to existence, and that it is precisely for the sake of clarifying it as inwardness or as subjectivity that this contrast is drawn. (K)
2. In this manner God certainly becomes a postulate, but not in the otiose manner in which this word is commonly understood. It becomes clear rather that the only way in which an existing individual comes into relation with God is when the dialectical contradiction brings his passion to the point of despair, and helps him to embrace God with the "category of despair" (faith). Then the postulate is so far from being arbitrary that it is precisely a life-necessity. It is then not so much that God is a postulate as that the existing individual's postulation of God is a necessity. (K)

important and necessary to a man which he feels to be his own, i.e., his own individual happiness.

And behold, in striving for the attainment of this, his own individual welfare, man perceives that his welfare depends upon other beings. And, upon watching and observing these other beings, man sees that all of them, both men and even animals, possess precisely the same conception of life as he himself. Each one of these beings, precisely as in his own case, is conscious only of his own life, and his own happiness, considers his own life alone of importance, and real, and the life of all other beings only as a means to his individual welfare. Man sees that every living being, precisely like himself, must be ready, for the sake of his petty welfare, to deprive all other beings of greater happiness and even of life.

And, having comprehended this, man involuntarily makes this calculation, that if this is so, and he knows that it is indubitably so, then, not one or not ten beings only, but all the innumerable beings in the world, for the attainment, each of his own object, are ready every moment to annihilate him, that man for whom alone life exists. And, having apprehended this, man sees that his personal happiness, in which alone he understands life, is not only not to be easily won by him, but that it will assuredly be taken from him.

The longer a man lives, the more firmly is this conviction confirmed by experience, and the man perceives that the life of the world in which he shares is composed of individualities bound together, desirous of exterminating and devouring each other, not only cannot be a happiness for him, but will, assuredly, be a great evil.

But, nevertheless, if the man is placed in such favorable conditions that he can successfully contend with other personalities, fearing nothing for his own, both experience and reason speedily show him, that even those semblances of happiness which he wrests from life, in the form of enjoyment for his own personality, do not constitute happiness, and are but specimens of happiness as it were, vouchsafed him merely in order that he may be the more vividly conscious of the suffering which is always bound up with enjoyment.

The longer man lives, the more plainly does he see that weariness, satiety, toils, and sufferings become ever greater and greater, and enjoyments ever less and less.

But this is not all. On beginning to become conscious of a decline of strength, and of ill-health, and gazing upon ill-health, age, and the death of others, he perceives this also in addition, that even his existence, in which alone he recognizes real, full life, is approaching weakness, old age, and death, with every hour, with every movement; that his life, besides being subject to thousands of chances of annihilation from other beings warring with him, and from ever increasing sufferings, is, in virtue of its very nature, nothing else than an incessant approach to death; to that condition which together with the life of the individual will, assuredly, be annihilated every possibility of any personal happiness. The man perceives that he, his own personality, is that in which alone he feels life, and that all he does is to struggle with those with whom it is impossible to struggle—with the whole world; that he is in search of enjoyments which give only the semblances of happiness, and which always terminate in sufferings, and he wishes to hold back life, which is impossible to hold back. The man perceives that he himself, his own personality, that for which, alone, he desires life and happiness, can have neither life nor happiness. And that which he desires to have—life and happiness—is possessed only by those beings who are strangers to him, whom he does not feel, and cannot feel, and of whose existence he cannot know and does not wish to know.

That which for him is the most important of all, and which alone is necessary to him, that which—as it seems to him—alone possesses life in reality, his personality, that which will perish, will become bones and worms, is not he; but that which is unnecessary for him, unimportant to him, all that world of ever changing and struggling beings, that is to say, real life, will remain, and will exist forever. So that the sole life which is felt by man, and which evokes all this activity, proves to be something deceptive and impossible; but the inward life, which he does not love, which he does not feel, of which he is ignorant, is the one real life.

That of which he is not conscious,—that alone possesses those qualities of which he would fain be the sole possessor. And this is not that which presents itself to a man in the evil moments of his gloomy moods, this is not a representation which it is possible for him not to have, but this is, on the contrary, such a palpable, indubitable truth, that if this thought once occurs to man, or if others explain it to him, he can never again free himself from it, he can never more force it out of his consciousness.

⚓ The Sole Aim of Life ⚓

The sole aim of life, as it first presents itself to man, is the happiness of himself as an individual, but individual happiness there cannot be; if there were anything resembling individual happiness in life, then that life in which alone happiness can exist, the life of the individual, is borne irresistibly, by every movement, by every breath, towards suffering, towards evil, towards death, towards annihilation.

And this is so self-evident and so plain that every thinking man, old or young, learned or unlearned, will see it.

This argument is so simple and natural that it presents itself to every reasoning man, and has been known to mankind ever since the most ancient times.

"The life of man as an individual, striving only towards his own happiness, amid an endless number of similar individuals, engaged in annihilating each other and in annihilating themselves, is evil and absurdity, and such real life cannot be." This is what man has been saying to himself from the most ancient times down to the present day, and this inward inconsistency of the life of man was expressed with remarkable force and clearness by the Indians, and the Chinese, and the Egyptians, and the Greeks, and the Jews, and from the most ancient times the mind of man has been directed to the study of such a happiness for man as should not be cancelled by the contest of beings among themselves, by suffering and by death. In the increasingly better solution of this indubitable, unavoidable contest, by sufferings and by death of the happiness of man, lies the constant movement in advance from that time when we know his life.

From the most ancient times, and among the most widely varying peoples, the great teachers of mankind have revealed to men more and more the clear definitions of life, solving its inward contradictions, and have pointed out the true happiness and true life which is proper to men.

And, since the position of all men in the world is identical, since the contradictions of his strivings after his personal welfare and the consciousness of his powerlessness are identical for every man, all the definitions of true happiness of life, and, hence, of the true revelation to men by the grandest minds of humanity, are identical.

"Life is the diffusion of that light which, for the happiness of men, descended upon them from heaven," said Confucius, six hundred years before Christ.

"Life is the peregrination and the perfection of souls, which attain to greater and ever greater bliss," said the Brahmins of the same day.

"Life is the abnegation of self, with the purpose of attaining blessed Nirvana," said Buddha, a contemporary of Confucius.

"Life is the path of peacefulness and lowliness, for the attainment of bliss," said Loa-dzi, also a contemporary of Confucius.

"Life is that which God breathed into man's nostrils, in order that he, by fulfilling his law, might receive happiness," says the Hebrew sage, Moses.

"Life is submission to the reason, which gives happiness to man," said the Stoics.

"Life is love towards God and our neighbor, which gives happiness to man," said Christ, summing up in his definition all those which had preceded it.

Such are the definitions of life, which, thousands of years before our day, pointing out to men real and indestructible bliss, in the place of the false and impossible bliss of individuality, solve the contradictions of human life and impart to it a reasonable sense.

It is possible not to agree with these definitions of life, it is possible to assume that these definitions can be expressed more accurately and more clearly; but it is impossible not to see that these definitions, equally with the acknowledgment of them, do away with the inconsistencies of life, and, replacing the aspiration for an unattainable bliss of individuality, by another aspiration, for a happiness indestructible by suffering and death, impart to life a reasonable sense. It is impossible not to see this also, that these definitions, being theoretically correct, are confirmed by the experience of life, and that millions and millions of men, who have accepted and who do accept such definitions of life, have, in fact, proved, and do prove, the possibility of replacing the aspiration towards individual welfare by an aspiration towards another happiness, of a sort which is not to be destroyed by suffering or death.

But, in addition to those men who have understood and who do understand the definitions of life, revealed to men by the great enlighteners of humanity, and who live by them, there always have been and there are now many people who, during a certain period of their life, and sometimes their whole life long, lead a purely animal existence, not only ignoring those definitions which serve to solve the contradictions of human life, but not even perceiving those contradictions which they solve. And there always have been and there now exist among those people men who, in consequence of their exclusively external position, regard themselves as called upon to guide mankind, and who, without themselves comprehending the meaning of human life, have taught and do teach other people life, which they themselves do not understand; to the effect that human life is nothing but individual existence.

Such false teachers have existed in all ages, and exist in our day also. Some confess in words the teachings of those enlighteners of mankind, in whose traditions they have been brought up, but, not comprehending their rational meaning, they convert these teachings into supernatural revelations as to the past and future life of men, and require only the fulfillment of ceremonial forms.

This is the doctrine of the Pharisees, in the very broadest sense, i.e., of the men who teach that a life preposterous in itself can be amended by faith in a future life, obtained by the fulfillment of external forms.

Others, who do not acknowledge the possibility of any other life than the visible one, reject every marvel and everything supernatural, and boldly affirm that the life of man is nothing but his animal existence from his birth to his death. This is the doctrine of the Scribes—of men who teach that there is nothing preposterous in the life of man, any more than in that of animals.

And both the former and the latter false prophets, in spite of the fact that the teaching of both is founded upon the same coarse lack of understanding of the fundamental inconsistency of human life, have always been at enmity with each other, and are still at enmity. Both these doctrines reign in our world, and, contending with each other, they fill the world with their dissensions—by those same dissensions concealing from men those definitions of life which reveal the path to the true happiness of men, and which were given to men thousands of years ago.

The Pharisees, not comprehending this definition of life, which was given to men by those teachers in whose traditions they were brought up, replace it with their false interpretations of a future life, and, in addition to this, strive to conceal from men the definition of life of other enlighteners of humanity, by presenting the latter to their disciples in the coarsest and harshest aspect, assuming that, by so doing, they will uphold the absolute authority of that doctrine upon which they found their interpretation.[1]

And the Scribes, not even suspecting in the teachings of the Pharisees those intelligent grounds from which they took their rise, flatly reject all doctrines, and boldly affirm that all these doctrines have no foundation whatever, but are merely remnants of the coarse customs of ignorance, and that the forward movement of mankind consists in not putting any questions whatever to one's self, concerning life, which overleap the bounds of the animal existence of man.

The Fear of Death is Only a Confession of the Unsolved Contradiction of Life

"There is no death," the voice of truth says to men. "I am the Resurrection and the Life; he that believeth in Me, though he were dead, yet shall he live. And every one that liveth and believeth in Me shall never die. Believest thou this?"

"There is no death," say all the great teachers of the world; and the same say millions of men who understand life, and bear witness to it with their lives. And every living man feels the same thing in his soul, at the moment when his consciousness clears up. But men who do not understand life cannot do otherwise than fear death. They see it, and believe in it.

"How is there no death?" cry these people in wrath and indignation. "This is sophistry! Death is before us; it has mowed down millions, and it will mow us down as well. And you may say as much as you please that it does not exist, it will remain all the same. Yonder it is!"

And they see that of which they speak, as a man mentally afflicted sees the vision which terrifies him. He cannot handle the vision, it has never touched him; of its intentions he knows nothing, but he is alarmed, and he suffers from this imaginary vision, which is deprived of the possibility of life. And it is the same with death. Man does not know his death, and never can know it; it has never yet touched him, of its intentions he knows nothing. Then what is it that he fears?

"It has never yet seized me, but it will seize me, that I surely know—it will seize me and annihilate me. And that is terrible," say men who do not understand life.

If men with false ideas of life could reason calmly, and think accurately on the basis of that conception which they have of life, they would be forced to the conclusion that in what is produced in my fleshly existence by the change which I see proceeding, incessantly, in all beings, and which I call death, there is nothing disagreeable or terrible.

I shall die. What is there terrible about that? How many changes have taken place, and are now in progress, in my fleshly existence, and I have not feared them? Why should I fear this change which has not yet come, and in which there is not only nothing repulsive to my reason and experience, but which is so comprehensible, so familiar, and so natural for me, that during the whole course of my life I have formed fancies, I still form them, in which the death both of animals and of people has been accepted by me as a necessary and often an agreeable condition of life. What is there terrible about it?

For there are but two strictly logical views of life: one false—that by which life is understood as those seeming phenomena which take place in my body from my birth to my death; and another, the true one—by which life is understood as that invisible consciousness of it which I bear within myself. One view is false, the other is true ; but both are logical, and men may hold either the one or the other, but in neither the one nor the other is the fear of death possible.

The first false view, which understands life as the visible phenomena in the body from birth to death, is as old as the world itself. This is not, as many think, a view of life which has been worked out by the materialistic science and philosophy of our day; the science and philosophy of our times have only carried this view to its extreme limits, by which it becomes more visible than hitherto how little this view corresponds to the fundamental demands of human life; but this is the ancient and primitive view of men who stood upon the lower steps of culture. It is expressed among the Chinese, among the Greeks, and among the Hebrews, in the Book of Job, and in the sentence: "Dust thou art, and to dust shalt thou return."

This view, in its present expression, runs as follows: Life is a chance play of forces in matter, manifesting itself in space and time. And what we call our consciousness is not life, but a certain delusion of the feelings, which makes it appear that life lies in this consciousness. Consciousness is the spark which flashes up from matter under certain conditions of the latter. This spark flashes up, burns, again grows feeble, and finally goes out. This spark, that is to say, consciousness, experienced by matter in the course of a certain time, between two endless spaces of time, is nothing. And, in spite of the fact that consciousness sees and passes judgment on itself and on all the infinite world, and beholds all the play of chance of this world,— and *chief of all*, in the contrary something that is not accidental, calls this play accident,—this consciousness itself is only the product of dead matter, a vision, appearing and disappearing without any trace or reason. All is the product of matter, infinitely varied; and what is called life is only a certain condition of dead matter.

Such is one view of life. This view is utterly false. According to this view, the rational consciousness of man is merely an accident, accompanying a certain condition of matter; and therefore, what we, in our consciousness, call life, is a phantom. The dead only exists. What we call life is the play of death. With such a view of life, death should not only not be terrible, but life ought to be terrible, as something unnatural and senseless, as it is among the Buddhists, and the new pessimists, Schopenhauer and Hartmann.

The other view of life is as follows. Life is only that which I recognize in myself. But I am always conscious of my life, not as I have been or as I shall be (when I meditate upon my life), but I am conscious of my life thus—that I am—that I never begin anywhere, that I shall never end anywhere. No comprehension of time and space is connected with my consciousness of life. My life is manifested in time, in space, but this is merely its manifestation. But the life itself of which I am conscious makes itself perceptible to me outside of time and space; so that, according to this view, it appears, not that the consciousness of life is a phantom, but all that which is dependent upon space and is visionary in time.

And, therefore, a curtailment of the bodily existence, so far as connected with time and space, has nothing wretched about it, according to this view, and can neither shorten nor destroy my true life. And, according to this view, death does not exist.

There could be no fear of death according to either view of life, if men held strictly to either the one or the other.

Neither as an animal, nor as a rational being, can man fear death; the animal has no consciousness of life and does not see death, and the rational being, having a consciousness of life, cannot see in the death of the animal anything except a natural and never ending movement of matter. But if man fears, what he fears is not death, which he does not know, but life, which alone he does know, and his animal and rational existence. That feeling which is expressed in men by the fear of death is only the consciousness of the inward contradiction of life; just as the fear of ghosts is merely a consciousness of a sickly mental condition.

"I shall cease to be, I shall die, all that in which I set my life will die," says one voice to a man.

"I am," says another voice, "and I cannot die, and I ought not to die. I ought not to die, and I am dying."

Not in death, but in this contradiction lies the cause of that terror which seizes upon a man, at the thought of death of the flesh: the fear of death lies not in the fact that man dreads the curtailment of his animal existence, but in the fact that it seems to him that that will die which cannot and must not die. The thought of future death is only a transference to the future of the death which takes place in the present. The phantom which presents itself of a future death of the flesh is not an awakening of the thought of death, but, on the contrary, an awakening of the thought of the life which a man should have and which he has not.

This feeling is similar to that which a man would experience on awaking to life in his grave, under ground. "There is life, but I am in death, and here it is, death!" He imagines that what is and must be will be annihilated. And the mind of man mourns and grows afraid. The best proof of the fact that the fear of death is not the fear of death, but of false life, is this, that men frequently kill themselves from the fear of death.

Men are not terrified by the thought of the death of the flesh because they are afraid that their life will end with it, but because the death of the flesh plainly demonstrates to them the necessity of a true life, which they do not possess. And this is why people who do not understand life are so disinclined to think of death. To think of death is exactly the same with them as to confess that they are not living as their rational consciousness demands.

People who fear death, fear it because it represents emptiness and darkness to them; but they behold emptiness and darkness because they do not see life.

Notes

1. The unity of the rational idea of the definition of life by other enlighteners of mankind does not present itself to them as proof of the truth of their teaching, since it injures faith in the senseless, false interpretations with which they replace the substance of doctrine.

Suggested Readings

Tolstoy, Leo. "The Death of Ivan Ilych" in *Great Short Works of Leo Tolstoy*. Trans. Louise and Aylmer Maude. New York, 1967.

Rowe, William. *Leo Tolstoy*. Boston: Twayne Publishers, 1986.

Simmons, Ernest. *Leo Tolstoy*. Boston: Little, Brown and Company, 1946.

Chapter 19

Reflections on War and Death

Sigmund Freud

Sigmund Freud, the father of the psychoanalytic method, was born in 1856 in Moravia. He belongs to an intellectual revolution beginning with Schopenhauer and Nietzsche which undermines the primacy of rationality. Man, according to Freud, is no longer the rational animal but is driven by unconscious libidinal forces which must of necessity be repressed. We stand as human beings in between our animal impulses (Id) and the civilizational forces which try to contain them (Super Ego). Freud will explain in this selection how our moral behavior and our attitude toward death are results of this conflict.

Our Attitude Towards Death

The second factor to which I attribute our present sense of estrangement in this once lovely and congenial world is the disturbance that has taken place in our attitude towards death, an attitude to which hitherto we have clung so fast.

This attitude was far from straightforward. We were of course prepared to maintain that death was the necessary outcome of life, that everyone owes a debt to Nature and must expect to pay the reckoning—in short, that death was natural, undeniable and unavoidable. In reality, however, we were accustomed to behave as if it were otherwise. We displayed an unmistakable tendency to "shelve" death, to eliminate it from life. We tried to hush it up; indeed we even have the saying, "To think of something as we think of death."[1] That is our own death, of course. Our own death is indeed unimaginable, and whenever we make the attempt to imagine it we can perceive that we really survive as spectators. Hence the psychoanalytic school could venture on the assertion that at bottom no one believes in his own death, or to put the same thing in another way, in the unconscious every one of us is convinced of his own immortality.

From *The Collected Papers*, Volume 4 by Sigmund Freud. Authorized translation under the supervision of Joan Riviere. Published by Basic Books, Inc. by arrangement with The Hogarth Press, Ltd. and The Institute of Psycho-Analysis, London. Reprinted by permission.

As to the death of another, the civilized man will carefully avoid speaking of such a possibility in the hearing of the person concerned. Children alone disregard this restriction; unabashed they threaten one another with the eventuality of death, and even go so far as to talk of it before one whom they love, as for instance: "Dear Mamma, it will be a pity when you are dead but then I shall do this or that." The civilized adult can hardly even entertain the thought of another's death without seeming to himself hard or evil-hearted; unless, of course, as a physician, lawyer or something of the sort, he has to deal with death professionally. Least of all will he permit himself to think of the death of another if with that event some gain to himself in freedom, means or position is connected. This sensitiveness of ours is of course impotent to arrest the hand of death; when it has fallen, we are always deeply affected, as if we were prostrated by the overthrow of our expectations. Our habit is to lay stress on the fortuitous causations of the death—accident, disease, infection, advanced age; in this way we betray our endeavour to modify the significance of death from a necessity to an accident. A multitude of simultaneous deaths appears to us exceedingly terrible. Towards the dead person himself we take up a special attitude, something like admiration for one who has accomplished a very difficult task. We suspend criticism of him, overlook his possible misdoings, issue the command: *De mortuis nil nisi bene,* and regard it as justifiable to set forth in the funeral-oration and upon the tombstone only that which is most favourable to his memory. Consideration for the dead, who no longer need it, is dearer to us than the truth, and certainly, for most of us, is dearer also than consideration for the living.

The culmination of this conventional attitude towards death among civilized persons is seen in our complete collapse when death has fallen on some person whom we love—a parent or a partner in marriage, a brother or sister, a child, a dear friend. Our hopes, our pride, our happiness, lie in the grave with him, we will not be consoled, we will not fill the loved one's place. We behave then as if we belonged to the tribe of the Asra, who must die too when those die whom they love.

But this attitude of ours towards death has a powerful effect upon our lives. Life is impoverished, it loses in interest, when the highest stake in the game of living, life itself, may not be risked. It becomes as flat, as superficial, as one of those American flirtations in which it is from the first understood that nothing is to happen, contrasted with a Continental love-affair in which both partners must constantly bear in mind the serious consequences. Our ties of affection, the unbearable intensity of our grief, make us disinclined to court danger for ourselves and for those who belong to us. We dare not contemplate a great many undertakings which are dangerous but quite indispensable, such as attempts at mechanical flight, expeditions to far countries, experiments with explosive substances. We are paralysed by the thought of who is to replace the son with his mother, the husband with his wife, the father with his children, if there should come disaster. The tendency to exclude death from our calculations brings in its train a number of other renunciations and exclusions. And yet the motto of the Hanseatic League declared: *"Navigare necesse est, vivere non necesse!"* (It is necessary to sail the seas, it is not necessary to live.)

It is an inevitable result of all this that we should seek in the world of fiction, of general literature and of the theatre compensation for the impoverishment of life. There we still find people who know how to die, indeed, who are even capable of killing someone else. There alone too we can enjoy the condition which makes it possible for us to reconcile Ourselves with death—namely, that behind all the vicissitudes of life we preserve our existence intact.

For it is indeed too sad that in life it should be as it is in chess, when one false move may lose us the game, but with the difference that we can have no second game, no return-match. In the realm of fiction we discover that plurality of lives for which we crave. We die in the person of a given hero, yet we survive him, and are ready to die again with the next hero just as safely.

It is evident that the war is bound to sweep away this conventional treatment of death. Death will no longer be denied; we are forced to believe in him. People really are dying, and now not one by one, but many at a time, often ten thousand in a single day. Nor is it any longer an accident. To be sure, it still seems a matter of chance whether a particular bullet hits this man or that; but the survivor may easily be hit by another bullet; and the accumulation puts an end to the impression of accident. Life has, in truth, become interesting again; it has regained its full significance.

Here a distinction should be made between two groups—those who personally risk their lives in battle, and those who have remained at home and have only to wait for the loss of their dear ones by wounds, disease, or infection. It would indeed be very interesting to study the changes in the psychology of the combatants, but I know too little about it. We must stop short at the second group, to which we ourselves belong. I have said already that in my opinion the bewilderment and the paralysis of energies, now so generally felt by us, are essentially determined in part by the circumstance that we cannot maintain our former attitude towards death, and have not yet discovered a new one. Perhaps it will assist us to do this if we direct our psychological inquiry towards two other relations with death—the one which we may ascribe to primitive, prehistoric peoples, and that other which in every one of us still exists, but which conceals itself, invisible to consciousness, in the deepest-lying strata of our mental life.

The attitude of prehistoric man towards death is known to us, of course, only by inferences and reconstruction, but I believe that these processes have furnished us with tolerably trustworthy information.

Primitive man assumed a very remarkable attitude towards death. It was far from consistent, was indeed extremely contradictory. On the one hand, he took death seriously, recognized it as the termination of life and used it to that end; on the other hand, he also denied death, reduced it to nothingness. This contradiction arose from the circumstance that he took up radically different attitudes towards the death of another man, of a stranger, of an enemy, and towards his own. The death of the other man he had no objection to; it meant the annihilation of a creature hated, and primitive man had no scruples against bringing it about. He was, in truth, a very violent being, more cruel and more malign than other animals. He liked to kill, and killed as a matter of course. That instinct which is said to restrain the other animals from killing and devouring their own species we need not attribute to him.

Hence the primitive history of mankind is filled with murder. Even to-day, the history of the world which our children learn in school is essentially a series of race-murders. The obscure sense of guilt which has been common to man since prehistoric times, and which in many religions has been condensed into the doctrine of original sin, is probably the outcome of a blood-guiltiness incurred by primitive man. In my book *Totem und Tabu* (1913) I have, following clues given by W. Robertson Smith, Atkinson and Charles Darwin, attempted to surmise the nature of this primal guilt, and I think that even the contemporary Christian doctrine enables us to deduce it. If the Son of God was obliged to sacrifice his life to redeem mankind from original sin, then by the law of the talion, the requital of like for like, that sin must have been a killing, a murder. Nothing else could call for the sacrifice of a life in expiation. And if the original sin was an offence against God the Father, the primal crime of mankind must have been a parricide, the killing of the primal father of the primitive human horde, whose image in memory was later transfigured into a deity.[2]

His own death was for primitive man certainly just as unimaginable and unreal as it is for any one of us to-day. But there was for him a case in which the two opposite attitudes towards death came into conflict and joined issue; and this case was momentous and productive of far-reaching results. It occurred when primitive man saw someone who belonged to him die— his wife, his child, his friend, whom assuredly he loved as we love ours, for love cannot be much younger than the lust to kill. Then, in his pain, he had to learn that one can indeed die oneself, an admission against which his whole being revolted; for each of these loved ones was, in very truth, a part of his own beloved ego. But even so, on the other hand such deaths had a rightfulness for him, since in each of the loved persons something of the hostile stranger had resided. The law of ambivalence of feeling, which to this day governs our emotional relations with those whom we love most, had assuredly a very much wider validity in primitive periods. Thus these beloved dead had also been enemies and strangers who had aroused in him a measure of hostile feeling.[3]

Philosophers have declared that the intellectual enigma presented to primitive man by the picture of death was what forced him to reflection, and thus that it became the starting-point of all speculation. I believe that here the philosophers think too philosophically, and give too little consideration to the primarily effective motives. I would therefore limit and correct this assertion: By the body of his slain enemy primitive man would have triumphed, without racking his brains about the enigma of life and death. Not the intellectual enigma, and not every death, but the conflict of feeling at the death of loved, yet withal alien and hated persons was what disengaged the spirit of inquiry in man. Of this conflict of feeling psychology was the direct offspring. Man could no longer keep death at a distance, for he had tasted of it in his grief for the dead; but still he did not consent entirely to acknowledge it, for he could not conceive of himself as dead. So he devised a compromise; he conceded the fact of death, even his own death, but denied it the significance of annihilation, which he had had no motive for contesting where the death of his enemy had been concerned. During his contemplation of his loved one's corpse he invented ghosts, and it was his sense of guilt at the satisfaction mingled with his sorrow that turned these new-born spirits into evil, dreaded demons. The changes wrought by death suggested to him the disjunction of the individuality into a body and a soul—first of all into several souls; in this way his train of thought ran parallel with the process of disintegration which sets in with death. The enduring remembrance of the dead became the basis for assuming other modes of existence, gave him the conception of life continued after apparent death.

The subsequent modes of existence were at first no more than appendages to that life which death had brought to a close—shadowy, empty of content, and until later times but slightly valued; they showed as yet a pathetic inadequacy. We may recall the answer made to Odysseus by the soul of Achilles:

> *Erst in the life on the earth, no less than a god we revered thee,*
> *We the Achaeans; and now in the realm of the dead as a monarch*
> *Here dost thou rule; then why should death thus grieve thee, Achilles?*
> *Thus did I speak: forthwith then answering thus he addressed me,*

> *Speak not smoothly of death, I beseech, O famous Odysseus,*
> *Better by far to remain on the earth as the thrall of another;*
> *E'en of a portionless man that hath means right scanty of living,*
> *Rather than reign sole king in the realm of the bodiless phantoms.*[4]

Or in the powerful, bitterly burlesque rendering by Heine, where he makes Achilles say that the most insignificant little Philistine at Stuckert-on-the-Neckar, in being alive, is far happier than he, the son of Peleus, the dead hero, the prince of shadows in the nether world.

It was not until much later that the different religions devised the view of this after-life as the more desirable, the truly valid one, and degraded the life which is ended by death to a mere preparation. It was then but consistent to extend life backward into the past, to conceive of former existences, transmigrations of the soul and reincarnation, all with the purpose of depriving death of its meaning as the termination of life. So early did the denial of death, which above we designated a convention of civilization, actually originate.

Beside the corpse of the beloved were generated not only the idea of the soul, the belief in immortality, and a great part of man's deep-rooted sense of guilt, but also the earliest inkling of ethical law. The first and most portentous prohibition of the awakening conscience was: Thou shalt not kill. It was born of the reaction against that hate-gratification which lurked behind the grief for the loved dead, and was gradually extended to unloved strangers and finally even to enemies.

This final extension is no longer experienced by civilized man. When the frenzied conflict of this war shall have been decided, every one of the victorious warriors will joyfully return to his home, his wife and his children, undelayed and undisturbed by any thought of the enemy he has slain either at close quarters or by distant weapons of destruction. It is worthy of note that such primitive races as still inhabit the earth, who are undoubtedly closer than we to primitive man, act differently in this respect, or did so act until they came under the influence of our civilization. The savage—Australian, Bushman, Tierra del Fuegan—is by no means a remorseless murderer; when he returns victorious from the war-path he may not set foot in his village nor touch his wife until he has atoned for the murders committed in war by penances which are often prolonged and toilsome. This may be presumed, of course, to be the outcome of superstition; the savage still goes in fear of the avenging spirits of the slain. But the spirits of the fallen enemy are nothing but the expression of his own conscience, uneasy on account of his blood-guiltiness; behind this superstition lurks a vein of ethical sensitiveness which has been lost by us civilized men.[5]

Pious souls, who cherish the thought of our remoteness from whatever is evil and base, will be quick to draw from the early appearance and the urgency of the prohibition of murder gratifying conclusions in regard to the force of these ethical stirrings, which must consequently have been implanted in us. Unfortunately this argument proves even more for the opposite contention. So powerful a prohibition can only be directed against an equally powerful impulse. What no human soul desires there is no need to prohibit;[6] it is automatically excluded. The very emphasis of the commandment *Thou shalt not kill* makes it certain that we spring from an endless ancestry of murderers, with whom the lust for killing was in the blood as possibly it is to this day with ourselves. The ethical strivings of mankind, of which we need not in the least depreciate the strength and the significance are an acquisition accompanying evolution; they have then become the hereditary possession of those human beings alive to-day, though unfortunately only in a very variable measure.

Let us now leave primitive man, and turn to the unconscious in our mental life. Here we depend entirely upon the psychoanalytic method of investigation, the only one which plumbs such depths. We ask what is the attitude of our unconscious towards the problem of death. The answer must be: Almost exactly the same as primitive man's. In this respect, as in many others, the man of prehistoric ages survives unchanged in our unconscious. Thus, our unconscious does not believe in its own death; it behaves as if immortal. What we call our "unconscious" (the deepest strata of our minds, made up of instinctual impulses) knows nothing whatever of negatives or of denials—contradictories coincide in it—and so it knows nothing whatever of our own death, for to that we can give only a negative purport. It follows that no instinct we possess is ready for a belief in death. This is even perhaps the secret of heroism. The rational explanation for heroism is that it consists in the decision that the personal life cannot be so precious as certain abstract general ideals. But more frequent, in my view, is that instinctive and impulsive heroism which knows no such motivation, and flouts danger in the spirit of Anzengruber's Hans the Road-Mender: "Nothing can happen to *me*." Or else that motivation serves but to clear away the hesitation which might delay an heroic reaction in accord with the unconscious. The dread of death, which dominates us oftener than we know, is on the other hand something secondary, being usually the outcome of the sense of guilt.

On the other hand, for strangers and for enemies, we do acknowledge death, and consign them to it quite as readily and unthinkingly as did primitive man. Here there does, indeed, appear a distinction which in practice shows for a decisive one. Our unconscious does not carry out the killing; it merely thinks it and wishes it. But it would be wrong entirely to depreciate this psychical reality as compared with actual reality. It is significant and pregnant enough. In our unconscious we daily and hourly deport all who stand in our way, all who have offended or injured us. The expression: "Devil take him!" which so frequently comes to our lips in joking anger, and which really means "Death take him!" is in our unconscious an earnest deliberate death-wish. Indeed, our unconscious will murder even for trifles; like the ancient Athenian law of Draco, it knows no other punishment for crime than death; and this has a certain consistency, for every injury to our almighty and autocratic ego is at bottom a crime of *lèse-majesté*.

And so, if we are to be judged by the wishes in our unconscious, we are, like primitive man, simply a gang of murderers. It is well that all these wishes do not possess the potency which was attributed to them by primitive men;[7] in the cross-fire of mutual maledictions mankind would long since have perished, the best and wisest of men and the loveliest and fairest of women with the rest.

Psychoanalysis finds little credence among laymen for assertions such as these. They reject them as calumnies which are confuted by conscious experience, and adroitly overlook the faint indications through which the unconscious is apt to betray itself even to consciousness. It is therefore relevant to point out that many thinkers who could not have been influenced by psychoanalysis have quite definitely accused our unspoken thoughts of a readiness, heedless of the murder-prohibition, to get rid of anyone who stands in our way. From many examples of this I will choose one very famous one:

In *Le Père Goriot*, Balzac alludes to a passage in the works of J. J. Rousseau where that author asks the reader what he would do if—without leaving Paris and of course without being discovered—he could kill, with great profit to himself, an old mandarin in Peking by a mere act of his will. Rousseau implies that he would not give much for the life of the dignitary. *"Tuer son mandarin"* has passed into a proverb for this secret readiness even on the part of ourselves to-day.

There is as well a whole array of cynical jests and anecdotes which testify in the same sense, such as, for instance, the remark attributed to a husband: "If one of us dies, I shall go and live in Paris." Such cynical jokes would not be possible unless they contained an unacknowledged verity which could not be countenanced if seriously and baldly expressed. In joke, as we know, even the truth may be told.

As for primitive man, so also for us in our unconscious, there arises a case in which the two contrasted attitudes towards death, that which acknowledges it as the annihilation of life and the other which denies it as ineffectual to that end, conflict and join issue—and this case is the same as in primitive ages—the death, or the endangered life, of one whom we love, a parent or partner in marriage, a brother or sister, a child or dear friend. These loved ones are on the one hand an inner possession, an ingredient of our personal ego, but on the other hand are partly strangers, even enemies. With the exception of only a very few situations, there adheres to the tenderest and closest of our affections a vestige of hostility which can excite an unconscious death-wish. But this conflict of ambivalence does not now, as it did then, find issue in theories of the soul and of ethics, but in neuroses, which afford us deep insight into normal mental life as well. How often have those physicians who practise psychoanalysis had to deal with the symptom of an exaggerated tender care for the well-being of relatives, or with entirely unfounded self-reproaches after the death of a loved person. The study of these cases has left them in no doubt about the extent and the significance of unconscious death-wishes.

The layman feels an extraordinary horror at the possibility of such feelings, and takes this repulsion as a legitimate ground for disbelief in the assertions of psychoanalysis. I think, mistakenly. No depreciation of our love is intended, and none is actually contained in it. It is indeed foreign to our intelligence as also to our feelings thus to couple love and hate, but Nature, by making use of these twin opposites, contrives to keep love ever vigilant and fresh, so as to guard it against the hate which lurks behind it. It might be said that we owe the fairest flowers of our love-life to the reaction against the hostile impulse which we divine in our breasts.

To sum up: Our unconscious is just as inaccessible to the idea of our own death, as murderously minded towards the stranger, as divided or ambivalent towards the loved, as was man in earliest antiquity. But how far we have moved from this primitive state in our conventionally civilized attitude towards death!

It is easy to see the effect of the impact of war on this duality. It strips us of the later accretions of civilization, and lays bare the primal man in each of us. It constrains us once more to be heroes who cannot believe in their own death; it stamps the alien as the enemy, whose death is to be brought about or desired; it counsels us to rise above the death of those we love. But war is not to be abolished; so long as the conditions of existence among the nations are so varied, and the repulsions between peoples so intense, there will be, must be, wars. The question then arises: Is it not we who must give in, who must adapt ourselves to them? Is it not for us to confess that in our civilized attitude towards death we are once more living psychologically beyond our means, and must reform and give truth its due? Would it not be better to give death the place in actuality and in our thoughts which property belongs to it, and to yield a little more prominence to that unconscious attitude towards death which we have hitherto so carefully suppressed? This hardly seems indeed a greater achievement, but rather a backward step in more than one direction, a regression; but it has the merit of taking somewhat more into account the true state of affairs, and of making life again more endurable for us. To endure life remains, when all is said, the first duty of all living beings. Illusion can have no value if it makes this more difficult for us.

We remember the old saying: *Si vis pacem, para bellum.* If you desire peace, prepare for war.

It would be timely thus to paraphrase it: *Si vis vitam, para mortem.* If you would endure life, be prepared for death.

Notes

1. [The German saying is used as an equivalent for "incredible" or "unlikely."—Trans.]
2. Cf. "Die infantile Wiederkehr des Totemismus," *Totem und Tabu.*
3. Cf. "Tabu and Ambivalez," *Totem und Tabu.*
4. *Odyssey*, xi. 484-491; translated by H.B. Cotterill.
5. Cf. *Totem und Tabu.*
6. Cf. the brilliant argument of Frazer quoted in *Totem und Tabu.*
7. Cf. "Allmacht der Gedanken," *Totem und Tabu.*

Suggested Readings

Starr, Anthony. *Freud.* Oxford: Oxford University Press, 1989.

Wollheim, Richard. *Freud.* London: Fontana, 1971.

Freud, Sigmund. A *General Selection From the Works of Sigmund Freud.* Ed. J. Rickman. New York: Doubleday Anchor, 1957.

VI

Contemporary Thought

Chapter 20

Do We Survive Death and How to Grow Old

Bertrand Russell

Bertrand Russell, 1872-1970, was born in Wales to an aristocratic family and was a towering, sometimes aloof yet magnanimous figure in the history of philosophy. He studied mathematics with Whitehead and together they wrote the foundational work on symbolic logic, Principia Mathematica. *He will be remembered not only for his urbane wit and intellectual generosity, but also for his tremendous influence on 20th century analytic philosophy. The following thoughts from Russell's older years will speak for themselves.*

✦ How to Grow Old ✦

In spite of the title, this article will really be on how *not* to grow old, which, at my time of life, is a much more important subject. My first advice would be to choose your ancestors carefully. Although both my parents died young, I have done well in this respect as regards my other ancestors. My maternal grandfather, it is true, was cut off in the flower of his youth at the age of sixty-seven, but my other three grandparents all lived to be over eighty. Of remoter ancestors I can only discover one who did not live to a great age, and he died of a disease which is now rare, namely, having his head cut off. A great-grandmother of mine, who was a friend of Gibbon, lived to the age of ninety-two, and to her last day remained a terror to all her descendants. My maternal grandmother, after having nine children who survived, one who died in infancy, and many miscarriages, as soon as she became a widow devoted herself to women's higher education. She was one of the founders of Girton College, and worked hard at opening the medical profession to women. She used to relate how she met in Italy an elderly gentleman who was looking very sad. She inquired the cause of his melancholy and he said that he had just parted from his two grandchildren. "Good gracious," she exclaimed, "I have seventy-two grandchildren, and if I were sad each time I parted from one of them, I should have a dismal existence!" "Madre snaturale," he replied. But speaking as one of the seventy-two, I prefer her recipe. After the age of eighty she found she had some difficulty in getting to sleep, so she habitually spent the hours from midnight to 3 a.m. in reading popular science. I do not believe that she ever had time to notice that she was growing old. This, I think, is the proper recipe for remaining young. If you have wide and keen interests and activities in which you can still be effective, you will have no reason to think about the merely statistical fact of the number of years you have already lived, still less of the probable brevity of your future.

As regards health, I have nothing useful to say since I have little experience of illness. I eat and drink whatever I like, and sleep when I cannot keep awake. I never do anything whatever on the ground that it is good for health, though in actual fact the things I like doing are mostly wholesome.

Psychologically there are two dangers to be guarded against in old age. One of these is undue absorption in the past. It does not do to live in memories, in regrets for the good old days, or in sadness about friends who are dead. One's thoughts must be directed to the future, and to things about which there is something to be done. This is not always easy; one's own past is a gradually increasing weight. It is easy to think to oneself that one's emotions used to be more vivid than they are, and one's mind more keen. If this is true it should be forgotten, and if it is forgotten it will probably not be true.

The other thing to be avoided is clinging to youth in the hope of sucking vigour from its vitality. When your children are grown up, they want to live their own lives, and if you continue to be as interested in them as you were when they were young, you are likely to become a burden to them, unless they are unusually callous. I do not mean that one should be without interest in them, but one's interest should be contemplative and, if possible, philanthropic, but not unduly emotional. Animals become indifferent to their young as soon as their young can look after themselves, but human beings, owing to the length of infancy, find this difficult.

I think that a successful old age is easiest for those who have strong impersonal interests involving appropriate activities. It is in this sphere that long experience is really fruitful, and it is in this sphere that the wisdom born of experience can be exercised without being oppressive. It is no use telling grown-up children not to make mistakes, both because they will not believe you, and because mistakes are an essential part of education. But if you are one of those who are incapable of impersonal interests, you may find that your life will be empty unless you concern yourself with your children and grandchildren. In that case you must realize that while you can still render them material services, such as making them an allowance or knitting them jumpers, you must not expect that they will enjoy your company.

Some old people are oppressed by the fear of death. In the young there is a justification for this feeling. Young men who have reason to fear that they will be killed in battle may justifiably feel bitter in the thought that they have been cheated of the best things that life has to offer. But in an old man who has known human joys and sorrows, and has achieved whatever work it was in him to do, the fear of death is somewhat abject and ignoble. The best way to overcome it—so at least it seems to me—is to make your interests gradually wider and more impersonal, until bit by bit the walls of the ego recede, and your life becomes increasingly merged in the universal life. An individual human existence should be like a river—small at first, narrowly contained within its banks, and rushing passionately past boulders and over waterfalls. Gradually the river grows wider, the banks recede, the waters flow more quietly, and in the end, without any visible break, they become merged in the sea, and painlessly lose their individual being. The man who, in old age, can see his life in this way, will not suffer from the fear of death, since the things he cares for will continue. And if, with the decay of vitality, weariness increases, the thought of rest will be not unwelcome. I should wish to die while still at work, knowing that others will carry on what I can no longer do, and content in the thought that what was possible has been done.

[REPRINTED FROM NEW HOPES FOR A CHANGING WORLD]

◢ Do We Survive Death? ◣

This piece was first published in 1936 in a book entitled
The Mysteries of Life and Death. The article by Bishop Barnes
to which Russell refers appeared in the same work.

Before we can profitably discuss whether we shall continue to exist after death, it is well to be clear as to the sense in which a man is the same person as he was yesterday. Philosophers used to think that there were definite substances, the soul and the body, that each lasted on from day to day, that a soul, once created, continued to exist throughout all future time, whereas a body ceased temporarily from death till the resurrection of the body.

The part of this doctrine which concerns the present life is pretty certainly false. The matter of the body is continually changing by processes of nutriment and wastage. Even if it were not, atoms in physics are no longer supposed to have continuous existence; there is no sense in saying: this is the same atom as the one that existed a few minutes ago. The continuity of a human body is a matter of appearance and behavior, not of substance.

The same thing applies to the mind. We think and feel and act, but there is not, in addition to thoughts and feelings and actions, a bare entity, the mind or the soul, which does or suffers these occurrences. The mental continuity of a person is a continuity of habit and memory: there was yesterday one person whose feelings I can remember, and that person I regard as myself of yesterday; but, in fact, myself of yesterday was only certain mental occurrences which are now remembered and are regarded as part of the person who now recollects them. All that constitutes a person is a series of experiences connected by memory and by certain similarities of the sort we call habit.

If, therefore, we are to believe that a person survives death, we must believe that the memories and habits which constitute the person will continue to be exhibited in a new set of occurrences.

No one can prove that this will not happen. But it is easy to see that it is very unlikely. Our memories and habits are bound up with the structure of the brain, in much the same way in which a river is connected with the riverbed. The water in the river is always changing, but it keeps to the same course because previous rains have worn a channel. In like manner, previous events have worn a channel in the brain, and our thoughts flow along this channel. This is the cause of memory and mental habits. But the brain, as a structure, is dissolved at death, and memory therefore may be expected to be also dissolved. There is no more reason to think otherwise than to expect a river to persist in its old course after an earthquake has raised a mountain where a valley used to be.

All memory, and therefore (one may say) all minds, depend upon a property which is very noticeable in certain kinds of material structures but exists little if at all in other kinds. This is the property of forming habits as a result of frequent similar occurrences. For example: a bright light makes the pupils of the eyes contract; and if you repeatedly flash a light in a man's eyes and beat a gong at the same time, the gong alone will, in the end, cause his pupils to contract. This is a fact about the brain and nervous system—that is to say, about a certain material structure. It will be found that exactly similar facts explain our response to language and our use of it, our memories and the emotions they arouse, our moral or immoral habits of behavior, and indeed everything that constitutes our mental personality, except the part determined by heredity. The part determined by heredity is handed on to our posterity but cannot, in the individual, survive the disintegration of the body. Thus both the hereditary and the acquired parts of a personality are, so far as our experience goes, bound up with the characteristics of certain bodily structures. We all know that memory may be obliterated by an injury to the brain, that a virtuous person may be rendered vicious by encephalitis lethargica, and that a clever child can be turned into an idiot by lack of iodine. In view of such familiar facts, it seems scarcely probable that the mind survives the total destruction of brain structure which occurs at death.

It is not rational arguments but emotions that cause belief in a future life.

The most important of these emotions is fear of death, which is instinctive and biologically useful. If we genuinely and wholeheartedly believed in the future life, we should cease completely to fear death. The effects would be curious, and probably such as most of us would deplore. But our human and subhuman ancestors have fought and exterminated their enemies throughout many geological ages and have profited by courage; it is therefore an advantage to the victors in the struggle for life to be able, on occasion, to overcome the natural fear of death. Among animals and savages, instinctive pugnacity suffices for this purpose; but at a certain stage of development, as the Mohammedans first proved, belief in Paradise has considerable military value as reinforcing, natural pugnacity. We should therefore admit that militarists are wise in encouraging the belief in immortality, always supposing that this belief does not become so profound as to produce indifference to the affairs of the world.

Another emotion which encourages the belief in survival is admiration of the excellence of man. As the Bishop of Birmingham says, "His mind is a far finer instrument than anything that had appeared earlier—he knows right and wrong. He can build Westminster Abbey. He can make an airplane. He can calculate the distance of the sun.... Shall, then, man at death perish utterly? Does that incomparable instrument, his mind, vanish when life ceases?"

The Bishop proceeds to argue that "the universe has been shaped and is governed by an intelligent purpose," and that it would have been unintelligent, having made man, to let him perish.

To this argument there are many answers. In the first place, it has been found, in the scientific investigation of nature, that the intrusion of moral or aesthetic values has always been an obstacle to discovery. It used to be thought that the heavenly bodies must move in circles because the circle is the most perfect curve, that species must be immutable because God would only create what was perfect and what therefore stood in no need of improvement, that it was useless to combat epidemics except by repentance because they were sent as a punishment for sin, and so on. It has been found, however, that, so far as we can discover, nature is indifferent to our values and can only be understood by ignoring our notions of good and bad. The Universe may have a purpose, but nothing that we know suggests that, if so, this purpose has any similarity to ours.

Nor is there in this anything surprising. Dr. Barnes tells us that man "knows right and wrong." But, in fact, as anthropology shows, men's views of right and wrong have varied to such an extent that no single item has been permanent. We cannot say, therefore, that man knows right and wrong, but only that some men do. Which men? Nietzsche argued in favor of an ethic profoundly different from Christ's, and some powerful governments have accepted his teaching. If knowledge of right and wrong is to be an argument for immortality, we must first settle whether to believe Christ or Nietzsche, and then argue that Christians are immortal, but Hitler and Mussolini are not, or vice versa. The decision will obviously be made on the battlefield, not in the study. Those who have the best poison gas will have the ethic of the future and will therefore be the immortal ones.

Our feelings and beliefs on the subject of good and evil are, like everything else about us, natural facts, developed in the struggle for existence and not having any divine or supernatural origin. In one of Aesop's fables, a lion is shown pictures of huntsmen catching lions and remarks that, if he had painted them, they would have shown lions catching huntsmen. Man, says Dr. Barnes, is a fine fellow because he can make airplanes. A little while ago there was a popular song about the cleverness of flies in walking upside down on the ceiling, with the chorus: "Could Lloyd George do it? Could Mr. Baldwin do it? Could Ramsay Mac do it? Why, No." On this basis a very telling argument could be constructed by a theologically-minded fly, which no doubt the other flies would find most convincing.

Moreover, it is only when we think abstractly that we have such a high opinion of man. Of men in the concrete, most of us think the vast majority very bad. Civilized states spend more than half their revenue on killing each other's citizens. Consider the long history of the activities inspired by moral fervor: human sacrifices, persecutions of heretics, witch-hunts, pogroms leading up to wholesale extermination by poison gases, which one at least of Dr. Barnes's episcopal colleagues must be supposed to favor, since he holds pacifism to be un-Christian. Are these abominations, and the ethical doctrines by which they are prompted, really evidence of an intelligent Creator? And can we really wish that the men who practiced them should live forever? The world in which we live can be understood as a result of muddle and accident; but if it is the outcome of deliberate purpose, the purpose must have been that of a fiend. For my part, I find accident a less painful and more plausible hypothesis.

Suggested Readings

Watling, J. *Bertrand Russell*. New York: British Book Center, 1971.
Ayer, A. J. *Bertrand Russell*. Chicago: University of Chicago Press, 1988.
Schilpp, Paul. *Philosophy of Bertrand Russell*. New York: Harper and Row, 1963.

Chapter **21**

Being-Towards-Death

Martin Heidegger

Martin Heidegger, 1889-1976, was born in the small town of Messkirch in the Black Forest region of Germany. Although his writing appears at first sight to be enigmatic and detached from the world, his thinking always stayed tied to the earth and the basic questions of existence and Being. As a young Catholic seminarian he studied Aristotle, the Classics and later did graduate work in both modern physics and Medieval logic. After meeting Husserl, the father of phenomenology, Heidegger began to apply the master's method of description to the analysis of human existence —Dasein. The selection below is from his 20th century masterpiece Being and Time.

◢ THE ONTICAL PRIORITY OF THE QUESTION OF BEING

Science in general may be defined as the totality established through an interconnection of true propositions.[1] This definition is not complete, nor does it reach the meaning of science. As ways in which man behaves, sciences have the manner of Being which this entity—man himself—possesses. This entity we denote by the term *"Dasein."* Scientific research is not the only manner of Being which this entity can have, nor is it the one which lies closest. Moreover, Dasein itself has a special distinctiveness as compared with other entities, and it is worth our while to bring this to view in a provisional way. Here our discussion must anticipate later analyses, in which our results will be authentically exhibited for the first time.

Dasein is an entity which does not just occur among other entities. Rather it is ontically distinguished by the fact that, in its very Being, that Being is an *issue* for it. But in that case, this is a constitutive state of Dasein's Being, and this implies that Dasein, in its Being, has a relationship towards that Being—a relationship which itself is one of Being.[2] And this means further that there is some way in which Dasein understands itself in its Being, and that to some degree it does so explicitly. It is peculiar to this entity that with and through its Being, this Being is disclosed to it. *Understanding of Being is itself a definite characteristic of Dasein's Being.* Dasein is ontically distinctive in that it is ontological.[3]

Here "Being-ontological" is not yet tantamount to "developing an ontology." So if we should reserve the term "ontology" for that theoretical inquiry which is explicitly devoted to the meaning of entities, then what we have had in mind in speaking of Dasein's "Being-ontological" is to be designated as something "pre-ontological." It does not signify simply "being-ontical," however, but rather "being in such a way that one has an understanding of Being."

That kind of Being towards which Dasein can comport itself in one way or another, and always does comport itself somehow, we call *"existence" [Existenz].* And because we cannot define Dasein's essence by citing a "what" of the kind that pertains to a subject-matter [*eines sachhaltigen Was*], and because its essence lies rather in the fact that in each case it has its Being to be, and has it as its own,[4] we have chosen to designate this entity as "Dasein," a term which is purely an expression of its Being [*als reiner Seinsausdruck*].

Dasein always understands itself in terms of its existence—in terms of a possibility of itself; to be itself or not itself. Dasein has either chosen these possibilities itself, or got itself into them, or grown up in them already. Only the particular Dasein decides its existence, whether it does so by taking hold or by neglecting. The question of existence never gets straightened out except through existing itself. The understanding of oneself which leads *along this way* we call *"existentiell."*[5] The question of existence is one of Dasein's ontical 'affairs.' This does not require that the ontological structure of existence should be theoretically transparent. The question about that structure aims at the analysis [*Auseinander-legung*] of what constitutes existence. The context [*Zusammenhang*] of such structures we call *"existentiality."* Its analytic has the character of an understanding which is not existentiell, but rather *existential.* The task of an existential analytic of Dasein has been delineated in advance, as regards both its possibility and its necessity, in Dasein's ontical constitution.

Preliminary Sketch of the
◢ Existential-ontological Structure of Death

From our considerations of totality, end, and that which is still outstanding, there has emerged the necessity of Interpreting the phenomenon of death as Being-towards-the-end, and of doing so in terms of Dasein's basic state. Only so can it be made plain to what extent Being-a-whole, as constituted by Being towards-the-end, is possible in Dasein itself in conformity with the structure of its Being. We have seen that care is the basic state of Dasein. The ontological signification of the expression "care" has been expressed in the 'definition': "ahead-of-itself-Being-already-in (the world) as Being-alongside entities which we encounter (within-the-world)." In this are expressed the fundamental characteristics of Dasein's Being: existence, in the "ahead-of-itself;" facticity, in the "Being-already-in;" falling, in the "Being-alongside." If indeed death belongs in a distinctive sense to the Being of Dasein, then death (or Being-towards-the-end) must be defined in terms of these characteristics.

We must, in the first instance, make plain in a preliminary sketch how Dasein's existence, facticity, and falling reveal themselves in the phenomenon of death.

The Interpretation in which the "not-yet—and with it even the uttermost "not-yet," the end of Dasein—was taken in the sense of something still outstanding, has been rejected as inappropriate in that it included the ontological perversion of making Dasein something present-at-hand. Being-at-an-end implies existentially Being-towards-the-end. The uttermost "not-yet" has the character of something *towards which* Dasein *comports itself*. The end is impending [*steht...bevor*] for Dasein. Death is not something not yet present-at-hand, nor is it that which is ultimately still outstanding but which has been reduced to a minimum. *Death is something that stands before us—something impending*.[6]

However, there is much that can impend for Dasein as Being-in-the-world. The character of impendence is not distinctive of death. On the contrary, this Interpretation could even lead us to suppose that death must be understood in the sense of some impending event encountered environmentally. For instance, a storm, the remodelling of the house, or the arrival of a friend, may be impending; and these are entities which are respectively present-at-hand, ready-to-hand, and there-with-us. The death which impends does not have this kind of Being.

But there may also be impending for Dasein a journey, for instance, or a disputation with Others, or the forgoing of something of a kind which Dasein itself can be—its own possibilities of Being, which are based on its Being with Others.

Death is a possibility-of-Being which Dasein itself has to take over in every case. With death, Dasein stands before itself in its ownmost potentiality-for-Being. This is a possibility in which the issue is nothing less than Dasein's Being-in-the-world. Its death is the possibility of no-longer being-able-to-be-there.[7] If Dasein stands before itself as this possibility, it has been *fully* assigned to its ownmost potentiality-for-Being. When it stands before itself in this way, all its relations to any other Dasein have been undone.[8] This ownmost non-relational[9] possibility is at the same time the uttermost one.

As potentiality-for-Being, Dasein cannot outstrip the possibility of death. Death is the possibility of the absolute impossibility of Dasein. Thus death reveals itself as that *possibility which is one's ownmost, which is non-relational, and which is not to be outstripped [unüberholbare]*. As such, death is something *distinctively* impending. Its existential possibility is based on the fact that Dasein is essentially disclosed to itself, and disclosed, indeed, as ahead-of-itself. This item in the structure of care has its most primordial concretion in Being-towards-death. As a phenomenon, Being-towards-the-end becomes plainer as Being towards that distinctive possibility of Dasein which we have characterized.

This ownmost possibility, however, non-relational and not to be outstripped, is not one which Dasein procures for itself subsequently and occasionally in the course of its Being. On the contrary, if Dasein exists, it has already been *thrown* into this possibility. Dasein does not, proximally and for the most part, have any explicit or even any theoretical knowledge of the fact that it has been delivered over to its death, and that death thus belongs to Being-in-the-world. Thrownness into death reveals itself to Dasein in a more primordial and impressive manner in that state-of-mind which we have called "anxiety." Anxiety in the face of death is anxiety 'in the face of' that potentiality-for-Being which is one's ownmost, nonrelational, and not to be outstripped. That in the face of which one has anxiety is Being-in-the-world itself. That about which one has this anxiety is simply Dasein's potentiality-for-Being. Anxiety in the face of death must not be confused with fear in the face of one's demise. This anxiety is not an accidental or random mood of 'weakness' in some individual; but, as a basic state-of-mind of Dasein, it amounts to the disclosedness of the fact that Dasein exists as thrown Being *towards* its end. Thus the existential conception of "dying" is made clear as thrown Being towards its ownmost potentiality-for-Being, which is non-relational and not to be outstripped. Precision is gained by distinguishing this from pure disappearance, and also from merely perishing, and finally from the 'Experiencing' of a demise.[10]

Being-towards-the-end does not first arise through some attitude which occasionally emerges, nor does it arise as such an attitude; it belongs essentially to Dasein's thrownness, which reveals itself in a state-of-mind (mood) in one way or another. The factical 'knowledge' or 'ignorance' which prevails in any Dasein as to its ownmost Being-towards-the-end, is only the expression of the existentiell possibility that there are different ways of maintaining oneself in this Being. Factically, there are many who, proximally and for the most part, do not know about death; but this must not be passed off as a ground for proving that Being-towards-death does not belong to Dasein 'universally.' It only proves that proximally and for the most part Dasein covers up its ownmost Being-towards-death, fleeing *in the face* of it. Factically, Dasein is dying as long as it exists, but proximally and for the most part, it does so by way of *falling*. For factical existing is not only generally and without further differentiation a thrown potentiality-for-Being-in-the-world, but it has always likewise been absorbed in the 'world' of its concern. In this falling Being-alongside, fleeing from uncanniness announces itself; and this means now, a fleeing in the face of one's ownmost Being-towards-death. Existence, facticity, and falling characterize Being-towards-the-end, and are therefore constitutive for the existential conception of death. *As regards its ontological possibility, dying is grounded in care.*

But if Being-towards-death belongs primordially and essentially to Dasein's Being, then it must also be exhibitable in everydayness, even if proximally in a way which is inauthentic.[11] And if Being-towards-the-end should afford the existential possibility of an existentiell Being-a-whole for Dasein, then this would give phenomenal confirmation for the thesis that "care" is the ontological term for the totality of Dasein's structural whole. If, however, we are to provide a full phenomenal justification for this principle, a *preliminary sketch* of the connection between Being-towards-death and care is not sufficient. We must be able to see this connection above all in that *concretion* which lies closest to Dasein—its everydayness.

BEING-TOWARDS-DEATH AND THE EVERYDAYNESS OF DASEIN

In setting forth average everyday Being-towards-death, we must take our orientation from those structures of everydayness at which we have earlier arrived. In Being-towards-death, Dasein comports itself *towards itself* as a distinctive potentiality-for-Being. But the Self of everydayness is the "they." The "they" is constituted by the way things have been publicly interpreted, which expresses itself in idle talk.[12] Idle talk must accordingly make manifest the way in which everyday Dasein interprets for itself its Being-towards-death. The foundation of any interpretation is an act of understanding, which is always accompanied by a state-of-mind, or, in other words, which has a mood. So we must ask how Being-towards-death is disclosed by the kind of understanding which, with its state-of-mind, lurks in the idle talk of the "they." How does the "they" comport itself understandingly towards that ownmost possibility of Dasein, which is non-relational and is not to be outstripped? What state-of-mind discloses to the "they" that it has been delivered over to death, and in what way?

In the publicness with which we are with one another in our everyday manner, death is 'known' as a mishap which is constantly occurring—as a 'case of death.'[13] Someone or other 'dies,' be he neighbour or stranger [*Nächste oder Fernerstehende*]. People who are no acquaintances of ours are 'dying' daily and hourly. 'Death' is encountered as a well-known event occurring within-the-world. As such it remains in the inconspicuousness[x] characteristic of what is encountered in an everyday fashion. The "they" has already stowed away [*gesichert*] an interpretation for this event. It talks of it in a 'fugitive' manner, either expressly or else in a way which is mostly inhibited, as if to say, "One of these days one will die too, in the end; but right now it has nothing to do with us."[14]

The analysis of the phrase 'one dies' reveals unambiguously the kind of Being which belongs to everyday Being-towards-death. In such a way of talking, death is understood as an indefinite something which, above all, must duly arrive from somewhere or other, but which is proximally *not yet present-at-hand* for oneself, and is therefore no threat. The expression 'one dies' spreads abroad the opinion that what gets reached, as it were, by death, is the "they." In Dasein's public way of interpreting, it is said that 'one dies,' because everyone else and oneself can talk himself into saying that "in no case is it I myself," for this "one" is *the "nobody."*[15] 'Dying' is levelled off to an occurrence which reaches Dasein, to be sure, but belongs to nobody in particular. If idle talk is always ambiguous, so is this manner of talking about death. Dying, which is essentially mine in such a way that no one can be my representative, is perverted into an event of public occurrence which the "they" encounters. In the way of talking which we have characterized, death is spoken of as a 'case' which is constantly occurring. Death gets passed off as always something 'actual;' its character as a possibility gets concealed, and so are the other two items that belong to it—the fact that it is non-relational and that it is not to be outstripped. By such ambiguity, Dasein puts itself in the position of losing itself in the "they" as regards a distinctive potentiality-for-Being which belongs to Dasein's ownmost Self. The "they" gives its approval, and aggravates the *temptation* to cover up from oneself one's ownmost Being-towards-death. This evasive concealment in the face of death dominates everydayness so stubbornly that, in Being with one another, the 'neighbours' often still keep talking the 'dying person' into the belief that he will escape death and soon return to the tranquillized everydayness of the world of his concern. Such 'solicitude' is meant to 'console' him. It insists upon bringing him back into Dasein, while in addition it helps him to keep his ownmost non-relational possibility-of-Being completely concealed. In this manner the "they" provides [*besorgt*] a *constant tranquillization about death*. At bottom, however, this is a tranquillization not only for him who is 'dying' but just as much for those who 'console' him. And even in the case of a demise, the public is still not to have its own tranquillity upset by such an event, or be disturbed in the carefreeness with which it concerns itself.[16] Indeed the dying of Others is seen often enough as a social inconvenience, if not even a downright tactlessness, against which the public is to be guarded.

But along with this tranquillization, which forces Dasein away from its death, the "they" at the same time puts itself in the right and makes itself respectable by tacitly regulating the way in which *one* has to comport oneself towards death. It is already a matter of public acceptance that 'thinking about death' is a cowardly fear, a sign of insecurity on the part of Dasein, and a sombre way of fleeing from the world. *The "they" does not permit us the courage for anxiety in the face of death*. The dominance of the manner in which things have been publicly interpreted by the "they," has already decided what state-of-mind is to determine our attitude towards death. In anxiety in the face of death, Dasein is brought face to face with itself as delivered over to that possibility which is not to be outstripped. The "they" concerns itself with transforming this anxiety into fear in the face of an oncoming event. In addition, the anxiety which has been made ambiguous as fear, is passed off as a weakness with which no self-assured Dasein may have any acquaintance. What is 'fitting' [*Was sich . . . "gehört"*] according to the unuttered decree of the "they," is indifferent tranquillity as to the 'fact' that one dies. The cultivation of such a 'superior' indifference *alienates* Dasein from its ownmost non-relational potentiality-for-Being.

But temptation, tranquillization, and alienation are distinguishing marks of the kind of Being called *"falling."* As falling, everyday Being-towards-death is a constant *fleeing in the face of death*. Being-*towards*-the-end has the mode of *evasion in the face of it*—giving new explanations for it, understanding it inauthentically, and concealing it. Factically one's own Dasein is always dying already; that is to say, it is in a Being-towards-its-end. And it hides this Fact from itself by recoining "death" as just a "case of death" in Others—an everyday occurrence which, if need be, gives us the assurance still more plainly that 'oneself' is still 'living.' But in thus falling and fleeing *in the face of* death, Dasein's everydayness attests that the very "they" itself already has the definite character of *Being-towards-death*, even when it is not explicitly engaged in 'thinking about death.' *Even in average everydayness, this ownmost potentiality-for-Being, which is non-relational and not to be outstripped, is constantly an issue for Dasein. This is the case when its concern is merely in the mode of an untroubled indifference* **towards** *the uttermost possibility of existence.*[17]

In setting forth everyday Being-towards-death, however, we are at the same time enjoined to try to secure a full existential conception of Being-towards-the-end, by a more penetrating Interpretation in which falling Being-towards-death is taken as an evasion *in the face of death. That in the face of which one flees* has been made visible in a way which is phenomenally adequate. Against this it must be possible to project phenomenologically the way in which evasive Dasein itself understands its death.

Everyday Being-towards-the-end, and
❧ the Full Existential Conception of Death

In our preliminary existential sketch, Being-towards-the-end has been defined as Being towards one's ownmost potentiality-for-Being, which is non-relational and is not to be outstripped. Being towards this possibility, as a Being which exists, is brought face to face with the absolute impossibility of existence. Beyond this seemingly empty characterization of Being-towards-death, there has been revealed the concretion of this Being in the mode of everydayness. In accordance with the tendency to falling, which is essential to everydayness, Being-towards-death has turned out to be an evasion in the face of death—an evasion which conceals. While our investigation has hitherto passed from a formal sketch of the ontological structure of death to the concrete analysis of everyday Being-towards-the-end, the direction is now to be reversed, and we shall arrive at the full existential conception of death by rounding out our Interpretation of everyday Being-towards-the-end.

In explicating everyday Being-towards-death we have clung to the idle talk of the "they" to the effect that "one dies too, sometime, but not right away."[18] All that we have Interpreted thus far is the 'one dies' as such. In the 'sometime, but not right away,' everydayness concedes something like a *certainty* of death. Nobody doubts that one dies. On the other hand, this 'not doubting' need not imply that kind of Being-certain which corresponds to the way death—in the sense of the distinctive possibility characterized above—enters into Dasein. Everydayness confines itself to conceding the 'certainty' of death in this ambiguous manner just in order to weaken that certainty by covering up dying still more and to alleviate its own thrownness into death.

By its very meaning, this evasive concealment in the face of death can *not* be *authentically* 'certain' of death, and yet it is certain of it. What are we to say about the 'certainty of death'?

To be certain of an entity means to *hold* it for true as something true.[19] But "truth" signifies the uncoveredness of some entity, and all uncoveredness is grounded ontologically in the most primordial truth, the disclosedness of Dasein. As an entity which is both disclosed and disclosing, and one which uncovers, Dasein is essentially 'in the truth.' *But certainty is grounded in the truth, or belongs to it equiprimordially.* The expression 'certainty,' like the term 'truth,' has a double signification. Primordially "truth" means the same as "Being-disclosive," as a way in which Dasein behaves. From this comes the derivative signification: "the uncoveredness of entities." Correspondingly, "certainty," in its primordial signification, is tantamount to "Being-certain," as a kind of Being which belongs to Dasein. However, in a derivative signification, any entity of which Dasein can be certain will also get called something 'certain.'

One mode of certainty is *conviction*. In conviction, Dasein lets the testimony of the thing itself which has been uncovered (the true thing itself) be the sole determinant for its Being towards that thing understandingly.[20] Holding something for true is adequate as a way of maintaining oneself in the truth, if it is grounded in the uncovered entity itself, and if, as Being towards the entity so uncovered, it has become transparent to itself as regards its appropriateness to that entity. In any arbitrary fiction or in merely having some 'view' ["Ansicht"] about an entity, this sort of thing is lacking.

The adequacy of holding-for-true is measured according to the truth-claim to which it belongs. Such a claim gets its justification from the kind of Being of the entity to be disclosed, and from the direction of the disclosure. The kind of truth, and along with it, the certainty, varies with the way entities differ, and accords with the guiding tendency and extent of the disclosure. Our present considerations will be restricted to an analysis of Being-certain with regard to death; and this Being-certain will in the end present us with a distinctive *certainty of Dasein*.

For the most part, everyday Dasein covers up the ownmost possibility of its Being—that possibility which is non-relational and not to be outstripped. This factical tendency to cover up confirms our thesis that Dasein, as factical, is in the 'untruth.' Therefore the certainty which belongs to such a covering-up of Being-towards-death must be an inappropriate way of holding-for-true, and not, for instance, an uncertainty in the sense of a doubting. In inappropriate certainty, that of which one is certain is held covered up. If 'one' understands death as an event which one encounters in one's environment, then the certainty which is related to such events does not pertain to Being-towards-the-end.

They say, "It is certain that 'Death' is coming."[21] *They say* it, and the "they" overlooks the fact that in order to be able to be certain of death, Dasein itself must in every case be certain of its ownmost non-relational potentiality-for-Being. They say, "Death is certain;" and in saying so, they implant in Dasein the illusion that it is *itself* certain of its death. And what is the ground of everyday Being-certain? Manifestly, it is not just mutual persuasion. Yet the 'dying' of Others is something that one experiences daily. Death is an undeniable 'fact of experience.'

The way in which everyday Being-towards-death understands the certainty which is thus grounded, betrays itself when it tries to 'think' about death, even when it does so with critical foresight—that is to say, in an appropriate manner. So far as one knows, all men 'die.' Death is probable in the highest degree for every man, yet it is not 'unconditionally' certain. Taken strictly, a certainty which is 'only' *empirical* may be attributed to death. Such certainty necessarily falls short of the highest certainty, the apodictic, which we reach in certain domains of theoretical knowledge.

In this 'critical' determination of the certainty of death, and of its impendence, what is manifested in the first instance is, once again, a failure to recognize Dasein's kind of Being and the Being-towards-death which belongs to Dasein—a failure that is characteristic of everydayness. *The fact that demise, as an event which occurs, is 'only' empirically certain, is in no way decisive as to the certainty of death.* Cases of death may be the factical occasion for Dasein's first paying attention to death at all. So long, however, as Dasein remains in the empirical certainty which we have mentioned, death, in the way that it 'is,' is something of which Dasein can by no means become certain. Even though, in the publicness of the "they," Dasein seems to 'talk' only of this 'empirical' certainty of death, *nevertheless at bottom* Dasein does *not* exclusively or primarily stick to those cases of death which merely occur. *In evading its death*, even everyday Being-towards-the-end is indeed certain of its death in another way than it might itself like to have true on purely theoretical considerations. This 'other way' is what everydayness for the most part veils from itself. Everydayness does not dare to let itself become transparent in such a manner. We have already characterized the every-day state-of-mind which consists in an air of superiority with regard to the certain 'fact' of death—a superiority which is 'anxiously' concerned while seemingly free from anxiety. In this state-of-mind, everydayness acknowledges a 'higher' certainty than one which is only empirical. One *knows* about the certainty of death, and yet 'is' not authentically certain of one's own. The falling everydayness of Dasein is acquainted with death's certainty, and yet evades *Being*-certain. But in the light of what it evades, this very evasion attests phenomenally that death must be conceived as one's ownmost possibility, non-relational, not to be outstripped, and—above all—*certain*.

One says, "Death certainly comes, but not right away." With this 'but . . .,' the "they" denies that death is certain. 'Not right away' is not a purely negative assertion, but a way in which the "they" interprets itself. With this interpretation, the "they" refers itself to that which is proximally accessible to Dasein and amenable to its concern. Everydayness forces its way into the urgency of concern, and divests itself of the fetters of a weary 'inactive thinking about death.' Death is deferred to 'sometime later,' and this is done by invoking the so-called 'general opinion' ["*allgemeine Ermessen*"]. Thus the "they" covers up what is peculiar in death's certainty—*that it is possible at any moment*. Along with the certainty of death goes the *indefiniteness* of its "when." Everyday Being-towards-death evades this indefiniteness by conferring definiteness upon it. But such a procedure cannot signify calculating when the demise is due to arrive. In the face of definiteness such as this, Dasein would sooner flee. Everyday concern makes definite for itself the indefiniteness of certain death by interposing before it those urgencies and possibilities which can be taken in at a glance, and which belong to the everyday matters that are closest to us.

But when this indefiniteness has been covered up, the certainty has been covered up too. Thus death's ownmost character as a possibility gets veiled—a possibility which is certain and at the same time indefinite—that is to say, possible at any moment.

Now that we have completed our Interpretation of the everyday manner in which the "they" talks about death and the way death enters into Dasein, we have been led to the characters of certainty and indefiniteness. The full existential-ontological conception of death may now be defined as follows: *death, as the end of Dasein, is Dasein's ownmost possibility—to non-relational, certain and as such indefinite, not to be outstripped. Death is,* as *Dasein's* end, in the Being of this entity *towards* its end.

Defining the existential structure of Being-towards-the-end helps us to work out a kind of Being of Dasein in which Dasein, *as Dasein,* can be a *whole.* The fact that even everyday Dasein already is *towards* its end—that is to say, is constantly coming to grips with its death, though in a 'fugitive' manner—shows that this end, conclusive [*abschliessende*] and determinative for Being-a-whole, is not something to which Dasein ultimately comes only in its demise. In Dasein, as being towards its death, its own uttermost "not-yet" has already been included—that "not-yet" which all others lie ahead of.[22] So if one has given an ontologically inappropriate Interpretation of Dasein's "not-yet" as something still outstanding, any formal inference from this to Dasein's lack of totality will not be correct. *The phenomenon of the "not-yet" has been taken over from the "ahead-of-itself;" no more than the care-structure in general, can it serve as a higher court which would rule against the possibility of an existent Being-a-whole; indeed this "ahead-of-itself" is what first of all makes such a Being-towards-the-end possible.* The problem of the possible Being-a-whole of that entity which each of us is, is a correct one if care, as Dasein's basic state, is 'connected' with death—the uttermost possibility for that entity.

Meanwhile, it remains questionable whether this problem has been as yet adequately worked out. Being-towards-death is grounded in care. Dasein, as thrown Being-in-the-world, has in every case already been delivered over to its death. In being towards its death, Dasein is dying factically and indeed constantly, as long as it has not yet come to its demise. When we say that Dasein is factically dying, we are saying at the same time that in its Being-towards-death Dasein has always decided itself in one way or another. Our everyday falling evasion *in the face of* death is an *inauthentic* Being-*towards*-death. But inauthenticity is based on the possibility of authenticity. Inauthenticity characterizes a kind of Being into which Dasein can divert itself and has for the most part always diverted itself, but Dasein does not necessarily and constantly have to divert itself into this kind of Being. Because Dasein exists, it determines its own character as the kind of entity it is, and it does so in every case in terms of a possibility which it itself is and which it understands.[23]

Can Dasein also *understand authentically* its ownmost possibility, which is non-relational and not to be outstripped, which is certain and, as such, indefinite? That is, can Dasein maintain itself in an authentic Being-towards-its-end? As long as this authentic Being-towards-death has not been set forth and ontologically defined, there is something essentially lacking in our existential Interpretation of Being-towards-the-end.

Authentic Being-towards-death signifies an existentiell possibility of Dasein. This ontical potentiality-for-Being must, in turn, be ontologically possible. What are the existential conditions of this possibility? How are they themselves to become accessible?

◢ Existential Projection of an Authentic Being-towards-death

Factically, Dasein maintains itself proximally and for the most part in an inauthentic Being-towards-death. How is the ontological possibility of an *authentic* Being-towards-death to be characterized 'Objectively,' if, in the end, Dasein never comports itself authentically towards its end, or if, in accordance with its very meaning, this authentic Being must remain hidden from the Others? Is it not a fanciful undertaking, to project the existential possibility of so questionable an existentiell potentiality-for-Being? What is needed, if such a projection is to go beyond a merely fictitious arbitrary construction? Does Dasein itself give us any instructions for carrying it out? And can any grounds for its phenomenal legitimacy be taken from Dasein itself? Can our analysis of Dasein up to this point give us any prescriptions for the ontological task we have now set ourselves, so that what we have before us may be kept on a road of which we can be sure?

The existential conception of death has been established; and therewith we have also established what it is that an authentic Being-towards-the-end should be able to comport itself towards. We have also characterized inauthentic Being-towards-death, and thus we have prescribed in a negative way [*prohibitiv*] how it is possible for authentic Being-towards-death *not* to be. It is with these positive and prohibitive instructions that the existential edifice of an authentic Being-towards-death must let itself be projected.

Dasein is constituted by disclosedness—that is, by an understanding with a state-of-mind. *Authentic* Being-towards-death can *not evade* its ownmost non-relational possibility, or *cover up* this possibility by thus fleeing from it, or *give a new explanation* for it to accord with the common sense of the "they." In our existential projection of an authentic Being-towards-death, therefore, we must set forth those items in such a Being which are constitutive for it as an understanding of death—and as such an understanding in the sense of Being towards this possibility without either fleeing it or covering it up.

In the first instance, we must characterize Being-towards-death as a *Being towards a possibility*—indeed, towards a distinctive possibility of Dasein itself. "Being towards" a possibility—that is to say, towards something possible—may signify "Being out for" something possible, as in concerning ourselves with its actualization. Such possibilities are constantly encountered in the field of what is ready-to-hand and present-at-hand—what is attainable, controllable, practicable, and the like. In concernfully Being out for something possible, there is a tendency to *annihilate the possibility* of the possible by making it available to us. But the concernful actualization of equipment which is ready-to-hand (as in producing it, getting it ready, readjusting it, and so on) is always merely relative, since even that which has been actualized is still characterized in terms of some involvements—indeed this is precisely what characterizes its Being. Even though actualized, it remains, as actual, something possible for doing something; it is characterized by an "in-order-to." What our analysis is to make plain is simply how Being out for something concernfully, comports itself towards the possible: it does so not by the theoretico-thematical consideration of the possible as possible, and by having regard for its possibility as such, but rather by looking *circumspectively away* from the possible and looking at that for which it is possible [*das Wofür-möglich*].

Manifestly Being-towards-death, which is now in question, cannot have the character of concernfully Being out to get itself actualized. For one thing, death as possible is not something possible which is ready-to-hand or present-at-hand, but a possibility of *Dasein's* Being.

So to concern oneself with actualizing what is thus possible would have to signify, "bringing about one's demise." But if this were done, Dasein would deprive itself of the very ground for an existing Being-towards-death.

Thus, if by "Being towards death" we do not have in view an 'actualizing' of death, neither can we mean "dwelling upon the end in its possibility." This is the way one comports oneself when one 'thinks about death,' pondering over when and how this possibility may perhaps be actualized. Of course such brooding over death does not fully take away from it its character as a possibility. Indeed, it always gets brooded over as something that is coming; but in such brooding we weaken it by calculating how we are to have it at our disposal. As something possible, it is to show as little as possible of its possibility. On the other hand, if Being-towards-death has to disclose understandingly the possibility which we have characterized, and if it is to disclose it *as a possibility,* then in such Being-towards-death this possibility must not be weakened: it must be understood *as a possibility,* it must be cultivated *as a possibility,* and we must *put up with* it *as a possibility,* in the way we comport ourselves towards it.

However, Dasein comports itself towards something possible in its possibility by *expecting* it [im *Erwarten*]. Anyone who is intent on something possible, may encounter it unimpeded and undiminished in its 'whether it comes or does not, or whether it comes after all.'[24] But with this phenomenon of expecting, has not our analysis reached the same kind of Being towards the possible to which we have already called attention in our description of "Being out for something" concernfully? To expect something possible is always to understand it and to 'have' it with regard to whether and when and how it will be actually present-at-hand. Expecting is not just an occasional looking-away from the possible to its possible actualization, but is essentially a *waiting for that actualization* [ein *Warten auf diese*]. Even in expecting, one leaps away from the possible and gets a foothold in the actual. It is for its actuality that what is expected is expected. By the very nature of expecting, the possible is drawn into the actual, arising out of the actual and returning to it.[25]

But Being towards this possibility, as Being-towards-death, is so to comport ourselves towards *death* that in this Being, and for it, death reveals itself *as a possibility.* Our terminology for such Being towards this possibility is *"anticipation" of this possibility.*[26] But in this way of behaving does there not lurk a coming-close to the possible, and when one is close to the possible, does not its actualization emerge? In this kind of coming close, however, one does not tend towards concernfully making available something actual; but as one comes closer understandingly, the possibility of the possible just becomes 'greater.' *The closest closeness which one may have in Being towards death as a possibility, is as far as possible from anything actual.* The more unveiledly this possibility gets understood, the more purely does the understanding penetrate into it *as the possibility of the impossibility of any existence at all.* Death, as possibility, gives Dasein nothing to be 'actualized,' nothing which Dasein, as actual, could itself *be.* It is the possibility of the impossibility of every way of comporting oneself towards anything, of every way of existing. In the anticipation of this possibility it becomes 'greater and greater;' that is to say, the possibility reveals itself to be such that it knows no measure at all, no more or less, but signifies the possibility of the measureless impossibility of existence. In accordance with its essence, this possibility offers no support for becoming intent on something, 'picturing' to oneself the actuality which is possible, and so forgetting its possibility. Being-towards-death, as anticipation of possibility, is what first *makes* this possibility *possible,* and sets it free as possibility.

Being-towards-death is the anticipation of a potentiality-for-Being of that entity whose kind of Being is anticipation itself.[27] In the anticipatory revealing of this potentiality-for-Being, Dasein discloses itself to itself as regards its uttermost possibility. But to project itself on its ownmost potentiality-for-Being means to be able to understand itself in the Being of the entity so revealed—namely, to exist. Anticipation turns out to be the possibility of understanding one's *ownmost* and uttermost potentiality-for-Being—that is to say, the possibility of *authentic existence*. The ontological constitution of such existence must be made visible by setting forth the concrete structure of anticipation of death. How are we to delimit this structure phenomenally? Manifestly, we must do so by determining those characteristics which must belong to an anticipatory disclosure so that it can become the pure understanding of that ownmost possibility which is non-relational and not to be outstripped—which is certain and, as such, indefinite. It must be noted that understanding does not primarily mean just gazing at a meaning, but rather understanding oneself in that potentiality-for-Being which reveals itself in projection.

Death is Dasein's *ownmost* possibility. Being towards this possibility discloses to Dasein its *ownmost* potentiality-for-Being, in which its very Being is the issue. Here it can become manifest to Dasein that in this distinctive possibility of its own self, it has been wrenched away from the "they." This means that in anticipation any Dasein can have wrenched itself away, from the "they" already. But when one understands that this is something which Dasein 'can' have done, this only reveals its factical lostness in the everydayness of the they-self.

The ownmost possibility is *non-relational*. Anticipation allows Dasein to understand that that potentiality-for-being in which its ownmost Being is an issue, must be taken over by Dasein alone. Death does not just 'belong' to one's own Dasein in an undifferentiated way; death *lays claim* to it as an *individual* Dasein. The non-relational character of death, as understood in anticipation, individualizes Dasein down to itself. This individualizing is a way in which the 'there' is disclosed for existence. It makes manifest that all Being-alongside the things with which we concern ourselves, and all Being-with Others, will fail us when our ownmost potentiality-for-Being is the issue. Dasein can be *authentically itself* only if it makes this possible for itself of its own accord. But if concern and solicitude fail us, this does not signify at all that these ways of Dasein have been cut off from its authentically Being-its-Self. As structures essential to Dasein's constitution, these have a share in conditioning the possibility of any existence whatsoever. Dasein is authentically itself only to the extent that, as concernful Being-alongside and solicitous Being-with, it projects itself upon its ownmost potentiality-for-Being rather than upon the possibility of the they-self. The entity which anticipates its non-relational possibility, is thus forced by that very anticipation into the possibility of taking over from itself its ownmost Being, and doing so of its own accord.

The ownmost, non-relational possibility is *not to be outstripped*. Being towards this possibility enables Dasein to understand that giving itself up impends for it as the uttermost possibility of its existence. Anticipation, however, unlike inauthentic Being-towards-death, does not evade the fact that death is not to be outstripped; instead, anticipation frees itself *for* accepting this. When, by anticipation, one becomes free *for* one's own death, one is liberated from one's lostness in those possibilities which may accidentally thrust themselves upon one; and one is liberated in such a way that for the first time one can authentically understand and choose among the factical possibilities lying ahead of that possibility which is not to be outstripped.[28] Anticipation discloses to existence that its uttermost possibility lies in giving itself up, and

The question of Dasein's authentic Being-a-whole and of its existential constitution still hangs in mid-air. It can be put on a phenomenal basis *which will* stand the test only if it can cling to a possible authenticity of its Being *which is* attested by Dasein itself. If we succeed in uncovering that attestation phenomenologically, together with what it attests, then the problem will arise anew as to *whether the anticipation of [zum] death, which we have hitherto projected only in its* **ontological** *possibility, has an essential connection with that authentic potentiality-for-Being which has been* **attested.**

Notes

1. '...das Ganze eines Begründungszusammenhanges wahrer Sätze...' See H. 357 below.
2. 'Zu dieser Seinsverfassung des Daseins gehört aber dann, dass es in seinem Sein zu diesem Sein ein Seinsverhältnis hat.' This passage is ambiguous and might also be read as" '...and this implies that Dasein, in its Being towards this Being, has a relationship of Being.'
3. '...dass es ontologisch *ist*.' As 'ontologisch' may be either an adjective or an adverb, we might also write: '...that it *is* ontologically.' A similar ambiguity occurs in the two following sentences, where we read "Ontologisch-sein' and 'ontisch-seiend' respectively.
4. '...das es je sein Sein als seiniges zu sein hat...'
5. We shall translate 'existenziell' by 'existentiell,' and 'existenzial' by 'existential.' There seems to be little reason for resorting to the more elaborate neologisms proposed by other writers.
6. '...sondern eher ein *Bevorstand*.' While we shall ordinarily use various forms of 'impend' to translate 'Bevorstand,' 'bevorstehen,' etc., one must bear in mind that the literal meaning of these expressions is one of 'standing before,' so that they may be quite plausibly contrasted with 'Ausstehen,' etc. ('standing out'). Thus we shall occasionally use forms of 'stand before' when this connotation seems to be dominant.
7. 'Nicht-mehr-dasein-könnens.' Notice that the expressions 'Seinkönnen' (our 'potentiality-for-Being') and 'Nichtmehrdasein' (our 'no-longer-Dasein') are here fused. Cf. H. 237-242.
8. 'So sich bevorstehend sind in ihm alle Bezüge zu anderem Dasein gelöst.'
9. 'unbezügliche.' This term appears frequently throughout the chapter, and, as the present passage makes clear, indicates that in death Dasein is cut off from relations with others. The term has accordingly been translated as 'non-relational,' in the sense of 'devoid of relationships.'
10. '...gegen ein "Erleben" des Ablebens.' (Cf. Section 49 above.)
11. '...dann muss es auch—wenngleich zunächst uneigentlich—in der Alltäglichkeit aufweisbar sein.' The earlier editions have another 'auch' just before 'in der Alltäglichkeit.'
12. '...das sich in der öffentlichen Ausgelegtheit konstituiert, die sich im Gerede ausspricht.' The earlier editions have '...konstituiert. Sie spricht sich aus im Gerede.'
13. 'Die Öffentlichkeit des alltäglichen Miteinander "kennt" den Tod als ständig vorkommendes Begegnis, als "Todesfall."'
14. '...man stirbt am Ende auch einmal, aber zunächst bleibt man selbst unbetroffen.'
15. 'Die öffentliche Daseinsauslegung sagt: "man stirbt," weil damit jeder andere und man selbst sich einreden kann: je nicht gerade ich; denn dieses Man ist das *Niemand*.' While we have usually followed the convention of translating the indefinite pronoun 'man' as 'one' and the expression 'das Man' as 'the "they,"' to do so here would obscure the point.
16. 'Und selbst im Falle des Ablebens noch soll die Öffentlichkeit durch das Ereignis nicht in ihrer besorgten Sorglosigkeit gestört und beunruhigt werden.'

17. '...wenn auch nur im Modus des Besorgens einer unbehelligten Gleichgültigkeit **gegen** die äusserste Möglichkeit seiner Existenz.' Ordinarily the expression 'Gleichgültigkeit gegen' means simply 'indifference towards.' But Heidegger's use of boldface type suggests that here he also has in mind that 'gegen' may mean 'against' or 'in opposition to.'

18. '...man stirbt auch einmal, aber vorläufig noch nicht.'

19. 'Eines Seienden gewiss-sein besagt: es als wahres für wahr *halten*.' The earlier editions have "Gewisssein" instead of 'gewiss-sein.' Our literal but rather unidiomatic translation of the phrase 'fur wahr halten' seems desirable in view of Heidegger's extensive use of the verb 'halten' ('hold') in subsequent passages where this phrase occurs, though this is obscured by our translating 'halten sich in...' as 'maintain itself in...' and 'halten sich an...' as 'cling to...' or 'stick to....'

20. 'In ihr lässt sich das Dasein einzig durch das Zeugnis der entdeckten (wahre) Sache selbst sein verstehendes Sein zu dieser bestimmen.' The connection between 'Uberzeugung' ('conviction') and 'Zeugnis' (testimony) is obscured in our translation.

21. 'Man sagt: es ist gewiss, dass "der" Tod kommt.'

22. '...dem alle anderen vorgelagert sind...' This clause is ambiguous, both in the German and in our translation, though the point is fairly clear. The ultimate 'not-yet' is not one which all others 'lie ahead of' in the sense that they lie beyond it or come after it; for nothing can 'lie ahead of it' in this sense. But they *can* 'lie ahead of it' in the sense that they might be actualized *before* the ultimate 'not-yet' has been actualized. (Contrast this passage with H. 302, where the same participle 'vorgelagert' is apparently applied in the *former* sense to death itself.)

23. 'Weil das Dasein existiert, bestimmt es sich als Seiendes, wie es ist, je aus einer Möglichkeit, die es selbst *ist* und versteht.'

24. 'Für ein Gespanntsein auf es vermag ein Mögliches in seinem "ob oder nicht oder schliesslich doch" ungehindert und ungeschmälert zu begegnen.'

25. 'Auch im Erwarten liegt ein Abspringen vom Möglichen und Fussfassen im Wirklichen, dafür das Erwartete erwartet ist. Vom Wirklichen aus und auf es zu wird das Mögliche in das Wirkliche erwartungsmässig hereingezogen.'

26. '...*Vorlaufen in die Möglichkeit.*' While we have used 'anticipate' to translate 'vorgreifen,' which occurs rather seldom, we shall also use it—less literally—to translate 'vorlaufen,' which appears very often in the following pages, and which has the special connotation of 'running ahead.' But as Heidegger's remarks have indicated, the kind of 'anticipation' which is involved in Being-towards-death, does not consist in 'waiting for' death or 'dwelling upon it' or 'actualizing' it before it normally comes; nor does 'running ahead into it' in this sense mean that we 'rush headlong into it.'

27. '...dessen Seinsart das Vorlaufen selbst ist.' The earlier editions have 'hat' instead of 'ist.'

28. '...die der unüberholbaren vorgelagert sind.' See note I, p. 303, H. 259 above.

29. 'Die gewisse Möglichkeit des Todes erschliesst das Dasein aber als Möglichkeit nur so, dass es vorlaufend zu ihr diese Möglichkeit als eigenstes Seinkönnen für sich *ermöglicht*.' While we have taken 'Die gewisse Möglichkeit des Todes' as the subject of this puzzling sentence, 'das Dasein' *may* be the subject instead. The use of the preposition 'zu' instead of the usual 'in' after 'vorlaufend' suggests that in 'anticipating' the possibility of death, Dasein is here thought of as 'running ahead' *towards* it or *up to* it rather than *into* it. When this construction occurs in later passages, we shall indicate it by subjoining 'zu' in brackets.

30. '*Die Befindlichkeit aber, welche die ständige und schlechthinnige, aus dem eigensten vereinzelten Sein des Dasiens aufsteigende Bedrohung seiner selbst offen zu halten vermag, ist die Angst.*' Notice that '*welche*' may be construed either as the subject or the direct object of the relative clause.

31. '...gehört zu diesem Sichverstehen des Daseins aus seinem Grunde die Grundbefindlichkeit der Angst.' It is not grammatically clear whether 'seinem' refers to "Sichverstehen" or to 'Daseins.'

Suggested Readings

Grene, Majorie. *Martin Heidegger.* New York: Hillary House, 1957.

Kockelman, J. A. *Heidegger: A First Introduction to His Philosophy.* Trans. T. Schrynemakers. Pittsburgh: Duquesne University Press, 1965.

Mehta, J. L. *Martin Heidegger: The Way and the Vision.* Honolulu: University Press, 1976.

Chapter **22**

Death

Thomas Nagel

Thomas Nagel (1937-   ) currently teaches at Princeton University and has written extensively on moral issues. The following selection is an example of a more analytic and argumentative approach to the question of whether death is an evil. Nagel thinks that since death deprives us of something desirable, it is definitely not a good thing.

> *The syllogism he had learnt from Kiesewetter's logic: "Caius is a man, men are mortal, therefore Caius is mortal," had always seemed to him correct as applied to Caius, but certainly not as applied to himself.... What did Caius know of the smell of that striped leather ball Vanya had been so fond of?*
>
> TOLSTOY, *THE DEATH OF IVAN ILYICH*

If, as many people believe, death is the unequivocal and permanent end of our existence, the question arises whether it is a bad thing to die. There is conspicuous disagreement about the matter: some people think death is dreadful; others have no objection to death *per se,* though they hope their own will be neither premature nor painful.

Those in the former category tend to think that those in the latter are blind to the obvious, while the latter suppose the former to be prey to some sort of confusion. On the one hand it can be said that life is all one has, and the loss of it is the greatest loss one can sustain. On the other hand it may be objected that death deprives this supposed loss of its subject, and that if one realizes that death is not an unimaginable condition of the persisting person, but a mere blank, one will see that it can have no value whatever, positive or negative.

Since I want to leave aside the question whether we are, or might be, immortal in some form, I shall simply use the word "death" and its cognates in this discussion to mean *permanent* death, unsupplemented by any form of conscious survival. I wish to consider whether death is in itself an evil; and how great an evil, and of what kind, it might be. This question should be of interest even to those who believe that we do not die permanently, for one's attitude toward immortality must depend in part on one's attitude toward death.

Clearly if death is an evil at all, it cannot be because of its positive features, but only because of what it deprives us of. I shall try to deal with the difficulties surrounding the natural view that death is an evil because it brings to an end all the goods that life contains.[1] An account of these goods need not occupy us here, except to observe that some of them, like perception, desire, activity, and thought, are so general as to be constitutive of human life. They are widely regarded as formidable benefits in themselves, despite the fact that they are conditions of misery as well as of happiness, and that a sufficient quantity of more particular evils can perhaps outweigh them. That is what is meant, I think, by the allegation that it is good simply to be alive, even if one is undergoing terrible experiences. The situation is roughly this: There are elements which, if added to one's experience, make life better; there are other elements which, if added to one's experience, make life worse. But what remains when these are set aside is not merely *neutral*: it is emphatically positive. Therefore life is worth living even when the bad elements of experience are plentiful, and the good ones too meager to outweigh the bad ones on their own. The additional positive weight is supplied by experience itself, rather than by any of its contents.

I shall not discuss the value that one person's life or death may have for others, or its objective value, but only the value it has for the person who is its subject. That seems to me the primary case, and the case which presents the greatest difficulties. Let me add only two observations. First, the value of life and its contents does not attach to mere organic survival: almost everyone would be indifferent (other things equal) between immediate death and immediate coma followed by death twenty years later without reawakening. And second, like most goods, this can be multiplied by time: more is better than less. The added quantities need not be temporarily continuous (though continuity has its social advantages). People are attracted to the possibility of long-term suspended animation or freezing, followed by the resumption of conscious life, because they can regard it from within simply as a *continuation* of their present life. If these techniques are ever perfected, what from outside appeared as a dormant interval of three hundred years could be experienced by the subject as nothing more than a sharp discontinuity in the character of his experiences. I do not deny, of course, that this has its own disadvantages. Family and friends may have died in the meantime; the language may have changed; the comforts of social, geographical, and cultural familiarity would be lacking. Nevertheless these inconveniences would not obliterate the basic advantage of continued, though discontinuous, existence.

If we turn from what is good about life to what is bad about death, the case is completely different. Essentially, though there may be problems about their specification, what we find desirable in life are certain states, conditions, or types of activity. It is *being* alive, *doing* certain things, having certain experiences, that we consider good. But if death is an evil, it is the *loss of life*, rather than the state of being dead, or nonexistent, or unconscious, that is objectionable.[2] This asymmetry is important. If it is good to be alive, that advantage can be attributed to a person at each point of his life. It is a good of which Bach had more than Schubert, simply because he lived longer. Death, however, is not an evil of which Shakespeare has so far received a larger portion than Proust. If death is a disadvantage, it is not easy to say when a man suffers it.

There are two other indications that we do not object to death merely because it involves long periods of nonexistence. First, as has been mentioned, most of us would not regard the *temporary* suspension of life, even for substantial intervals, as in itself a misfortune. If it develops that people can be frozen without reduction of the conscious lifespan, it will be inappropriate to pity those who are temporarily out of circulation. Second, none of us existed before we were born (or conceived), but few regard that as a misfortune. I shall have more to say about this later.

The point that death is not regarded as an unfortunate *state* enables us to refute a curious but very common suggestion about the origin of the fear of death. It is often said that those who object to death have made the mistake of trying to imagine what it is like to *be* dead. It is alleged that the failure to realize that this task is logically impossible (for the banal reason that there is nothing to imagine) leads to the conviction that death is a mysterious and therefore terrifying prospective *state*. But this diagnosis is evidently false, for it is just as impossible to imagine being totally unconscious as to imagine being dead (though it is easy enough to imagine oneself, from the outside, in either of those conditions). Yet people who are averse to death are not usually averse to unconsciousness (so long as it does not entail a substantial cut in the total duration of waking life).

If we are to make sense of the view that to die is bad, it must be on the ground that life is a good and death is the corresponding deprivation or loss, bad not because of any positive features but because of the desirability of what it removes. We must now turn to the serious difficulties which this hypothesis raises, difficulties about loss and privation in general, and about death in particular.

Essentially, there are three types of problem. First, doubt may be raised whether *anything* can be bad for a man without being positively unpleasant to him: specifically, it may be doubted that there are any evils which consist merely in the deprivation or absence of possible goods, and which do not depend on someone's *minding* that deprivation. Second, there are special difficulties, in the case of death, about how the supposed misfortune is to be assigned to a subject at all. There is doubt both as to *who* its subject is, and as to *when* he undergoes it. So long as a person exists, he has not yet died, and once he has died, he no longer exists; so there seems to be no time when death, if it is a misfortune, can be ascribed to its unfortunate subject. The third type of difficulty concerns the asymmetry, mentioned above, between our attitudes to posthumous and prenatal nonexistence. How can the former be bad if the latter is not?

It should be recognized that if these are valid objections to counting death as an evil, they will apply to many other supposed evils as well. The first type of objection is expressed in general form by the common remark that what you don't know can't hurt you. It means that even if a man is betrayed by his friends, ridiculed behind his back, and despised by people who treat him politely to his face, none of it can be counted as a misfortune for him so long as he does not suffer as a result. It means that a man is not injured if his wishes are ignored by the executor of his will, or if, after death, the belief becomes current that all the literary works on which his fame rests were really written by his brother, who died in Mexico at the age of 28. It seems to me worth asking what assumptions about good and evil lead to these drastic restrictions.

All the questions have something to do with time. There certainly are goods and evils of a simple kind (including some pleasures and pains) which a person possesses at a given time simply in virtue of his condition at that time. But this is not true of all the things we regard as good or bad for a man. Often we need to know his history to tell whether something is a misfortune or not; this applies to ills like deterioration, deprivation, and damage. Sometimes his experimental *state* is relatively unimportant—as in the case of a man who wastes his life in the cheerful pursuit of a method of communicating with asparagus plants. Someone who holds that all goods and evils must be temporarily assignable states of the person may of course try to bring difficult cases into line by pointing to the pleasure or pain that more complicated goods and evils cause. Loss, betrayal, deception, and ridicule are on this view bad because people suffer when they learn of them. But it should be asked how our ideas of human value would have to be constituted to accommodate these cases directly instead. One advantage of such an account might be that it would enable us to explain *why* the discovery of these misfortunes causes suffering—in a way that makes it reasonable. For the natural view is that the discovery of betrayal makes us unhappy because it is bad to be betrayed—not that betrayal is bad because its discovery makes us unhappy.

It therefore seems to me worth exploring the position that most good and ill fortune has as its subject a person identified by his history and his possibilities, rather than merely by his categorical state of the moment—and that while this subject can be exactly located in a sequence of places and times, the same is not necessarily true of the goods and ills that befall him.[3]

These ideas can be illustrated by an example of deprivation whose severity approaches that of death. Suppose an intelligent person receives a brain injury that reduces him to the mental condition of a contented infant, and that such desires as remain to him can be satisfied by a custodian, so that he is free from care. Such a development would be widely regarded as a severe misfortune, not only for his friends and relations, or for society, but also, and primarily, for the person himself. This does not mean that a contented infant is unfortunate. The intelligent adult who has been *reduced* to this condition is the subject of the misfortune. He is the one we pity, though of course he does not mind his condition—there is some doubt, in fact, whether he can be said to exist any longer.

The view that such a man has suffered a misfortune is open to the same objections which have been raised in regard to death. He does not mind his condition. It is in fact the same condition he was in at the age of three months, except that he is bigger. If we did not pity him then, why pity him now; in any case, who is there to pity? The intelligent adult has disappeared, and for a creature like the one before us, happiness consists in a full stomach and a dry diaper.

If these objections are invalid, it must be because they rest on a mistaken assumption about the temporal relation between the subject of a misfortune and the circumstances which constitute it. If, instead of concentrating exclusively on the oversized baby before us, we consider the person he was, and the person he *could* be now, then his reduction to this state and the cancellation of his natural adult development constitute a perfectly intelligible catastrophe.

This case should convince us that it is arbitrary to restrict the goods and evils that can befall a man to nonrelational properties ascribable to him at particular times. As it stands, that restriction excludes not only such cases of gross degeneration, but also a good deal of what is important about success and failure, and other features of a life that have the character of processes. I believe that we can go further, however. There are goods and evils which are irreducibly relational; they are features of the relations between a person, with spatial and temporal boundaries of the usual sort, and circumstances which may not coincide with him either in space or in time. A man's life includes much that does not take place within the boundaries of his body and his mind, and what happens to him can include much that does not take place within the boundaries of his life. These boundaries are commonly crossed by the misfortunes of being deceived, or despised, or betrayed. (If this is correct, there is a simple account of what is wrong with breaking a deathbed promise. It is an injury to the dead man. For certain purposes it is possible to regard time as just another type of distance.) The case of mental degeneration shows us an evil that depends on a contrast between the reality and the possible alternatives. A man is the subject of good and evil as much because he has hopes which may or may not be fulfilled, or possibilities which may or may not be realized, as because of his capacity to suffer and enjoy. If death is an evil, it must be accounted for in these terms, and the impossibility of locating it within life should not trouble us.

When a man dies we are left with his corpse, and while a corpse can suffer the kind of mishap that may occur to an article of furniture, it is not a suitable object for pity. The man, however, is. He has lost his life, and if he had not died, he would have continued to live it, and to possess whatever good there is in living. If we apply to death the account suggested for the case of dementia, we shall say that although the spatial and temporal locations of the individual who suffered the loss are clear enough, the misfortune itself cannot be so easily located. One must be content just to state that his life is over and there will never be any more of it. That *fact*, rather than his past or present condition, constitutes his misfortune, if it is one. Nevertheless if there is a loss, someone must suffer it, and *he* must have existence and specific spatial and temporal location even if the loss itself does not. The fact that Beethoven had no children may have been a cause of regret to him, or a sad thing for the world, but it cannot be described as a misfortune for the children that he never had. All of us, I believe, are fortunate to have been born. But unless good and ill can be assigned to an embryo, or even to an unconnected pair of gametes, it cannot be said that not to be born is a misfortune. (That is a factor to be considered in deciding whether abortion and contraception are akin to murder.)

This approach also provides a solution to the problem of temporal asymmetry, pointed out by Lucretius. He observed that no one finds it disturbing to contemplate the eternity preceding his own birth, and he took this to show that it must be irrational to fear death, since death is simply the mirror image of the prior abyss. That is not true, however, and the difference between the two explains why it is reasonable to regard them differently. It is true that both the time before a man's birth and the time after his death are times when he does not exist. But the time after his death is time of which his death deprives him. It is time in which, had he not died then, he would be alive. Therefore any death entails the loss of *some* life that its victim would have led had he not died at that or any earlier point. We know perfectly well what it would be for him to have had it instead of losing it, and there is no difficulty in identifying the loser.

But we cannot say that the time prior to a man's birth is time in which he would have lived had he been born not then but earlier. For aside from the brief margin permitted by premature labor, he *could* not have been born earlier: anyone born substantially earlier than he was would have been someone else. Therefore the time prior to his birth is not time in which his subsequent birth prevents him from living. His birth, when it occurs, does not entail the loss to him of any life whatever.

The direction of time is crucial in assigning possibilities to people or other individuals. Distinct possible lives of a single person can diverge from a common beginning, but they cannot converge to a common conclusion from diverse beginnings. (The latter would represent not a set of different possible lives of one individual, but a set of distinct possible individuals, whose lives have identical conclusions.) Given an identifiable individual, countless possibilities for his continued existence are imaginable, and we can clearly conceive of what it would be for him to go on existing indefinitely. However inevitable it is that this will not come about, its possibility is still that of the continuation of a good for him, if life is the good we take it to be.[4]

We are left, therefore, with the question whether the nonrealization of this possibility is in every case a misfortune, or whether it depends on what can naturally be hoped for. This seems to me the most serious difficulty with the view that death is always an evil. Even if we can dispose of the objections against admitting misfortune that is not experienced, or cannot be assigned to a definite time in the person's life, we still have to set some limits on *how* possible a possibility must be for its nonrealization to be a misfortune (or good fortune, should the possibility be a bad one). The death of Keats at 24 is generally regarded as tragic; that of Tolstoy at 82 is not. Although they will both be dead forever, Keats's death deprived him of many years of life which were allowed to Tolstoy; so in a clear sense Keats's loss was greater (though not in the sense standardly employed in mathematical comparison between infinite quantities). However, this does not prove that Tolstoy's loss was insignificant. Perhaps we record an objection only to evils which are gratuitously added to the inevitable; the fact that it is worse to die at 24 than at 82 does not imply that it is not a terrible thing to die at 82, or even at 806. The question is whether we can regard as a misfortune any limitation, like mortality, that is normal to the species. Blindness or near-blindness is not a misfortune for a mole, nor would it be for a man, if that were the natural condition of the human race.

The trouble is that life familiarizes us with the goods of which death deprives us. We are already able to appreciate them, as a mole is not able to appreciate vision. If we put aside doubts about their status as goods and grant that their quantity is in part a function of their duration, the question remains whether death, no matter when it occurs, can be said to deprive its victim of what is in the relevant sense a possible continuation of life.

A man's sense of his own experience, on the other hand, does not embody this idea of a natural limit. His existence defines for him an essentially open-ended possible future, containing the usual mixture of goods and evils that he has found so tolerable in the past. Having been gratuitously introduced to the world by a collection of natural, historical, and social accidents, he finds himself the subject of a *life*, with an indeterminate and not essentially limited future. Viewed in this way, death, no matter how inevitable, is an abrupt cancellation of indefinitely extensive possible goods. Normality seems to have nothing to do with it, for the fact that we will all inevitably die in a few score years cannot by itself imply that it would not be good to live longer. Suppose that we were all inevitably going to die in *agony*—physical agony lasting six months. Would inevitability make *that* prospect any less unpleasant? And why should it be different for a deprivation? If the normal lifespan were a thousand years, death at 80 would be a tragedy. As things are, it may just be a more widespread tragedy. If there is no limit to the amount of life that it would be good to have, then it may be that a bad end is in store for us all.

Notes

1. As we shall see, this does not mean that it brings to an end all the goods that a man can possess.
2. It is sometimes suggested that what we really mind is the process of *dying*. But I should not really object to dying if it were not followed by death.
3. It is certainly not true in general of the things that can be said of him. For example, Abraham Lincoln was taller than Louis XIV. But when?
4. I confess to being troubled by the above argument, on the ground that it is too sophisticated to explain the simple difference between our attitudes to prenatal and posthumous nonexistence. For this reason I suspect that something essential is omitted from the account of the badness of death by an analysis which treats it as a deprivation of possibilities. My suspicion is supported by the following suggestion of Robert Nozick. We could imagine discovering that people developed from individual spores that had existed indefinitely far in advance of their birth. In this fantasy, birth never occurs naturally more than 100 years before the permanent end of the spore's existence. But then we discover a way to trigger the premature hatching of these spores, and people are born who have thousands of years of active life before them. Given such a situation, it would be possible to imagine *oneself* having come into existence thousands of years previously. If we put aside the question whether this would really be the same person, even given the identity of the spore, then the consequence appears to be that a person's birth at a given time *could* deprive him of many earlier years of possible life. Now while it would be cause for regret that one had been deprived of all those possible years of life by being born too late, the feeling would differ from that which many people have about death. I conclude that something about the future prospect of permanent nothingness is not captured by the analysis in terms of denied possibilities. If so, then Lucretius' argument still awaits an answer.

Suggested Readings

Fischer, John, (Ed). *The Metaphysics of Death.* Stanford University Press, 1993.

Nagel, Thomas. "Birth, Death and the Meaning of Life" in *The View From Nowhere.* Oxford: Oxford University Press, 1986.

Nagel, Thomas. "Mind-body Identity, a Side Issue?" in *The Mind-Brain Identity Theory: A Collection of Papers.* New York: St. Martin's Press, 1970.

Chapter 23

Reflections on the Tedium
of Immortality

Bernard Williams

Bernard Williams (1929-   ) taught at Cambridge University and is currently teaching at the University of California at Berkeley. He has written numerous books and articles on ethics and questions concerning the self. In the article selected below Williams argues that given what we know about human desires and happiness, too long a life, or worse, immortality, would not be desirable.

⚜ The Makropulos Case ⚜

This essay started life as a lecture in a series "on the immortality of the soul or kindred spiritual subject."[1] My kindred spiritual subject is, one might say, the mortality of the soul. Those among previous lecturers who were philosophers tended, I think, to discuss the question whether we are immortal; that is not my subject, but rather what a good thing it is that we are not. Immortality, or a state without death, would be meaningless, I shall suggest; so, in a sense, death gives the meaning to life. That does not mean that we should not fear death (whatever force that injunction might be taken to have, anyway). Indeed, there are several very different ways in which it could be true at once that death gave the meaning to life and that death was, other things being equal, something to be feared. Some existentialists, for instance, seem to have said that death was what gave meaning to life, if anything did, just because it was the fear of death that gave meaning to life; I shall not follow them. I shall rather pursue the idea that from facts about human desire and happiness and what a human life is, it follows both that immortality would be, where conceivable at all, intolerable, and that (other things being equal) death is reasonably regarded as an evil. Considering whether death can reasonably be regarded as an evil is in fact as near as I shall get to considering whether it should be feared: they are not quite the same question.

My title is that, as it is usually translated into English, of a play by Karel Capek which was made into an opera by Janáček and which tells of a woman called Elina Makropulos, *alias* Emilia Marty, *alias* Ellian Macgregor, *alias* a number of other women with the initials EM, on whom her father, the court physician to a sixteenth-century emperor, tried out an elixir of life. At the time of the action she is aged 342. Her unending life has come to a state of boredom, indifference, and coldness. Everything is joyless: "in the end it is the same," she says, "singing and silence." She refuses to take the elixir again; she dies, and the formula is deliberately destroyed by a young woman among the protests of some older men.

EM's state suggests at least this, that death is not necessarily an evil, and not just in the sense in which almost everybody would agree to that, where death provides an end to great suffering, but in the more intimate sense that it can be a good thing not to live too long. It suggests more than that, for it suggests that it was not a peculiarity of EM's that an endless life was meaningless. That is something I shall follow out later. First, though, we should put together the suggestion of EM's case, that death is not necessarily an evil, with the claim of some philosophies and religions that death is necessarily not an evil. Notoriously, there have been found two contrary bases on which that claim can be mounted: death is said by some not to be an evil because it is not the end, and by others, because it is. There is perhaps some profound temperamental difference between those who find consolation for the fact of death in the hope that it is only the start of another life, and those who equally find comfort in the conviction that it is the end of the only life there is. That both such temperaments exist means that those who find a diagnosis of the belief in immortality, and indeed a reproach to it, in the idea that it constitutes a consolation, have at best only a statistical fact to support them. While that may be just about enough for the diagnosis, it is not enough for the reproach.

Most famous, perhaps, among those who have found comfort in the second option, the prospect of annihilation, was Lucretius, who, in the steps of Epicurus, and probably from a personal fear of death which in some of his pages seems almost tangible, addresses himself to proving that death is never an evil. Lucretius has two basic arguments for this conclusion, and it is an important feature of them both that the conclusion they offer has the very strong consequence—and seems clearly intended to have the consequence—that, for oneself at least, it is all the same whenever one dies, that a long life is no better than a short one. That is to say, death is never an evil in the sense not merely that there is no-one for whom dying is an evil, but that there is no time at which dying is an evil—sooner or later, it is all the same.

The first argument (*De rerum natura,* 3.870ff., 898ff.) seeks to interpret the fear of death as a confusion, based on the idea that we shall be there after death to repine our loss of the *praemia vitae,* the rewards and delights of life, and to be upset at the spectacle of our bodies burned, and so forth. The fear of death, it is suggested, must necessarily be the fear of some experiences had when one is dead. But if death is annihilation, then there are no such experiences: in the Epicurean phrase, when death is there, we are not, and when we are there, death is not. So, death being annihilation, there is nothing to fear. The second argument (1091) addresses itself directly to the question of whether one dies earlier or later, and says that one will be the same time dead however early or late one dies, and therefore one might as well die earlier as later. And from both arguments we can conclude *nil igitur mors est ad nos, neque pertinet hilum*—death is nothing to us, and does not matter at all (830).

The second of these arguments seems even on the face of things to contradict the first. For it must imply that if there *were* a finite period of death, such that if you died later you would be dead for less time, then there *would* be some point in wanting to die later rather than earlier. But that implication makes sense, surely, only on the supposition that what is wrong with dying consists in something undesirable about the condition of being dead. And that is what is denied by the first argument.

More important than this, the oddness of the second argument can help to focus a difficulty already implicit in the first. The first argument, in locating the objection to dying in a confused objection to being dead, and exposing that in terms of a confusion with being alive, takes it as genuinely true of life that the satisfaction of desire, and possession of the *praemia vitae*, are good things. It is not irrational to be upset by the loss of home, children, possessions—what is irrational is to think of death as, in the relevant sense, *losing* anything. But now if we consider two lives, one very short and cut off before the *praemia* have been acquired, the other fully provided with the *praemia* and containing their enjoyment to a ripe age, it is very difficult to see why the second life, by these standards alone, is not to be thought better than the first. But if it is, then there must be something wrong with the argument which tries to show that there is nothing worse about a short life than a long one. The argument locates the mistake about dying in a mistake about consciousness, it being assumed that what commonsense thinks about the worth of the *praemia vitae* and the sadness of their (conscious) loss is sound enough. But if the *praemia vitae* are valuable—even if we include as necessary to that value consciousness that one possesses them—then surely getting to the point of possessing them is better than not getting to that point, longer enjoyment of them is better than shorter, and more of them, other things being equal, is better than less of them. But if so, then it just will not be true that to die earlier is all the same as to die later, nor that death is never an evil—and the thought that to die later is better than to die earlier will not be dependent on some muddle about thinking that the dead person will be alive to lament his loss. It will depend only on the idea, apparently sound, that if the *praemia vitae* and consciousness of them are good things, then longer consciousness of more *praemia* is better than shorter consciousness of fewer *praemia*.

Is the idea sound? A decent argument, surely, can be marshalled to support it. If I desire something, then, other things being equal, I prefer a state of affairs in which I get it to one in which I do not get it, and (again, other things being equal) plan for a future in which I get it rather than not. But one future, for sure, in which I would not get it would be one in which I was dead. To want something, we may also say, is to that extent to have reason for resisting what excludes having that thing: and death certainly does that, for a very large range of things that one wants.[2] If that is right, then for any of those things, wanting something itself gives one a reason for avoiding death. Even though, if I do not succeed, I will not know that, nor what I am missing, from the perspective of the wanting agent it is rational to aim for states of affairs in which his want is satisfied, and hence to regard death as something to be avoided; that is, to regard it as an evil.

It is admittedly true that many of the things I want, I want only on the assumption that I am going to be alive; and some people, for instance some of the old, desperately want certain things when nevertheless they would much rather that they and their wants were dead. It might be suggested that not just these special cases, but really all wants, were conditional on being alive; a situation in which one has ceased to exist is not to be compared with others with respect to desire-satisfaction—rather, if one dies, all bets are off. But surely the claim that all desires are in this sense conditional must be wrong. For consider the idea of a rational forward-looking calculation of suicide; there can be such a thing, even if many suicides are not rational, and even though with some that are, it may be unclear to what extent they are forward-looking (the obscurity of this with regard to suicides of honour is an obscurity in the notion of shame). In such a calculation, a man might consider what lay before him, and decide whether he did or did not want to undergo it. If he does decide to undergo it, then some desire propels him on into the future, and *that* desire at least is not one that operates conditionally on his being alive, since it itself resolves the question of whether he is going to be alive. He has an unconditional or (as I shall say) a *categorical* desire.

The man who seriously calculates about suicide and rejects it only just has such a desire, perhaps. But if one is in a state in which the question of suicide does not occur, or occurs only as total fantasy—if, to take just one example, one is happy—one has many such desires, which do not hang from the assumption of one's existence. If they did hang from that assumption, then they would be quite powerless to rule out that assumption's being questioned, or to answer the question if it is raised; but clearly they are not powerless in those directions—on the contrary they are some of the few things, perhaps the only things, that have power in that direction. Some ascetics have supposed that happiness required reducing one's desires to those necessary for one's existence, that is, to those that one has to have, granted that one exists at all; rather, it requires that some of one's desires should be fully categorical, and one's existence itself wanted as something necessary to them.

To suppose that one can in this way categorically want things implies a number of things about the nature of desire. It implies, for one thing, that the reason I have for bringing it about that I get what I want is not merely that of avoiding the unpleasantness of not getting what I want. But that must in any case be right—otherwise we should have to represent every desire as the desire to avoid its own frustration, which is absurd.

About what those categorical desires must be, there is not much of great generality to be said, if one is looking at the happy state of things: except, once more against the ascetic, that there should be not just enough, but more than enough. But the question might be raised, at the impoverished end of things, as to what the minimum categorical desire might be. Could it be *just* the desire to remain alive? The answer is perhaps "no." In saying that, I do not want to deny the existence, the value, or the basic necessity of a sheer reactive drive to self-preservation: humanity would certainly wither if the drive to keep alive were not stronger than any perceived reasons for keeping alive. But if the question is asked, and it is going to be answered calculatively, then the bare categorical desire to stay alive will not sustain the calculation—that desire itself, when things have got that far, has to be sustained or filled out by some desire for something else, even if it is only, at the margin, the desire that future desires of mine will be born and satisfied. But the best insight into the effect of categorical desire is not gained at the impoverished end of things, and hence in situations where the question has actually come up. The question of life being desirable is certainly transcendental in the most modest sense, in that it gets by far its best answer in never being asked at all.

None of this—including the thoughts of the calculative suicide—requires my reflection on a world in which I never occur at all. In the terms of "possible worlds" (which can admittedly be misleading), a man could, on the present account, have a reason from his own point of view to prefer a possible world in which he went on longer to one in which he went on for less long, or—like the suicide—the opposite; but he would have no reason of this kind to prefer a world in which he did not occur at all. Thoughts about his total absence from the world would have to be of a different kind, impersonal reflections on the value *for the world* of his presence or absence: of the same kind, essentially, as he could conduct (or, more probably, not manage to conduct) with regard to anyone else. While he can think egoistically of what it would be for him to live longer or less long, he cannot think egoistically of what it would be for him never to have existed at all. Hence the sombre words of Sophocles "Never to have been born counts highest of all..." (*Oedipus at Colonus* 1224ff.) are well met by the old Jewish reply—"how many are so lucky? Not one in ten thousand."

Lucretius' first argument has been interestingly criticised by Thomas Nagel on lines different from those that I have been following. Nagel claims that what is wrong with Lucretius' argument is that it rests on the assumption that nothing can be a misfortune for a man unless he knows about it, and that misfortunes must consist in something nasty *for* him. Against this assumption that nothing can be a misfortune for a man unless he knows about it, which would normally be thought to constitute a misfortune, though those to whom they happen are and remain ignorant of them (as, for instance, certain situations of betrayal). The difference between Nagel's approach and mine does not, of course, lie in the mere point of whether one admits misfortunes which do not consist of or involve nasty experiences: anyone who rejects Lucretius' argument must admit them. The difference is that the reasons which a man would have for avoiding death are, on the present account, grounded in desires—categorical desires—which he has; he, on the basis of these, has reason to regard possible death as a misfortune to be avoided, and we, looking at things from his point of view, would have reason to regard his actual death as his misfortune. Nagel, however, if I understand him, does not see the misfortune that befalls a man who dies as necessarily grounded in the issue of what desires or sorts of desires he had; just as in the betrayal case, it could be a misfortune for a man to be betrayed, even though he did not have any desire not to be betrayed. If this is a correct account, Nagel's reasoning is one step further away from Utilitarianism on this matter than mine,[3] and rests on an independent kind of value which a sufficiently Utilitarian person might just reject; while my argument cannot merely be rejected by a Utilitarian person, it seems to me, since he must if he is to be consistent, and other things being equal, attach disutility to any situation which he has good reason to prevent, and he certainly has good reason to prevent a situation which involves the non-satisfaction of his desires. Thus, granted categorical desires, death has a disutility for an agent, although that disutility does not, of course, consist in unsatisfactory experiences involved in its occurrence.

The question would remain, of course, with regard to any given agent, whether he had categorical desires. For the present argument, it will do to leave it as a contingent fact that most people do: for they will have a reason, and a perfectly coherent reason, to regard death as a misfortune, while it was Lucretius' claim that no-one could have a coherent reason for so regarding it. There may well be other reasons as well; thus Nagel's reasoning, though different from the more Utilitarian type of reason I have used against Lucretius, seems compatible with it and there are strong reasons to adopt his kind of consideration as well. In fact, further and deeper thought about this question seems likely to fill up the apparent gap between the two sorts of arguments; it is hard to believe, for one thing, that the supposed contingent fact that people have categorical desires can really be as contingent as all that. One last point about the two arguments is that they coincide in not offering—as I mentioned earlier—any considerations about worlds in which one does not occur at all; but there is perhaps an additional reason why this should be so in the Utilitarian-type argument, over and above the one it shares with Nagel's. The reason it shares with Nagel's is that the type of misfortune we are concerned with in thinking about X's death is X's misfortune (as opposed to the misfortunes of the state or whatever); and whatever sort of misfortune it may be in a given possible world that X does not occur in it, it is not X's misfortune. They share the feature, then, that for anything to be X's misfortune in a given world, X must occur in that world. But the Utilitarian-type argument further grounds the misfortune, if there is one, in certain features of X, namely his desires; and if there is no X in a given world, then *a fortiori* there are no such grounds.

But now, if death, other things being equal, is a misfortune; and a longer life is better than a shorter life; and we reject the Lucretian argument that it does not matter when one dies: then it looks as though—other things always being equal—death is at any time an evil, and it is always better to live than to die. Nagel indeed, from his point of view, does seem to permit that conclusion, even though he admits some remarks about the natural term of life and the greater misfortune of dying in one's prime. But wider consequences follow. For if all that is true, then it looks as though it would be not only always better to live, but better to live always: that is, never to die. If Lucretius is wrong, we seem committed to wanting to be immortal. That would be, as has been repeatedly said, with other things equal. No-one need deny that since, for instance, we grow old and our powers decline, much may happen to increase the reasons for thinking death a good thing. But these are contingencies. We might not age; perhaps, one day, it will be possible for some of us not to age. If that were so, would it not follow then that, more life being *per se* better than less life, we should have reason so far as that went (but not necessarily in terms of other inhabitants) to live for ever? EM indeed bears strong, if fictional, witness against the desirability of that; but perhaps she still laboured under some contingent limitations, social or psychological, which might once more be eliminated to bring it about that really other things were equal. Against this, I am going to suggest that the supposed contingencies are not really contingencies; that an endless life would be a meaningless one; and that we could have no reason for living eternally a human life. There is no desirable or significant property which life would have more of, or have more unqualifiedly, if we lasted for ever. In some part, we can apply to life Aristotle's marvellous remark about Plato's Form of the Good: "nor will it be any the more good for being eternal: that which lasts long is no whiter than that which perishes in a day" (*Ethica Nicomachea* 1096B4). But only in part; for, rejecting Lucretius, we have already admitted that more days may give us more than one day can.

If one pictures living for ever as living as an embodied person in the world rather as it is, it will be a question, and not so trivial as may seem, of what age one eternally is. EM was 342; because for 300 years she had been 42. This choice (if it was a choice) I am personally, and at present, well disposed to salute—if one had to spend eternity at any age, that seems an admirable age to spend it at. Nor would it necessarily be a less good age for a woman: that at least was not EM's problem, that she was too old at the age she continued to be at. Her problem lay in having been at it for too long. Her trouble was, it seems, boredom: a boredom connected with the fact that everything that could happen and make sense to one particular human being of 42 had already happened to her. Or, rather, all the sorts of things that could make sense to one woman of a certain character; for EM has a certain character, and indeed, except for her accumulating memories of earlier times, and no doubt some changes of style to suit the passing centuries, she seems always to have been much the same sort of person.

There are difficult questions, if one presses the issue, about this constancy of character. How is this accumulation of memories related to this character which she eternally has, and to the character of her existence? Are they much the same kind of events repeated? Then it is itself strange that she allows them to be repeated, accepting the same repetitions, the same limitations—indeed, *accepting* is what it later becomes, when earlier it would not, or even could not, have been that. The repeated patterns of personal relations, for instance, must take on a character of being inescapable. Or is the pattern of her experiences not repetitious in this way, but varied? Then the problem shifts, to the relation between these varied experiences, and the fixed character: how can it remain fixed, through an endless series of very various experiences? The experiences must surely happen to her without really affecting her; she must be, as EM is, detached and withdrawn.

EM, of course, is in a world of people who do not share her condition, and that determines certain features of the life she has to lead, as that any personal relationship requires peculiar kinds of concealment. That, at least, is a form of isolation which would disappear if her condition were generalised. But to suppose more generally that boredom and inner death would be eliminated if everyone were similarly becalmed, is an empty hope: it would be a world of Bourbons, learning nothing and forgetting nothing, and it is unclear how much could even happen.

The more one reflects to any realistic degree on the conditions of EM's unending life, the less it seems a mere contingency that it froze up as it did. That it is not a contingency, is suggested also by the fact that the reflections can sustain themselves independently of any question of the particular character that EM had; it is enough, almost, that she has a human character at all. Perhaps not quite. One sort of character for which the difficulties of unending life would have less significance than they proved to have for EM might be one who at the beginning was more like what she is at the end: cold, withdrawn, already frozen. For him, the prospect of unending cold is presumably less bleak in that he is used to it. But with him, the question can shift to a different place, as to why he wants the unending life at all; for, the more he is at the beginning like EM is at the end, the less place there is for categorical desire to keep him going, and to resist the desire for death. In EM's case, her boredom and distance from life both kill desire and consist in the death of it; one who is already enough like that to sustain life in those conditions may well be one who had nothing to make him want to do so. But even if he has, and we conceive of a person who is stonily resolved to sustain for ever an already stony existence, his possibility will be of no comfort to those, one hopes a larger party, who want to live longer because they want to live more.

To meet the basic anti-Lucretian hope for continuing life which is grounded in categorical desire, EM's unending life in this world is inadequate, and necessarily so relative to just those desires and conceptions of character which go into the hope. That is very important, since it is the most direct response, that which should have been adequate if the hope is both coherent and what it initially seemed to be. It also satisfied one of two important conditions which must be satisfied by anything which is to be adequate as a fulfillment of my anti-Lucretian hope, namely that it should clearly be *me* who lives for ever. The second important condition is that the state in which I survive should be one which, to me looking forward, will be adequately related, in the life it presents, to those aims which I now have in wanting to survive at all. That is a vague formula, and necessarily so, for what exactly that relation will be must depend to some extent on what kind of aims and (as one might say) prospects for myself I now have. What we can say is that since I am propelled forward into longer life by categorical desires, what is promised must hold out some hopes for those desires. The limiting case of this might be that the promised life held out some hope just to that desire mentioned before, that future desires of mine will be born and satisfied; but if that were the only categorical desire that carried me forward into it, at least this seems demanded, that any image I have of those future desires should make it comprehensible to me how in terms of my character they could be my desires.

This second condition the EM kind of survival failed, on reflection, to satisfy; but at least it is clear why, before reflection, it looked as though it might satisfy the condition—it consists, after all, in just going on in ways in which we are quite used to going on. If we turn away now from EM to more remote kinds of survival, the problems of those two conditions press more heavily right from the beginning. Since the major problems of the EM situation lay in the indefinite extension of one life, a tempting alternative is survival by means of an indefinite series of lives. Most, perhaps all, versions of this belief which have actually existed have immediately failed the first condition: they get nowhere near providing any consideration to mark the difference between rebirth and new birth. But let us suppose the problem, in some way or another, removed; some conditions of bodily continuity, minimally sufficient for personal identity, may be supposed satisfied. (Anyone who thinks that no such conditions could be sufficient, and requires, for instance, conditions of memory, may well find it correspondingly difficult to find an alternative for survival in this direction which both satisfies the first requirement, of identity, and also adequately avoids the difficulties of the EM alternative.) The problem remains of whether this series of psychologically disjoint lives could be an object of hope to one who did not want to die. That is, in my view, a different question from the question of whether it will be he—which is why I distinguished originally two different requirements to be satisfied. But it is a question; and even if the first requirement be supposed satisfied, it is exceedingly unclear that the second can be. This will be so, even if one were to accept the idea, itself problematical, that one could have reason to fear the future pain of someone who was merely bodily continuous with one as one now is.[4]

There are in the first place certain difficulties about how much a man could consistently be allowed to know about the series of his lives, if we are to preserve the psychological disjointness which is the feature of this model. It might be that each would in fact have to seem to him as though it were his only life, and that he could not have grounds for being sure what, or even that, later lives were to come. If so, then no comfort or hope will be forthcoming in this model to those who want to go on living. More interesting questions, however, concern the man's relation to a future life of which he did get some advance idea. If we could allow the idea that he could fear pain which was going to occur in that life, then we have at least provided him with one kind of reason which might move him to opt out of that life, and destroy himself (being recurrent, under conditions of bodily continuity, would not make one indestructible). But physical pain and its nastiness are to the maximum degree independent of what one's desires and character are, and the degree of identification needed with the later life to reject that aspect of it is absolutely minimal. Beyond that point, however, it is unclear how he is to bring this later character and its desires into a relation to his present ones, so as to be satisfied or the reverse with this marginal promise of continued existence. If he can regard this future life as an object of hope, then equally it must be possible for him to regard it with alarm, or depression, and—as in the simple pain case—opt out of it. If we cannot make sense of his entertaining that choice, then we have not made sense of this future life's being adequately related to his present life, so that it could, alternatively, be something he might want in wanting not to die. But can we clearly make sense of that choice? For if we—or he—merely wipe out his present character and desires, there is nothing left by which he can judge it at all, at least as something *for him;* while if we leave them in, we—and he—apply something irrelevant to that future life, since (to adapt the Epicurean phrase), when they are there, it is not, and when it is there, they are not. We might imagine him considering the future prospects, and agreeing to go on if he found them congenial. But that is a muddled picture. For whether they are congenial to him as he is now must be beside the point, and the idea that it is not beside the point depends on carrying over into the case features that do not belong to it, as (perhaps) that he will remember later what he wanted in the earlier life. And when we admit that it is beside the point whether the prospects are congenial, then the force of the idea that the future life could be something that he *now* wanted to go on to, fades.

There are important and still obscure issues here,[5] but perhaps enough has been said to cast doubt on this option as coherently satisfying the desire to stay alive. While few will be disposed to think that much can be made of it, I must confess that out of the alternatives it is the only one which for me would, if it made sense, have any attraction—no doubt because it is the only one which has the feature that what one is living at any given point is actually *a life.* It is singular that those systems of belief that get closest to actually accepting recurrence of this sort seem, almost without exception, to look forward to the point when one will be released from it. Such systems seem less interested in continuing one's life than in earning one the right to a superior sort of death.

The serial and disjoint lives are at least more attractive than the attempt which some have made, to combine the best of continuous and of serial existence in a fantasy of very varied lives which are nevertheless cumulatively effective in memory. This might be called the *Teiresias* model. As that case singularly demonstrates, it has the quality of a fantasy, of emotional pressure trying to combine the uncombinable. One thing that the fantasy has to ignore is the connexion, both as cause and as consequence, between having one range of experiences rather than another, wishing to engage in one sort of thing rather than another, and having a character. Teiresias cannot have a character, either continuously through these proceedings, or cumulatively at the end (if there were to be an end) of them: he is not, eventually, a person but a phenomenon.

In discussing the last models, we have moved a little away from the very direct response which EM's case seemed to provide to the hope that one would never die. But perhaps we have moved not nearly far enough. Nothing of this, and nothing much like this, was in the minds of many who have hoped for immortality; for it was not in this world that they hoped to live for ever. As one might say, their hope was not so much that they would never die as that they would live after their death, and while that in its turn can be represented as the hope that one would not really die, or, again, that it was not really oneself that would die, the change of formulation could point to an after-life sufficiently unlike this life, perhaps, to earth the current of doubt that flows from EM's frozen boredom.

But in fact this hope has been and could only be modelled on some image of a more familiar untiring or unresting or unflagging activity or satisfaction; and what is essentially EM's problem, one way or another, remains. In general we can ask what it is about the imagined activities of an eternal life which would stave off the principal hazard to which EM succumbed, boredom. The Don Juan in Hell joke, that heaven's prospects are tedious and the devil has the best tunes, though a tired fancy in itself, at least serves to show up a real and (I suspect) a profound difficulty, of providing any model of an unending, supposedly satisfying, state or activity which would not rightly prove boring to anyone who remained conscious of himself and who had acquired a character, interests, tastes, and impatiences in the course of living, already, a finite life. The point is not that for such a man boredom would be a tiresome consequence of the supposed states or activities, and that they would be objectionable just on the utilitarian or hedonistic ground that they had this disagreeable feature. If that were all there was to it, we could imagine the feature away, along no doubt with other disagreeable features of human life in its present imperfection. The point is rather that boredom, as sometimes in more ordinary circumstances, would be not just a tiresome effect, but a reaction almost perceptual in character to the poverty of one's relation to the environment. Nothing less will do for eternity than something that makes boredom *unthinkable*. What could that be? Something that could be guaranteed to be at every moment utterly absorbing? But if a man has and retains a character, there is no reason to suppose that there is anything which could be that. If, lacking a conception of the guaranteedly absorbing activity, one tries merely to think away the reaction of boredom, one is no longer supposing an improvement in the circumstances, but merely an impoverishment in his consciousness of them. Just as being bored can be a sign of not noticing, understanding, or appreciating enough, so equally not being bored can be a sign of not noticing, or not reflecting, enough. One might make the immortal man content at every moment, by just stripping off from him consciousness which would have brought discontent by reminding him of other times, other interests, other possibilities. Perhaps, indeed, that is what we have already done, in a more tempting way, by picturing him just now as at every moment totally absorbed—but that is something we shall come back to.

Of course there is in actual life such a thing as justified but necessary boredom; Thus—to take a not entirely typical example—someone who was, or who thought himself, devoted to the radical cause might eventually admit to himself that he found a lot of its rhetoric excruciatingly boring. He might think that he ought not to feel that, that the reaction was wrong, and merely represented an unworthiness of his, an unregenerate remnant of intellectual superiority. However, he might rather feel that it would not necessarily be a better world in which no-one was bored by such rhetoric and that boredom was, indeed, a perfectly worthy reaction to this rhetoric after all this time; but for all that, the rhetoric might be necessary. A man at arms can get cramp from standing too long at his post, but sentry-duty can after all be necessary. But the threat of monotony in eternal activities could not be dealt with in that way, by regarding immortal boredom as an unavoidable ache derived from standing ceaselessly at one's post. (This is one reason why I said that boredom in eternity would have to be *unthinkable*.) For the question would be unavoidable, in what campaign one was supposed to be serving, what one's ceaseless sentry-watch was for.

Some philosophers have pictured an eternal existence as occupied in something like intense intellectual enquiry. Why that might seem to solve the problem, at least for them, is obvious. The activity is engrossing, self-justifying, affords, as it may appear, endless new perspectives, and by being engrossing enables one to lose oneself. It is that last feature that supposedly makes boredom unthinkable, by providing something that is, in that earlier phrase, at every moment totally absorbing. But if one is totally and perpetually absorbed in such an activity, and loses oneself in it, then as those words suggest, we come back to the problem of satisfying the conditions that it should be me who lives for ever, and that the eternal life should be in prospect of some interest. Let us leave aside the question of people whose characteristic and most personal interests are remote from such pursuits, and for whom, correspondingly, an immortality promised in terms of intellectual activity is going to make heavy demands on some theory of a "real self" which will have to emerge at death. More interesting is the content and value of the promise for a person who is, in this life, disposed to those activities. For looking at such a person as he now is, it seems quite unreasonable to suppose that those activities would have the fulfilling or liberating character that they do have for him, if they were in fact all he could do or conceive of doing. If they are genuinely fulfilling, and do not operate (as they can) merely as a compulsive diversion, then the ground and shape of the satisfactions that the intellectual enquiry offers him, will relate to *him*, and not just to the enquiry. The *Platonic introjection*, seeing the satisfactions of studying what is timeless and impersonal as being themselves timeless and impersonal, may be a deep illusion, but it is certainly an illusion.

We can see better into that illusion by considering Spinoza's thought, that intellectual activity was the most active and free state that a man could be in, and that a man who had risen to such activity was in some sense most fully individual, most fully himself. This conclusion has been sympathetically expounded by Stuart Hampshire, who finds on this point a similar doctrine in Spinoza and in Freud: in particular, he writes, "[one's] only means of achieving this distinctness as an individual, this freedom in relation to the common order of nature, is the power of the mind freely to follow in its thought an intellectual order."[6] The contrast to this free intellectual activity is "the common condition of men that their conduct and their judgments of value, their desires and aversions, are in each individual determined by unconscious memories"—a process which the same writer has elsewhere associated with our having any character at all as individuals.[7]

Hampshire claims that in pure intellectual activity the mind is most free because it is then least determined by causes outside its immediate states. I take him to mean that rational activity is that in which the occurrence of an earlier thought maximally explains the occurrence of a later thought, because it is the rational relation between their contents which, granted the occurrence of the first, explains the occurrence of the second. But even the maximal explanatory power, in these terms, of the earlier thought does not extend to total explanation: for it will still require explanation why this thinker on this occasion continued on this rational path of thought at all. Thus I am not sure that the Spinozist consideration which Hampshire advances even gives a very satisfactory sense to the *activity* of the mind. It leaves out, as the last point shows, the driving power which is needed to sustain one even in the most narrowly rational thought. It is still further remote from any notion of creativity, since that, even within a theoretical context, and certainly in an artistic one, precisely implies the origination of ideas which are not fully predictable in terms of the content of existing ideas. But even if it could yield one sense for "activity," it would still offer very little, despite Spinoza's heroic defence of the notion, for *freedom*. Or—to put it another way—even if it offered something for freedom of the intellect, it offers nothing for freedom of the individual. For when freedom is initially understood as the absence of "outside" determination, and in particular understood in those terms as an unquestionable *value*, my freedom is reasonably not taken to include freedom from my past, my character, and my desires. To suppose that those are, in the relevant sense, "outside" determinations, is merely to beg the vital question about the boundaries of the self, and not to prove from premises acceptable to any clear-headed man who desires freedom that the boundaries of the self should be drawn round the intellect. On the contrary, the desire for freedom can, and should, be seen as the desire to be free in the exercise and development of character, not as the desire to be free of it. And if Hampshire and others are right in claiming that an individual character springs from and gets its energies from unconscious memories and unclear desires, then the individual must see them too as within the boundaries of the self, and themselves involved in the drive to persist in life and activity.

With this loss, under the Spinozist conception, of the individual's character, there is, contrary to Hampshire's claim, a loss of individuality itself, and certainly that could make an eternity of intellectual activity, so construed, a reasonable object of interest to one concerned with individual immortality. As those who totally wish to lose themselves in the movement can consistently only hope that the movement will go on, so the consistent Spinozist—at least on this account of Spinozism—can only hope that the intellectual activity goes on, something which could be as well realised in the existence of Aristotle's prime mover, perhaps, as in anything to do with Spinoza or any other particular man.

Stepping back now from the extremes of Spinozist abstraction, I shall end by returning to a point from which we set out, the sheer desire to go on living, and shall mention a writer on this subject, Unamuno, whose work *The Tragic Sense of Life*[8] gives perhaps more extreme expression than anyone else has done to that most basic form of the desire to be immortal, the desire not to die.

> *I do not want to die—no, I neither want to die nor do I want to want to*
> *die; I want to live for ever and ever and ever. I want this "I" to live—this*
> *poor "I" that I am and that I feel myself to be here and now, and therefore the*
> *problem of the duration of my soul, of my own soul, tortures me [p. 60].*

Although Unamuno frequently refers to Spinoza, the spirit of this is certainly far removed from that of the "sorrowful Jew of Amsterdam." Furthermore, in his clear insistence that what he desperately wants is this life, the life of this self, not to end, Unamuno reveals himself at equal removes from Manicheanism and from Utilitarianism; and that is correct, for the one is only the one-legged descendant of the other. That tradition—Manichean, Orphic, Platonic, Augutinian—which contrasts the spirit and the body in such a sense that the spiritual aims at eternity, truth and salvation, while the body is adjusted to pleasure, the temporary, and eventual dissolution, is still represented, as to fifty per cent, by secular Utilitarianism: it is just one of the original pair of boots left by itself and better regarded now that the other has fallen into disrepair. Bodies are all that we have or are: hence for Utilitarianism it *follows* that the only focus of our arrangements can be the efficient organisation of happiness. Immortality, certainly, is out, and so life here should last as long as we determine—or eventually, one may suspect, others will determine—that it is pleasant for us to be around.

Unamuno's outlook is at the opposite pole to this and, whatever else may be wrong with it, it salutes the true idea that the meaning of life does not consist either in the management of satisfactions in a body or in an abstract immortality without one. On the one hand he had no time for Manicheanism, and admired the rather brutal Catholic faith which could express its hopes for a future life in the words which he knew on a tombstone in Bilbao:

> *Aunque estamos en polvo convertidos*
> *en Ti, Señor, nuestra esperanza fía,*
> *que tornaremos a vivir vestidos*
> *con la carne y la piel que nos cubria [p. 79].*

At the same time, his desire to remain alive extends an almost incomprehensible distance beyond any desire to continue agreeable experiences: "For myself I can say that as a youth and even as a child I remained unmoved when shown the most moving pictures of hell, for even then nothing appeared quite so horrible to me as nothingness itself" (p. 28). The most that I have claimed earlier against Lucretius is not enough to make that preference intelligible to me. The fear of sheer nothingness is certainly part of what Lucretius rightly, if too lightly, hoped to exorcise; and the *mere* desire to stay alive, which is here stretched to its limit, is not enough (I suggested before) to answer the question, once the question has come up and requires an answer in rational terms. Yet Unamuno's affirmation of existence even through limitless suffering[9] brings out something which is implicit in the claim against Lucretius. It is not necessarily the prospect of pleasant times that creates the motive against dying, but the existence of categorical desire, and categorical desire can drive through both the existence and the prospect of unpleasant times.

Suppose, then, that categorical desire does sustain the desire to live. So long as it remains so, I shall want not to die. Yet I also know, if what has gone before is right, that an eternal life would be unliveable. In part, as EM's case originally suggested, that is because categorical desire will go away from it: in those versions, such as hers, in which I am recognisably myself, I would eventually have had altogether too much of myself. There are good reasons, surely, for dying before that happens. But equally, at times earlier than that moment, there is reason for not dying. Necessarily, it tends to be either too early or too late. EM reminds us that it can be too late, and many, as against Lucretius, need no reminding that it can be too early. If that is any sort of dilemma, it can, as things still are and if one is exceptionally lucky, be resolved, not by doing anything, but just by dying shortly before the horrors of not doing so become evident. Technical progress may, in more than one direction, make that piece of luck rarer. But as things are, it is possible to be, in contrast to EM, *felix opportunitate mortis*—as it can be appropriately mistranslated, lucky in having the chance to die.

Notes

1. At the University of California, Berkeley, under a benefaction in the names of Agnes and Constantine Foerster. I am grateful to the committee for inviting me to give the 1972 lecture in this series.
2. Obviously the principle is not exceptionless. For one thing, one can want to be dead: the content of that desire may be obscure, but whatever it is, a man presumably cannot be *prevented* from getting it by dying. More generally, the principle does not apply to what I elsewhere call *non-I desire*: for an account, see my "Egoism and Altruism," *Problems of the Self,* pp. 260ff. They do not affect the present discussion, which is within the limits of egoistic rationality.
3. Though my argument does not in any sense imply Utilitarianism; for some further considerations on this, see the final paragraphs of this paper.
4. One possible conclusion from the dilemma discussed in my "The Self and the Future." For the point, mentioned below, of the independence of physical pain from psychological change, see *Problems of the Self,* p. 54.
5. For a detailed discussion of closely related questions, though in a different framework, see Derek Parfitt, "Personal Identity," *Philosophical Review,* 80 (1971), 3-27.

6. "Spinoza and the Idea of Freedom," reprinted in *Freedom of Mind* (Oxford: Clarendon, 1972), pp. 183ff.; the two quotations are from pp. 206-7.
7. "Disposition and Memory," *ibid.*, pp. 160ff.; see esp. pp. 176-77.
8. *Del sentimiento trágico de la vida*, trans. J. E. Crawford Flitch (London, 1921). Page references in the text are to the 1962 Fontana Library edition.
9. An affirmation which takes on a special dignity retrospectively in the light of his own death shortly after his courageous speech against Millán Astray and the obscene slogan "¡Viva la Muerte!" (see Hugh Thomas, *The Spanish Civil War* [Harmondsworth: Pelican, 1961], pp. 442-44).

Suggested Readings

J. E. J. Altham and Ross Harrison, ed. *World, Mind, and Ethics: Essays on the Ethical Philosophy of Bernard Williams*. New York: Cambridge University Press, 1995.

Fischer, John, (Ed). *The Metaphysics of Death*. Stanford University Press, 1993.

Williams, Bernard. "Practical Necessity" in *The Philosophical Frontiers of Christian Theology*. Ed. Brian Hebblethwaite and Steward Sutherland. New York: Cambridge University Press, 1982.

Chapter 24

The Conquest of Death

Roland Puccetti

Roland Puccetti (1924-   ) taught at Dalhousie University and authored the book
Persons: A Study of Possible Moral Agents in the Universe. *The article by Puccetti
included in this anthology is an example of what in the introduction was called Reductive
immortality. He disagrees with Williams that death is a welcome event and argues that a
cyborg form of immortality is not only possible but desirable. Puccetti also argues that
from a psychological point of view, apart from spiritual concerns, we in fact desire to live.*

Except for the religiously inclined, like Donne, it seems fatuous to talk of conquering death. Death is not the last disease mankind will have to overcome. It is what follows when the organism finally succumbs to disease or injury, the absence of life where there was life before. One does not, after everything else has happened, catch death too: if that were the case people would sometimes recover from death; but in this world, at least, they never do.

Does that mean men *must* die? This cannot be a logical "must." The familiar premiss "All men are mortal" is hardly analytic, since children who understand they are human are sometimes surprised to learn they will die. The statement must be empirical, an inductive generalisation of some sort. What evidence do we have for its truth? Just that all men we have known have died except those now living. Could anyone *know* it is true? I do not see how. The last man alive could know he is dying, but never that he had died.

However, this point cuts both ways. There seems no way a man could know he is not mortal, either. If Zeus or a voice from the heavens proclaimed to me that I had been given the gift of immortality, accompanied by suitable displays of miraculous powers, I might have good psychological reasons for expecting an open-ended personal future. But no amount of assurances could make this a necessary truth. There never could be a time when, having survived so long, I could be sure of living on still another day.

But then what shall we say about the notion of conquering death? If it does not convey immortality because nothing can logically guarantee this, is it an empty phrase? I shall take it to mean just the indefinite prolongation of life. And since as I argued nothing in our logical conventions or even our conceptual scheme rules this out, it is a meaningful concept.

But is it theoretically as well as logically possible? Here the analogy with disease may not be entirely misleading. For we do speak of, and understand, the "conquest" of diseases like malaria and cholera where we do not mean they have been wholly eradicated, but that in some parts of the world at least they have been brought under medical control to a degree that few people ever have fatal encounters with them. Similarly, the notion of conquering death can be pared down to this: the idea that we might some day be able so to prolong life that few of us would die over very long time-spans, and then only by bizarre accidents. Is this conceivable? Could death itself become as rare as, say, death by tetanus or influenza is today? And would that be desirable?

I want to discuss this possibility at length, but first we have to get clear what the death of a human being amounts to.

⚓ The Physiology of Death ⚓

Looked at biologically, a human being like any organism above unicellular level is an integrated four-dimensional clone of cells. Obviously if all the cells constituting a human being die, he is dead too. But this cannot be our criterion of death, since some cells (e.g. cartilage cells) go on living for hours after a man's death; and no one would say we are burying him alive because part of, say, his left knee is living as we lower him into the grave. For the same reason we do not say a man is dead when a peripheral part of his body has died, e.g. a foot after severe frostbite. In both cases there has not been involvement of the central integrating organs, the life or death of which determines our judgment of the individual's continued survival.

What are these organs? First, there are the major supporting organs that keep the brain alive and conscious: heart and lungs. Second, the brain itself. Normally these function so interdependently that there is little point in distinguishing them with regard to the death of a man. Lung failure or heart failure or both together prevent oxygen-carrying blood from reaching the brain; hypoxia in the brain causes rapid destruction of tissue; and when the reticular core of the brainstem is damaged, there can be no recovery of consciousness. However, it must not be thought that these organs have a rough parity of importance to human life. Strictly speaking, it is not true that men die of heart attacks or drowning or lung cancer. Rather, these events cause paralysis or destruction of respiratory and cardiac functions, which causes anoxia in the brain; and it is *this* which in turn causes death of the brain and person. The point can be made this way: a bullet through the heart kills within minutes, but a bullet through the upper brainstem kills instantaneously. Admittedly, the distinction will seem picayune to someone facing a firing squad; but as we shall now see, it can have great importance in some controversial medical contexts.

live again, perhaps unendingly.[7] Certainly this proposal will do no harm, if you can afford $10,000 and particularly like the idea of permanent embalment: the advantage of believing in any kind of resurrection is that you will never find out you were wrong. However, there can be no serious expectation of surgeons' "restoring" thousands of millions of destroyed and missing neurons with all the precise interconnections they had before you died so that *you*, an individual person, would live again; how could they, since the pattern of neocortical connections disappeared *before* you were frozen?

The second school, recognising this fact, is more modest. It urges research in cryogenics so that some day *suspended animation* may be achieved in mammals, eventually in men, without the present-day hazards of ventricular fibrillation, cellular destruction by formation of ice crystals, and other problems. It is, in other words, the "Freeze Alive" school of thought. But it, too, banks on one's being reawakened centuries later when, in one author's words, "All disease and aging are cured—relegated to history."[8] Here, of course, there is an explicit assumption that genetic engineering will allow us to change the genotype itself. Without this being achieved, "hybernauts" of the future will not gain greater longevity by suspended animation; seventy or so years of conscious life is still no more than seventy years if you live half of it in the twentieth century and half in the twenty-second.

Can the genotype be changed? Sir Macfarlane Burnet, discussing the publicity accompanying Kornberg's successful synthesis of DNA in 1967, has this to say:

> What they [Kornberg and Tatum] were envisaging in principle was that in due course it could become possible to extract from normal human cells the sequence of DNA that was missing from or wrongly made in the patient. Once isolated these could be used as the pattern, the template, for the synthesis by bacterial enzymes of numerous replicas of itself. This is acceptable as a possibility of the foreseeable future. The next step would be the crucial and probably impossible one: to incorporate the gene into the genetic mechanism of a suitable virus vehicle in such a fashion that the virus in its turn will transfer the gene it is carrying to cells throughout the body and in the process precisely replace the faulty gene with the right one. I should be willing to state in any company that the chance of doing this will remain infinitely small to the last syllable of recorded time.[9]

But Sir Macfarlane was talking only of *one* faulty gene responsible, say, for a specific hereditary defect like harelip. If senescence and hence greater vulnerability to fatal injury or disease is due to most of the human body's organs' not being programmed to sustain optimum efficiency beyond maturity, then to "cure" aging would involve altering a vast number of genes such that all these organs never falter or wear out. I conclude, always tentatively, that as long as we have bodies we shall grow old and die, and that no amount of scientific optimism will change this.

But must we have bodies? I said earlier that conscious human life—the only sort worth having—is rooted in neocortical function, sustained and alerted to consciousness by the reticular formation in the brainstem and associated structures. It follows that an intact human brain kept *in vitro* but nourished by a properly oxygenated and glucose-supplied blood flow mechanically pumped into it through the severed arteries could support conscious life; indeed there is partial support for this claim in the fact that monkey brains have been kept alive for several days *in vitro*: the EEG recordings indicated periods of consciousness.[10]

However, an isolated human brain, devoid of neural inputs and unable to affect anything with its motor commands, would have an unenviable life. It would see nothing, hear nothing, feel nothing. When conscious it could only feed on its memories of an embodied past and, eerily, talk to itself, an endless silent monologue. (Theologians will recognise in this description the physiological analogue of continued existence as a disembodied soul.) It would appear that to live a genuinely human life, a body is necessary after all.

But need it be a *human* body, hence vulnerable to aging and death? Need it even be a *living* body? I do not see why. After all, the body is just the means by which our brains interact with the extrabodily environment. In principle, though it is technologically very far-fetched, we could someday build prosthetic bodies housing portable, miniaturised heart-and-lung machines that keep the brain—comfortably installed in the head cavity—well-nourished with blood and glucose, etc. Descending neural pathways from the brain would end at, say, the medulla oblongata, where the electrical charges they emit could activate a miniaturised digital computer to perform limb movements. Conversely, receptors in the prosthetic body would send messages up to the computer, which could in turn fire the proper sequence of ascending nerve fibres that transform these into proprioceptive, kinesthetic, somesthetic, and tactile sensations in the brain. It is important to note that these sensations would be qualitatively indistinguishable from those we now experience. A touch or caress upon the surface of the prosthetic body would be felt by the person whose brain it is as *his* bodily sensation: One must not think one would be sacrificing all the pleasures of having a body by exchanging the one he now has for an inanimate replica body. And indeed for aesthetic and psychological reasons, as well as satisfying third person criteria of personal identity, this prosthetic body should be modeled on his own: he might, however, introduce one or two long-desired cosmetic changes.

What I have just described is technically outrageous, but it does not require overriding any physiological realities.[11] Even vision and hearing could be achieved with a prosthetic body of sufficient sophistication, by having mechanical sensors fire the appropriate neurons in the visual and auditory cortices directly, thus bypassing the normal optic and auditory nerve pathways: indeed in the case of vision that would only be an extension of present research.[12] But I shall leave further details to the imagination. I am not sure, for example, whether it would be worthwhile to develop mechanical digestive and excretory systems, just in order not to forgo the pleasures of the table; or whether one should sacrifice some surface sensitivity in the prosthetic body to avoid risk of activating pain mechanisms in the brain. These are complications we can afford to neglect.

The idea of escaping the evolutionary limitations of our present bodies by having our brains transplanted at postmaturity into bodies which, being inorganic, do not age or deteriorate, has a prima facie attractiveness about it. If I am correct that death amounts to destruction of the neocortex, then the most common causes of this—failure of supportive organs due to conditions like heart disease or lung cancer—would not kill cyborg man. Indeed a great number of widely held theories about the mechanisms of senescence in higher animals would have no application to him. These include those which emphasise the increase of collagen, a fibrous protein, in the body;[13] the theory that capillary breakdown due to circulatory deficiency is the culprit;[14] the decline-in-endocrine-gland approach; that version of the waste product theory which blames faulty metabolism and the increase of toxic substances in the blood;[15] and the theory that failing autoimmunological surveillance related to a diminishing thymus is responsible.[16] Even such general restrictions on longevity as the "Hayflick Limitation," which limits the number of times an embryonic human cell can divide in tissue culture (about fifty),[17] seems irrelevant to the postmitotic cells of the brain. Radiation, of course, can destroy the chromosomal integrity of any cell, including those of the human brain, but at less than cytoxic levels it does not seem to have any effect on ageing.[18]

The greatest challenge to any hope of vastly prolonging human life by corporeal prosthesis is found in *Abnutzungstheorie,* the "wear and tear" view of aging. For if this is right the brain of cyborg man would, just like any bodily organ, wear out in time. And certainly the large (statistically established) loss of brain weight between ages thirty and seventy-five mentioned earlier supports this pessimism. However, it is far from clear how, if at all, this loss contributes to death. For one thing, cellular fallout appears to begin at puberty rather than middle age, while both physical strength and intellectual growth are still increasing. What is more, it seems to *taper* off in the last decade of a normal lifespan. A recent study by Tomlinson suggests that there is no significant difference in the proportionate brain weight of intellectually unimpaired people who die at sixty-five and those who die at seventy-five. Speaking of twenty-eight cases, he says: "As a group, loss of brain weight and the degree of cerebral atrophy was relatively slight, and the lateral ventricles were only slightly larger than those of normal young adults. Indeed all the brain weights fell within the normal limits for young adults and many brains showed no apparent cortical atrophy or significant ventricular dilation."[19]

Dayan has made a thorough review of evidence for pathological change in the aging human brain and it is surprising how difficult it is to say in what these changes consist. Atrophy clearly occurs, but the nature of the loss is unknown since suggested anatomical sites for the loss have been disproven at almost every place where exact counts have been made. Argyrophilic plaques appear in the cortex in the sixth or seventh decade of life, and neurofibrillary tangles at about the same time: these are independent idiopathic degenerative processes, but they do not appear to affect the most important neuronal processes. Neuroaxonal dystrophy is another invariable finding, but of very limited functional significance; and the same appears to be true of amyloid deposits around small blood vessels in the cortex and of intra-neuronal inclusions.[20] Other types of brain lesions associated with aging are too variable to be significant. It is true that lipofucins build up in brain cells (and in heart muscle cells) with age; another version of the waste product theory holds this to be responsible for senescence. However, artificially induced concentrations of these substances in rats did not alter their life-span,[21] and there is some evidence this pigment can be decreased by chemical treatment.[22]

But even if cellular fallout and cortical atrophy are not themselves clearly fatal, it is true that with age our brains become more and more susceptible to disorders of cerebral blood flow that can cause fatal brain trauma such as atheroma of the arteries, thrombosis, embolisms, aneurysms, sclerosis, etc. However, it is not known to what degree circulatory deficiencies reflect degenerative changes in the aging brain, or are due primarily to failing cardiac/respiratory support systems in an aging body.[23] If the latter is the case, cyborg man's brain might very well retain efficient blood circulation indefinitely, because of superior artificial (and easily replaceable) support systems. Even if, as now appears the case,[24] cerebrovascular insufficiency in the elderly is due to malfunctioning central ganglion cells, leading to decreased oxygen and glucose uptake, it has been shown that brain metabolism is responsive to pharmaceutical treatment.[25] In cyborg man autoregulatory mechanisms of the brain could be monitored by computer and appropriate chemicals injected into the blood stream when needed. About all one can say in our present state of knowledge is that we just do not know whether, under these idealised conditions, the human brain could survive the aging process for an indefinite period of time.

☙ The Intellect of Cyborg Man ❧

Senility is so often associated with senescence in our experience of elderly people that one might legitimately wonder if, even if cyborg man's brain did not die with age, it would not become so intellectually deteriorated that the whole exercise would be futile. What is the point of keeping a man alive and conscious in a youthful-looking prosthetic body if he becomes doddering, absent-minded, amnesic, cranky, etc., *anyway?*

Bromley[26] and Welford[27] have independently shown that there is a decline in intellectual ability with normal aging, which they attribute to deterioration in the central processing functions of cognition. However, this relates to intelligence testing of a large number of individuals from all walks of life. One would expect that in the creative professions the gain from experience, learning, and refinement of judgment outweighs this mild decline in general capacity. After all, the value to us of a playwright or paleontologist or painter is not measured by his performance on the WAIS over the years, but on the quality and quantity of his output. Even if this also declines between, say, ages fifty and sixty-five, that may not be disconnected from the fact that he is then becoming but two-thirds or so of the man he was in terms of organic, physiological efficiency. Cyborg man would not show physiological deterioration like this; it remains to be proved that he would *nevertheless* decline intellectually. Even Bromley admits that effects of aging appear to be *less* conspicuous in the brain than some other systems of the body.[28] Without deleterious changes in the body at all, why should the brain begin to fail?

And indeed if not, if cyborg man's brain neither died nor deteriorated with age, think of what this could mean to society. Imagine that we had been able to do hundreds of years ago what I am suggesting we may be able to do hundreds of years from now. Who can say that the geniuses of the seventeenth century would not have done two, three, any number of times as much great work had they lived on in good health to age 200, 300, or more years? Shakespeare might not have gone into voluntary retirement; Newton's life might have overlapped with

Einstein's; and Beethoven might be with us still. True, even cyborg man could perish in the accidents of life. A hard enough blow to the prosthetic head would dispatch him as easily as it does us. He could still drown or get run over or have an irate husband shoot him. But once the principal causes of human mortality are eliminated, the genius has as good an opportunity to live half a millennium as to live half a hundred years.

⚔ Is Death Desirable? ⚔

Leon Kass has said that death is "not only inevitable, but also biologically, psychologically, and spiritually desirable."[29] I hope I have said enough to show that one may rationally doubt whether it is inevitable. Dr. Kass offers no argument for the rest of his statement. That death should be *biologically* desirable suggests Weismann's old argument that "Worn-out individuals are not only valueless to the species, but they are even harmful, for they take the place of those which are sound."[30] Alex Comfort's rejoinder to this is worth quoting: "This argument both assumes what it sets out to explain, that the survival of an individual decreases with increasing age, and denies its own premiss, by suggesting that worn-out individuals threaten the existence of the young."[31] However, Kass may only have meant that in most species *overpopulation* would result from this. That is true; but the difficulty and expense of creating cyborg men are such that either (1) only few individuals of great promise would be preserved this way, somewhat like the system of academic tenure today, *or* (2) in a society which could afford to give every mature male and female this option, overpopulation would have been solved by birth control, planetary and stellar migration, etc., long before.

That death is *spiritually* desirable is incomprehensible to me since in many of the great living religions, at least, it is the (other-worldly) conquest of death which gives them much of their attraction and *rationale*. But of course in another sense what Kass says is true: for some religions it is terribly important that you experience complete *physical* death before, with luck and merit, you are allowed to live again. But since I am not concerned in this essay with spiritual matters, I shall let that pass.

That death is *psychologically* desirable is a more interesting suggestion. On the surface it has a certain appeal. There are certainly moments when, peering vaguely ahead into our lives, Marcus Aurelius' plaintive question *"Quousque tandem?"* takes on real meaning. Death appears as the darkness at the end of a cone of diminishing light, and it is not unwelcome. It equals perfect rest, the end of tribulations. But apart from those unfortunates whose continued lives have become circled in pain or stress, we show a remarkable reluctance to step into the shadows. We cling on, and scream against the dying light. Perhaps that is just selfishness; but how many of us, in good health and with undiminished intellectual powers, would really say: "Well, tomorrow is all right with me"? Surely on the morrow we would want to say the same. It is only because the cone stretches far ahead that the shadows seem welcome.

But I do not like to think of death just in my own case. We must all have had friends, or at least one friend, who was personally so valuable to us that his decline and death seems an irreparable loss to ourselves and everyone who knew him. Such a person, bright and warm and enriching to the end, was in fact based in a well-functioning neocortex being slowly more threatened with death from an aging supportive body system. We need only ask ourselves this question: If I could have *him*, or *her*, sitting here with me in my study tonight, joking and commenting on the latest news or theory or what have you, would it matter greatly that he or she was there in a prosthetic body? And if he or she could have been installed in such a body when he or she was thirty-five or forty, would that be worse than the cruel image Shakespeare etched in our racial memory with these words?

...and his big manly voice
Turning again toward childish treble, pipes
And whistles in his sound. Last scene of all,
That ends this strange eventful history,
Is second childishness and mere oblivion—
Sans teeth, sans eyes, sans taste, sans everything.

—As You Like It

Notes

1. Alex Comfort, *Ageing: The Biology of Senescence* (London: Routledge & Kegan Paul, 1964), fig. 72 p. 272, pp. 275, 88.
2. G. P. Bidder, "Senescence," *British Medical Journal,* 11 (1932), 5831; see also Comfort, *Ageing,* Ch. 8.
3. Nathan W. Shock, "The Physiology of Aging," *Scientific American* (January 1962), 100-10.
4. It is true that the maximum work rate drops 30% between ages 30 and 75, and the maximum work rate for short bursts as much as 60% (Shock, 101). But that is *physical* work. My remarks obviously do not apply to unskilled manual labour, or to professional sports.
5. Comfort, *Ageing,* p. 183.
6. *Theory and Therapeutics of Aging,* ed. Ewald W. Busse (New York: Medcom Press, 1973), Chap. 1.
7. R. C. W. Ettinger, *The Prospect of Immortality* (New York: Doubleday, 1964), pp. 29-30.
8. Robert W. Prehoda, *Suspended Animation* (Philadelphia: Chilton, 1969), p. 126.
9. Macfarlane Burnet, *Genes, Dreams and Realities* (New York: Penguin, 1973), p.81.
10. Robert J. White, Maurice S. Albin, and Javier Verdura, "Preservation of Viability in the Isolated Monkey Brain Utilizing a Mechanical Extracorporeal Circulation," *Nature,* 202 (1964), 1082-83.
11. A special problem, however, would be finding a way to prevent degeneration of the severed nerve endings in the lower brainstem above the break: in higher vertebrates this always occurs. Some technique of artificial nerve regeneration is the major requirement here.
12. G. S. Brindley and W. S. Lewin, "The Sensations Produced by Electrical Stimulation of the Visual Cortex," *Journal of Physiology,* 196 (1968), 479-93.
13. T. Verzar, "Aging of Connective Tissue," *Gerontologia,* 1 (1957), 363-78.
14. N. Seyle and P. Prioreschi, "Stress Theory of Aging," *Aging: Some Social and Biological Aspects,* ed. N. W. Shock (Washington: American Association for the Advancement of Science, 1960), pp. 261-72.
15. A. Carrell and A. H. Ebeling, "Antagonistic Growth Activity and Growth Inhibiting Principles in Serum," *Journal of Experimental Medicine,* 37 (1923), 653-59.
16. R. W. Walford, "Auto-immunity and Aging," *Journal of Gerontology,* 17 (1962), 281-85.
17. T. Hayflick, "The Limited *in vitro* Lifetime of Human Diploid Cell Strains," *Experimental Cellular Research,* 37 (1965), 614-36.
18. P. Alexander, "Is There a Relationship Between Aging, the Shortening of Life Span by Radiation and the Induction of Somatic Mutations?" in *Perspectives in Experimental Gerontology,* ed. N. W. Shock (Springfield: Thomas, 1966), Chap. 20.

conclusion: that is to say accept that man was born entirely from the world—not only his flesh and bones but his incredible power of thought.[1]

Let us consider him, without reducing his stature, as a phenomenon. This will *ipso facto* change the face of the universe.

The point of departure for this metamorphosis is that life, manifested in man, reveals itself as a property *sui generis* of the cosmos. In the history of the physical sciences, there are periodic discoveries of 'characteristic phenomena' which by their apparent anomaly reveal a fundamental property of things. Among these have been the activity of radium and the inability of experiment to detect a movement of the globe through the ether.[2] The greatest mistake that science could have made when confronted with these facts would have been to consign them to the realm of tiresome freaks. If we had done so we should have no knowledge of the vast realm of radiations, and the far-reaching theories of relativity. Man 'the thinker,' generally regarded as an 'irregularity' in the universe, is precisely one of those special phenomena by which one of the most basic aspects of the cosmos is revealed to us with a degree of intensity that renders it immediately recognizable. Below man, life, despite the singular properties of its constituents and its general evolution, might at a pinch have been consigned to an obscure department of chemistry. By confining it, most artificially moreover, to its lowest and most mechanical terms (that is to say to forms scarcely emerged from, or in process of re-immersion in matter) biology might attempt to reduce it to tactisms and tropisms. With man something new, which science had hitherto been able to contain if only by violent means, burst forth irresistibly. At the level of humanity, there can be no more temporizing. We must make up our minds, by virtue of the general perspectives of evolution themselves, to make a special place in the physics of the universe for the powers of consciousness, spontaneity and improbability represented by life. This is inevitable, or man remains unexplained—excluded from a cosmos of which he manifestly forms a part. But then, and this is the *second step* towards the light, the moment one tries to determine this place it inevitably proves both vast and fundamental. Life, in fact, is not a partial, limited property of matter, analogous to some vibratory or molecular effect: it is rather a sort of inverse of everything that habitually serves us as a definition of matter. Consequently life is not a fixed and static relationship between elements of the world; it clearly appears, on the contrary, as the sign of a universal process; terrestrial life being a function of the sidereal evolution of the globe, which is itself a function of total cosmic evolution. Hence the dilemma: either life, completed by thought, is merely an illusion in the world, or else, once it is granted the least physical reality, it tends to occupy a universal, central and exigent position in it. *This is the true scientific situation.*

Once life has encroached so far, only one reality (in so far as it truly exists) remains to confront it, and can be compared to it in size and universality: this is entropy, that mysterious *involution* by which the world tends progressively to refurl on itself, in unorganized plurality and increasing probability, the layer of cosmic energy. And then, before our enquiring minds, a final duel is fought between life (thought) and entropy (matter) for the domination of he universe. Are life and entropy the two opposite but equivalent faces of a single fundamental reality in eternal equipoise? Or radically has one of them the natural advantage of being more primal and durable than the other?

No, the cosmos could not possibly be explained as a dust of unconscious elements, on which life, for some incomprehensible reason, burst into flower—as an accident or as a mould. But it is *fundamentally and primarily* living, and its complete history is ultimately nothing but an immense psychic exercise; the slow but progressive attaining of a diffused consciousness—a gradual escape from the 'material' conditions which, *secondarily*, veil it in an initial state of extreme plurality. From this point of view man is nothing but the point of emergence in nature, at which this deep cosmic evolution culminates and declares itself. From this point onwards man ceases to be a spark fallen by chance on earth and coming from another place. He is the flame of a general fermentation of the universe[3] which breaks out suddenly on the earth. He is no longer a sterile enigma or discordant note in nature. He is the key of things and the final harmony. In him everything takes shape and is explained.

The world is like a maze before us. Many entrances, but only one path that leads to the centre. Because we approach at the wrong angle or from the wrong direction nature resists our efforts to reach it. Let us make a better choice of our known and unknown quantities. Let us put our x in the proper place, that is to say in the material and the plural; and let us recognize that *evidences of consciousness and freedom are primordial and defy analysis*. Then we find the right order. No more closed doors or blind alleys. The Ariadne's thread that can guide us through the universe is the 'birth of the spirit,' and the hand from which we receive it is the faithful recognition of the 'phenomenon of man.'

⚓ Spiritualization ⚓

If we wish to appreciate the phenomenon of spirit at its true value, we must first of all familiarize ourselves with the idea of its real breadth. At first sight the conscious portion of the world presents itself in the form of discontinuous, tiny and ephemeral fragments: a bright dust of individualities, a flight of shooting stars. In the second chapter of this essay we shall have to return with a keener eye to the meaning and value inherent in each of these sparks. For the moment it suits us to assume the greatest possible distance from their distracting and minimizing singularity. What are the dimensions of the magnitude that we call 'spirit,' *if* we *take it as a whole?* I am going to show that, rightly regarded, they are the dimensions of the universe itself.

⚓ THE SPIRIT'S PRESENT

If we wish to discern the phenomenon of spirit in its entirety, we must first educate our eyes to perceiving collective realities. Because we are ourselves individuals, life around us affects us principally on the individual scale. Atoms ourselves, we at first see only other atoms. But it does not require much reflexion to discover that animate bodies are not as separate from one another as they appear. Not only are they all, by the mechanism of reproduction, related by birth. But by the very process of their development, a network of living connexions (psychological, economic, social, etc.) never for a moment ceases to hold them in a single tissue, which becomes more complicated and tenacious the further they evolve. Like drops of water scattered in the sand and subjected to the same pressure, that of the layer to which they belong; like electrical charges distributed along a single conductor and subjected to the same potential;

a First. As regards our individual destinies we can see a justification ahead for our hope of a personal immortality, which seems to be the *necessary* natural compensation, for thinking beings, of a death that *they have become capable of foreseeing*. On the one hand, the irresistible and infallible spiritualization of the world would not succeed if the conscious particle represented by each one of us were not to pass into an irreversible and totalizing term of transformation; and on the other hand this passage of what is us into what is other, far from threatening our ego, has precisely the effect of consolidating it. Death, in which we seem to disappear, thus reveals itself as representing a simple phase of growth; it marks our accession into a super-human sphere of self-consciousness, of personality.

b Second. As regards the final nature of the spirit into which all spirituality converges, that is to say all the personality in the world, we see that its supreme simplicity contains a prodigious complexity. In that spirit, on the one hand, all the elements into which the personal consciousness of the world appeared in the beginning to be broken up (that is to say at the moment of hominization) are carried to their maximum individual differentiation by maximum union with the All, and then extended without becoming confused with one another. And on the other hand, in this spirit, essentially needed for the unification without confusion of these *unmixable* centres, a distinct and autonomous centre is discovered as necessary, which is itself personal and radiates over the myriad of inferior personalities: the sum of all the past and the ultimate focal point of the future.

c Third. As regards the direction of our present activity, we observe that, to complete ourselves, we must pass into a greater than ourselves. Survival and also 'super-life' await us in the direction of a growing consciousness and love of the universal. All our action should be organized—that is to say our morality should be shaped—towards reaching (and at the same time bringing into being) this pole.

⚘ Moral Application ⚘

Two conditions are necessary (and in fact sufficient) to make us accept and co-operate with the demands of evolution: the universal and superhuman end to which it is taking us must present itself to us as at the same time *incorruptible* and *personal*. And that it is so I should like to show.

First, incorruptible. Death has been tirelessly examined by man in the partings and humiliations that accompany it. Tirelessly, the moralists have used the power ascribed to it to throw salutary cold water on the fever of our passions. But have we ever sufficiently examined the power it has of lighting the most distant horizons of human energy? Death is probably almost nothing to an animal; absorbed in its actions, it never leaves the present moment. But what proportions does this phenomenon not take when transported into the surroundings of the noosphere? How will the being react, once confronted and for the whole of his life with an end in which he appears to perish completely? Resignation? Stoicism? Not at all, I say, but *legitimate* revolt and desertion, unless death reveals the form or condition of a new progress. To act is to create, and creation is for ever. Reflective action and the expectation of total disappearance are therefore *cosmically incompatible*. The association, therefore, in a single evolutionary current of thought and death raises a fundamental conflict which must end in the destruction of one of these two contradictory ends. Either spirit will see that it has been deceived and retire from the game. Or else death, lifting its veil of annihilation, will take on the features of life. Now the first alternative would involve the absurdity of a universe victorious over unconsciousness as far as man, yet successfully bringing reflexion to birth in him only to show itself, the universe, incapable of sustaining it. There remains the second alternative, that death leaves some part of ourselves existing in some way, to which we can turn with devotion and interest, as to a portion of the absolute. The final fate to which we must be destined by our incorporation in the universe must, *in order to be such,* appear to our hopes as *imperishable.* That, as I have already stated, is a first condition *sine qua non* for the deployment of human energy.

Incorruptibility, therefore. But also, I added, *personality.* Certainly men—I have known several—who have felt the need of finding some extension to our existences try to console themselves for their eventual disappearance with the thought that their ashes will rejoin and disappear in the great stream of matter. Matter in its simplest and most imperishable forms would in that case be the unchangeable environment in which we shall finally rest. A moment's reflection is enough to show the disadvantage of this prospect. Elementary matter might, it is supposed, represent the form of equilibrium to which the stuff of the noosphere tends to drift and fix. But this is impossible for two reasons. First, permanent though they appear in relation to our life-span, the physico-chemical elements, as we now know, are themselves in process of breaking up; there is a death of matter. Moreover, and this is more serious still, formless energy to which the pantheisms of the inanimate try to cling as the basis of stability in no way resembles (even supposing it to be indestructible) the ideal legitimately expected by our conscious endeavours. Born of a dispersion or general release of things, pure matter stands at the antipodes of the 'centre of psychic convergence' required and foreshadowed by all the inner demands and by all the recorded developments of the noosphere. What death, in order to be death no longer, must let through, is not a residue but the most precious essence of our beings; not the most primitive and the most unconscious, but the most evolved and the most reflective parts of ourselves. And each of us, by the long labour of the past in the first place, and secondly, thanks to our individual liberty, is gradually forming a nucleus for vision and action, an 'I,' a *person.*

The idea in common circulation that the universal is opposed to the personal, seems to have its instinctive origin in the fact that 'personality' only manifests itself to our experience in connexion with individuals, and its scientific origin in the modern discovery of those vast diffused unities of energy and matter, in which, as we have said, it has been possible for us to believe we have found the stable and definite form of the All. But this idea (we ought rather to say this impression) does not stand up to analysis. The totality of a sphere is just as present in its centre, which takes the form of a point, as spread over its whole surface; in fact it really lies only in that point. Now why should it be strange for the universe to have a centre, that is to say to collect itself to the same degree in a single consciousness, if its totality is already partially reflected in each of our particular consciousnesses? To conceive of an ultimate centre of thought is after all only a matter of extending along the same line the process by which the human soul was born.[5] In order that, in a given world, the appearance of a personal-universal not only can but must take place, it is sufficient for the world in question to be 'structurally convergent.' That our universe is precisely of such a structure is revealed by the very existence of our individual centres of thought.

We are now faced with the second aspect of the paradox. To establish the possibility, and even the necessity, of a personal-universal at the summit of evolution, we have just assumed that an ultra-concentration in a higher consciousness could and must be produced from human personal elements. But is such a transformation in fact intrinsically realizable? At first it would seem that it is not. At a first view, we can only see two imaginable processes which could lead to the formation of a universal centre: either the absorption of the lower centres in a more powerful unity that will absorb them, or a coalescence of these centres in a resulting unity born of their assemblage. Now neither of these two mechanisms shows itself capable of assuring, as would be necessary, a progress of the elements *in cohesion* and *in distinction at once.* By nature, the elementary 'I's,' once formed, can no longer advance in being except by an increase of the interior concentration from which they were born. How therefore could they be absorbed or melt into anything without proportionately shrinking back on themselves? We have accepted that, to be more personal, the human nuclei would have to unite in another or among themselves. But the point is that they cannot fuse without, apparently, to the same extent contracting their personality. Is it possible to escape this contradiction? Yes, we must reply, and indeed very easily. In order to see the paradox vanish, it is sufficient to turn the last, fallacious proposition upside down. One personality, we have just said, seems unable to join itself with another personality except by losing something of its own personality. But precisely the reverse is true. Let us observe any unification by *convergence* that operates in the field of our experience: a grouping of cells in a living body, a grouping of individuals and functions in a social organism, a grouping of souls under the influence of a great love. And we come to a factual conclusion that easily proves the theory. It is this: the phenomena of fusion or dissolution are in nature only the sign of a return to fragmentation in homogeneity. Union, the true upward union in the spirit, ends by establishing the elements it dominates in their own perfection. *Union differentiates.* In virtue of this fundamental principle, elementary personalities can, and can *only* affirm themselves by acceding to a psychic unity or higher soul. But this always on one condition: that the higher centre to which they come to join *without mingling together* has its own autonomous reality. *Since there is no fusion or dissolution* of the elementary personalities the centre in which they join *must necessarily be distinct from them, that is to say have its own personality.*

Hence we have the following formula for the supreme goal towards which human energy is tending: an organic plurality the elements of which find the consummation of their own personality in a paroxysm of mutual union and limpidity: the whole body being supported by the unifying influence of a *distinct centre* of super-personality.

This last condition or qualification has considerable importance. It demonstrates that the noosphere in fact *physically* requires, for its maintenance and functioning, the existence in the universe of a true pole of psychic convergence: a centre different from all the other centres which it 'super-centres' by assimilation: a personality distinct from all the personalities it perfects by uniting with them. The world would not function if there did not exist, somewhere ahead in time and space, 'a cosmic point Omega' of total synthesis.

Notes

1. For the Christian transformist, God's creative action is no longer conceived as an intrusive thrusting of His works into the midst of pre-existent beings, but as a *bringing to birth* of the successive stages of His work in the heart of things. It is no less essential, no less universal, no less intimate either on that account. (Author's note on 'The Transformist Paradox,' *The Vision of the Past*, p. 102.)

2. An absolute movement through inter-sidereal space.

3. Sustained, of course, by some deep creative force. If we do not speak more explicitly of this force, it is, we repeat, because our purpose is to follow the shape of the apparent curve of phenomena without examining the metaphysical conditions of its existence. (Author's note on the subject of 'Hominization,' *The Vision of the Past*, p. 73.)

4. 'From a purely scientific and empirical standpoint,' as is said in the preceding paragraph. (*Ed.*)

5. In so far as the existence of the soul, in the course of development of creation, is linked with the appearance of the body. (*Ed.*)

Suggested Readings

Knight, Alice Valle. *The Meaning of Teilhard de Chardin: A Primer.* Old Greenwich (Conn): Devin-Adair, 1974.

Aller, Catherine. *The Challenge of Pierre Teilhard de Chardin.* New York: Exposition Press, 1967.

Grau, Joseph. *Morality and the Human Future In the Thought of Teilhard de Chardin: A Critical Study.* New York: Seabury Press, 1981.

Appendix

A

Culture
Criticism

Introduction

Since we live and die in a capitalist system, it seems only fitting and proper that we end our anthology with a cultural critique of the funeral ritual. In her book *The American Way of Death* Jessica Mitford, the British born "Queen of the Muckrakers," reveals the grotesque underbelly, pardon the pun, of the funeral parlor. I once heard a relative express her preference for a certain parlor because "they served cold cuts" after the ceremony. Apart from the hors d'oeuvres, why is it that we indulge in this strange ritual of pharaonic mummification?

In hope of answering this question we have followed the Mitford article with selections from the writings of Karl Marx. For Marx, a scathing critic of capitalism, the forces of production (the way we labor with tools) create the relations of production (the way we think and act toward self and others). Under the capitalist mode of labor, the worker not only makes commodities, but these commodities are taken from him in trade for the funny stuff we call money. In the end the worker is himself treated and traded like any other commodity on the market. In this alienated condition the worker can only fill his emptiness with things—even unto death.

Although the Marxist critique is still relevant in terms of alienation and certain inherent contradictions within the capitalist system, it is, nevertheless, tied to the conditions of the industrial age and the Enlightenment ideals of revolution, liberty and progress through rational means. Marx should have known better—things change! Revolution? Who would come? And even if anybody showed up for one, we would end up helping to sell soap, or cell phones, on the evening news. Marx failed to see that the ubiquitous and all consuming nature of the capitalist schizoid machine would gobble up any opposition and spit it out as amusement and advertisement. In fact, we now prefer and like the world of simulation, imagery and amusement far better than any real natural object or commodity—we are now beyond commodities and in the age of the hyperreal. To understand this new condition and how it affects our view of death, we end with a postmodern critique of the funeral.

Chapter 26

The American Way of Death

Jessica Mitford

How long, I would ask, are we to be subjected to the tyranny of custom and undertakers? Truly, it is all vanity and vexation of spirit—a mere mockery of woe, costly to all, far, far beyond its value; and ruinous to many; hateful, and an abomination to all, yet submitted to by all, because none have the moral courage to speak against it and act in defiance of it.

—Lord Essex

O DEATH, where is thy sting? O grave, where is thy victory? Where, indeed. Many a badly stung survivor, faced with the aftermath of some relative's funeral, has ruefully concluded that the victory has been won hands down by a funeral establishment—in disastrously unequal battle.

Much has been written of late about the affluent society in which we live, and much fun poked at some of the irrational "status symbols" set out like golden snares to trap the unwary consumer at every turn. Until recently, little has been said about the most irrational and weirdest of the lot, lying in ambush for all of us at the end of the road—the modem American funeral.

The drama begins to unfold with the arrival of the corpse at the mortuary.

Alas, poor Yorick! How surprised he would be to see how his counterpart of today is whisked off to a funeral parlor and is in short order sprayed, sliced, pierced, pickled, trussed, trimmed, creamed, waxed, painted, rouged and neatly dressed—transformed from a common corpse into a Beautiful Memory Picture. This process is known in the trade as embalming and restorative art, and is so universally employed in the United States and Canada that the funeral director does it routinely, without consulting corpse or kin. He regards as eccentric those few who are hardy enough to suggest that it might be dispensed with. Yet no law requires embalming, no religious doctrine commends it, nor is it dictated by considerations of health, sanitation, or even of personal daintiness. In no part of the world but in Northern America is it widely used. The purpose of embalming is to make the corpse presentable for viewing in a suitably costly container; and here too the funeral director routinely, without first consulting the family, prepares the body for public display.

Is all this legal? The processes to which a dead body may be subjected are after all to some extent circumscribed by law. In most states, for instance, the signature of next of kin must be obtained before an autopsy may be performed, before the deceased may be cremated, before the body may be turned over to a medical school for research purposes; or such provision must be made in the decedent's will. In the case of embalming, no such permission is required nor is it ever sought. A textbook, *The Principles and Practices of Embalming,* comments on this: "There is some question regarding the legality of much that is done within the preparation room." The author points out that it would be most unusual for a responsible member of a bereaved family to instruct the mortician, in so many words, to *"embalm"* the body of a deceased relative. The very term "embalming" is so seldom used that the mortician must rely upon custom in the matter. The author concludes that unless the family specifies otherwise, the act of entrusting the body to the care of a funeral establishment carries with it an implied permission to go ahead and embalm.

Embalming is indeed a most extraordinary procedure, and one must wonder at the docility of Americans who each year pay hundreds of millions of dollars for its perpetuation, blissfully ignorant of what it is all about, what is done, how it is done. Not one in ten thousand has any idea of what actually takes place. Books on the subject are extremely hard to come by. They are not to be found in most libraries or bookshops.

In an era when huge television audiences watch surgical operations in the comfort of their living rooms, when, thanks to the animated cartoon, the geography of the digestive system has become familiar territory even to the nursery school set, in a land where the satisfaction of curiosity about almost all matters is a national pastime, the secrecy surrounding embalming can, surely, hardly be attributed to the inherent gruesomeness of the subject. Custom in this regard has within this century suffered a complete reversal. In the early days of American embalming, when it was performed in the home of the deceased, it was almost mandatory for some relative to stay by the embalmer's side and witness the procedure. Today, family members who might wish to be in attendance would certainly be dissuaded by the funeral director. All others, except apprentices, are excluded by law from the preparation room.

A close look at what does actually take place may explain in large measure the undertaker's intractable reticence concerning a procedure that has become his major *raison d'être.* Is it possible he fears that public information about embalming might lead patrons to wonder if they really want this service? If the funeral men are loath to discuss the subject outside the trade, the reader may, understandably, be equally loath to go on reading at this point. For those who have the stomach for it, let us part the formaldehyde curtain.

The body is first laid out in the undertaker's morgue—or rather, Mr. Jones is reposing in the preparation room—to be readied to bid the world farewell.

The preparation room in any of the better funeral establishments has the tiled and sterile look of a surgery, and indeed the embalmer-restorative artist who does his chores there is beginning to adopt the term "dermasurgeon" (appropriately corrupted by some mortician-writers as "demi-surgeon") to describe his calling. His equipment, consisting of scalpels, scissors, augurs, forceps, clamps, needles, pumps, tubes, bowls and basins, is crudely imitative of the surgeon's, as is his technique, acquired in a nine- or twelve-month post-high-school course in an embalming school. He is supplied by an advanced chemical industry with a bewildering array of fluids, sprays, pastes, oils, powders, creams, to fix or soften tissue, shrink or distend it as needed, dry it here, restore the moisture there. There are cosmetics, waxes and paints to fill and cover features, even plaster of Paris to replace entire limbs. There are ingenious aids to prop and stabilize the cadaver: a Vari-Pose Head Rest, the Edwards Arm and Hand Positioner, the Repose Block (to support the shoulders during the embalming), and the Throop Foot Positioner, which resembles an old-fashioned stocks.

Mr. John H. Eckels, president of the Eckels College of Mortuary Science, thus describes the first part of the embalming procedure: "In the hands of a skilled practitioner, this work may be done in a comparatively short time and without mutilating the body other than by slight incision—so slight that it scarcely would cause serious inconvenience if made upon a living person. It is necessary to remove the blood, and doing this not only helps in the disinfecting, but removes the principal cause of disfigurements due to discoloration."

Another textbook discusses the all-important time element: "The earlier this is done, the better, for every hour that elapses between death and embalming will add to the problems and complications encountered...." Just how soon should one get going on the embalming? The author tells us, "On the basis of such scanty information made available to this profession through its rudimentary and haphazard system of technical research, we must conclude that the best results are to be obtained if the subject is embalmed before life is completely extinct—that is, before cellular death has occurred. In the average case, this would mean within an hour after somatic death." For those who feel that there is something a little rudimentary, not to say haphazard, about this advice, a comforting thought is offered by another writer. Speaking of fears entertained in early days of premature burial, be points out, "One of the effects of embalming by chemical injection, however, has been to dispel fears of live burial." How true; once the blood is removed, chances of live burial are indeed remote.

To return to Mr. Jones, the blood is drained out through the veins and replaced by embalming fluid pumped in through the arteries. As noted in *The Principles and Practices of Embalming,* "every operator has a favorite injection and drainage point—a fact which becomes a handicap only if be fails or refuses to forsake his favorites when conditions demand it." Typical favorites are the carotid artery, femoral artery, jugular vein, subclavian vein. There are various choices of embalming fluid. If Flextone is used, it will produce a "Mild, flexible rigidity. The skin retains a velvety softness, the tissues are rubbery and pliable. Ideal for women and children." It may be blended with B. and G. Products Company's Lyf-Lyk tint, which is guaranteed to reproduce "nature's own skin texture...the velvety appearance of living tissue." Suntone comes in three separate tints: Suntan; Special Cosmetic Tint, a pink shade "especially indicated for young female subjects"; and Regular Cosmetic Tint, moderately pink.

About three to six gallons of a dyed and perfumed solution of formaldehyde, glycerin, borax, phenol, alcohol and water is soon circulating through Mr. Jones, whose mouth has been sewn together with a "needle directed upward between the upper lip and gum and brought out through the left nostril," with the corners raised slightly "for a more pleasant expression." If he should be bucktoothed, his teeth are cleaned with Bon Ami and coated with colorless nail polish. His eyes, meanwhile, are closed with flesh-tinted eye caps and eye cement.

The next step is to have at Mr. Jones with a thing called a trocar. This is a long, hollow needle attached to a tube. It is jabbed into the abdomen, poked around the entrails and chest cavity, the contents of which are pumped out and replaced with "cavity fluid." This done, and the hole in the abdomen sewn up, Mr. Jones's face is heavily creamed (to protect the skin from burns which may be caused by leakage of the chemicals), and he is covered with a sheet and left unmolested for a while. But not for long—there is more, much more, in store for him. He has been embalmed, but not yet restored, and the best time to start the restorative work is eight to ten hours after embalming, when the tissues have become firm and dry.

The object of all this attention to the corpse, it must be remembered, is to make it presentable for viewing in an attitude of healthy repose. "Our customs require the presentation of our dead in the semblance of normality...unmarred by the ravages of illness, disease or mutilation," says Mr. J. Sheridan Mayer in his *Restorative Art*. This is rather a large order since few people die in the full bloom of health, unravaged by illness and unmarked by some disfigurement. The funeral industry is equal to the challenge: "In some cases the gruesome appearance of a mutilated or disease-ridden subject may be quite discouraging. The task of restoration may seem impossible and shake the confidence of the embalmer. This is the time for intestinal fortitude and determination. Once the formative work is begun and affected tissues are cleaned or removed, all doubts of success vanish. It is surprising and gratifying to discover the results which may be obtained."

The embalmer, having allowed an appropriate interval to elapse, returns to the attack, but now he brings into play the skill and equipment of sculptor and cosmetician. Is a hand missing? Casting one in plaster of Paris is a simple matter. "For replacement purposes, only a cast of the back of the hand is necessary; this is within the ability of the average operator and is quite adequate." If a lip or two, a nose or an ear should be missing, the embalmer has at hand a variety of restorative waxes with which to model replacements. Pores and skin texture are simulated by stippling with a little brush, and over this cosmetics are laid on. Head off? Decapitation cases are rather routinely handled. Ragged edges are trimmed, and head joined to torso with a series of splints, wires and sutures. It is a good idea to have a little something at the neck—a scarf or high collar—when time for viewing comes. Swollen mouth? Cut out tissue as needed from inside the lips. If too much is removed, the surface contour can easily be restored by padding with cotton. Swollen necks and cheeks are reduced by removing tissue through vertical incisions made down each side of the neck. "When the deceased is casketed, the pillow will hide the suture incisions...as an extra precaution against leakage, the suture may be painted with liquid sealer."

The opposite condition is more likely to present itself—that of emaciation. His hypodermic syringe now loaded with massage cream, the embalmer seeks out and fills the hollowed and sunken areas by injection. In this procedure the backs of the hands and fingers and the under-chin area should not be neglected.

Positioning the lips is a problem that recurrently challenges the ingenuity of the embalmer. Closed too tightly, they tend to give a stern, even disapproving expression. Ideally, embalmers feel, the lips should give the impression of being ever so slightly parted, the upper lip protruding slightly for a more youthful appearance. This takes some engineering, however, as the lips tend to drift apart. Lip drift can sometimes be remedied by pushing one or two straight pins through the inner margin of the lower lip and then inserting them between the two front upper teeth. If Mr. Jones happens to have no teeth, the pins can just as easily be anchored in his Armstrong Face Former and Denture Replacer. Another method to maintain lip closure is to dislocate the lower jaw, which is then held in its new position by a wire run through holes which have been drilled through the upper and lower jaws at the midline. As the French are fond of saying, *il faut souffrir pour être belle.*[1]

If Mr. Jones has died of jaundice, the embalming fluid will very likely turn him green. Does this deter the embalmer? Not if he has intestinal fortitude. Masking pastes and cosmetics are heavily laid on, burial garments and casket interiors are color-correlated with particular care, and Jones is displayed beneath rose-colored lights. Friends will say, "How *well* he looks."

Death by carbon monoxide, on the other hand, can be rather a good thing from the embalmer's viewpoint: "One advantage is the fact that this type of discoloration is an exaggerated form of a natural pink coloration." This is nice because the healthy glow is already present and needs but little attention.

The patching and filling completed, Mr. Jones is now shaved, washed and dressed. Cream-based cosmetic, available in pink, flesh, suntan, brunette and blond, is applied to his hands and face, his hair is shampooed and combed (and, in the case of Mrs. Jones, set), his hands manicured. For the horny-handed son of toil special care must be taken; cream should be applied to remove ingrained grime, and the nails cleaned. "If he were not in the habit of having them manicured in life, trimming and shaping is advised for better appearance—never questioned by kin."

Jones is now ready for casketing (this is the present participle of the verb "to casket"). In this operation his right shoulder should be depressed slightly "to turn the body a bit to the right and soften the appearance of lying flat on the back." Positioning the hands is a matter of importance, and special rubber positioning blocks may be used. The hands should be cupped slightly for a more lifelike, relaxed appearance. Proper placement of the body requires a delicate sense of balance. It should lie as high as possible in the casket, yet not so high that the lid, when lowered, will hit the nose. On the other hand, we are cautioned, placing the body too low "creates the impression that the body is in a box."

Jones is next wheeled into the appointed slumber room where a few last touches may be added—his favorite pipe placed in his hand or, if he was a great reader, a book propped into position. (In the case of little Master Jones a Teddy bear may be clutched.) Here he will hold open house for a few days, visiting hours 10 A.M. to 9 P.M.

All now being in readiness, the funeral director calls a staff conference to make sure that each assistant knows his precise duties. Mr. Wilber Krieger writes: "This makes your staff feel that they are a part of the team, with a definite assignment that must be properly carried out if the whole plan is to succeed. You never heard of a football coach who failed to talk to his entire team before they go on the field. They have drilled on the plays they are to execute for hours and days, and yet the successful coach knows the importance of making even the bench-warming third-string substitute feel that he is important if the game is to be won." The winning of *this* game is predicated upon glass-smooth handling of the logistics. The funeral director has notified the pallbearers whose names were furnished by the family, has arranged for the presence of clergyman, organist, and soloist, has provided transportation for everybody, has organized and listed the flowers sent by friends. In *Psychology of Funeral Service* Mr. Edward A. Martin points out: "He may not always do as much as the family thinks he is doing, but it is his helpful guidance that they appreciate in knowing they are proceeding as they should.... The important thing is how well his services can be used to make the family believe they are giving unlimited expression to their own sentiment."

The religious service may be held in a church or in the chapel of the funeral home; the funeral director vastly prefers the latter arrangement, for not only is it more convenient for him but it affords him the opportunity to show off his beautiful facilities to the gathered mourners. After the clergyman has had his say, the mourners queue up to file past the casket for a last look at the deceased. The family is *never* asked whether they want an open-casket ceremony; in the absence of their instruction to the contrary, this is taken for granted. Consequently well over 90 per cent of all American funerals feature the open casket—a custom unknown in other parts of the world. Foreigners are astonished by it. An English woman living in San Francisco described her reaction in a letter to the writer:

> *I myself have attended only one funeral here—that of an elderly fellow worker of mine. After the service I could not understand why everyone was walking towards the coffin (sorry, I mean casket), but thought I had better follow the crowd. It shook me rigid to get there and find the casket open and poor old Oscar lying there in his brown tweed suit, wearing a suntan makeup and just the wrong shade of lipstick. If I had not been extremely fond of the old boy, I have a horrible feeling that I might have giggled. Then and there I decided that I could never face another American funeral—even dead.*

The casket (which has been resting throughout the service on a Classic Beauty Ultra Metal Casket Bier) is now transferred by a hydraulically operated device called Porto-Lift to a balloon-tired, Glide Easy casket carriage which will wheel it to yet another conveyance, the Cadillac Funeral Coach. This may be lavender, cream, light green—anything but black. Interiors, of course, are color-correlated, "for the man who cannot stop short of perfection."

At graveside, the casket is lowered into the earth. This office, once the prerogative of friends of the deceased, is now performed by a patented mechanical lowering device. A "Lifetime Green" artificial grass mat is at the ready to conceal the sere earth, and overhead, to conceal the sky, is a portable Steril Chapel Tent ("resists the intense heat and humidity of summer and the terrific storms of winter...available in Silver Grey, Rose or Evergreen"). Now is the time for the ritual scattering of earth over the coffin, as the solemn words "earth to earth, ashes to ashes, dust to dust are pronounced by the officiating cleric. This can today be accomplished "With a mere flick of the wrist with the Gordon Leak-Proof Earth Dispenser. No grasping of a handful of dirt, no soiled fingers. Simple, dignified, beautiful, reverent! The modern way!" The Gordon Earth Dispenser (at $5) is of nickel-plated brass construction. It is not only "attractive to the eye and long wearing"; it is also "one of the 'tools' for building better public relations" if presented as "an appropriate non-commercial gift" to the clergyman. It is shaped something like a saltshaker.

Untouched by human hand, the coffin and the earth are now united.

It is in the function of directing the participants through this maze of gadgetry that the funeral director has assigned to himself his relatively new role of "grief therapist." He has relieved the family of every detail, he has revamped the corpse to look like a living doll, he has arranged for it to nap for a few days in a slumber room, he has put on a well-oiled performance in which the concept of *death* has played no part whatsoever—unless it was inconsiderately mentioned by the clergyman who conducted the religious service. He has done everything in his power to make the funeral a real pleasure for everybody concerned. He and his team have given their all to score an upset victory over death.

Notes

1. In 1963 *Mortuary Management* reports a new development: "Natural Expression Formers,' an invention of Funeral Directors Research Company. "They may be used to replace one or both artificial dentures, or over natural teeth; have 'bite-indicator' lines as a closure guide...Natural Expression Formers also offer more control of facial expression."

Chapter 27

Capitalism and Commodification

Karl Marx

⚒ The Premisses of the Materialist Method ⚒

The premisses from which we begin are not arbitrary ones, not dogmas, but real premisses from which abstraction can only be made in the imagination. They are the real individuals, their activity and the material conditions under which they live, both those which they find already existing and those produced by their activity. These premisses can thus be verified in a purely empirical way.

The first premiss of all human history is, of course, the existence of living human individuals. Thus the first fact to be established is the physical organization of these individuals and their consequent relation to the rest of nature. Of course, we cannot here go either into the actual physical nature of man, or into the natural conditions in which man finds himself—geological, oro-hydrographical, climatic, and so on. The writing of history must always set out from these natural bases and their modification in the course of history through the action of men.

Men can be distinguished from animals by consciousness, by religion, or anything else you like. They themselves begin to distinguish themselves from animals as soon as they begin to produce their means of subsistence, a step which is conditioned by their physical organization. By producing their means of subsistence men are indirectly producing their actual material life.

The way in which men produce their means of subsistence depends first of all on the nature of the actual means of subsistence they find in existence and have to reproduce. This mode of production must not be considered simply as being the production of the physical existence of the individuals. Rather it is a definite form of activity of these individuals, a definite form of expressing their life, a definite mode of life on their part. As individuals express their life, so they are. What they are, therefore, coincides with their production, both with *what* they produce and with *how* they produce. The nature of individuals thus depends on the material conditions determining their production.

The production of ideas, of conceptions, of consciousness, is at first directly interwoven with the material activity and the material intercourse of men, the language of real life. Conceiving, thinking, the mental intercourse of men, appear at this stage as the direct efflux of

From *Karl Marx: Selected Writings* edited by David McLellan (1977). Reprinted by permission of Oxford University Press.

their material behaviour. The same applies to mental production as expressed in the language of politics, laws, morality, religion, metaphysics, etc. of a people. Men are the producers of their conceptions, ideas, etc.—real, active men, as they are conditioned by a definite development of their productive forces and of the intercourse corresponding to these, up to its furthest forms. Consciousness can never be anything else than conscious existence, and the existence of men is their actual life-process. If in all ideology men and their circumstances appear upside-down as in a *camera obscura*, this phenomenon arises just as much from their historical life-process as the inversion of objects on the retina does from their physical life-process.

In direct contrast to German philosophy which descends from heaven to earth, here we ascend from earth to heaven. That is to say, we do not set out from what men say, imagine, conceive, nor from men as narrated, thought of, imagined, conceived, in order to arrive at men in the flesh. We set out from real, active men, and on the basis of their real life-process we demonstrate the development of the ideological reflexes and echoes of this life-process. The phantoms formed in the human brain are also, necessarily, sublimates of their material life-process, which is empirically verifiable and bound to material premises. Morality, religion, metaphysics, all the rest of ideology and their corresponding forms of consciousness, thus no longer retain the semblance of independence. They have no history, no development; but men, developing their material production and their material intercourse, alter, along with this their real existence, their thinking and the products of their thinking. Life is not determined by consciousness, but consciousness by life. In the first method of approach the starting-point is consciousness taken as the living individual; in the second method, which conforms to real life, it is the real living individuals themselves, and consciousness is considered solely as their consciousness.

This method of approach is not devoid of premises. It starts out from the real premises and does not abandon them for a moment. Its premises are men, not in any fantastic isolation and rigidity, but in their actual, empirically perceptible process of development under definite conditions. As soon as this active life-process is described, history ceases to be a collection of dead facts as it is with the empiricists (themselves still abstract), or an imagined activity of imagined subjects, as with the idealists.

Where speculation ends—in real life—there real, positive science begins: the representation of the practical activity, of the practical process of development of men. Empty talk about consciousness ceases, and real knowledge has to take its place.

The ideas of the ruling class are in every epoch the ruling ideas, i.e. the class which is the ruling material force of society is at the same time its ruling intellectual force. The class which has the means of material production at its disposal, has control at the same time over the means of mental production, so that thereby, generally speaking, the ideas of those who lack the means of mental production are subject to it. The ruling ideas are nothing more than the ideal expression of the dominant material relationships, the dominant material relationships grasped as ideas; hence of the relationships which make the one class the ruling one, therefore, the ideas of its dominance. The individuals composing the ruling class possess among other things consciousness, and therefore think. In so far, therefore, as they rule as a class and determine the extent and compass of an epoch, it is self-evident that they do this in its whole range, hence among other things rule also as thinkers, as producers of ideas, and regulate the production and distribution of the ideas of their age: thus their ideas are the ruling ideas of the epoch. For instance, in an age and in a country where royal power, aristocracy, and bourgeoisie are contending for mastery and where, therefore, mastery is shared, the doctrine of the separation of powers proves to be the dominant idea and is expressed as an 'eternal law'...

Social relations are closely bound up with productive forces. In acquiring new productive forces men change their mode of production; and in changing their mode of production, in changing the way of earning their living, they change all their social relations. The hand-mill gives you society with the feudal lord; the steam-mill, society with the industrial capitalist.

The same men who establish their social relations in conformity with their material productivity, produce also principles, ideas, and categories in conformity with their social relations.

Thus these ideas, these categories, are as little eternal as the relations they express. They are historical and transitory products.

There is a continual movement of growth in productive forces, of destruction in social relations, of formation in ideas; the only immutable thing is the abstraction of movement—*mors immortalis*.

⚓ Alienated Labour ⚓

We started from the presuppositions of political economy. We accepted its vocabulary and its laws. We presupposed private property, the separation of labour, capital, and land, and likewise of wages, profit, and ground rent; also division of labour; competition; the concept of exchange value, etc. Using the very words of political economy we have demonstrated that the worker is degraded to the most miserable sort of commodity; that the misery of the worker is in inverse proportion to the power and size of his production; that the necessary result of competition is the accumulation of capital in a few hands, and thus a more terrible restoration of monopoly; and that finally the distinction between capitalist and landlord, and that between peasant and industrial worker disappears and the whole of society must fall apart into the two classes of the property owners and the propertyless workers.

We start with a contemporary fact of political economy:

The worker becomes poorer the richer is his production, the more it increases in power and scope. The worker becomes a commodity that is all the cheaper the more commodities he creates. The depreciation of the human world progresses in direct proportion to the increase in value of the world of things. Labour does not only produce commodities; it produces itself and the labourer as a commodity and that to the extent to which it produces commodities in general.

What this fact expresses is merely this: the object that labour produces, its product, confronts it as an alien being, as a power independent of the producer. The product of labour is labour that has solidified itself into an object, made itself into a thing, the objectification of labour. The realization of labour is its objectification. In political economy this realization of labour appears as a loss of reality for the worker, objectification as a loss of the object or slavery to it, and appropriation as alienation, as externalization.

The realization of labour appears as a loss of reality to an extent that the worker loses his reality by dying of starvation. Objectification appears as a loss of the object to such an extent that the worker is robbed not only of the objects necessary for his life but also of the objects of his work. Indeed, labour itself becomes an object he can only have in his power with the greatest of efforts and at irregular intervals. The appropriation of the object appears as alienation to such an extent that the more objects the worker produces, the less he can possess and the more he falls under the domination of his product, capital.

All these consequences follow from the fact that the worker relates to the product of his labour as to an alien object. For it is evident from this presupposition that the more the worker externalizes himself in his work, the more powerful becomes the alien, objective world that he creates opposite himself, the poorer he becomes himself in his inner life and the less he can call his own. It is just the same in religion. The more man puts into God, the less he retains in himself. The worker puts his life into the object and this means that it no longer belongs to him but to the object. So the greater this product the less he is himself. The externalization of the worker in his product implies not only that his labour becomes an object, an exterior existence but also that it exists outside him, independent and alien, and becomes a self-sufficient power opposite him, that the life that he has lent to the object affronts him, hostile and alien.

Let us now deal in more detail with objectification, the production of the worker, and the alienation, the loss of the object, his product, which is involved in it.

The worker can create nothing without nature, the sensuous exterior world. It is the matter in which his labour realizes itself, in which it is active, out of which and through which it produces.

But as nature affords the means of life for labour in the sense that labour cannot live without objects on which it exercises itself, so it affords a means of life in the narrower sense, namely the means for the physical subsistence of the worker himself.

Thus the more the worker appropriates the exterior world of sensuous nature by his labour, the more he doubly deprives himself of the means of subsistence, firstly since the exterior sensuous world increasingly ceases to be an object belonging to his work, a means of subsistence for his labour; secondly, since it increasingly ceases to be a means of subsistence in the direct sense, a means for the physical subsistence of the worker.

Thus in these two ways the worker becomes a slave to his object: firstly he receives an object of labour, that is he receives labour, and secondly, he receives the means of subsistence. Thus it is his object that permits him to exist first as a worker and secondly as a physical subject. The climax of this slavery is that only as a worker can he maintain himself as a physical subject and it is only as a physical subject that he is a worker.

(According to the laws of political economy the alienation of the worker in his object is expressed as follows: the more the worker produces the less he has to consume, the more values he creates the more valueless and worthless he becomes, the more formed the product the more deformed the worker, the more civilized the product, the more barbaric the worker, the more powerful the work the more powerless becomes the worker, the more cultured the work the more philistine the worker becomes and more of a slave to nature.)

What does the externalization of labour consist of then?

Firstly, that labour is exterior to the worker, that is, it does not belong to his essence. Therefore he does not confirm himself in his work, he denies himself, feels miserable instead of happy, deploys no free physical and intellectual energy, but mortifies his body and ruins his mind. Thus the worker only feels a stranger. He is at home when he is not working and when he works he is not at home. His labour is therefore not voluntary but compulsory, forced labour. It is therefore not the satisfaction of a need but only a means to satisfy needs outside itself. How alien it really is is very evident from the fact that when there is no physical or other compulsion, labour is avoided like the plague. External labour, labour in which man externalizes himself, is a labour of self-sacrifice and mortification. Finally, the external character of labour for the worker shows itself in the fact that it is not his own but someone else's, that it does not belong to him, that he does not belong to himself in his labour but to someone else. As in religion the human imagination's own activity, the activity of man's head and his heart, reacts independently on the individual as an alien activity of gods or devils, so the activity of the worker is not his own spontaneous activity. It belongs to another and is the loss of himself.

The result we arrive at then is that man (the worker) only feels himself freely active in his animal functions of eating, drinking, and procreating, at most also in his dwelling and dress, and feels himself an animal in his human functions.

Eating, drinking, procreating, etc. are indeed truly human functions. But in the abstraction that separates them from the other round of human activity and makes them into final and exclusive ends they become animal.

The animal is immediately one with its vital activity. It is not distinct from it. They are identical. Man makes his vital activity itself into an object of his will and consciousness. He has a conscious vital activity. He is not immediately identical to any of his characterizations. Conscious vital activity differentiates man immediately from animal vital activity. It is this and this alone that makes man a species-being. He is only a conscious being, that is, his own life is an object to him, precisely because he is a species-being. This is the only reason for his activity being free activity. Alienated labour reverses the relationship so that, just because he is a conscious being, man makes his vital activity and essence a mere means to his existence.

The practical creation of an objective world, the working-over of inorganic nature, is the confirmation of man as a conscious species-being, that is, as a being that relates to the species as to himself and to himself as to the species. It is true that the animal, too, produces. It builds itself a nest, a dwelling, like the bee, the beaver, the ant, etc. But it only produces what it needs immediately for itself or its offspring; it produces one-sidedly whereas man produces universally; it produces only under the pressure of immediate physical need, whereas man produces freely from physical need and only truly produces when he is thus free; it produces only itself whereas man reproduces the whole of nature. Its product belongs immediately to its physical body whereas man can freely separate himself from his product. The animal only fashions things according to the standards and needs of the species it belongs to, whereas man knows how to produce according to the measure of every species and knows everywhere how to apply its inherent standard to the object; thus man also fashions things according to the laws of beauty.

Thus it is in the working over of the objective world that man first really affirms himself as a species-being. This production is his active species-life. Through it nature appears as his work and his reality. The object of work is therefore the objectification of the species-life of man; for he duplicates himself not only intellectually, in his mind, but also actively in reality and thus can look at his image in a world he has created. Therefore when alienated labour tears from man the object of his production, it also tears from him his species-life, the real objectivity of his species and turns the advantage he has over animals into a disadvantage in that his inorganic body, nature, is torn from him.

Now, therefore, for the first question: What are wages? How are they determined?

If workers were asked: 'How much are your wages?' one would reply: 'I get a mark a day from my employer'; another, 'I get two marks,' and so on. According to the different trades to which they belong, they would mention different sums of money which they receive from their respective employers for the performance of a particular piece of work, for example, weaving a yard of linen or type-setting a printed sheet. In spite of the variety of their statements, they would all agree on one point: wages are the sum of money paid by the capitalist for a particular labour time or for a particular output of labour.

The capitalist, it seems, therefore, buys their labour with money. They sell him their labour for money. For the same sum with which the capitalist has bought their labour, for example, two marks, he could have bought two pounds of sugar or a definite amount of any other commodity. The two marks, with which he bought two pounds of sugar, are the price of the two pounds of sugar. The two marks, with which he bought twelve hours' use of labour, are the price of twelve hours' labour. Labour, therefore, is a commodity, neither more nor less than sugar. The former is measured by the clock, the latter by the scales.

The workers exchange their commodity, labour, for the commodity of the capitalist, for money, and this exchange takes place in a definite ratio. So much money for so much labour. For twelve hours' weaving, two marks. And do not the two marks represent all the other commodities which I can buy for two marks? In fact, therefore, the worker has exchanged his commodity, labour, for commodities of all kinds and that in a definite ratio. By giving him two marks, the capitalist has given him so much meat, so much clothing, so much fuel, light, etc., in exchange for his day's labour. Accordingly, the two marks express the ratio in which labour is exchanged for other commodities, the exchange value of his labour.

Wages are, therefore, not the worker's share in the commodity produced by him. Wages are the part of already existing commodities with which the capitalist buys for himself a definite amount of productive labour.

Labour is, therefore, a commodity which its possessor, the wage-worker, sells to capital. Why does he sell it? In order to live.

But the exercise of labour is the worker's own life-activity, the manifestation of his own life. And this life-activity he sells to another person in order to secure the necessary means of subsistence. Thus his life-activity is for him only a means to enable him to exist. He works in order to live. He does not even reckon labour as part of his life, it is rather a sacrifice of his life. It is a commodity which he has made over to another.

◢ On Money ◣

What I have thanks to money, what I pay for, i.e. what money can buy, that is what I, the possessor of the money, am myself. My power is as great as the power of money. The properties of money are my—(its owner's)—properties and faculties. Thus what I am and what I am capable of is by no means determined by my individuality. I am ugly, but I can buy myself the most beautiful women. Consequently I am not ugly, for the effect of ugliness, its power of repulsion, is annulled by money. As an individual, I am lame, but money can create twenty-four feet for me; so I am not lame; I am a wicked, dishonest man without conscience or intellect, but money is honoured and so also is its possessor. Money is the highest good and so its possessor is good. Money relieves me of the trouble of being dishonest; so I am presumed to be honest. I may have no intellect, but money is the true mind of all things and so how should its possessor have no intellect? Moreover he can buy himself intellectuals and is not the man who has power over intellectuals not more intellectual than they? I who can get with money everything that the human heart longs for, do I not possess all human capacities? Does not my money thus change all my incapacities into their opposite?

If money is the bond that binds me to human life, that binds society to me and me to nature and men, is not money the bond of all bonds? Can it not tie and untie all bonds? Is it not, therefore, also the universal means of separation? It is the true agent both of separation and of union, the galvano-chemical power of society.

Shakespeare brings out two particular properties of money:

1. It is the visible god-head, the transformation of all human and natural qualities into their opposites, the general confusion and inversion of things; it makes impossibilities fraternize.
2. It is the universal whore, the universal pander between men and peoples.

The inversion and confusion of all human and natural qualities, the fraternization of impossibilities, this divine power of money lies in its being the externalized and self-externalizing species-being of man. It is the externalized capacities of humanity.

What I cannot do as a man, thus what my individual faculties cannot do, this I can do through money. Thus money turns each of these faculties into something that it is not, i.e. into its opposite.

If I long for a meal, or wish to take the mail coach because I am not strong enough to make the journey on foot, then money procures the meal and the mail coach for me. This means that it changes my wishes from being imaginary, and translates them from their being in thought, imagination, and will into a sensuous, real being, from imagination to life, from imaginary being to real being. The truly creative force in this mediation is money.

Demand also exists for the man who has no money but his demand is simply an imaginary entity that has no effective existence for me, for a third party or for other men and thus remains unreal and without an object. The difference between a demand that is based on money and effective and one that is based on my needs, passions, wishes, etc. and is ineffective is the difference between being and thought, between a representation that merely exists within me and one that is outside me as a real object.

The mode of production in which the product takes the form of a commodity, or is produced directly for exchange, is the most general and most embryonic form of bourgeois production. It therefore makes its appearance at an early date in history, though not in the same predominating and characteristic manner as nowadays. Hence its Fetish character is comparatively easy to be seen through. But when we come to more concrete forms, even this appearance of simplicity vanishes. Whence arose the illusions of the monetary system? To it gold and silver, when serving as money, did not represent a social relation between producers, but were natural objects with strange social properties. And modern economy, which looks down with such disdain on the monetary system, does not its superstition come out as clear as noonday, whenever it treats of capital? How long is it since economy discarded the physiocratic illusion that rents grow out of the soil and not out of society?

Suggested Readings

Fromm, Erich. *Marx's Concept of Man.* New York: Ungar, 1969.
Singer, Peter. *Marx.* New York and Oxford: Oxford University Press, 1983.
Wolfson, M. *Karl Marx.* New York: Columbia University Press, 1971.

Chapter 28

A Postmodern View of Death:
à la Baudrillard

D. J. Ciraulo

If Marx is at least partially correct in thinking that the future can be read in the actual material and economic tendencies of the present, then we denizens, we won't say citizens, of Silicon Valley will categorically reject death. Death is certainly a reality, but it is precisely the concept of "reality" which no longer counts. According to Baudrillard the real has been canceled out in favor of the hyperreal. Since the question of the "real" self has become philosophically problematic anyway, what matters most now is that we have a simulacrum of the self. What we want is something much better than the banality of a putatively real self. We will be content only with the hyperreal self—an authentic fake which makes no reference to anything outside its own appearance and simulation.

It was announced on the news that scientists have discovered all the letters of the human genetic alphabet. We are now on the verge of completing the final reduction of the human being to its essential template and code (shades of an inverted Platonism) for the possible endless reproduction and manipulation of ourselves. This code, for Baudrillard, is the ultimate digital prosthetic device: with it we will be able to extend and morph our bodies far beyond the external and superficial face-lift and biotechnics of today. And soon the genetic code will pharmaceutically worm its way into the brain in a way which not only makes psychotropic drugs obsolete, but also plays havoc with the whole notion of existential freedom. The question of freedom and agency will be in serious trouble not merely from the internal threat of biochemical reductionism, but from the external operation of the digital dream machine: with Michael Jackson, Madonna, Hulk Hogan, Cicciolina and Dolly the sheep as protean archetypes of prosthetic simulacra, we will recreate ourselves endlessly—subjective freedoms freely choosing to objectify ourselves thereby annihilating and trading our freedom for a sign of ourselves.

But what is in store for us is far better than this somewhat narcissistic aestheticism which, after all, is still tied to the vicissitudes of the body. This is much too real! We would still be making reference to the body and to a subject. The age of the hyperreal announces the death of all referents, subjective and objective, and the subsequent apotheosis of the sign in its continual flux. No, the genetic code, as prosthetic device, promises something much more! By way of historical precedent, there is a story about Prince Louis Francois de Conte, a decadent aristocrat who before dying stretched out in his coffin and complained that it was too tight. The good old Prince was a forerunner of the hyperreal and like us desired something much more satisfying than the usual coffin and hope of immortality beyond. But first, what is all this talk about the death of the referent? If Nietzsche's pronouncement on the "death of God" means that metaphysical foundations are gone and must now be understood as stories to be told—grand narratives, and Foucault's "end of man" displaces the notion of man as a free autonomous subject at the center of things to the more humble peripheral status of an object who is prodded, probed and scrutinized by the power discourses of theology and science, then what does Baudrillard mean by this new death—the "death of the referent?"

It has been supposed since Plato that words and signs, if they are to be truthful and meaningful, must refer or correspond to some objective state of affairs, that is, that there must be an extra-linguistic reality, or signified, which is being mapped or mirrored by our language. One did not have to wait for Derrida or Rorty to understand that Saussure and the later Wittgenstein of the *Investigations* already severed the necessary link between the sign and its meaning—signifier and the signified (referent). Wittgenstein says:

> *"Now what do the words of this language signify?—What is*
> *supposed to show they signify, if not the kind of use they have?"*[1]

Following Wittgenstein, the postmodernists see language as a game where the meaning of a word is generated not by an outside referent, but by the internal relation between the words and signs themselves. This is much like a game of chess where the king and queen have meaning only in terms of the rules which guide their moves. To put it simply, the sound "dog" emanating from the hole in the lower part of one's head has no intrinsic and necessary connection to the furry creature in the room, but takes on its meaning in terms of other sounds (signifiers) like "cat" and "rat" in the shared social communicative system (game) in which we speak. The "death of the referent" means that language and signs have been cut loose from what was thought to be their natural moorings in the physical world and we have, like Alice, entered a wonderland—or better Disneyland—of disconnected signifiers where unlike Alice we now prefer the world of the rabbit hole—the fake—and refuse to go back to the parking lot.

Marx thought something of the same sort of disjuncture between object and meaning, signifier and signified, was happening in the capitalist economy, that is, that we live in a kind of wonderland of work believing that the objects we consume have real value beyond their use. Marx first noticed this strange and arbitrary attachment of values to ordinary objects in his analysis of the commodity fetish in *Capital*. Nobody would question the use-value, or intrinsic utility of an object like a coat to keep us warm, but something extraordinary and magical happens when we add surplus-value to the coat through the process of exchange: the useful object now takes on a supernatural and spectral quality beyond its utility and the labor it took to make it. In our eyes, the commodity is imbued with a meaning and value which does not intrinsically belong to it—it has become a fetish! (And today it is even worse. The "market" is now taking on anthropomorphic qualities: an economist interviewed by the stock market cheerleader and anchorman on CNN says things like "the market has decided," and "the market is going to fall into a sense of compromise." What is going on here? Like the German Romantics who felt themselves to be the jinns and voice of the World Spirit, the capitalist pundits now speak the Will of the Market). Marx hoped that the contradictions inherent in the forces of production, like the elimination of alienated labor through the advance of robotics and technology, would ultimately prove fatal to the capitalist system; and that the elimination of money as a universal standard of exchange would rid us of the illusory fetishistic mist in which we live. In short, he believed that the abstract spectral quality of commodities—their signification—would be demystified leaving behind the "real" concrete world of commodities to be used in a natural way without the surplus value attached for the purpose of exploitation. This stripping down of the commodity to its "real" qualities would finally end the nightmarish history of our addiction and enslavement to the quasi-supernatural ideology of capitalism.

But Marx was wrong! The advanced capitalist machine, which by the way is now driverless and without a head, has become victorious over any nostalgic return or reference to the real. Technological advances have actually neutralized the dialectical tensions within the forces of production through the digitalization of the medium of labor. Do we really have a worker and a commodity anymore? Or, has the worker, like all of us now, become an interactive information processor who is himself processed as a receptacle nodal point in the system where the old commodities of labor have been replaced by digital representations—simulacra? There are certainly commodities, but they are, like cigarettes, merely the delivery vehicle for the dope. We are now hooked to the simulacra of the real—to the rosy euphoria of the fake. It is not the industrial factory which is paradigmatic for economics, but Disneyland!

For Marx, the fetishistic halo of smoke and mirrors, although fake, still surrounded a real object or commodity; and the economy, however perverse, was still related to some real social activity. But today, with the help of the digital code as prosthetic device, both the economy and its halo have been blasted into hyperspace. We now have an orbital economy with its free floating signifiers disconnected from the real. As Habermas would say, the system is separating from the life-world. What economist today believes that the market has anything to do with what pork chops one buys?—anything to do with the natural law of supply and demand? Rather, the demand is supplied!—dictated to us from outer space through the media which is merely the capitalist machine reflecting on itself as its own propaganda.

One can now see that the process of commodification going on today in funeral parlors, with the usual accoutrements of tuxedo, casket and embalming, is a pseudo-morphic ritual belonging to the industrial age where one still believed in the value of the commodity—in this case the funeralized dead body as commodity. But as was stated earlier, the digital code as prosthetic device promises much more than the funeral parlors can deliver. Along with the economy, the national debt, information of all sorts and the nuclear threat, we in our postmortem state will go orbital and exist in a parallel universe. The digital code promises nothing less than the ersatz of transcendence: our deaths will be the birth of our virtual self—a complete fake and simulacrum of ourselves frozen in time and kept safe, like superman, in an electronic matrix/palace of ice.

The funeral of today is still part of the old pharaonic imaginary which preserved the body for its journey to the other world. But with new and improved software and the ongoing reduction of the self to a database, we can skip this step and go straight into orbit—virtual immortality.

> "In its electronic and digital form, the database is perfectly transferable in
> space, indefinitely preservable in time, it may last forever everywhere."[2]

Our postmortem condition will be a Western techno-version of the Hindu metaphysical doctrine of the subtle body with its cyclical reincarnations; we, however, will be on a sort of electronic wheel of samsara where instead of occupying a spiritual dimension, the cyber-self will orbit about the earth more like space junk; but unlike space junk, which will burn up upon reentry, the cyber-self will be preprogrammed to beam itself down like a Bodhisattva incarnating and intruding into our world. Now a hologram, the Bodhisattva, or better, the Bodhisinatra will be able to appear in our frontrooms looking better than ever, a never aging sight for sore eyes repetitively singing, "I did it my way." (I am sure the reader will be incredulous about the technological wherewithal to pull off such a feat, but one can rest assured that the details are being worked out.)

The industrial age of the spectacle and the spectator is over! We are now in the interactive age. Funerals still belong to the simulacra of the spectacle where one respectfully observes the body as a sublime signifier for the absence of the person—the lost referent. But with the death of all referents, and therefore deference to the other, the new postmortem relationship will be modeled more on the proud shamelessness of the Jerry Springer show. What I bequeath to the world upon my death is an image, a fake—a simulacrum of all that I would have liked to have said and done endlessly interacting with you in complete and shimmering electrical transparency—a complete obscenity!

Notes

1. Wittgenstein, Ludwig. *Philosophical Investigations*. New York: Macmillan Publishing, 1958, p. 99.
2. Poster, Mark. "Databases as Discourse, or Electronic Interpellations." In *Critical Essays Michel Foucault*. Ed. Kalis Racevskis. New York: GK Hall and Co., 1999, p. 277.

Suggested Readings

Best, Steven and Kellner, Douglas (Ed). *Postmodern Theory: Critical Interrogations*. New York: Guildford Press, 1991.

Baudrillard, Jean. *Selected Writings*. Ed. Mark Poster. Stanford: Stanford University Press, 1988.

Baudrillard, Jean. *The Transparency of Evil: Essays on Extreme Phenomena*. London: Verso, 1993.

Eco, Umberto. *Travels in Hyperreality*. New York: Harcourt Brace Jovanovich, 1983.

Appendix

B

Guiding Questions

⚔ **Plato** ⚔

I. Apology

1. What are the charges brought against Socrates by his Athenian accusers and what is his reply concerning the sort of wisdom he in fact possesses?

2. What does Socrates say is his greatest service to the city?

3. What fate is worse than death for Socrates?

4. What prophetic statement does Socrates make to his accusers?

5. What are the two arguments Socrates gives to his friends for why one should not fear death? Are they convincing?

II. Crito

1. Concerning his escape, what does Socrates say about listening to the opinion of the many?

2. How does Socrates depict the individual's relationship to the State?

3. Why does Socrates say it would be unjust to escape the death penalty?

III. Phaedo

1. Why is suicide not an option for Socrates?

2. How does Socrates explain the idea that a true philosopher is always pursuing death?

3. How does Socrates use the argument from opposites to prove the immortality of the soul?

4. Explain the theory of recollection and show how Socrates thinks it proves the preexistence of the soul.

5. How does Socrates explain the relation between the soul and the body in terms of the unchangeable and changeable?

6. What is the philosophers attitude toward the pleasures of the body and the attainment of true happiness?

ᴀ Epicurus ᴄ

1. In terms of his materialistic view of reality, how does Epicurus explain the nature and composition of the soul?

2. Given his theory of sensation, how does Epicurus explain the relation between the soul and the body?

3. Why, for Epicurus, would we be better off not believing in life after death?

4. What is the nature of the good life according to Epicurean principles?

5. How does the Epicurean view of life and death differ from the Platonic conception?

ᵫ Marcus Aurelius ᵫ

1. If man is simply a part of the larger whole which is nature, what then for Marcus Aurelius is the cause of evil?

2. Given the Stoic view, what would Marcus Aurelius say about Epicurean Hedonism?

3. Why for Marcus Aurelius would there be no difference between a long and short life?

4. What are the five ways Aurelius says that the soul does damage to itself?

5. How does philosophy assist us in the conduct of life and the acceptance of death?

Hindu Upanishads

1. What does the King of Death say about the difference between the pleasant and the good?

2. Explain the nature of the Universal Self in terms of the analogy of the charioteer.

3. How would you explain the relation between Brahman and the self?

4. How does one gain eternal peace and escape the cycle of death and rebirth?

⚓ Hindu Bhagavad Gita ⚓

1. What is the painful dilemma Prince Arjuna faces?

2. Krishna councils Arjuna to fight. What are his reasons and explain how they are consistent with Hindu philosophy?

3. What does Krishna mean by the concept of Atman?

Heinrich Zimmer

1. Explain the Four Noble Truths and show how this doctrine is more like a medical diagnosis than a speculative philosophy.

2. What is the root cause of all suffering? How is this like the Socratic view of evil?

3. How is Nirvana explained through the analogy of the ferryboat?

4. Compare the Buddhist way of coping with death with the Socratic and Epicurean ways.

Buddhaghosa

1. The Buddhaghosa gives eight ways to meditate on death. What does one achieve by this and how would it affect one's life?

2. Can you compare the Buddhaghosa with the Stoic view of Marcus Aurelius? In what way would Buddhism differ from the Stoic view?

3. How would the Buddhaghosa's recollection of death differ from the Socratic view of recollection?

Confucius

1. What is the connection Confucius makes between dying content and proper Li, or ritual?

2. What kind of ritual does Confucius think we need?

3. Why is Confucius more interested in the social relations of the living than in life after death? (see Fingarette article)

﹅ Herbert Fingarette ﹅

1. It is a moral commonplace that one should not use another person. How does Fingarette explain this problem in terms of the Confucian metaphor of the Holy Vessel?

2. How does the metaphor of the Holy Vessel explain what Confucius means by proper Li?

3. How does Fingarette explain the Confucian notion of the individual, and how would it differ from the typical Western view?

4. How might our Western notion of individuality effect the way we die?

⚔ Mencius ⚔

1. For Mencius, what is the true sign of one's humanity (Jen)?

2. Mencius thinks we have an original and common mind. How does this affect the way we think of death?

↘ Chuang Tzu ↙

1. How does the philosophical relativism of Chuang Tzu help one in terms of death?

2. How does understanding that the Tao (The Way) is a process of transformation guide us in our attitudes towards life and death?

3. How would you compare the Confucianist view of death with its emphasis on social propriety (Li) with the more cosmological view of the Taoist (Yin/Yang)?

St. Augustine

1. How does the death of Augustine's friend help to initiate a turn around in his life? What does he realize?

2. How does Christianity change Augustine's view of friendship?

3. Augustine was very much influenced by Platonism. Compare and contrast the Augustinian view of worldly beauty with the Socratic idea of recollection.

4. How does Augustine describe the difference between faith and reason?

5. What does Augustine mean by the second death?

6. Augustine holds to a dualistic conception of body and soul. How does this answer the question of death and explain the problem of evil?

7. In what essential ways does the Augustinian Christian view of the meaning of life differ from the Hindu? In what ways are they similar?

Meister Eckhart

See What Love

1. What does Meister Eckhart mean by the two births of man?

2. Concerning suffering, is there a point of comparison between the Stoicism of Aurelius and the mysticism of Meister Eckhart? Explain this likeness and how they differ.

Blessed are the Poor

1. What are the two kinds of poverty and what constitutes a truly poor man for Eckhart?

2. Explain how Eckhart's mystical notion of true poverty is much like the Hindu concept of Atman?

Montaigne

1. Why does Montaigne say that the good and happy life can only be judged on our last day?

2. How does Montaigne synthesize the Platonic notion of virtue with Epicurean hedonism?

3. Would you say that Montaigne's view on death is closer to the Greek or the Christian, and why?

4. How does Montaigne suggest that we come to grips with the inevitability of death?

Blaise Pascal

1. If our lives are as precarious as Pascal suggests, in what can we ground our human dignity?

2. How does Pascal differ from Montaigne on death and the immortality of the soul?

3. What does Pascal think about a person who is not concerned about death nor God?

4. Explain Pascal's wager. What are his reasons?

⚔ G.W.F. Hegel ⚔

1. How does Hegel describe the main characteristics of spirit in opposition to matter?

2. What does Hegel say about the evolution of freedom in history? Give some examples of what he means.

3. How is death important for the process of world history and the evolution of spirit?

4. What is the individual's relation to the collective or to what Hegel calls national spirit?

5. In terms of our own individual mortality, can we find solace in the immortality of Hegel's World Spirit?

Soren Kierkegaard

1. How does Kierkegaard explain the difference between an objective and a subjective relation to God?

2. What is the relationship between Kierkegaard's notion of subjective passion and immortality? How does he relate this to the case of society?

3. How does Kierkegaard disagree with Hegel on the concepts of the individual, truth and spirituality?

ᴁ Leo Tolstoy ᴁ

1. How would you sum up what Tolstoy means by the basic contradiction of human life?

2. What mistake does Tolstoy think we make in terms of our individuality and the true meaning of life and happiness?

3. According to Tolstoy, what are the two views of life? Why is one true and the other false?

4. Can you make a comparison between Tolstoy's view and the Hindu concept of Atman?

5. What according to Tolstoy constitutes the real fear of death? How might he suggest that we live our lives?

✄ Sigmund Freud ✄

1. Summarize what Freud thinks of as our conventional view of death.

2. What is the effect that war has on our attitude towards death?

3. How does Freud describe the inherent contradiction in prehistoric man's view of death?

4. How does primitive man resolve the above contradiction?

5. What does Freud say is our unconscious attitude towards death, and how is it related to our instinctual impulses?

⚜ Bertrand Russell ⚜

Do We Survive Death?

1. How does Russell argue that life after death is not very likely?

2. What are the causes for our belief in life after death? What is Russell's response?

How to Grow Old?

1. What does Russell think is the recipe for staying young?

2. What are the dangers to be guarded against in old age?

3. How for Russell do we overcome the fear of death? Can Russell's materialistic view be compared to what Socrates says in the Phaedo?

✒ Martin Hiedegger ✒

1. Can you explain what Heidegger means by Dasein? How is it different from other entities? What does it mean to say that the essence of Dasein is existence?

2. How does the possibility of death differ from other possibilities?

3. How does the "everydayness" of the "they" help Dasein to evade its being-towards-death?

4. How does "everyday" Dasein understand the certainty of death? How does this way of seeing our death fail to recognize Dasein's authentic being-towards-death?

5. What does anticipation have to do with Dasein's authentic being-towards-death? What role does anxiety play?

ᵆ Thomas Nagel ᵇ

1. How does Nagel argue that it is not death per se, or nonexistence, which is a problem but the loss of life?

2. What are the three types of problems Nagel raises in regard to death?

3. What does Nagel mean that the boundaries of good and evil are not confined to the spatial-temporal location of the body? How does he relate this to death?

4. How does Nagel argue against Epicurus and Montaigne that death is not the same as our nonexistence before birth?

5. Why is the confrontation with death ambiguous for Nagel? What does this ambiguity have to do with a first person verses a third person account?

⚔ **Bernard Williams** ⚔

1. What does Williams mean by a categorical desire? How would he disagree with Epicurus?

2. Why does Williams say that EM's boredom is not contingent, or just dependent on her situation, but necessary?

3. What would make the boredom of eternal life unthinkable?

4. What conclusion does Williams come to concerning the ambiguity between our desire to live and the boredom of living too long?

Roland Puccetti

1. Is "conquering death" a meaningful concept? If so, what would it mean for Puccetti?

2. Why does Puccetti think that the human condition is a deplorable one?

3. What does Puccetti think is wrong with the Great Postponement solution to death?

4. Is becoming cyborg man the answer to death? What is the up and down side to this solution?

Teilhard De Chardin

1. Chardin holds an emergent evolutionist view of the cosmos. What is the difference between matter and life, and what is man's place in the scheme of things?

2. How does Chardin explain the phenomenon of spirit in terms of its present and its past? How does his view differ from Creationism?

3. If consciousness is headed for what Chardin calls a superpersonalized collective phenomenon, how does he explain the Christian notion of individual immortality?

4. Chardin states two reasons which he thinks will help us to "accept and co-operate with the demands of evolution." What are these reasons, and do you think they give meaning to our mortality?

5. Compare and contrast Hegel and Chardin on the issues of matter and spirit, and the individual and the collective.

6. Does process theology offer another way to view life and death? If not, what are the problems?

⚞ Karl Marx ⚟

1. Can you explain what Marx means when he says that "life is not determined by consciousness, but consciousnesses by life?"

2. Can you give some examples of how the owners of the forces of production have something to do with what we find meaningful in life?

3. With alienated labor Marx thinks we become commodities and are reduced to animality. How is this so, and is it true for our high-tech world of labor?

4. Explain what Marx means when he says that money is the inversion and confusion of all natural qualities.

5. What does Marx mean by the fetish character of a commodity? Can you see any connection between this concept and the way we view our deaths. (see the previous article by Mitford)